PHILOSOPHY OF MIND IN THE TWENTIETH AND TWENTY-FIRST CENTURIES

While the philosophical study of mind has always required philosophers to attend to the scientific developments of their day, from the twentieth century onwards it has been especially influenced and informed by psychology, neuroscience, and computer science.

Philosophy of Mind in the Twentieth and Twenty-First Centuries provides an outstanding survey of the most prominent themes in twentieth-century and contemporary philosophy of mind. It also looks to the future, offering cautious predictions about developments in the field in the years to come.

Following an introduction by Amy Kind, twelve specially commissioned chapters by an international team of contributors discuss key topics, thinkers, and debates, including:

- the phenomenological tradition,
- the mind–body problem,
- theories of consciousness,
- theories of perception,
- theories of personal identity,
- mental causation,
- intentionality,
- Wittgenstein and his legacy,
- cognitive science, and
- future directions for philosophy of mind.

Essential reading for students and researchers in philosophy of mind and philosophy of psychology, *Philosophy of Mind in the Twentieth and Twenty-First Centuries* is also a valuable resource for those in related disciplines such as psychology and cognitive science.

Amy Kind is Russell K. Pitzer Professor of Philosophy at Claremont McKenna College, USA. Her research interests lie broadly in the philosophy of mind, but most of her work centers on issues relating to imagination and phenomenal consciousness. In addition to authoring the introductory textbook *Persons and Personal Identity* (2015), she has edited *The Routledge Handbook of Philosophy of Imagination* (2016) and co-edited *Knowledge Through Imagination* (2016).

The History of the Philosophy of Mind
General Editors: Rebecca Copenhaver and Christopher Shields

The History of the Philosophy of Mind is a major six-volume reference collection, covering the key topics, thinkers, and debates within philosophy of mind, from Antiquity to the present day. Each volume is edited by a leading scholar in the field and comprises chapters written by an international team of specially commissioned contributors.

Including a general introduction by Rebecca Copenhaver and Christopher Shields, and fully cross-referenced within and across the six volumes, *The History of the Philosophy of Mind* is an essential resource for students and researchers in philosophy of mind, and will also be of interest to those in many related disciplines, including Classics, Religion, Literature, History of Psychology, and Cognitive Science.

VOL. 1 PHILOSOPHY OF MIND IN ANTIQUITY
edited by John E. Sisko

VOL. 2 PHILOSOPHY OF MIND IN THE EARLY AND
HIGH MIDDLE AGES
edited by Margaret Cameron

VOL. 3 PHILOSOPHY OF MIND IN THE LATE MIDDLE AGES AND
RENAISSANCE
edited by Stephan Schmid

VOL. 4 PHILOSOPHY OF MIND IN THE EARLY MODERN
AND MODERN AGES
edited by Rebecca Copenhaver

VOL. 5 PHILOSOPHY OF MIND IN THE NINETEENTH CENTURY
edited by Sandra Lapointe

VOL. 6 PHILOSOPHY OF MIND IN THE TWENTIETH AND
TWENTY-FIRST CENTURIES
edited by Amy Kind

PHILOSOPHY OF MIND IN THE TWENTIETH AND TWENTY-FIRST CENTURIES

The History of the Philosophy of Mind, Volume 6

Edited by Amy Kind

LONDON AND NEW YORK

First published 2019
by Routledge
2 Park Square, Milton Park, Abingdon, Oxon OX14 4RN

and by Routledge
711 Third Avenue, New York, NY 10017

Routledge is an imprint of the Taylor & Francis Group, an informa business

© 2019 selection and editorial matter, Amy Kind; individual chapters, the contributors

The right of Amy Kind to be identified as the editor of the editorial material, and of the authors for their individual chapters, has been asserted in accordance with sections 77 and 78 of the Copyright, Designs and Patents Act 1988.

All rights reserved. No part of this book may be reprinted or reproduced or utilised in any form or by any electronic, mechanical, or other means, now known or hereafter invented, including photocopying and recording, or in any information storage or retrieval system, without permission in writing from the publishers.

Trademark notice: Product or corporate names may be trademarks or registered trademarks, and are used only for identification and explanation without intent to infringe.

British Library Cataloguing-in-Publication Data
A catalogue record for this book is available from the British Library

Library of Congress Cataloging-in-Publication Data
Names: Kind, Amy, editor.
Title: Philosophy of mind in the twentieth and twenty-first centuries / edited by Amy Kind.
Description: New York : Routledge, 2018. | Series: The history of the philosophy of mind ; Volume 6 | Includes bibliographical references and index.
Identifiers: LCCN 2017060258 | ISBN 9781138243972 (hardback : alk. paper) | ISBN 9780429508127 (e-book)
Subjects: LCSH: Philosophy of mind—History—20th century. | Philosophy of mind—History—21st century.
Classification: LCC BD418.3 .P4846 2018 | DDC 128/.20904—dc23
LC record available at https://lccn.loc.gov/2017060258

ISBN: 978-1-138-24397-2 (Vol VI, hbk)
ISBN: 978-0-429-50812-7 (Vol VI, ebk)

ISBN: 978-1-138-24392-7 (Vol I, hbk)
ISBN: 978-0-429-50821-9 (Vol I, ebk)
ISBN: 978-1-138-24393-4 (Vol II, hbk)
ISBN: 978-0-429-50819-6 (Vol II, ebk)
ISBN: 978-1-138-24394-1 (Vol III, hbk)
ISBN: 978-0-429-50817-2 (Vol III, ebk)
ISBN: 978-1-138-24395-8 (Vol IV, hbk)
ISBN: 978-0-429-50815-8 (Vol IV, ebk)
ISBN: 978-1-138-24396-5 (Vol V, hbk)
ISBN: 978-0-429-50813-4 (Vol V, ebk)
ISBN: 978-1-138-92535-9 (6-volume set, hbk)

Typeset in Times New Roman
by Apex CoVantage, LLC

CONTENTS

List of contributors		vii
General introduction		x
REBECCA COPENHAVER AND CHRISTOPHER SHIELDS		
Introduction to volume 6: twentieth-century philosophy of mind: themes, problems, and scientific context		1
AMY KIND		
1 Philosophy of mind in the phenomenological tradition		21
PHILIP J. WALSH AND JEFF YOSHIMI		
2 The mind-body problem in 20th-century philosophy		52
AMY KIND		
3 A short history of philosophical theories of consciousness in the 20th century		78
TIM CRANE		
4 20th-century theories of perception		104
NICO ORLANDI		
5 20th-century theories of personal identity		126
JENS JOHANSSON		
6 Introspecting in the 20th century		148
MAJA SPENER		
7 The mental causation debates in the 20th century		175
JULIE YOO		

CONTENTS

8 Intentionality: from Brentano to representationalism   200
   MICHELLE MONTAGUE

9 Wittgenstein and his legacy   233
   SEVERIN SCHROEDER

10 The boundaries of the mind   256
    KATALIN FARKAS

11 The rise of cognitive science in the 20th century   280
    CARRIE FIGDOR

12 How philosophy of mind can shape the future   303
    SUSAN SCHNEIDER AND PETE MANDIK

   Index   320

CONTRIBUTORS

Tim Crane is professor of philosophy at the Central European University, Budapest. He has written on a number of topics in the philosophy of mind, including intentionality, consciousness, perception, mental causation, and physicalism. His books include *The Mechanical Mind* (1995, 3rd edition 2015), *Elements of Mind* (2001), *The Objects of Thought* (2013), *Aspects of Psychologism* (2014), *The Meaning of Belief* (2017), and (as editor) *The Contents of Experience* (1992) and *A Debate on Dispositions* (1996). He is the Philosophy Consultant Editor of the *TLS*.

Katalin Farkas is professor of philosophy at the Central European University, Budapest. Her main interests are the philosophy of mind and epistemology. Her book *The Subject's Point of View* (OUP 2008) defends an internalist conception of the boundaries of the mind.

Carrie Figdor is associate professor at the University of Iowa, Department of Philosophy and Interdisciplinary Graduate Program in Neuroscience. She publishes on topics at the intersection of philosophy of mind, science, and language, on epistemology and ethics of journalism, and on metaphysics. Her monograph *Pieces of Mind: The Proper Domain of Psychological Predicates* is forthcoming with Oxford University Press, and her work has appeared in *The Journal of Philosophy, Philosophy of Science, Topics in Cognitive Science, Mind & Language, Frontiers in Communication*, among others. She co-hosts "New Books in Philosophy" (http://newbooksnetwork.com/category/philosophy/) a podcast that features interviews with philosophers about their new books.

Jens Johansson is Professor of Practical Philosophy at Uppsala University. He has published a number of essays on the philosophy of death, personal identity, and related issues, and co-edited *The Oxford Handbook of Philosophy of Death* (2013, with Ben Bradley and Fred Feldman).

Amy Kind is Russell K. Pitzer Professor of Philosophy at Claremont McKenna College. Her research interests lie broadly in the philosophy of mind, but most of her work centers on issues relating to imagination and to phenomenal consciousness. In addition to authoring the introductory textbook *Persons and*

Personal Identity (Polity, 2015), she has edited *The Routledge Handbook of Philosophy of Imagination* (Routledge, 2016) and she has co-edited *Knowledge through Imagination* (Oxford University Press, 2016).

Pete Mandik is professor of philosophy at William Paterson University of New Jersey. He is author of *This Is Philosophy of Mind* (2013) and *Key Terms in Philosophy of Mind* (2010).

Michelle Montague is Associate Professor of philosophy at the University of Texas, Austin. Her work focuses on the philosophy of mind, primarily on consciousness and intentionality. In addition to publishing numerous articles in these areas, she is the author of *The Given: Experience and Its Content* (Oxford University Press, 2016), the co-editor with Tim Bayne of *Cognitive Phenomenology* (Oxford University Press, 2011), and the co-editor with Galen Strawson of *Philosophical Writings* by P. F. Strawson (Oxford University Press, 2011).

Nico Orlandi is associate professor of philosophy at the University of California, Santa Cruz. Nico specializes in philosophy of mind and philosophy of psychology and neuroscience, and has published several articles in addition to a book, *The Innocent Eye: Why Vision Is Not a Cognitive Process*.

Susan Schneider teaches at the University of Connecticut and is a member of the technology and ethics group at Yale and the Institute for Advanced Study in Princeton. Schneider writes about matters involving the metaphysics of mind, AI, and philosophy of cognitive science. She also writes opinion pieces for venues like *The New York Times*, *Nautilus*, and *Scientific American*. Her work wrestles with vexed questions about the metaphysical nature of the self and mind. Her books include the *Blackwell Companion to Consciousness* (with Max Velmans), *Science Fiction and Philosophy* and *The Language of Thought: A New Philosophical Direction*, as well as a forthcoming trade book, *Future Minds*. Her website SchneiderWebsite.com features many online lectures, interviews, and papers.

Severin Schroeder is Associate Professor in Philosophy at the University of Reading. He has written three monographs on Wittgenstein: *Wittgenstein: The Way Out of the Fly Bottle* (Polity, 2006), *Wittgenstein Lesen* (Frommann-Holzboog, 2009), and *Das Privatsprachen-Argument* (Schöningh/Mentis, 1998). He is the editor of *Wittgenstein and Contemporary Philosophy of Mind* (Palgrave 2001) and *Philosophy of Literature* (Wiley-Blackwell 2010). He is currently working on a book on Wittgenstein's philosophy of mathematics (Routledge).

Maja Spener is a lecturer in the Department of Philosophy at the University of Birmingham (UK). She is writing a book on introspective method in philosophy and scientific psychology.

CONTRIBUTORS

Philip J. Walsh is a post-doctoral teaching fellow at Fordham University. His research focuses on phenomenology and philosophy of mind. His published work includes articles on Husserl and Merleau-Ponty, as well as contemporary debates about perception, thought, expression, agency, and social cognition.

Julie Yoo is an Associate Professor of Philosophy at the California State University, Northridge. She has published articles in philosophy of mind and philosophy of language. Her research areas also include metaphysics and feminist philosophy.

Jeff Yoshimi is an Associate Professor of philosophy and cognitive science in the Cognitive and Information Science department at UC Merced. He is a founding faculty member, having arrived in 2004, before the campus opened. He does work in phenomenology, philosophy of mind and cognitive science, neural networks, dynamical systems theory, and visualization of complex processes.

GENERAL INTRODUCTION

Rebecca Copenhaver and Christopher Shields

How far back does the history of philosophy of mind extend? In one sense, the entire history of the discipline extends no further than living memory. Construed as a recognized sub-discipline of philosophy, philosophy of mind seems to have entered the academy in a regular way only in the latter half of the twentieth century. At any rate, as an institutional matter, courses listed under the name 'Philosophy of Mind' or 'The Mind-Body Problem' were rare before then and seem not to have become fixtures of the curriculum in Anglo-American universities until the 1960s.[1] More broadly, construed as the systematic self-conscious reflection on the question of how mental states and processes should be conceived in relation to physical states and processes, one might put the date to the late nineteenth or early twentieth century.

One might infer on this basis that a six-volume work on *The History of Philosophy of Mind* extending back to antiquity is bound to be anachronistic: we cannot, after all, assume that our questions were the questions of, say, Democritus, working in Thrace in the fifth century BC, or of Avicenna (Ibn-Sînâ), active in Persia in the twelfth century, or of John Blund, the Oxford- and Paris-trained Chancellor of the see of York from 1234–1248, or, for that matter, of the great German philosopher and mathematician Leibniz (1646–1716). One might on the contrary think it *prima facie* unlikely that thinkers as diverse as these in their disparate times and places would share very many preoccupations either with each other or with us.

Any such immediate inference would be unduly hasty and also potentially misleading. It would be misleading not least because it relies on an unrealistically unified conception of what *we* find engaging in this area: philosophy of mind comprises today a wide range of interests, orientations, and methodologies, some almost purely *a priori* and others almost exclusively empirical. It is potentially misleading in another way as well, heading in the opposite direction. If we presume that the only thinkers who have something useful to say to us are those engaging the questions of mind we find salient, using idioms we find congenial, then we will likely overlook some surprising continuities as well as instructive discontinuities across these figures and periods.

Some issues pertinent to mental activity may prove perennial. Of equal importance, however, are the differences and discontinuities we find when we investigate questions of mind assayed in earlier periods of thought. In some cases, it is true, we find it difficult to determine without careful investigation whether difference in idiom suffices for difference in interest or orientation. For instance, it was once commonplace to frame questions about mental activity as questions about the soul, where today questions posed about the nature of the soul and its relation to the body are apt to sound to many outmoded or at best quaintly archaic. Yet when we read what, for instance, medieval philosophers investigated under that rubric, we are as likely as not to find them reflecting on such core contemporary concerns as the nature of perception, the character of consciousness, the relation of mental faculties to the body, and the problem of intentionality – and to be doing so in a manner immediately continuous with some of our own preoccupations.

That said, even where upon examination we find little or no continuity between present-day and earlier concerns, this very difference can be illuminating. Why, for instance, is the will discussed so little in antiquity? Hannah Arendt suggests an answer: the will was not discussed in antiquity because it was not discovered before St. Augustine managed to do so in the third century.[2] Is she right? Or is the will in fact discussed obliquely in antiquity, enmeshed in a vocabulary at least initially alien to our own? On the supposition that Arendt is right, and the will is not even a topic of inquiry before Augustine, why should this be so? Should this make us less confident that we have a faculty rightly called 'the will'? Perhaps Augustine not so much discovered the will as *invented* it, to give it pride of place in his conception of human nature. A millennium later Thomas Aquinas contended that the will is but one power or faculty of the soul, as an intellectual appetite for the good (*ST* I 82, resp.). Is he right? Is the will as examined by Augustine and Aquinas the same will of which we ask, when we do, whether our will is free or determined?

A study of the history of philosophy of mind turns up, in sum, some surprising continuities, some instructive partial overlaps, and some illuminating discontinuities across the ages. When we reflect on the history of the discipline, we bring into sharper relief some of the questions we find most pressing, and we inevitably come to ask new and different questions, even as we retire questions which we earlier took to be of moment. Let us reflect first then on some surprising continuities. Three illustrations will suffice, but they could easily be multiplied.

First, consider some questions about minds and machines: whether machines can be conscious or otherwise minded, whether human intelligence is felicitously explicated in terms of computer software, hardware, or functional processes more generally. Surely such questions belong to our era uniquely? Yet we find upon reading some early modern philosophy that this is not so. In Leibniz, for instance, we find this striking passage, known as 'Leibniz's mill':

> Imagine there were a machine whose structure produced thought, feeling, and perception; we can conceive of its being enlarged while maintaining

the same relative proportions, so that we could walk into it as we can walk into a mill. Suppose we do walk into it; all we would find there are cogs and levers and so on pushing one another, and never anything to account for a perception. So perception must be sought in simple substances, not in composite things like machines. And that is all that can be found in a simple substance – perceptions and changes in perceptions; and those changes are all that the internal actions of simple substances can consist in.

(*Monadology* §17)

Leibniz offers an argument against mechanistic conceptions of mental activity in this passage, one with a recognizably contemporary counterpart. His view may be defensible or it may be indefensible; but it is certainly relevant to questions currently being debated.

Similarly, nearly every course in philosophy of mind these days begins with some formulation of the 'mind-body problem', usually presented as a descendant of the sort of argument Descartes advanced most famously in his *Meditations*, and defended most famously in his correspondence with Elisabeth of Bohemia. Centuries before Descartes, however, we encounter the Islamic polymath Avicenna (Ibn-Sînâ) wondering in detail about the question of whether the soul has or lacks quantitative extension, deploying a striking thought experiment in three separate passages, one of which runs:

One of us must suppose that he was just created at a stroke, fully developed and perfectly formed but with his vision shrouded from perceiving all external objects – created floating in the air or in space, not buffeted by any perceptible current of the air that supports him, his limbs separated and kept out of contact with one another, so that they do not feel each other. Then let the subject consider whether he would affirm the existence of his self. There is no doubt that he would affirm his own existence, although not affirming the reality of any of his limbs or inner organs, his bowels, or heart or brain or any external thing. Indeed he would affirm the existence of this self of his while not affirming that it had any length, breadth or depth. And if it were possible for him in such a state to imagine a hand or any other organ, he would not imagine it to be a part of himself or a condition of his existence.

(Avicenna, '*The Book of Healing*')

Avicenna's 'Floating Man', or 'Flying Man', reflects his Neoplatonist orientation and prefigures in obvious ways Descartes' more celebrated arguments of *Meditations* II. Scholars dispute just how close this parallel is,[3] but it seems plain that these arguments and parables bear a strong family resemblance to one another, and then each in turn to a yet earlier argument by Augustine,[4] more prosaically put, but engaging many of the same themes.

The point is not to determine who won the race to this particular argument, nor to insist that these authors arrive at precisely the same finish line. Rather, when we study each expression in its own context, we find illuminating samenesses and differences, which in turn assist us in framing our own questions about the character of the quantitative and qualitative features of mind, about the tenability of solipsism, and about the nature of the human self. One would like to know, for instance, whether such a narrow focus on the internal states of human consciousness provides a productive method for the science of mind. Or have our philosophical forebears, as some today think, created impediments by conceiving of the very project in a way that neglects the embodied characteristics of cognition? From another angle, one may wonder whether these approaches, seen throughout the history of the discipline, lead inexorably to Sartre's conclusion that 'consciousness is a wind blowing from nowhere towards objects'.[5] One way to find out is to study each of these approaches in the context of its own deployment.

For a final example, we return to the birthplace of Western philosophy to reflect upon a striking argument of Democritus in the philosophy of perception. After joining Leucippus in arguing that the physical world comprises countless small atoms swirling in the void, Democritus observes that *only* atoms and the void are, so to speak, really real. All else exists by convention: 'by convention sweet and by convention bitter, by convention hot, by convention cold, by convention colour; but in reality atoms and void' (DK 68B9). This remark evidently denies the reality of sensible qualities, such as sweetness and bitterness, and even colour. What might Democritus be thinking? By judging this remark alongside his remaining fragments, we see that he is appealing to the variability of perception to argue that if one perceiver tastes a glass of wine and finds it sweet, while another perceiver tastes the same glass and finds it bitter, then we must conclude – on the assumption that perceptual qualities are real – that either one or the other perceiver is wrong. After all, they cannot both be right, and there seems little point in treating them as both wrong. The correct conclusion, Democritus urges, is that sensible qualities, in contrast to atoms and the void, are not real. The wine is neither sweet nor bitter; sweetness and bitterness are wholly subjective states of perceivers.

Readers of seventeenth- and eighteenth-century British philosophy will recognize this argument in Locke and Berkeley. Locke presents the argument to support his distinction between primary and secondary qualities: primary qualities being those features of objects that are (putatively) *in* objects, independently of perception, such as number, shape, size, and motion; secondary qualities being those features of objects subject to the variability of perception recognized by Democritus. Locke struggles with the reality of secondary qualities, sometimes treating them as ideas in our minds and other times as dispositions of the primary qualities of objects that exist independently of us. Democritus, by contrast, aligning the real with the objective, simply banishes them to the realm of convention. And Berkeley appeals to the same phenomenon on which Locke founds his famous distinction – the variability of perception – to argue that the distinction is unsustainable and thus embraces the anti-Democritean option: the real is the ideal.

We may ask which if any of these philosophers deserves to be followed. As an anecdotal matter, when beginning philosophy students grasp the point of arguments from the variability of perception, they become flummoxed, because before having their attention focussed on the phenomenon of variability, most tend to think of sensible qualities as intrinsic monadic properties of the external objects of perception. This issue in the philosophy of perception, straddling as it does different periods and idioms, remains a live one, proving as vivid for us as it was for Democritus and Locke.

When we find similar philosophical arguments and tropes recurring in radically different periods and contexts throughout the history of philosophy, that is usually at least a strong *prima facie* indication that we are in an area demanding careful scrutiny. Unsurprisingly, arguments concerning the nature of perception and perceptible qualities offer one telling illustration. Still, we should resist the temptation to find continuities where none exists, especially where none exists beyond the verbal or superficial. We should moreover resist, perhaps more strongly still, the tendency to minimize or overlook differences where they appear. One of the intellectual joys of studying the history of philosophy resides precisely in uncovering and appreciating the deep discontinuities between disparate times and contexts.

On this score, examples abound, but one suffices to illustrate our point. The title of a widely read article written in the 1960s posed a provocative question: 'Why Isn't the Mind-Body Problem Ancient?'.[6] This question, of course, has a presupposition, namely that the mind-body problem is in fact *not* ancient. It also seems to betray a second presupposition, namely that there is *a* mind-body problem: a single problem that that engages philosophers of the modern era but that escaped the ancients. This presupposition raises the question: what *is* the single, unified, mind-body problem that the ancients failed to recognize? In fact, when we turn to the range of questions posed in this domain, we find a family of recognizably distinct concerns: the hard problem, the explanatory gap, mental causation, and so on. Not all these questions have a common orientation, even if they arise from a common anxiety that the mind and the body are at once so dissimilar that inquiring into their relationship may already be an error, and yet so similar in their occupation and operation as to obliterate any meaningful difference.

We might call this anxiety *categorial*. That is, it has seemed to various philosophers in various eras that there is some basic categorial distinction to be observed in the domain of the mental, to the effect that mental states belong to one category and physical states to another. That by itself might be true without, however, there being any attendant problem. After all, we might agree that there is a categorial distinction between, say, biological properties and mathematical properties, and even that these families of properties are never co-instantiable. After all, no number can undergo descent with modification, and no animal can be a cosine. That is hardly a problem: no one expects numbers to be biological subjects, and no one would ever mistake an organism for a mathematical function. The problem in the domain of the mental and physical seems to arise only when we assume that some objects – namely ourselves – exhibit both mentality and physicality, and do so in a way that is systematic and unified. Bringing these thoughts together we arrive at a mind-body problem: if mental and physical properties are categorially exclusive while we ourselves are mental and physical at once, we must be what we cannot be, namely subjects of properties that cannot coincide.

In this sense, Cartesian dualism might be regarded as a solution to the mind-body problem, at least *this* mind-body problem, one which simply concedes its conclusion by affirming that minds and bodies are irredeemably different sorts of substances displaying different sorts of properties. Needless to say, this 'solution' invites a series of still more intractable problems concerning the interaction of these postulated disparate substances, about the location of the mental, and so forth. Even so, when the Cartesian expedient is rejected on these or other grounds, the old problem re-emerges, in one guise yielding an equally desperate seeming sort of solution, namely the total elimination of the mental as ultimately not amenable to a purely physicalistic characterization.[7] Eliminativism, no less than Cartesianism, solves the mind-body problem effectively by concession.

One should accordingly look afresh at the problem as formulated. In fact, when one asks *what* these purportedly mutually excluding properties may be, several candidates come to the fore. Some think properties such as *being conscious* are mental and cannot possibly be physical, perhaps because conscious states are ineliminably subjective, whereas all physical properties are objective, or because mental properties are essentially qualitative, whereas physical properties are only quantitative. Descartes' own reasons, though disputed, seem to have been largely epistemic: possibly one can doubt the existence of one's body, whereas it is impossible, because self-defeating, to doubt the existence of one's own mind or mental states (*Meditation* II). If these property-differences obtain in these domains and are in fact such as to be mutually exclusive, then we do now have the makings of a mind-body problem.

Returning, then, to the question pertinent to our study of the ancient period, we may ask: do the ancients draw these sorts of categorial distinctions? If so, why do they fail to appreciate the problems we find so familiar and obvious? Or do they in fact fail to draw these categorial distinctions in the first place? If they do not, then one would like to know why not. One can imagine a number of different options here: one could fault the ancients for failing to pick up on such starkly categorial differences; one could credit them for astutely avoiding the conceptual muddles of Cartesianism. Some argue, for instance, that Aristotelian hylomorphism embraces a framework of explanation within which Cartesian questions simply cannot arise, thereby obviating an array of otherwise intractable problems.[8] Although we do not attempt to litigate these issues here, one can appreciate how an investigation into ancient approaches to philosophy of mind yields palpable benefits for some modern questions, even if and perhaps precisely because such questions were not ancient.

Needless to say, we never know in advance of our investigations whether the benefits of such study will be forthcoming. To make such discoveries as can be made in this area, then, we need ask a set of questions similar to those we asked regarding the mind-body problem, *mutatis mutandis*, for other philosophical problems in the mental domain, broadly construed, as they arise in other periods of philosophy beyond ancient philosophy as well.

If we proceed in this way, we find that the study of the history of philosophy of mind offers the contemporary philosopher perspectives on the discipline which, however far below the surface, may yet guide our own inquiries into the mental and physical, and into the character of mental and physical states and processes. This is, of course, but one reason to engage the studies these six volumes contain. Other researchers with a more purely historical orientation will find a wealth of material in these pages as well, ranging across all periods of western philosophy, from antiquity to that part of the discipline that resides in living memory. Our historical and philosophical interests here may, of course, be fully complementary: the history of philosophy of mind takes one down some odd by-ways off some familiar boulevards, into some dead-ends and cul-de-sacs, but also along some well-travelled highways that are well worth traversing over and again.

Notes

1 A perusal of the course offerings of leading universities in the US tends to confirm this. To take but one example, which may be multiplied, a search of the archives of the University of Notre Dame lists one course in 'Philosophy of Mind' offered as an advanced elective in 1918 and 1928, 1929, but then no further course until 1967, when 'The Mind-Body Problem,' began to be offered yearly off and on for two decades. In the 1970s, various electives such as 'Mind and Machines' were offered intermittently, and a regular offering in 'Philosophy of Mind' began only in 1982. This offering continues down to the present. While we have not done a comprehensive study, these results cohere with archive searches of several other North American universities.
2 Arendt sees prefigurations in St. Paul and others, but regards Augustine as 'the first philosopher of the will and the only philosopher the Romans ever had' (1978, vol. ii, 84).
3 For an overview of these issues, see Marmura (1986).
4 On the relation between Descartes and Augustine, see the instructive treatment in Matthews (1992).
5 Sartre (1943: 32–33).
6 Matson (1966). Citing Matson's question, King (2007) went on to pose a continuing question of his own: 'Why Isn't the Mind-Body Problem Medieval?'. In so doing, King meant to oppose Matson, who had claimed that the one should not assume that medieval philosophers, although writing in a recognizably Aristotelian idiom, similarly failed to engage any mind-body problem. After all, he noted, in addition to their Aristotelianism, they accepted a full range of theistic commitments alien to Aristotle.
7 Eliminativism about the mental has a long and chequered history, extending at least as far back as Broad (1925) (who rejects it), but has its most forceful and accessible formulation in Churchland (1988).
8 Charles (2008) has advanced this sort of argument on behalf of hylomorphism.

Bibliography

Arendt, Hannah. 1978. *The Life of the Mind*, vols. i and ii. New York: Harcourt Brace Jovanovich.
Broad, C. D. 1925. *The Mind and Its Place in Nature*. London: Routledge & Kegan.

Charles, David. 2008. "Aristotle's Psychological Theory". *Proceedings of the Boston Area Colloquium in Ancient Philosophy* **24**: 1–29.

Churchland, P. M. 1988. *Matter and Consciousness*. Cambridge, MA: MIT Press.

King, Peter. 2007. "Why Isn't the Mind-Body Problem Medieval?" In *Forming the Mind: Essays on the Internal Senses and the Mind/Body Problem From Avicenna to the Medical Enlightenment*, 187–205. Berlin: Springer.

Marmura, Michael. 1986. "Avicenna's Flying Man in Context". *The Monist* **69** (3): 383–395.

Matson, Wallace. 1966. "Why Isn't the Mind-Body Problem Ancient?" In *Mind, Matter, and Method: Essays in Philosophy and Science in Honor of Herbert Feigl*, 92–102. St. Paul: University of Minnesota Press.

Matthews, Gareth. 1992. *Thought's Ego in Augustine and Descartes*. Ithaca: Cornell University Press.

Sartre, Jean-Paul. 1943. "Une Idée fondamentale de la phénoménologie de Husserl: L'intentionalité". In *Situations I*. Paris: Gallimard.

INTRODUCTION TO VOLUME 6
Twentieth-century philosophy of mind: themes, problems, and scientific context

Amy Kind

The six volumes in this series aim to take a historical look at philosophy of mind from the very beginnings of philosophical discussion up to the present day. From the vantage point of these early years of the 21st century, however, it's hard to be sure that we yet have enough distance and perspective to accurately and adequately reflect on 20th-century philosophy of mind through a historical lens. For many of these debates, the dust has not yet settled. Moreover, the issues from the past century that now look to us to be of central importance may in the end not prove to be of lasting interest, while there may be other issues of significance that we now fail to identify as such. That said, the first eleven essays in this volume take up themes and debates that seem to have had particular prominence in 20th century philosophy of mind. Then turning finally from the past to the future, the volume concludes with an essay that offers some cautious predictions about developments we are likely to see in philosophy of mind in years to come.

This introduction aims to provide some important background for the thematic discussions that follow by situating 20th-century of mind in a broader context and, in particular, in a scientific context. While the philosophical study of mind has always required philosophers to attend to the scientific developments of their day, philosophy of mind in the 20th century was especially influenced by such work – perhaps more so than at any other point in its history. The influence came largely from three different areas of research: psychology, neuroscience, and computer science. As psychologists came to attend more closely to the connection between mind and behavior, as scientists came to better understand neural function, and as the mid-century work of Alan Turing ushered in the computer revolution, our understanding of a diverse range of issues in philosophy of mind – and indeed, even our very approach to those issues – was deeply affected.

In the first three sections of this introduction, I attempt to provide a brief overview of these three different areas of philosophically influential scientific research. Obviously, an introductory piece of this sort cannot provide anything even close to a comprehensive examination of such wide scientific terrain, but my selective discussion should nonetheless help to provide some important context for the essays of this volume. Thus, in the final section of this introduction, I turn to those essays themselves. There my aim will be twofold: first, to sketch the themes discussed in these chapters, and second, to highlight some of the interconnections between them.

1. Behaviorism

Philosophy of mind in the 20th century has been affected by its cognate discipline of psychology in many ways, but perhaps nothing in this domain has been more influential than the psychological behaviorism that ushered in the 20th century. While the psychologists of the late 19th century had relied heavily on introspectionist methods in their investigations, the behaviorists denied that introspection had any role to play in the collection of scientific data. In their view, for psychology to be a proper science – for it to be empirical in its orientation – it must concern itself not with consciousness but with human behavior.

The term "behaviorism" was introduced in 1913 by the American psychologist John Watson in "Psychology as the Behaviorist Sees It," an article often referred to as the behaviorist manifesto. As Watson there articulated it, behaviorism sees psychology as "a purely objective, experimental branch of natural science which needs introspection as little as do the sciences of chemistry and physics" (Watson 1913, 176). For the behaviorist, the theoretical goal of psychology concerns the prediction and control of human behavior. At the center of the behaviorist program was the notion of stimulus-response, and correspondingly, the behaviorist divided psychological questions into two broad forms. Given a stimulus, the psychologist aims to determine what response will result; given a response, the psychologist aims to determine what stimulus brought it about. By proceeding in this way, the behaviorist works to identify the objective laws governing human behavior.

Watson's behaviorism can be seen largely as a theory about psychological methodology. Though he urged that psychology "must discard all references to consciousness," this was a claim about the proper focus of psychology and not a denial that consciousness exists. In later years, more radical behaviorists such as B. F. Skinner went further, dismissing feelings, ideas, and other features of mental life as "mental fictions" that play no helpful explanatory role (Skinner 1974, 18). By doing so, Skinner claimed, behaviorism "directs attention to the genetic and personal histories of the individual and to the current environment, where the real causes of behaviour are to be found" (Skinner 1987, 75).

Skinner's most famous experimental work involved pigeons, and it was in conjunction with his pigeon studies that he developed an approach known as *operant conditioning*. Prior to any conditioning, a pigeon will produce certain spontaneous pieces of behavior – what Skinner called *operants* – such as pecking at a key. By rewarding a certain type of operant with food or water, Skinner found that he could reinforce it, i.e., he could cause it to increase in frequency. Skinner then applied these lessons from the shaping of pigeon behavior to human behavior, behavior that he saw as shaped by the physical and social environment in which we live: "Through operant conditioning, the environment builds the basic repertoire with which we keep our balance, walk, play games, handle instruments and tools, talk, write, sail a boat, drive a car, or fly a plane" (Skinner 1953, 66).

Like Skinner, most of the behaviorists based their conclusions about human behavior on their work with animals. Watson's own development of behaviorism was heavily influenced by Ivan Pavlov, a Russian physiologist who had shown that dogs could be conditioned to respond not only to food but also to a stimulus such as a bell that had been paired with it. (Pavlov's studies produced laws now known as *classical conditioning*). In addition to Skinner's work with pigeons, other leading behaviorists of the time such as Clark Hull and Edwin R. Guthrie worked with rats and cats. Much of this work suggested that the original stimulus-response paradigm was overly simplistic, and it consequently resulted in the addition of intervening variables. For example, Hull thought that factors such as drive and habit strength needed to be added to any predictive/explanatory laws of behavior.

Following Watson's manifesto, behaviorism dominated psychology for several decades, and it wasn't until the late 1950s that it fell out of favor. Ultimately, though behaviorists were successful in developing experimental techniques that would move psychology away from its reliance on introspection and towards objective methods of investigation, they were considerably less successful in providing any genuine explanation of human behavior. The theory proved especially problematic when it came to explaining thought and language. Skinner attempted to rectify this latter problem by applying the behaviorist framework to linguistic behavior in his *Verbal Behavior* (1957), but this attempt was largely seen as unsuccessful. One especially notable criticism came in a scathing 1959 review by the linguist Noam Chomsky. In fact, this review is often cited as a key turning point in the fortunes of behaviorism. As Chomsky persuasively argued, an explanation of linguistic acquisition and competence that ignores entirely the contribution of innate mechanisms is doomed to failure. The acquisition and production of language is far too sophisticated to be explained solely in terms of responses to stimuli.

Though behaviorism is now out of vogue, contemporary psychology owes much to its teachings. At the theoretical level, the behaviorists' careful attention to experimental design and the measurement of variables has had a lasting impact on psychological research methods. At the clinical level, many contemporary therapies aimed at treating conditions such as addiction or PTSD can be traced to behaviorist models of the shaping of behavior. We can also see a deep behavioristic legacy in a vast array of social practices – from educational practices to job training. For our purposes, however, perhaps what's most important is behaviorism's philosophical legacy. In ways both direct and indirect, as well as both positive and negative, psychological behaviorism cast a long shadow over many of the debates that occupied philosophers of mind in the 20th century. From discussions of the relation between mind and body (Chapters 2 and 7), to discussions about consciousness (Chapter 3), perception (Chapter 4), and introspection (Chapter 5), to the development of Wittgenstein's philosophical views on mind (Chapter 9), we consistently see the influence of behaviorism, and even in these early years of the 21st century, we still find behavioristic traces in many areas of philosophical theorizing about the mind.

2. Neural localization

The 20th century brought about extraordinary progress in our understanding of the brain. One particularly important area of progress concerns neural localization (sometimes also called *brain mapping*): the attempt to identify which neural regions correlate with which cognitive functions. While there has been a very recent explosion of progress in this area with the advent of the sophisticated neural imaging techniques starting in the 1990s, there were significant developments throughout the century even before these advanced imaging techniques became available.

The story of neural localization might be said to begin in the early 19th century with the work of Franz Joseph Gall, an Austrian physician and neuroanatomist. Today Gall is perhaps most famous for his advocacy of *phrenology*, a view according to which the shape of the skull determines various personality and character traits such as spirituality, secretiveness, and self-esteem. Indeed, Gall's phrenological drawings mapped out as many as forty-two distinct areas of the skull and the underlying cerebral cortex that corresponded to different intellectual and emotional capacities. While Gall himself did not rely on any of the empirical brain research available at the time in developing these cranial maps, and while phrenology itself has long been rejected as mere pseudoscience, he can nonetheless be credited with setting forth two key principles that remain influential today: (1) that mental function arises from the brain, and (2) that the brain does not operate as a single organ but instead can be divided into numerous smaller organs, each of which bears responsibility for different cognitive functions.

Gall's work came under attack in the 1820s by the French physiologist Pierre Flourens. Flourens rejected not only Gall's phrenology but also the principles of localization underlying it. Denying that different parts of the brain had discrete functions, Flourens instead proposed what's become known as a *holistic* approach to the brain. According to the holistic view, each part of a cerebral hemisphere is capable of performing all of the functions of that hemisphere. Holism remained popular until the middle of the 19th century when several different developments began to swing the pendulum back in the direction of localization. Work by the French neurologist Paul Broca and later by the German neurologist Carl Wernicke showed that language function could be traced to the left frontal cortex. Working with patients who suffered from various linguistic deficits, both Broca and Wernicke used postmortem analysis to identify the locations of neural damage. Also worth noting is the famous case of Phineas Gage, a construction worker who was seriously injured during an explosion in 1848 when his brain and skull were impaled by an iron rod over an inch thick. Though Gage recovered and had no subsequent difficulties with either motor function or speech, he experienced a dramatic personality change. A responsible and polite man before the accident, thereafter he became profane, irreverent, and untrustworthy. Lack of autopsy results prevented the full significance of the Gage case from being revealed at the time, but an analysis by John Harlow in the 1860s correlated Gage's cognitive and behavioral changes with a specific area of the prefrontal cortex.[1]

The start of the 20th century brought further evidence in support of the localization paradigm through the work of German anatomist Korbinian Brodmann. Brodmann attempted to differentiate the functional areas of the brain by analyzing cell shapes, their distribution, and their arrangement into patterns such as clusters and columns. This new approach – known as the *cytoarchitectonic method* – enabled Brodmann to identify forty-three distinct functional areas of the cortex, and even now the cortical map he developed still proves influential. At the time, however, not everyone accepted Brodmann's work, and the holistic view continued to enjoy pockets of support in the early years of the 20th century. Advocates included Pavlov, whom we encountered above in our discussion of behaviorism, and the American psychologist Karl Lashey, whose work running rats through mazes led him to the conclusion that what mattered was the size of a brain lesion rather than its location. But by mid-century, as the empirical case for localization continued to strengthen, support for holism declined and localization became the prevailing view. It has remained so to this day.

While the empirical evidence for localization in the 19th and early 20th centuries came largely from postmortem studies of the brain, mid-century medical advances allowed for the collection of data from living patients. Largely because of the efforts of the pioneering Canadian neurosurgeon Wilder Penfield and his colleagues who were working to treat patients with epilepsy, techniques were developed that enabled the direct stimulation of cortical tissue of conscious patients during brain surgery. This enabled surgeons to better identify the areas responsible for the seizures and in turn allowed for the collection of data about brain function in real time.

Around the same time, an entirely different surgical procedure aimed at treating epilepsy led to further lessons about neural function. Starting in the late 1940s, a group of patients who suffered from a particularly severe and uncontrollable form of epilepsy underwent surgery to sever the corpus callosum, the bundle of nerve fibers connecting the brain's two hemispheres. By breaking this connection, doctors hoped to be able to prevent the epileptic seizures from spreading from one hemisphere of the brain to the other. Ultimately, approximately 100 such operations were performed. The patients who underwent these surgeries – often referred to post surgery as *split-brain subjects* – presented researchers with a unique opportunity to learn about brain function, and subsequent studies by the neuropsychologists Roger Sperry and Michael Gazzaniga revealed considerable new insights not only into hemispheric specialization but also into the ability of the hemispheres to coordinate their activities and to function independently of one another.

The state of scientific knowledge about the brain by mid-century was thus considerable. A staggering amount of progress had been made in just a hundred years' time. But even greater advances were yet to come. Perhaps nothing has been as important to our understanding of neural function as the late 20th-century development of noninvasive neural-imagining techniques. Starting with the development of X-ray computed tomography (CT scans) in the early 1970s, scientists could for the first time work with three-dimensional images – a development that, as Marcus Raichle puts it, "quite literally changed the way in which we looked at the human brain" (Raichle 2008, 120).

Many of the modern imaging technologies work by measuring *hemodynamic* changes, i.e., they measure the changes in blood flow and the levels of oxygenation in the blood following neural activity. Though scientific research had revealed an important relationship between blood flow and brain function as early as the 1870s, it took almost 100 years for the significance of this fact to be fully appreciated and implemented for effective neural imaging by way of the development of positron emission tomography (PET) and magnetic resonance imaging (MRI). Finally, one more important step forward occurred in the late 1980s with the development of functional magnetic resonance imaging (fMRI) – a development that opened up a new avenue of research that was almost wholly responsible for the birth of cognitive neuroscience. Unlike previous neural imagining techniques, fMRI technology allows for relatively high-resolution images of the brain to be collected very quickly, with a whole brain scan being possible in less than three seconds.[2]

So how has philosophy of mind in the 20th century been influenced by all of this neuroscientific research? As we have learned more and more about the brain, how has that influenced our philosophical understanding of the mind? Interestingly, some philosophers have suggested that for most of the century it has had very little effect at all.[3] In their article on "The Philosophy of Neuroscience" in *The Stanford Encyclopedia of Philosophy*, John Bickle, Peter Mandik, and Anthony Landreth argue that "actual neuroscientific discoveries have exerted little influence on the details of materialist philosophies of mind." While granting that the late 20th-century "neuroscientific milieu" has had some sway in discouraging dualism, they note that most 20th-century materialists – including even the empirically oriented identity theorists of the 1950s (see Chapter 2) – have relied very little on actual neuroscientific details. Moreover, as they go on to suggest, the rise of functionalism in the 1970s has been accompanied by a neglect of neuroscientific research not only in practice but also in principle. Functionalists suggested that mental states are to be understood in terms of their function. But since the function of a state does not depend on physical mechanisms in which it is realized, functionalists have tended to think that we cannot understand the nature of mind by way of neuroscience.

To my mind, however, this pessimistic assessment of the influence that neuroscience has had on philosophy is problematic. Granted, philosophers' continued fixation on c-fibers in discussion of pain (see Chapter 2), even in the face of evidence that this association is overly simplistic, may seem to indicate a clear neuroscientific indifference – and this is how Bickle et al. take it.[4] But there are numerous other cases in which specific neuroscientific findings have played a key role in philosophical debates about the mind. Take the split-brain studies, for example. Introduced to philosophers largely by way of Thomas Nagel's "Brain Bisection and the Unity of Consciousness" (1971), the empirical results generated by Sperry and Gazzaniga have played a direct role in a variety of different philosophical debates from questions about consciousness (see Chapter 3) to questions about personal identity (see Chapter 5). Empirical findings about the relation between perceptual processing and electrical brain fields contributed to the demise of gestaltist views of perception (see Chapter 4), while empirical results concerning our sensorimotor capabilities have given rise to philosophical views of embodied cognition (see Chapter 10).

Perhaps more importantly, even when philosophers have not been focused on the specific details of neuroscientific research, they have still been tremendously influenced by the more general lessons that emerged during the course of the 20th-century investigation of the brain. The "neuroscientific milieu" referenced by Bickle et al. has significantly shaped a variety of philosophical debates about the mind in the 20th century. Philosophical inquiries into the nature of the mind, of consciousness, of mental causation, of perception, etc. have all been conducted against the backdrop of the continuing success of the brain mapping project. Philosophers working on mental causation, for example, may not be focused on particular findings about mental-physical correlations, but it's become a starting point in much of that discussion that such correlations exist (see Chapter 7). Moreover, as we move forward in the 21st century, there is every indication that the influence of neuroscience on philosophy of mind will continue to grow even stronger.

3. Alan Turing and the computer revolution

In this section, I turn from neuroscience to computer science, and in particular, to the seminal work of Alan Turing (1912–1954), a British mathematician who racked up many significant accomplishments during his short life. During World War II, he was part of the team of cryptographers who managed to decrypt the German code machine Enigma. He is widely credited with creating the field of artificial intelligence. And, though he was not trained as a philosopher, his paper "Computing Machinery and Intelligence," published in *Mind* in 1950, has been hugely influential in 20th-century philosophy of mind.[5]

In fact, there are four distinct elements of Turing's work that have proved especially important to philosophers of mind: (1) his development of what is typically referred to as a *Turing machine*, not an actual machine but rather an abstract model for a universal computing machine; (2) his subsequent contributions to the actual construction of some of the first digital computers; (3) his work on the mathematical notion of computability, and in particular, the result now often referred to as the *Church-Turing thesis* (see Chapter 11); and (4) his articulation of a framework – what he himself referred to as an *imitation game* but which is now widely referred to as the *Turing test* – for determining whether computers can think. Here I will focus on this last element of Turing's work,[6] but all four of these elements are part and parcel of what has sometimes been called the *computer revolution* – a revolution that parallels previous scientific revolutions associated with figures such as Copernicus, Darwin, and Freud. As Luciano Floridi has argued, the computer revolution has forced us to reconceptualize the world in which we live:

> Computer science and the issuing technological applications . . . have not only provided unprecedented epistemic and engineering powers over natural and artificial realities; by doing so they have also cast new light on who we are, how we are related to the world and hence how we understand ourselves.
>
> (Floridi 2012, 3540)

When approaching the question of whether machines can think, it is easy to get bogged down in definitional matters such as what we mean by "machine" and what we mean by "thinking" – so much so that the very question itself may seem a meaningless one. To bypass this difficulty, Turing proposed that we instead approach the question by judging the machine's performance in an imitation game. Consider a set-up involving a neutral interviewer and two systems – one human and one machine. The interviewer asks questions of each system, not knowing which is which, via some kind of remote relay. (Turing described this in terms of a teleprinter connecting the rooms, but today it is easy to imagine the set-up in terms of texting or some other kind of instant messaging.) With no limit placed on the type of questions allowed, the interviewer is then given some set amount of time – five minutes, say – and is charged with determining which system is the human and which system is the machine. Having described this imitation game, Turing suggests we discard the meaningless question "Can machines think?" and instead ask: "Are there imaginable machines that can do well at the imitation game" (Turing 1950, 442)?

Turing himself gave an affirmative answer to this question, and he famously predicted that by the end of the 20th century, machines would be developed that would be able to reliably succeed at the imitation game. While this prediction has not yet come true, machines have exhibited considerable mastery across a diverse range of seemingly intelligent domains. Not only have machines been able to beat humans at games such as chess, Go, and Jeopardy!, but we now also have unmanned drones in our skies, driverless cars about to populate our highways, and programs like Siri and Cortana that organize our lives.[7] To many, it seems only a matter of time – perhaps only a very short matter of time – before the Turing test is passed. (See Chapter 12 for discussion of the likely future of artificial intelligence.)

However the future unfolds, it's hard to overstate the importance played in the late 20th century by the framework for thinking about machine intelligence that Turing's imitation game provided. In particular, this framework was almost solely responsible for the initial wave of artificial intelligence in the 1950s and 1960s. As Blay Whitby has noted, in those years it served as "a source of inspiration to all concerned with AI" (Whitby 1996, 53).[8] Indeed, writing in 1964, Alan Ross Anderson notes that more than 1,000 papers had been published since 1950 on the question of whether machines can think (Anderson 1964, 1).

Criticism of the Turing test has tended to come from two very different directions. On the one hand, some have charged that the test does not set a high enough bar for intelligence: Couldn't a machine pass simply by "simulating" thinking rather than by actually thinking? (See, e.g., Searle 1980). Often these sorts of worries can be traced to the behaviorist presuppositions that seem to be underlying the test: The Turing test seems to reduce thinking to behavior, a reduction that many have found problematic. On the other hand, some have charged that the test sets too high a bar for machine thought: Couldn't there be intelligent machines that would be unable to pass the Turing test? In assessing this second criticism, it's important to note that Turing seemed to intend that his test be a *sufficient* but not *necessary* condition for machine thought. While a machine's ability to pass the test licenses the conclusion that it thinks, a machine's inability to pass the test does not license the conclusion that it doesn't think. Even so, some have suggested that the test sets such an unrealistically rigorous standard that it fails to be at all useful. Consider an example offered by Robert French (1990). If you are trying to determine what counts as flying, you might adopt the Seagull test: Anything that can fool a panel of investigators into thinking that it is a seagull counts as flying. Insisting that this is only a sufficient condition for flying does not make this test any more helpful when it gives false negatives on objects like 747s, mosquitoes, and hummingbirds – and likewise for the potentially false negatives issued by the Turing test. More generally, we might worry that the very set-up of the Turing test, a set-up that involves the imitation of humans, mistakenly constrains machine intelligence to a human mold.

Even this brief overview of the Turing test indicates that Turing's work played a seminal role in the development of cognitive science, a topic taken up in Chapter 11 of this volume. It's perhaps also already clear how his work would influence 20th-century philosophical thinking about the mind-body problem and the problem of consciousness: The emergence of functionalism – and, more generally, the computational model of mind – in the second half of the century owes directly to the computer revolution for which he was largely responsible (see Chapters 2 and 3). Because the computational model of mind is at work in 20th-century discussions of perception (Chapter 4), intentionality (Chapter 8), and questions about the boundaries of the mind (Chapter 10), we see a similar influence on many of the other philosophical problems and themes traced in this volume. To give just one more example, we might note the impact that Turing had on Wittgenstein, whose lectures on the philosophy of mathematics he attended at the University of Cambridge in 1939. Indeed, there are various indications throughout Wittgenstein's work that he was grappling with Turing's ideas.[9] (For a discussion of Wittgenstein's philosophy of mind, see Chapter 9.)

4. The essays

It was against this scientific backdrop – from psychology to neuroscience to computer science – that the philosophical debates discussed in this volume played out. Not all of these debates were influenced by these empirical developments in the same way, and in some cases the influence is significantly more pronounced than in others. But as I turn now to the twelve chapters of this volume, it should become clear that many of the preoccupations of 20th-century philosophy of mind are deeply influenced by the science of the century.

The volume begins with Phillip Walsh and Jeff Yoshimi's discussion of the phenomenological tradition initiated by Edmund Husserl and then developed by figures such as Martin Heidegger, Emmanuel Levinas, Maurice Merleau-Ponty, and Simone de Beauvoir. As the study of phenomena – things as they *appear* as opposed to things as they really *are* – phenomenology is essentially the study of consciousness. Though the work of the phenomenologists and the work of analytic philosophers of mind developed in isolation from one another for most of the 20th century, there is considerable thematic overlap between them and, as Walsh and Yoshimi show, there was also an increasing convergence between these areas of study by century's end.

After providing a comprehensive overview of the phenomenological tradition in 20th-century philosophy, Walsh and Yoshimi turn to philosophical issues in which the intersection between phenomenology and philosophy of mind is particularly salient. The first concerns perceptual content, where the work of Husserl and Merleau-Ponty has interesting points of contact with contemporary debates about non-conceptual content and the plausibility of representationalism. While these points of contact have been increasingly explored in recent years, the second issue discussed by Walsh and Yoshimi – that of the phenomenology of the mind-body debate – still remains largely unexplored. As Walsh and Yoshimi convincingly show, Husserl's own phenomenology of the mind-body problem can help to elucidate the space of possibilities available for philosophical consideration. In particular, by rejecting unlimited supervenience and endorsing only *partial* supervenience – by claiming, that is, that only some of an agent's mental processes supervene on that agent's physical processes – Husserl opens the door to a wider range of possible positions than was usually accepted in 20th-century philosophy of mind. (Here Walsh and Yoshimi's discussion connects nicely with the themes explored by Julie Yoo in Chapter 7.)

In Chapter 2, I trace the discussion of the mind-body problem in 20th-century philosophy. The dualist consensus that had dominated philosophical thinking about the relation between the mind and the brain since Descartes' work in the 17th century came under significant pressure throughout most of the 20th century. The story told here is perhaps well known – early in the century, philosophers were inclined towards various versions of behaviorism, which then was supplanted in mid-century by the development of the identity theory, which was in turn largely supplanted in the 60s and 70s by functionalism. In this chapter, however, I attempt to flesh out this standard story by showing how the problems and objections that beset each theory directly gave rise to the next. I also aim to show how dissatisfaction with these theories led to a renewed focus on the qualitative aspects of mind in the final decades of the century.

All three areas of scientific research outlined in the earlier sections of this introduction manifest their influence throughout the discussion in Chapter 2. The philosophical behaviorism of the early 20th century was very much influenced by what was happening in psychology at the time, and as psychological behaviorism fell into disfavor largely because of the work of Chomsky, so too did philosophical behaviorism. Increased understanding of the workings of the brain – and in particular, increasing optimism about neural localization – helped to give rise to the identity theorist's conviction that mental states could be identified with particular brain states. Finally, the computer revolution ushered in by Turing's seminal work helped give rise to functionalism and, more generally, to computational models of mind.

Tim Crane takes up a topic closely related to the mind-body problem in Chapter 3 when he traces the development of 20th-century thinking about consciousness. As Crane notes, at the beginning of the century philosophers across the spectrum – from perceptual realists to pragmatists to phenomenologists – accepted two basic tenets about consciousness: that consciousness is the defining feature of the mind, and that consciousness and thought (intentionality) are inextricably connected and thus cannot be treated in isolation from one another (for similar discussion, see Chapter 8). By the end of the century, both of these tenets had been largely rejected. Moreover, while philosophers at the start of the century took the primary problem of consciousness to be one of explaining the nature of our access to the mind-independent world, philosophers at century's end took the primary problem of consciousness to be one of explaining how any physical thing could be conscious.

Crane's concern in this chapter is to diagnose how this change came about. Starting with the notion of "givenness" that characterized consciousness at the start of the century, Crane shows how philosophers began to conceive of consciousness as primarily a sensory phenomenon – where the sensory element itself is seen as ineffable. This conception of consciousness, what Crane calls *the phenomenal residue* conception, naturally leads to a bifurcated characterization of mental phenomena: On the one hand, there are essentially unconscious propositional attitudes, and, on the other hand, there are sensory qualia. Though this division was treated as inevitable for much of the second half of the century, Crane argues that it should be rejected.

In Chapter Four, Nico Orlandi explores the history of philosophical reflection about perception in the last century. Her discussion treats perception in two guises. First, we can think of perception as a *conscious relation*. In this guise, perception is taken to be a means of acquainting perceivers with the mind-independent world. Twentieth-century work on perception involved a sustained defense of this assumption, which is often referred to as *perceptual realism*. Orlandi traces its development from sense data theorists such as G. E. Moore and Bertrand Russell at the start of the century, to intentionalists such as G.E.M. Anscombe in mid-century, to disjuncitivists such as John McDowell in the latter half of the century.

Second, we can think of perception as a subconscious process, i.e., as whatever process enables us to perceive the world as we do. Here philosophers have been greatly influenced by research in psychology and, more broadly, in cognitive science. At the beginning of the century, gestalt theorists such as the psychologists Max Wertheimer, Wolfang Köhler, and Kurt Koffka rejected the structuralism and atomism that dominated at the end of the nineteenth century and argued that percepts cannot always be decomposed into more basic sensory parts. Rather, we must adopt a more holistic picture. Though gestaltism largely fell out of favor by mid-century, it nonetheless exerted an important influence on subsequent philosophical work. The second half of the century was marked by the emergence of two different views. According to constructivism, perception essentially involves an internal inference, one that supplements the initial sensory stimulation. In vision, for example, the retinal image is processed by using hidden assumptions to reach perceptual conclusions about the environment. In contrast to constructivism, the ecological views that emerged in the second half of the century focused not on internal procedures but on environmental interactions. While the constructivist tends to see perception as a static process, ecological theorists like J. J. Gibson see perception as dynamic. For Gibson, the perceptual act is an active engagement with the world.

In different ways, both of these views gain support from the developments in artificial intelligence discussed earlier in section 3 of this introduction. Constructivism, for example, gains plausibility from the computational theory of mind. As Orlandi notes,

> If we recognize symbols as information-carrying structures, and algorithms as containing assumptions and rules to process the symbols, then viewing the perceptual process as computational pretty much amounts to viewing it the way the constructivist does – as an inference from some informational states to others.
>
> (this volume, p. 116)

In contrast, ecological views gain plausibility from more recent developments in connectionism. Connectionist networks, which attune to the world by spreading levels of activation, seem to work in the dynamic way predicted by the ecological view and without the internal inference process posited by constructivism.

While the first four chapters of the volume can be seen as tracing back to problems that were brought to the forefront of philosophical inquiry by Descartes, the topic of the fifth chapter traces back instead to a problem that was brought to the forefront by Locke. In this chapter, Jens Johansson takes up the topic of personal identity and, in particular, the question of what it takes for us to persist through time. Locke's answer, proposed in the 17th century, was that someone existing at one time is identical to someone existing at a later time if and only if the latter individual can remember something the former person experienced at the earlier time. Though Locke's contemporaries pointed out several deep problems with this view, 20th-century interest in it was reignited when, in the early 1940s, H. P. Grice proposed a particularly sophisticated version of the Lockean view that avoided previous objections. After further modifications, Locke's emphasis on memory has given way to interest in psychological connections more broadly considered, and the view has developed into what's commonly known as the *psychological continuity view*. As Johansson notes, much of the discussion of personal identity in 20th-century philosophy has centered on the plausibility of this view. One persistent challenge comes from the fission problem, i.e., from the fact that it seems that one person can be psychologically continuous with two (or more) future individuals. More recently, other challenges have come from animalism, a view that sees us fundamentally as human animals. On this view, our persistence conditions are the persistence conditions of animals. Thus, our continued existence through time consists not in psychological continuity but in the continuity of the human organism.

The debate about personal identity is one that bridges both philosophy of mind and metaphysics, and it has a very different character from the debates discussed in the previous chapters of this volume. But here too we can see influence from some of the empirical developments discussed earlier in this chapter. First, our increasing knowledge about the brain (and particularly, about neural localization of function) has helped to inform other thought experiments that have played an influential role in philosophical discussion of the problem of personal identity. Here recall the split-brain patients discussed in section 2. Lessons learned from such patients give rise to particular manifestations of the fission problem; we might imagine, for example, that someone's brain is severed and each half is then implanted into a new android body. Secondly, and relatedly, the emergence of artificial intelligence and the corresponding computational theory of mind may well have given rise to intuitions that help to support the psychological continuity theory. Once we see the mind computationally, as a pattern of information, it then becomes easier to think of ourselves surviving when the information-pattern is uploaded into a different body or even to a machine.

In Chapter Six, Maja Spener explores the role that introspection played in 20th-century theorizing about the mind. Focusing on the use of introspection in both philosophy and psychology, Spener attempts to analyze some of the persisting influences these disciplines had on one another in this context. In doing so, however, she also highlights the peculiar lack of influence in some contexts. In particular, though the behaviorists largely succeeded in purging introspectionist methods from psychology in the first part of the century (see Section 1 above), philosophers – particularly philosophers of perception – continued to rely heavily and unashamedly on introspection in developing their philosophical theories. As Spener shows, this lack of influence also led to a surprising result: Despite sophisticated debates about introspection at the beginning of the century, the end of the century saw philosophers working with a surprisingly rudimentary conception of the proper role of introspection. Though there were indeed some lessons learned about introspection over the course of the 20th century, Spener also shows that there were many lessons lost.

Spener begins her discussion with the philosophical use of introspection by sense-data theorists such as G. E. Moore, C. I. Lewis, and H. H. Price. While such theorists often pointed out that introspection can lead us astray, and while they often accused their opponents of misusing introspection, they themselves were happy to invoke introspective data in defense of their own theory. Spener next turns to an extended discussion of the use of introspection in psychology – from introspectionists like Wundt, Titchener, and Külpe to Gestalt theorists like Koffka and Köhler. (See also the discussion of Gestalt psychology in Chapter 4). As she carefully shows, psychologists of the early 20th century tended to accept that introspection can be usefully employed in a study of the conscious mind, but they also were careful to distinguish different kinds of introspection, not all of which they found equally suitable for experimental investigation. In the final section of her paper, Spener turns to late 20th-century philosophical theorizing and, in particular, to theorizing about the so-called transparency thesis. Roughly put, the thesis is that, when one reflects on the phenomenal character of one's experience, one "looks through" the experience to what it is about, namely, to ordinary objects in the world. As Spener shows, discussions about transparency tend to take for granted that we have introspective access to our experiences and, moreover, that such access yields judgments appropriate for employment in theorizing. At the end of the century, unlike at its start, there was no longer any sense that we need to differentiate types of introspective access.

As we saw earlier, the discussion of Chapter Two attends to what's often referred to as the mind-body problem. But talk of *the* mind-body problem is perhaps misleading. Alongside the problem of how to account for the structural relation between mental states and their underlying neural states, there is also the problem of how to account for the causal relation between them. Julie Yoo takes up this problem – often referred to as the problem of mental causation – in Chapter 7.

The first part of Yoo's discussion concerns three responses to mental interaction that were prevalent in the early 20th century: epiphenomenalism, panpsychism, and emergentism. While there are considerable differences between these three accounts, they share amongst them a broadly naturalistic focus. Thinkers surveyed in this part of the chapter include Thomas Huxley, William James, Bertrand Russell, and Samuel Alexander (among others). Yoo next turns to a form of skepticism about mental causation that arose in mid-century as an outgrowth of behaviorism, ordinary language philosophy, and the rise of Wittgensteinism (see Chapter Nine). According to thinkers such as Gilbert Ryle, it is a mistake to think of reasons as causes and hence also a mistake to think of the mind as something that can wield causal powers. Finally, the third and longest section of Yoo's article focuses on what she calls the "golden age" of mental causation debates, an age that was largely ushered in by Donald Davidson's argument for anomalous monism in 1970. This argument gave rise to what Yoo calls the *Anomalism Problem*:

If events can be causally related only if there are laws that cover them, then the absence of psychological or psychophysical laws raises doubts about mental events' causal efficacy.

An explosion of interest in mental causation as the result of discussion of the Anomalism Problem in turn led to two other problems of mental causation. The Exclusion Problem, owing to the work of Jaegwon Kim, questions how mental events can be causally efficacious given the causal closure of the physical domain. Given causal closure, every event or action has a fully sufficient physical cause that "excludes" other causes, such as mental causes, in bringing about the action. The other problem arises from worries about externalism. According to content externalism (see the extensive discussion in Chapter 10), representational states are not solely "in the head." Rather, their content depends on social and environmental factors. But if this is true, then unless we are prepared to accept some kind of spooky action at a distance, mental contents do not look like they play a role in causing behavior. As Yoo discusses, the last decades of the 20th century witnessed careful attention to all three of these problems.

In Chapter Eight, Michelle Montague takes up the notion of intentionality, i.e., the respect in which our mental states are object-directed. Her discussion focuses on Franz Brentano, a philosopher whose work has been enormously influential in 20th- and 21st-century theorizing about the topic. Brentano's work aimed to establish two central claims about intentionality. First, he claimed that intentionality is the "mark" of the mental, i.e., that all and only mental states are intentional. Second, he claimed that consciousness and intentionality are constitutively related to one another. While much of 20th-century discussion of intentionality was preoccupied with what's often referred to as *the problem of intentionality* – the problem of how we can think about nonexistent objects – Montague argues that a focus on this problem obscures our understanding of Brentano's position and leads to misinterpretations of it.

Montague begins with a detailed explication of Brentano's theories of consciousness and intentionality in his *Psychology from an Empirical Standpoint*, published in 1874. She then discusses the shift in his views evident in the publication of the 1911 Appendix to this work. As Montague shows, Brentano moves from thinking about intentionality as involving *reference to something as object* to thinking of it explicitly as a *relation*. Her discussion then moves to other philosophers who were influenced by Brentano, and she shows the impact that his work has had on subsequent philosophical discussions of intentionality. She starts with Kazimierz Twardowski and Alexius Meinong, two students of Brentano's who attempted to develop and improve upon their teacher's original theory. She then turns to Roderick Chisholm, the philosopher largely responsible for generating interest in Brentano's work within contemporary analytic philosophy. Chisholm's focus on our apparent ability to think about nonexistent objects set the terms for much of the subsequent discussion about intentionality in the second half of the 20th century. Montague argues that much of that discussion – and in particular, the separatist assumptions that treated intentionality and consciousness in isolation from one another for much of the second half of the century – proved to be a departure from Brentano's own thinking about intentionality. In the final decades of the 20th century (and continuing now in these early years of the 21st century), an increasing skepticism about and then rejection of separatism brought philosophers of mind back to something closer Brentano's own treatment of intentionality. In the final section of her chapter, Montague discusses contemporary theories of consciousness such as representationalism, higher-order theories, "consciousness first" views, and the phenomenal intentionality program. (Here Montague's discussion connects nicely with Crane's discussion of these theories in Chapter 3.) In the course of this discussion, she shows how such theories do – and do not – succeed in recapturing Brentano's original insights about intentionality.

Much as Chapter 8 serves as a chapter on the work and subsequent legacy of a towering figure in late 19th- and early 20th-century philosophy, Chapter 9 serves as a chapter on the work and subsequent legacy of a towering figure in early and mid-20th-century philosophy. In this chapter, Severin Schroeder focuses on Ludwig Wittgenstein, particularly on his criticism of Cartesian dualism and the various misunderstandings that attend it. Because it is difficult to understand these criticisms unless one understands Wittgenstein's distinctive approach to philosophy, Schroeder begins his discussion with an introduction to Wittgenstein's overall methodology. The chapter then ends with a discussion of Wittgenstein's influence on subsequent philosophy of mind, an influence that has been particularly prominent in the development of functionalist views. (For more on functionalism, see Chapter 2.)

Wittgenstein's anti-Cartesianism is particularly evident in his trenchant criticisms of the inner-object model – a model according to which thoughts and feelings are taken to be mental objects analogous to physical objects such as rocks and tables. In the course of this chapter, Schroeder aims to elucidate Wittgenstein's attempts to show the problematic consequences of the inner-object model with respect to sensations and other minds, understanding, thinking, and voluntary action. Consider, for example, Wittgenstein's famous private-language argument. Here Wittgenstein targets the assumption that sensations and other mental states are private, inner objects, inaccessible to others; his general strategy is to show that this assumption leads to absurd consequences – consequences such as the problem of other minds, i.e., our inability to have any way of knowing what others think and feel (and even if they think and feel), or the problem of communication, i.e., our inability to communicate anything about our thoughts and feelings to anyone else. Schroeder reconstructs in detail four of Wittgenstein's principal objections to the inner-object view of sensations. Likewise, in his discussion of Wittgenstein's attack on the inner-object view of voluntary action, a view presupposed not only by Descartes but also by British Empiricists such as John Locke, Schroeder differentiates three different objections posed by Wittgenstein. Though the details differ, all three of these objections aim to show that words like "willing" do not pick out some distinctive mental occurrence that either precedes or accompanies a movement and thereby makes it a voluntary one.

Thus far we have seen various ways in which 20th-century philosophy developed in reaction to Cartesian dualism. In Chapter 10, Katalin Farkas takes up the 20th-century reaction to a different aspect of the Cartesian conception of mind, namely, individualism. According to individualism, the content of mental states can be individuated wholly in terms of properties of the subject of those states. Consider the Evil Demon thought experiment of the First Meditation, where Descartes worries that a powerful and malicious force might be deceiving him into thinking there is an external world. As Descartes argues, even if he were the victim of radical deception, he would still be a thinking thing and, moreover, he would still have exactly the same mental features as those he has when he is not deceived. This claim – that we could have the very same thoughts and experiences absent an external world, that our thoughts would have the very same *content* absent an external world – came under intense scrutiny in the second half of the 20th century.

After an introductory sketch of the Cartesian conception of mind, Farkas turns to the externalism (or anti-individualism) that has its origins in Frege's distinction between sense and reference and grew more directly out of the work of Hilary Putnam and Tyler Burge in the 1970s. Putnam and Burge proposed thought experiments that suggested that two qualitatively identical individuals placed in different environments might mean different things by a natural kind term like "water" and likewise have different concepts and different thoughts. To use Putnam's famous phrase, both meanings and the content of thoughts "ain't in the head." In addition to her discussion of Putnam and Burge, Farkas also considers the two-dimensionalism associated with David Kaplan and later developed by David Chalmers and also the alternate externalist framework of Gareth Evans and John McDowell. Then, turning to naturalist conceptions of mind, Farkas discusses two other themes that arise in thinking about the boundaries of the mind: (1) the "active externalism" of the extended mind thesis, and (2) embodied cognition views. According to the extended mind thesis, external devices such as notebooks or smart phones may play the same role in our cognitive processes as non-occurrent beliefs, and hence may be literally said to be part of the mind. According to views of embodied cognition – views that draw heavily on the sorts of empirical research we considered earlier – our cognitive processes fundamentally depend upon our bodies and, in particular, on our bodies' sensorimotor capacities. Discussion of these views leads Farkas to a more general discussion of the different ways that 20th-century philosophers have conceived of the boundaries of the mind.

Perhaps nowhere in the volume is the connection to Turing's legacy more apparent than in Chapter 11. Here Carrie Figdor provides a conceptual history of the rise of cognitive science in the 20th century. Cognitive science is the multidisciplinary study of individual agents, both what they are and how they function. Figdor organizes her discussion around five central innovations of the 20th century that constitute what she calls the "basic explanatory package" of cognitive science.

The first four pieces of the package came together in relatively short succession in the 1930s and 1940s. First, Turing's development of the universal Turing Machine showed how a sequence of simple internal state transitions could produce rational behavior. Second, the proposal by McCulloch and Pitts that we should think of neurons as biological logic gates enabled cognitive scientists to understand how those simple internal state transitions might be thought to occur in the brain. (A logic gate is a unit whose operations can be explained in terms of the truth tables for conjunction and disjunction.) This work also led to the development of connectionist networks, often referred to as *neural* nets. Third, Wiener's work showed how systems could learn. While Turing's original model did not address the question of how system rules could be modified, Wiener showed how we could incorporate feedback control into the model. This helps to account for learning. On Wiener's model, learning occurs when an agent appropriately modifies its behavior in response to experience that is itself a consequence of prior behavior. Fourth, Shannon's work helped us to understand what was meant by "information" in discussions of information processing. In particular, Shannon showed that the statistical or probabilistic structure inherent in communication elucidates and indeed quantifies the notion of information.

The final element of the conceptual package did not emerge until David Marr's work in the 1980s. Marr was a vision scientist, but his approach to explanation helped to unify cognitive science research across its many disciplines. In particular, Marr identified three different kinds of questions we need to answer in order to explain the workings of an information-processing system. The first question concerns computation: What is the problem that the system needs to solve? The second question concerns algorithm: What sorts of representations and rules are utilized in solving the problem? And the third question concerns implementation: In what physical mechanisms are these representations (and the processes in which they are involved) realized?

Figdor's chapter concludes by noting that "the basic conceptual package for explaining agency will soon be fully elaborated in outline if not in its empirical details," and she predicts that, with respect to cognitive science, the 21st century will likely be the century of the social, i.e., it will involve intense study of social cognition. In the final chapter of the book, Susan Schneider and Pete Mandik directly take up the question of what lies ahead in the 21st century. Their discussion begins with findings from the artificial intelligence community that strongly suggests that sophisticated artificial intelligence will be here by 2070, if not earlier. This looming development suggests that philosophy of mind will have a very important role to play in the decades ahead. Though discussing this role requires Schneider and Mandik to make some predictions, their chapter is better viewed as *prescriptive* than as *predictive*, as their primary concern is to suggest ways that philosophy of mind can positively impact the future that lies before us.

Consider, for example, the fact that a dizzying array of neural enhancements will likely soon be widely available. Philosophical work on the extended mind – and here recall Farkas' discussion in Chapter 10 – can help us to better understand and navigate these emerging technologies. Or consider the fact that one may soon be able to upload one's consciousness and thereby in some way "migrate" to a cloud-based existence. In this context, Johansson's discussion of the problem of personal identity in Chapter 6 becomes particularly relevant: Would such a migration constitute survival? Here again, Schneider and Mandik suggest ways that philosophy of mind can help people of the late 21st century make sense of the decisions with which they will be confronted. Finally, consider also the challenges that lie ahead as we confront the possibility of AI consciousness. Analogous to what's often referred to as the hard problem of consciousness (see Crane's discussion in Chapter 3) is the hard problem of AI consciousness, a problem that concerns how we determine whether there is something that it is like to be an AI system. Do such systems really feel pain when they are damaged? Can they experience suffering? The need to make progress on such questions seems particularly pressing when we recognize the ethical obligations we have to creatures that have the capacity to suffer.

In a sense, Schneider and Mandik's chapter – a chapter that concludes not only this volume but also all six volumes of this series on philosophy of mind – serves as a vindication of the discipline itself. As they convincingly argue, the problems that lie ahead are problems that philosophy of mind is distinctively qualified to address. While scientists and artificial intelligence researchers will develop the coming technologies, philosophers of mind will be needed to help understand and assess the implications such technologies present. In doing so, future philosophers will have a very long and fruitful history upon which to draw.

Notes

1 These findings would later be corroborated in the 20th century; see Damasio et al. (1994).
2 For a useful survey of the advances made in neural imaging techniques in the second half of the 20th century, see Savoy (2001). In particular, this article provides a helpful and relatively accessible overview of techniques such as PET, MRI, and fMRI.
3 They take the publication of Patricia Churchland's *Neurophilosophy* (1986) to be the turning point.
4 Alternatively, one might see philosophers' use of "c-fiber" as explicitly serving a placeholder function. See the discussion in Chapter 2.
5 As of this writing in 2016, Google scholar lists this paper as having been cited more than 8400 times. (For comparison, J.J.C. Smart's influential paper "Sensations and Brain Processes," published in *Philosophical Review* in 1959, is listed as having been cited just over 1300 times.)
6 All four of these elements of Turing's work are discussed in the papers collected in Millican and Clark (1996).
7 Indeed, programs like Siri are referred to as "intelligent personal assistants."
8 It's worth noting that, having made this assessment, Whitby goes on to argue that focus on the Turing test eventually became a distraction from other promising avenues of AI research.
9 Wittgenstein (1967; 1980) explicitly addressed the notion of Turing machines.

Bibliography

Anderson, Alan (ed.). (1964). *Minds and Machines*. Englewood Cliffs, NJ: Prentice-Hall.
Bickle, John, Mandik, Peter and Landreth, Anthony. (2012). "The Philosophy of Neuroscience," in Zalta, Edward N. (ed.), *The Stanford Encyclopedia of Philosophy* (Summer 2012 Edition). http://plato.stanford.edu/archives/sum2012/entries/neuroscience/.

Churchland, Patricia (1986). *Neurophilosophy*. Cambridge, MA: The MIT Press.

Damasio, Hanna, et al. (1994) "The Return of Phineas Gage: Clues About the Brain from the Skull of a Famous Patient," *Science*, 264: 1102–1105.

Floridi, Luciano (2012) "Turing's Three Philosophical Lessons and the Philosophy of Information," *Philosophical Transactions of the Royal Aristotelian Society*, 370: 3536–3542.

French, Robert (1990). "Subcognition and the Limits of the Turing Test," *Mind*, 99: 53–65.

Millican, P.J.R., and Clark, A. (eds.). (1996). *Machines and Thought: The Legacy of Alan Turing*, vol. I. Oxford: Clarendon Press.

Nagel, Thomas (1971) "Brain Bisection and the Unity of Consciousness," *Synthese*, 22: 396–413.

Raichle, Marcus (2008). "A Brief History of Human Brain Mapping," *Trends in Neurosciences*, 32(2): 118–126.

Savoy, Robert L. (2001). "History and Future Directions of Human Brain Mapping and Functional Neuroimaging," *Acta Psychologica*, 107: 9–42.

Searle, John (1980). "Minds, Brains, and Programs," *Behavioral and Brain Sciences*, 3: 417–424.

Skinner, B.F. (1953). *Science and Human Behavior*. New York: Macmillan Publishing Co.

Skinner, B.F. (1974). *About Behaviorism*. New York: Alfred A. Knopf, Inc.

Skinner, B.F. (1987). "Behaviorism, Skinner On," in Gregory, Richard L. (ed.), *Oxford Companion to the Mind*. New York: Oxford University Press.

Turing, A.M. (1950). "Computing Machinery and Intelligence," *Mind*, 59: 433–460.

Watson, John B. (1913). "Psychology as the Behaviorist Views It," *Psychological Review*, 20: 158–177.

Whitby, Blay (1996). "The Turing Test: AI's Biggest Blind Alley," in Millican and Clark (eds.): 53–62.

Wittgenstein, Ludwig (1967). *Zettel*. Edited by G.E.M. Anscombe and G. H. von Wright. Oxford: Blackwell.

Wittgenstein, Ludwig (1980) *Remarks on the Philosophy of Psychology*, 2 vols. Edited by G.E.M Anscombe, G. H. von Wright, and H. Nyman. Oxford: Blackwell.

1

PHILOSOPHY OF MIND IN THE PHENOMENOLOGICAL TRADITION

Philip J. Walsh and Jeff Yoshimi

1. Introduction

Contemporary phenomenology and philosophy of mind are vast areas of research. In the PhilPapers database, phenomenology has over 34,000 entries, and philosophy of mind contains over 92,000 entries, distributed across consciousness, intentionality, perception, and metaphysics of mind, among others.[1] The two areas come together at many points – think of two galaxies colliding. But the metaphor is not quite apt. They are not independent bodies of research that happen to overlap but are rather two phases of a continuous tradition that diverged for a time and are now, at least partially, reintegrating (the image of a diverging and reconverging flock of starlings – a murmuration – comes to mind).

Philosophy of mind in the 20th century is typically understood in terms of a certain historical progression (cf. Chapter 2): after rejecting introspection as unreliable, the behaviorists of the 1930s–1950s sought to understand the mind strictly in terms of publicly available data. But behaviorism cannot account for certain inner feelings and states, so the identity theory emerged in the late 1950s as a viable physicalist alternative (Place 1956; Feigl 1958; Smart 1959). The identity theory posits a strict, reductive identity between brain states and mental states. However, the one-to-one link between psychological terms and corresponding physical terms was problematic, since terms like "pain" seem to have a one-many relation to physical kinds (many types of system can feel pain). To address this issue, functionalists described mental states as states of a kind of finite state machine or probabilistic automaton, defined by a pattern of relationships between inputs, outputs, and other internal states (Fodor 1974; Putnam 1967). These systems have the attractive feature that they can be multiply realized in different physical systems. Thus, octopi and humans can be in pain. It is "non-reductive" physicalism because it does not posit a 1–1 identity relation between mental states and brain state types, but rather a many-one implementation relation (Stoljar 2015). Functionalism continues to be a dominant theory of mind.

However, problems with functionalism – which were essentially *phenomenological* problems – emerged beginning in the 1970s. Nagel (1974), and later Block (1980), Searle (1980), and Jackson (1982), pointed out that purely formal relations between states leave out the first-person, subjective character of consciousness. By the 1990s, consciousness had become a central topic in philosophy of mind (Searle 1992; Flanagan 1992; Chalmers 1996; also see Chapter 3 on 20th-century theories of consciousness), and since then, more and more aspects of the mental are being addressed from a standpoint that does not try to reduce or analyze away consciousness.[2]

So contemporary philosophy of mind has rediscovered phenomenology, albeit in an (until recently) fairly impoverished form. Contemporary philosophers of mind often address "the phenomenology" of a particular form of experience by inquiring whether "there is something that it is like" to undergo it. The phrase is suggestive, but it has led to an austere phenomenology, an account of the "small mental residue" that materialist theories leave unexplained (Kim 2010, 333). This narrow conception of phenomenology has, however, been expanding. "Liberal" accounts of phenomenal character include emotional-affective, agentive, and cognitive experience (Bayne and Montague 2011). Intentionality has been pursued in an increasingly phenomenological way (Horgan and Tienson 2002; Kriegel 2013). These and related projects come closer to phenomenology as historically conceived, which was extremely rich in terms of its method, scope, and conceptual apparatus.

In what follows, we use the term "phenomenology" in two senses. In one sense, "phenomenology" is a method – the study of consciousness using first-person reflection. It studies the phenomenal character of mental states, or "what it is like" to experience them from the first-person perspective. In another sense, "phenomenology" is an explicit research program initiated by Edmund Husserl (1859–1938) and developed in different and sometimes inconsistent ways by Martin Heidegger (1889–1976), Maurice Merleau-Ponty (1908–1961), Simone de Beauvoir (1908–1986), and others.

In the next section, we give an overview of the phenomenological tradition. In section 3, we survey some of the many ways phenomenology overlaps philosophy of mind: they have shared historical origins in Brentano, Frege, and Husserl; there are numerous areas of thematic overlap; and there are also active collaborations, especially in the recent literature. In sections 4 and 5, we develop two case studies that show in more detail how phenomenology and philosophy mind can interact. In section 4, we describe a detailed phenomenological approach to perceptual content, and in section 5 we outline Husserl's phenomenological analysis of mind-body relations.

2. Overview of phenomenology

Phenomenology is often defined as the study of consciousness, or sometimes, the study of phenomena, i.e. things as they appear as opposed to things as they really are. Although there are problems with this definition (Husserl and Heidegger would have quibbles with it), it is helpful as a first pass way of understanding what phenomenology is.

The first of the classical phenomenologists, Husserl, developed the following first-person reflective method. He begins with the *phenomenological reduction* (Husserl 2014, §32ff.). The idea is to focus on lived experience in the "natural attitude" of daily life, and to describe it as accurately as possible. To do this, take some episode of everyday life, put it in "brackets" (i.e. do not make any extraneous assumptions about it, but simply treat it as a phenomenon to be studied) and describe it. Perhaps you are aware of a book page or a computer screen as you read these words, as well as pictures or people in the background. Perhaps you are aware of music playing, an itch in your body, or a lingering emotional state. You arguably have some sense of yourself and your body as separate from the things around you. You probably assume the things around you exist. Most of us are thus naïve realists in the natural attitude (in this way the method is supposed to differ from Descartes'; there is no active doubting, there is simply a description of whatever our epistemic attitude happens to be at a time).

Husserl dissected these conscious states into their various kinds of parts, using mereology, the study of parts and wholes, which he helped to develop (Varzi 2015). For example, within the total field of consciousness he distinguishes intentional experiences or "acts" of consciousness as entities that can be further analyzed (which, following his teacher Brentano, were an emphasis throughout his career; cf. Chapter 8 on Intentionality). Within intentional experiences of physical objects, Husserl distinguishes their sensory character from their more cognitive components (the way the cup looks vs. my knowledge that it is a cup, that it was given to me at Christmas last year, etc.). He also distinguishes one's sense of an object as an external object, from one's sense of herself as perceiving the object. Several of the distinctions that Husserl made in his careful mereological analyses of perceptual experience foreshadow contemporary debates about the metaphysics and epistemology of perceptual experience. For example, Husserl claims that perceptual experience consists of non-intentional sensory stuff (which he referred to as *hyle*) in need of conceptual "interpretation" or "apprehension", a topic that tracks several current debates (see section 4 below).

One of Husserl's main innovations is his account of how the objects given in intentional experience are "constituted" in "webs of partial intentions", characterized by "motivation" relations and "horizon" structures (Husserl 2001a, §10; 1989, §56).[3] The idea is that my seeing a thing as being a certain way is founded on a pattern of counterfactual sensori-motor relationships between my current sensory experience and my immanent anticipations. As I turn the cup in my hands or move around it, my current sense of the front of the cup "motivates" a range of further perspectives (Walsh 2013). The totality of my motivated expectations forms a kind of "horizon" of understanding, which captures my overall sense of how I think the thing will look from different perspectives. When I move the cup, these motivated expectations will either be fulfilled or frustrated by what I actually do see. When expectations are frustrated, I update my horizon understanding of the cup. When I learn something about the cup this information is "sedimented" in to my understanding of it. These changes in how I see things are studied by "genetic phenomenology." In these and other ways, reality is "constituted" for a person in flowing streams of experience. The study of how different features of experienced reality are related to conscious processes is what Husserl calls "constitutive phenomenology." Much of Husserl's vast output – 40,000 pages of research manuscripts – takes up questions relating to particular domains of constitutive phenomenology: the constitution of space, time, living beings, animals, other people, social, worlds, cultural institutions, fictional worlds, abstract domains like mathematics, etc. In section 5, we consider one of these areas – Husserl's account of the constitution of mind-body relations relative to our *experiences* of minds, bodies, and mind-body interactions – in relation to the contemporary metaphysics of mind.

Husserl makes a distinction between two general types of phenomenological process (Yoshimi 2009). On the one hand, there is a level of passive or pre-predicative constitution, which does not involve attention (hence "passive") or language (hence "pre-predicative"). Simply by interacting with things, we get a sense of how they work. As we walk around a neighborhood, interact with a cat, or practice skiing, we become familiar with how the neighborhood is laid out, or how the cat or skis tend to behave. As surprises occur, we update our knowledge of these things: we change what we expect at a turn in the neighborhood, or how we expect the cat to respond to a new person. Husserl refers to this as a process of "passive genesis", by which our intuitive, pre-attentive understanding of things is updated (Husserl 1969; 1973; 2001c). Whenever we see a thing, we tacitly bring all this implicitly acquired understanding to it, via what Husserl calls "passive synthesis". When, by contrast, we start to talk about things, using the explicit conceptual resources of a language, a second set of dynamics – which is active and predicative – becomes involved. Husserl describes in great detail how, in acts of comparing, contrasting, explicating, counting, relating, and so forth, we develop a more explicit, linguistically mediated sense of things. This cat is named Lily. She is a Balinese, and Balinese cats are known to be playful. These conceptual structures have their own horizon-structures, a kind of linguistic web of associations and patterns that further inform how we experience things. These two processes have been used to understand Husserl's relation to social and embodied cognition (Walsh 2014), cognitive science (Yoshimi 2009), and perceptual content (Hopp 2008, see section 4 below).

Husserl also describes essences or *eide*, which are invariant features of a class of objects constituted in experience. He does so using a variational method, which may have derived from the mathematical theory of calculus of variations (*Variationsrechnung*) he wrote his Ph.D. dissertation on (Yoshimi 2007). The idea is to take some object given in the field of experience, e.g. a perceived cup or passage of music, and then imagine arbitrary variations to it, while remaining in some larger region of being (e.g. physical things in general, sounds in general). The cup could be larger, a different color, etc., but still remain a physical thing. Features of the thing that remain constant through the variation are essences. Husserl says, for example, that it is an essence of perceived physical things that we never perceive them all at once: no matter how we alter the cup, we are always perceiving only one part of it. This is the essential "one-sidedness" of perception (Husserl 2014, 12; see also Husserl 2014, §42). Essences impose necessary constraints on how the members of a given class of objects or processes must appear in consciousness. Eidetic phenomenology studies these essences. Essences are known *a priori* and are necessarily true, according to Husserl. There are interesting questions about the viability of eidetic phenomenology (Kasmier 2010) and its relation to rationalism, conceptual analysis, and contemporary epistemology.[4] In section 5, we consider Husserl's eidetic analysis of the phenomenology of the mind-body problem, a kind of conceptual analysis of what is necessary, and what is left open, when one experiences minds in relation to bodies.

Husserl thought of phenomenology as an active, collaborative research program and not as a static doctrine. In *Logical Investigations*, he refers to the "zig-zag" (*Zickzack*) manner of phenomenological inquiry: "since the close interdependence of our various epistemological concepts leads us back again and again to our original analyses, where the new confirms the old, and the old the new" (Husserl 2001b, 175). A testament to this ethos can be found in the way his students have carried on this discussion, developing Husserl's ideas across a wide range of topics. In the remainder of this section, we overview some of the major phenomenological figures after Husserl.

Heidegger began as Husserl's assistant and envisioned protégé. He dedicated *Being and Time* to Husserl "with friendship and gratitude" (Husserl later added in marginal comments near this dedication: *Amicus Plato, sed magis amica veritas*; "Plato is a friend, but truth is a greater friend" Husserl 1997). Heidegger had a distinctive vision of phenomenology and was increasingly critical of Husserl as their professional relationship unfolded. He eventually broke with Husserl completely, joining the Nazi party and, as rector of Freiburg, ostracizing Husserl, and removing the dedication to Husserl from *Being and Time*.

Heidegger's background and bearing are much different than Husserl's. Where Husserl was a mathematician by training, Heidegger was trained in theology and history of philosophy. Where Husserl was sanguine about the prospects of a rational foundation for all knowledge by way of eidetic analysis of pure consciousness, Heidegger came to distrust the very concept of consciousness, and the terms and categories of Western philosophy more generally. He advocated "destroying the history of ontology" (Heidegger 1962, 41), and developed a new vocabulary for describing human existence. Rather than referring to human beings or conscious agents, for example, he refers to "*Dasein*", literally "there-being", which he defines as that being whose "being is an issue for it". Where Husserl emphasizes experiences of physical things like trees and ink blotters, Heidegger emphasizes what is meaningful in a person's life, that "for the sake of which" a person lives. The cup is rarely perceived as such, but is rather a tool, ready-to-hand, there "in-order-to" provide refreshment and energy while writing or reading papers, which is something one does "for the sake of" being an academic. These more existential dimensions of everyday experience are Heidegger's emphasis in phenomenology. Heidegger takes up all the classical phenomenological themes – space, time, things, language, other persons, etc. – but always with new language and emphases, and with fascinating results. Heidegger's approach to phenomenology has been influential in philosophy of mind and cognitive science, especially via the work of Hubert Dreyfus and his students (Dreyfus and Hall 1982; Dreyfus 1992; Wrathall and Malpas 2000).

Some notable students of Husserl include Edith Stein and Aron Gurwitsch. Stein's dissertation, *On the Problem of Empathy* (1916/1989), conducted under Husserl's supervision, provides a concise analysis of a variety of phenomena related to contemporary discussions of social cognition and the problem of other minds (see, e.g., Stueber 2006; Goldman 2006). Further links between Husserl's theory of meaning and the social world were taken up by Alfred Schutz, who integrated phenomenology with Max Weber's sociology. Husserl praised Schutz's *The Phenomenology of the Social World* (Schutz 1932/1967), which remains relevant in contemporary discussions of collective intentionality and intersubjectivity (Gilbert 1989; Mathiesen 2005; Chelstrom 2013).

Aron Gurwitsch was a philosopher and psychologist who did early work connecting phenomenology with Gestalt psychology and clinical psycho-pathology. After World War I, he worked with brain-injured veterans at a special institute set up by the Prussian government (Embree 1972). He began meeting with Husserl in the late 1920s and early 1930s, and later became close friends with Schutz, with whom he carried on an extensive and illuminating correspondence (Grathoff 1989). In the 1930s, he fled the Nazis to France, where he gave a series of lectures attended by Maurice Merleau-Ponty that may have influenced Merleau-Ponty's way of interpreting psychological data (in particular, psycho-pathological cases) using phenomenology.[5] He fled again to America in the 1940s, where he (along with others, like Schutz and Farber) helped establish phenomenology as a field of philosophical research (Kaelin and Schrag 1989). He is perhaps best known for his "field theory of consciousness", which studies the overall organization of consciousness into different parts – including inner thoughts, bodily experiences, and a sense of some part of the physical world – and the way these parts change their organization in time. This theory has been applied to the study of bodily awareness (de Vignemont 2011), attention (Arvidson 2006), and cognitive science (Embree 2004).

One of the first figures to bring phenomenology to France was Emmanuel Levinas. Levinas attended Husserl's lectures in Freiburg in 1928–1929, around the same time Gurwitsch and Schutz began studying Husserl's work. Levinas' dissertation (Levinas 1930/1995) was devoted to Husserl's theory of intuition, and he subsequently translated Husserl's lectures at the Sorbonne, *Cartesian Meditations*, from German into French (Husserl 1931/1960). Levinas' mature work on the ethical dimensions of experience stems from his critical engagement with Husserl's phenomenological analyses of empathy and intersubjectivity, and develops an account that emphasizes the experience of looking at another conscious being (human or animal) in the face. Although Levinas is not typically understood as doing philosophy of mind, his work can be understood as making phenomenological contributions to topics in social cognition and moral psychology (Overgaard 2007; Levin 1998; Atterton 2011).

It is said that Sartre was converted to phenomenology when Raymond Aron pointed at a cocktail and said, "You see, my dear fellow, if you were a phenomenologist, you could talk about this cocktail and make a philosophy out of it", after which Sartre immediately went looking for a copy of Levinas' book on Husserl's theory of intuition (Flynn 2014). Sartre went on to study Husserlian phenomenology in Berlin in 1933–1934. His early works are primarily interpretations of Husserl, but he went on to develop a distinctive approach to phenomenology. His point of departure is the phenomenological analysis of self-awareness and the structure of subjectivity. In *The Transcendence of the Ego* (Sartre 1937/1991), *Being and Nothingness* (Sartre 1943/2003), and elsewhere, Sartre develops an account of subjectivity, or the "ego", whereby the world-directed intentionality of experience necessarily includes a pre-reflexive form of self-awareness (D. W. Smith 1986). On Sartre's account, the self is not defined by any fixed essence, but is rather a kind of "nihilating" force, which surges forward, transcending its own concrete circumstances and historical situations (its "facitity") and creating values by its radically free acts. Sartre also develops an original account of human emotions like shame, which on his account is a form of self-relation through which the self becomes aware of itself *as an object*, i.e. as something fixed and visible to others. Shame "is not a feeling of being this or that guilty object but in general of being *an* object" (Sartre 2003, 312; qtd. in Zahavi 2014).

Simone de Beauvoir studied philosophy alongside Sartre and Merleau-Ponty at the Sorbonne, and engaged in a life-long personal and philosophical parternship with Sartre. She contributed to a wide range of philosophical topics from a phenomenological perspective. *The Second Sex* (Beauvoir 1949/2011) is perhaps the most richly interdisciplinary work of classical phenomenology. Rather than relying solely on phenomenological reflection, Beauvoir draws on literary, historical, biological, and psychological sources to elaborate what the actual lived experiences of women have been at different times and places, and in different concrete circumstances. Going beyond Merleau-Ponty's brief analysis of sexuality in *Phenomenology of Perception*, Beauvoir connects phenomena such as menstruation and pregnancy to the intersubjective manner in which one's subjectivity is shaped by the norms and expectations of others (Murphy 2009). It has been argued that her main interest in the book is phenomenological: "Instead of putting forward a sociohistorical theory or a liberalist thesis, Beauvoir presents a phenomenological description. The phenomenon that she describes is the reality named *woman*, and her aim is to analyze the meanings involved in this reality" (Heinämaa 1999, 115).

Merleau-Ponty's *Phenomenology of Perception* (1945/2013) has been increasingly influential in recent philosophy of mind.[6] Developing a complex dialectic between rationalism and empiricism, judgment and sensation, Merleau-Ponty weaves together concepts from Husserl, Heidegger, and empirical psychology (among other sources) to develop an account of the essentially bodily nature of perception and of intentionality in general. For Merleau-Ponty, what is fundamental in experience is not the patterns of sensation emphasized by empiricists, or the abstract rules emphasized by rationalists, or the behavioral tendencies emphasized by psychologists, but rather the concrete situation a person or organism finds itself in, which is structured around its bodily existence and what is significant in a situation. Merleau-Ponty is notable for his detailed examination of clinical cases, for example Schneider, a patient with visual agnosia (a case which Gurwitsch first described to Merleau-Ponty on the basis of his work at the Prussian institute). Schneider could do concrete things like swatting away a mosquito or grabbing his nose, but could not identify abstract locations on his body. He was no longer sexually stimulated by direct bodily contact, but was aroused by suggestions of an intimate situation. These cases highlight the fundamental importance of our embodied existence in a meaningful world, where whole situations matter far more than discrete locations or explicit rules.

Husserl's influence on 20th-century philosophy extends even further than this. Theodor Adorno (1956/1982), Jacques Derrida (1967/2011), and Paul Ricouer (Ricoeur 1967/2007) – central figures in contemporary continental philosophy – devoted their earliest monographs to extending and critiquing Husserl's ideas. Husserl's understanding of mind and consciousness, whether sympathetically elaborated upon or critically deconstructed, has thereby formed the basis of a great deal of 20th-century philosophy.

3. Phenomenology in relation to philosophy of mind

The phenomenological tradition is related to the philosophy of mind in several broad ways, which we survey here.[7] First, we describe their shared historical origins in late 19th-century thought, and some of the surprising ways this shared history continued in to the 20th-century. Second, we describe a few philosophical areas (e.g. mereology, the study of parts and wholes) that have phenomenological origins and that are today used by philosophers of mind. Third, we survey the many areas of thematic overlap between phenomenology and contemporary philosophy of mind.

Phenomenology and philosophy of mind have a shared history. Philosophy of mind is generally considered to be part of analytic philosophy, and analytic philosophy originated in the same milieu as phenomenology, an "Anglo-Austrian tradition" (Dummett 1993, 2) encompassing Bolzano, Brentano, Frege, Husserl, and others. Husserl's early work is distinctively analytic in its tone and content. Husserl makes fine-grained distinctions, resolves equivocations, and engages in the same issues of logic, language, and meaning as other early analytic philosophers. He was in close dialogue with Frege and his ideas were familiar to Russell and Wittgenstein.[8]

Phenomenology continued to be interwoven with analytic philosophy during the period of logical positivism and the Vienna school (D. W. Smith 2013; Rollinger 1999; Livingston 2002). Carnap took seminars with Husserl at Freiburg, and his foundational program was rooted in phenomenological considerations, an effort to derive all knowledge claims from an analysis of "the given" (the

Aufbau refers several times to Husserl in this connection). Husserl has been called "Carnap's unknown master" (Haddock 2008). The verificationist idea that statements are meaningful only if they can be verified in immediate experience also has obvious affinities to phenomenology, since verification chains are themselves phenomenological constructs (D. W. Smith and McIntyre 1982; Lübcke 1999).[9]

There were also premonitions of the analytic/continental split in this period. Carnap (1931) famously critiqued Heidegger's account of the "nothing" as a paradigm example of nonsense (interestingly, Carnap probably inherited his concept of nonsense from Husserl; Bar-Hillel 1957; Vrahimis 2013). Schlick vigorously disputed Husserl's idea that non-sensory intuition of essences is possible (Livingston 2002). Later, as behaviorism – the view that internal mental states don't exist or aren't amenable to observation – took hold first among psychologists and then analytic philosophers like Wittgenstein and Ryle, all mention of private conscious states became suspect; "the air was laced with a certain suspicion of 'inner' mental states behind behavior and speech" (D. W. Smith and Thomasson 2005, 2). Overt references to consciousness – or worse, transcendental subjectivity – were clearly out of the question by the middle of the 20th century – as was the dense, opaque style of prose associated with Heidegger and his followers.

Nonetheless, leading figures in early philosophy of mind, even in this period, maintained an interest in phenomenology.[10] Ryle went to Freiburg to meet Husserl and study with Heidegger (Thomasson 2002, 116), and then began his career at Oxford teaching phenomenology and related ideas. His first two publications were reviews of phenomenological texts. Over the course of his career Ryle wrote six papers "focused entirely on the phenomenological tradition" (Thomasson 2002, 116). Ryle's conception of the scope and method of philosophy is, Thomasson argues, due in large part to Brentano's and Husserl's influence. All three sharply distinguished the methods of empirical science (and psychology in particular) from the methods of philosophy. All three thought of philosophy as a distinctive form of inquiry, that should proceed independently of experimental results or inductive generalizations. Ryle's specific approach to conceptual analysis was influenced by Husserl. In the *Logical Investigations* Husserl described a method for identifying categories of meaning by asking which terms could be substituted in to a sentence without producing some form of nonsense. Ryle's concept of a category mistake seems to have been a direct application and broadening of this type of "nonsense detection" (more on this connection shortly), as do his efforts in *The Concept of Mind* to examine the logical relationships between different types of mental concepts (he himself described the book as "a sustained essay in phenomenology"; Thomasson, 122). Ryle was also influenced by Heidegger. Ryle's critique of Cartesianism and associated talk of "inner" mental states is clearly resonant with Heidegger, as is Ryle's method of ordinary language philosophy, which emphasizes everyday practice over theoretical reflection. Based on these and other observations, Thomasson concludes that "the very idea of analytic philosophy and its proper role" (123) and "some of its characteristic methods" (134) owe more to phenomenology than is generally acknowledged.

Sellars was also trained in phenomenology. While pursuing his MA at SUNY Buffalo, Sellars met Marvin Farber, a student of Husserl's who was one of the primary people to bring phenomenology to America (Kaelin and Schrag 1989). Sellars would later say, "For longer than I care to remember I have seen philosophical analysis (and synthesis) as akin to phenomenology (Thomasson 2002, 123). Sellars defended a kind of "outer observation" account of appearance-talk, which may have been influenced by Husserl's method of phenomenological reduction. On this account, appearance-talk is parasitic on world-talk: "the concept of *looking green*, the ability to recognize that something *looks green*, presupposes the concept of *being green*" (Sellars, quoted in Thomasson 2005, 120). Compare Husserl's method of phenomenological reduction, which, as we saw, begins with the naïve realism of everyday life. In everyday life, we simply assume that things *are* certain ways. Husserl and Sellars both note that it is only by a complex and derivative procedure (e.g., coming to doubt our ability to judge colors in different lighting conditions) that we come to think of things in terms of their "appearances" (we return to these issues in section 4).

One general source of Husserl's influence on 20th-century philosophy of mind – already noted in the discussion of Ryle – is his work on "pure grammar" in the fourth logical investigation. Husserl distinguishes word sequences that are formally ungrammatical (e.g. "a man and is") with word sequences that are grammatical but describe impossible situations (e.g. "round square" or "wooden iron"). The former are nonsense or *Unsinn*; the latter are countersense or *Widersinn*. Husserl's grammatical analyses influenced Ryle, Carnap, and, perhaps indirectly, Chomsky. As we saw, there is evidence that Carnap's concept of nonsense derived from Husserl (Vrahimis 2013), and it has also been suggested that *Logical Syntax of Language* was written under Husserl's influence (Bar-Hillel 1957). Ryle's account of category mistakes – cases where one category is mixed with another incompatible one – can plausibly be viewed as a refinement of Husserl's account of countersense (Thomasson 2002). Husserl's account of pure grammar is in several ways similar to Chomsky's linguistic theory (Edie 1977).[11]

Beyond these historical interconnections, phenomenology is related to philosophy of mind via concepts and tools that now have independent philosophical interest. Examples include formal ontology (the study of the basic categories of being – object, property, fact, etc. – and their inter-relations; B. Smith 1998), mereology (the study of parts and wholes; Varzi 2015; Simons 1987), facts (Mulligan and Correia 2013), and ontological dependence (Correia 2008). All of these originate in part in Husserl (each has other sources as well), and have become a standard part of the philosopher's metaphysical toolkit. These tools have been applied in various ways to philosophy of mind. Mereology is relevant to the question of how unified mental states can be parsed in to distinct "experiential parts" (Brook and Raymont 2014). Ontological dependence and formal ontology have been deployed in the literature on mental-physical relations like supervenience, dependence, and grounding (Yoshimi 2010; Correia and Schnieder 2012).

Finally, and for our purposes most importantly, there are many areas of direct thematic overlap between phenomenology and philosophy of mind. In these cases, we find both the explicit application of insights from the phenomenological tradition to philosophy of mind, as well as more implicit traces of phenomenology (both as tradition and method) in pursuit of contemporary topics. Examples include the structure of intentionality (D. W. Smith and McIntyre 1982; McIntyre 1986; Dreyfus and Hall 1982; Kriegel 2011; Strawson 1994; Crane 1998); the twin-earth thought experiment and semantic externalism (Beyer 2013; Føllesdal 2018); Davidson's anomalous monism (D. W. Smith 1995; Zhok 2011); the overlap between Husserl and John Searle's philosophy of language, mind, and the social world (what some have called the "Searle in Husserl");[12] functionalism and artificial intelligence;[13] first-person knowledge (Thomasson 2005), supervenience and metaphysics of mind (Yoshimi 2010); one-order and higher-order theories of consciousness (Kriegel 2009; Kriegel and Williford 2006); representational theories of mind (McIntyre 1986; Shim 2011); and non-conceptual content (Hopp 2010; Barber 2008; Dahlstrom 2007).

In some areas, phenomenology and philosophy of mind are actively collaborating, as in discussions of self and structure of self-awareness (D. W. Smith 1986; Kriegel 2009; Strawson 2009; Zahavi 2005; Siewert 2013), the study of social cognition, the problem of other minds, empathy, and collective intentionality (Schutz and Natanson 1970; Overgaard 2007; Gallagher and Zahavi 2007; Carr 1986; Mathiesen 2005; Schmid 2003; Zahavi 2014), embodied, enactive, and situated approaches to cognition (Gallagher 2005; Noë 2004; Thompson 2007; Hurley 1998; Rowlands 2010; ch. 10 on Boundaries of the mind in this volume), time-consciousness (Dainton 2000), bodily awareness (de Vignemont 2011), whether non-sensory purely "cognitive phenomenology" exists (Siewert 1998; Strawson 1994; Pitt 2004; Bayne and Montague 2011; Smithies 2013; Chudnoff 2015; Breyer and Gutland 2016), and in debates in the philosophy of perception about disjunctivism, representationalism, and direct realism (A. D. Smith 2008; Hopp 2011; Overgaard 2013).

We now consider two specific cases to further illustrate how phenomenology and philosophy of mind interact.

4. Perceptual content

Suppose you enter a room with a round black dining table in the center. As you approach the table, you are looking down at it from an oblique angle. Sunlight streams through an open window, creating variegated shades and tones across the surface of the table. What do you see? Or, to put the question differently, what is the *content* or your perceptual experience? On one hand, answering this question is straightforward: you see a table. On the other hand, it provokes further questions regarding *how*, precisely, one is aware of the table. For example, does the table look round? Or, given the angle of your perspective, does it appear elliptical? Do you see it as being a uniform shade of black? Or are you unaware of the blackness, since the sunlight presents the table as a variegated set of shades and tones? What is the relationship between what is phenomenally manifest in the experience and what the experience represents as being the case? These questions about content, representation, and phenomenal character are at the center of several live debates in contemporary philosophy of mind (cf. Orlandi, Chapter 4 of this volume). Relative to these debates, we believe that Husserl developed a fairly rich view, whereby perceptual experience is built up from multiple non-conceptual and conceptual layers or strata. In what follows we distinguish four layers of perceptual experience: (1) what is intuitively given or "sensorily manifest" in the experience; (2) an "immanent horizon" of felt associations; (3) a "counter-factual horizon" of ways we expect an object to be relative to different movements with respect to it; and (4) a linguistically/conceptually mediated stratum of "active" and "predicative" understandings of things. As we will see, these strata play different representational roles and are more or less phenomenally prominent in experience. We will also see that (1)–(4) involve different types of conceptual and non-conceptual content: (1) and (2) are "linguistically non-conceptual" and also "discriminatively non-conceptual". (3) is linguistically non-conceptual but discriminatively conceptual. And (4) is both linguistically and discriminatively conceptual.

On Husserl's account, objects dominate experience. We *live through* perceptions, but *experience things* (recall his emphasis on constitutive phenomenology, on how the objects that appear to us are constituted in experiential processes). This emphasis on objects is sometimes referred to as the "transparency" of consciousness (Kind 2010). As Lycan puts it, "We normally 'see right through' perceptual states to external objects and do not even notice that we are *in* perceptual states" (Lycan 2014, sec. 3.3; see also Harman 1990; Tye 1995; 2000).

For Husserl, as for many contemporary authors, this object-centered feature of experience can be described in terms of perceptual *content*. Husserl describes the content of an act as that part of it which "*prescribes* – represents or presents – the object of my perception" (D. W. Smith 2007, 208); it "specifies the object of perception" (D. W. Smith 2007, 209). This object-prescribing content is distinct from the full experiential act that contains it, whose overall phenomenology seems to outstrip the object-prescribing content, as we will see. The content is also distinct from the actual object it refers to.[14] As Husserl said as early as the *Investigations*:

> We must distinguish . . . between *the object as it is intended* [the intentional object] . . . and the *object which is intended* [the actual object]. In each act an object is presented as determined in this or that manner.
> (Husserl 2001a, 113)

Although objects dominate experience, for Husserl, perceptual phenomenology includes an implicit sense of our embodied relation to the world (this is related to Husserl's phenomenology of the mind-body problem; more in section 5). We see the pattern of shading on the table, and know that it is the result of light playing off the table. Even with no scientific knowledge, we have an implicit understanding of how light works and how it interacts with things. The variegated shades (what Husserl calls "intuitive content") are *sensorily manifest*. In a similar way, we understand that as the car moves in the distance it gets smaller in our visual field, because of how objects interact with our eyes. These features of perception are not what we initially focus on, but on reflection we can in some sense identify that the table was "viewed as" elliptical, and as being colored in different shades due to lighting conditions.[15]

Within this sensorily manifest intuitive content, Husserl distinguishes non-intentional sensations or what he later calls "*hyle*", from an interpretive element that "animates" them.[16] He makes this distinction using a variational method.[17] The contribution made by the interpretive part of perception can be varied independently of what is sensorily manifest, and vice versa. Thus, on the one hand, different patterns of sensation can yield the same perceptual sense you have of the table. As the lighting changes slightly, the same table appears. On the other hand, the sensory contents can remain the same as perceptual contents vary. For this case, Husserl describes the interpretive shift that occurs when perceiving a figure in a wax museum initially as another person, and then as a wax figure or mannequin (Husserl 2001a, Inv. 5, Sec. 27). The part that is different between these experiences – the part that *exceeds* their sensory character – is the "interpretation", "act character", or "apprehensional character" of the perceptual act.

Husserl associates this apprehensional character with several additional layers of structure in the perceptual act, which are in various ways conceptual and non-conceptual. To make these connections between Husserl's account of perceptual content and conceptual structures, we distinguish two senses of "conceptual". In one sense, concepts are the constituents of propositional contents – the stuff of language and thought. If one thinks that the table is black, one does so in virtue of the concepts "table" and "black". We will call these "linguistically structured concepts". In another sense, a concept is a kind of discriminative ability available to non-linguistic animals. Insofar as an animal can differentially respond to humans vs. non-human objects, or to perishable vs. unperishable food sources, animals have concepts in this sense (Margolis and Laurence 2011). We will call these "discriminative concepts". Notice that both types of concept allow for a kind of detachment from the intuitively given object. One can think about the black table using the words "black" and "table" and thus be intentionally related to a black table, without seeing any tables. Arguably an animal could imagine one of *those things* (i.e. a table, a human, or a piece of food), absent any actual table, human or food, and thereby be non-intuitively related to something.

Husserl describes several structures that are non-conceptual relative to *both* of these senses of "conceptual". First, the sensorily manifest intuitive content of the act – i.e. how the object appears to sensory experience – is non-conceptual in a classical sense. The table is presented as having a very specific shape and color (not the pattern of light on it, but what we take to be the *actual color and shape* of the given table, e.g., the precise pattern of knots and grains visible in the wood beneath the paint). This detail far exceeds what the linguistically structured concept "black table" prescribes. When we think "black table" we are thinking at a level of generality that, on Husserl's account, is consistent with many different intuitive contents, many different ways an actual table could be given (Hopp 2010). The sensorily manifest also seems to be discriminatively non-conceptual, insofar as a perceiver would not be able to reliably discriminate between each subtle variation in the pattern of shading of the table.

Second, there is a kind of penumbra of felt associations between the current object and other profiles of the object, and other features of the object – an "immanent horizon". This is the level of passively synthesized motivations, which develop via passive genesis (cf. section 2). This penumbra of motivations is phenomenally manifest – according to Husserl – and contributes to how we take the object to be, but also exceeds what can be given in any kind of conceptualized experience. The motivation relations that comprise this stratum of experience are developed in Husserl's early analyses in the *Logical Investigations*, and later in his lectures on *Active and Passive Synthesis* (Husserl 2001c). He describes them as a kind of experienced indication relation, a species of association (Walsh 2013). He is explicit, however, that this is not to be understood in terms of Hume's discussion of discrete impressions causally "triggering" subsequent impressions. Rather,

> If A summons B into consciousness, we are not merely simultaneously or successively conscious of both A and B, but we usually *feel* their connection forcing itself upon us, a connection in which the one points to the other and seems to belong to it.
>
> (Husserl 2001b, 187)

The phenomenal character of "felt-belonging" connects the phenomenal features of a momentary perceptual profile of a table to those subsequent profiles that are most imminent in the temporal flow of experience, i.e. what he calls "adumbrations" or "protentions".[18] As with intuitive content, the penumbra does not rely on linguistically-structured concepts. A dog need not have any concept of a table in order to experience this kind of felt penumbra of associations. So the immanent horizon is linguistically non-conceptual (whether it is discriminatively non-conceptual is less clear; we will not take up the issue further here).

A next level of structure is the level of counterfactual horizon structure (cf. section 2), which further unpacks what apprehensional character is, e.g. what changes when we go from seeing an object as a mannequin to seeing it as a human. The horizon of an experience of a thing is the set of further possible experiences of that thing, which extends "in infinitely many directions in a *systematically and firmly rule-governed manner*, and . . . in each direction without end" (Husserl 2014, 78). That is, our overall understanding of a thing can be understood in terms of rule-governed patterns connecting how we interact with a thing with how we expect it to respond. When you see the figure first as a human, then as a mannequin, this shift in representational content can be explicated by analyzing the way the horizon of the experience changes. If I see a *mannequin*, I expect it not to move, to have a specific feel when I touch it. If I see a *human*, I expect the skin to give, and be warmer. I expect a living person to move and notice me. These expectations extend "in infinitely many directions" and "without end" and can thus be thought of as systems of counterfactuals describing chains of possible interactions and expected experiences (D. W. Smith and McIntyre 1982; Yoshimi 2009).

Counterfactual horizon structures are linguistically non-conceptual, but discriminatively conceptual. Horizon structure does not require that we have linguistic concepts: pre-linguistic animals and children have a sense of how things will behave relative to our movements and interactions. So horizons are in that sense non-conceptual (cf. Hopp 2010). However, horizons *are* conceptual insofar as concepts are discriminative structures. A dog can approach what it takes to be a real person in the store, and have a specific set of expectations as a result. When it begins to suspect it is not a real person, and just an inanimate object, it will activate a different set of expectations and thereby behave differently. These features of experience are clearly part of the content of an act – the full accuracy conditions for an act must specify how we expect it to be – but are not phenomenally present in the same way intuitive contents and the penumbra of motivations are. So we have a subtle layer of meaning: a further layer of content that is in one sense conceptual, in another sense non-conceptual. This layer is important for analyzing the representational content of experience in that it is essential for understanding the relation between what is phenomenally manifest in the experience and one's dispositions. It is not, however, part of the occurrent phenomenal character of the experience in the same manner as the intuitively given content and the immanent horizon of motivations. This horizon of expectations is far too detailed (it says what will be surprising or not relative to *all possible movements with respect* to an object) to plausibly be included in the phenomenology of an experience.

Finally, Husserl describes a layer of structure which is explicitly conceptual in the linguistic sense. This is the layer of predicative structures where we talk and think about things; we compare them, explicate their properties, relate them to other things, read about them, and so forth (cf. section 2). We learn about the history of mannequins; we compare mannequins in terms of their weight, age, and cost; we talk to someone who worked with mannequins in a warehouse. In these ways, we create layers or "sediments" of linguistic conceptual structure on top of the pre-given object, which is already endowed with the more passive motivational and horizon structures described above. Whereas many animals may possess the nonlinguistic discriminative concepts described above, it is plausible that only human perceptual experience includes this kind of explicitly conceptual stratum. It is in virtue of the former that both the dog and I share a basic horizon of expectation regarding how the mannequin might look or move, and in virtue of the latter that I, and not the dog, experience the mannequin as a cultural object of a specific kind. These sedimented predicative structures have their own kind of horizons and motivation relations, e.g. the "arithmetical horizon" (Husserl 2014, sec. 28), the space of possible thoughts about numbers and transitions between these thoughts. Thus Husserl acknowledges – and in our view, expands on – the considerations that drive conceptualism (McDowell 1994; Brewer 1999), i.e. that what is given in perception must be able to connect in an appropriate way with the space of reasons, the logical space of language and thought.

Husserl's account of perceptual content overlaps with contemporary discussions in philosophy of mind in several ways beyond those already mentioned. His idea that perceptual content prescribes an object resonates with contemporary discussions of representational content in terms of "accuracy conditions." For Husserl, perceptual content "prescribes" an object in that it conveys how the object *is* – i.e. what properties the object instantiates, and how it will behave relative to our interactions with it – rather than simply presenting us with how the object *appears* (from here, in this light, etc.). This view of content is akin to Siegel's (2010) "content view", whereby perceptual content is not like the contents of a bucket, but rather like the contents of a newspaper – the information conveyed by the experience (Siegel 2015). As we have seen with his analysis of the hyletic component of perceptual act, however, Husserl does not think that the phenomenal character of experience is fully determined by its representational content. As Shim (2011) argues, this puts Husserl at odds with "representationalist" or "intentionalist" views (Harman 1990; Dretske 1995; Tye 1995; 2000; Byrne 2001).

Husserl's analysis of (in contemporary terms) perceptual content was also taken up and extended in interesting ways by Merleau-Ponty. Merleau-Ponty understood his project in *Phenomenology of Perception* as a continuation of Husserl's work. He was among the first to visit the Husserl archives in Leuven the year they opened (Vongehr 2007). At the archives, he may have been the first person (outside of Husserl's personal circle) to see *Ideas II*, where Husserl's sensori-motor account is worked out in detail.[19] Merleau-Ponty explains pre-predicative (i.e. linguistically non-conceptual) sense by appealing to the way perceptual experience is intertwined with our bodily form. He thereby expands on Husserl's horizon level of analysis, describing systematic correlations between what is visually given and our ongoing proprioceptive and kinesthetic sense of our bodies. Unlike Husserl (on some readings), Merleau-Ponty locates content in a kind of perceptual norm or optimum (cf. Dreyfus 2002; Crowell 2013, ch. 6; Kelly 2005). When you see the table from an oblique angle and it appears elliptical to you, the content of your perception represents it as being round since it would appear round from an optimal view (directly overhead). The normativity of this perceptual optimum is established by facts about how our bodies are structured and how our perceptual systems operate in relation to the world, and not necessarily by anything consciously accessible to us in the phenomenological reduction. This emphasis on sensori-motor contingencies is central to the enactivist account of perception (Noë 2004; O'Regan 2001; Hurley 1998), a thriving area of contemporary philosophy of mind and cognitive science (cf. the references in section 3).

5. The phenomenology of the mind-body problem

Whereas the issue of perceptual content in relation to phenomenology has been explored in some depth already, there is a largely unexplored area of overlap between phenomenology and the mind-body problem, which we briefly describe here.

In texts written around 1910, Husserl develops what can be called a "phenomenology of the mind-body problem" or more generally, a "phenomenology of the metaphysics of mind". Rather than directly asking what mental states and physical states are, and how they are related, he asks how people *experience* mental states, physical states, and their relationship (Yoshimi 2010).[20] That is, he considers how mental states, physical states, and mental-physical relationships are themselves constituted in the flux of experience. Husserl's phenomenology of the mind-body problem does not decide the philosophical issues, but rather sheds light on the space of possibilities available for philosophical consideration. Thus, Husserl's phenomenology can be viewed as a kind of transcendental or eidetic analysis of the mind-body problem, a framework within which any analysis of mind-body relations must unfold (recall that essences or *eide* are necessary constraints on the appearance of a given class of objects or processes). On Husserl's eidetic analysis, one can't have a position on the mind-body problem *except* relative to some prior experience of mind-body relations. Experiences of mind, body, and their relation are constrained by certain essential structures. Eidetic phenomenology lays out what these constraints are. Empirical considerations can further restrict the space of possible theories of mind and brain.[21] Again, this does not decide the philosophical issues, but rather helps delineate what the space of possible philosophical positions on the mind-body problem is for creatures like us.

We will begin by describing Husserl's analysis of how sensory states are experienced as supervening on brain states. His analysis is quite similar to standard physicalist accounts of mental states. However, unlike physicalists, Husserl does not believe that *all* mental phenomena are experienced as supervening on physical states. His view can be thought of as involving a kind of "partial-supervenience". We end by considering the range of positions on the mind body problem left open by Husserl's eidetic analysis.

According to Husserl, we experience sensations as arising from physical processes.[22] He calls this an "experience of psycho-physical conditionality" (Husserl 1989, 78) or "physiological dependences" (*physiologische Abhängigkeiten*; 143). For example, we know that running an object over the surface of the skin produces a determinate succession of sensings, which can be repeated: "If an object moves mechanically over the surface of my skin, touching it, then I obviously have a succession of sensings ordered in a determinate way" (161–162). He calls this a "phenomenal if-then". If the body is put in a certain state, then certain phenomenal states will arise. Husserl also notes that we do not always understand how these experienced mental-physical connections or "conditionalities" work; we just have an understanding that somehow there is such a relationship (272).

Husserl describes a phenomenological form of supervenience between sensory states and physical states.[23] He says that we experience the physical states of organisms as determining their sensory states. If two experienced agents or "animate organisms" are experienced as physically indiscernible, they will also be experienced as mentally indiscernible:[24]

> the sensibility presents itself [to consciousness] in such a way that we can say that if the animate organism is the same . . . with regard to its materiality and its material states, then . . . the stratum of sensation would also have to be the same.
>
> (Husserl 1980, 120)

So, sensations are experienced as supervening on physical processes. If two agents are experienced as having the same physical properties, they will also be experienced as having the same "stratum of sensation" (i.e. sensory properties). Other phenomenological features are experienced as supervening on physical states of the brain, including "phantasy" (which includes imagination and memory), feelings, instincts, and "the proper character, the rhythm, of higher consciousness" (Husserl 1989, 308–309).

Thus far we have a picture of mind-body relations that is similar to a standard contemporary physicalist conception. According to this picture, mental properties are related to physical properties via synchronic "vertical" supervenience relations (think of how a pattern of atoms at a time determines a unique molecular pattern at that same time). See Figure 1.1. Physical processes are related by dynamic or diachronic "horizontal" causal processes, where one state of (say) the brain gives rise to successive states, relative to an environment and a set of physical laws. The lower-level dynamics then induce higher level dynamics via the supervenience relations (Yoshimi 2012). For example, when a brain changes from state P to P* at the neural level, this gives rise to parallel changes from M to M* at the psychological level, in virtue of the supervenience relation.

On the basis of this overall picture of mental-physical relations, many contemporary philosophers deny that true mental causation is possible (cf. Chapter 7

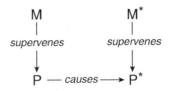

Figure 1.1 A standard account of mental-physical relations. Physical processes like P to P* unfold dynamically and are shown as proceeding horizontally. Physical to mental supervenience relations occur synchronically and are shown as vertical lines.[25]

Adapted from Kim (2003).

on mental causation). All apparent causal processes are ultimately driven by bottom-level physical processes; the appearance of mental causation is an epiphenomenon. This has come to be known as the "causal exclusion argument"; think of low-level process "excluding" high level process from doing anything (Kim 2007). This argument has been addressed by physicalists in a variety of ingenious ways, which seek to preserve mental causation in a physicalist framework (Bennett 2008; Wilson 2009).

However, although we experience many mental properties as being fixed by physical properties, it is not clear that we experience *all* mental properties as being fixed by physical properties (Husserl 1980, 16). For some mental phenomena, Husserl thinks it is unclear whether there is an assumed physical basis, and concludes that it is an empirical question which mental phenomena are experienced as having a physical basis and which aren't: "obviously, how far all this extends can only be decided empirically and if possible by means of experimental psychology" (Husserl 1989, 308). He goes on to a give an argument that some properties relating to time-consciousness *must not* supervene on physical processes.[26] Husserl thus defends a form of *partial supervenience*: the idea that some, but not all mental properties are fixed by an agent's physical properties. This variant on the supervenience relation is novel to Husserl's account, and is of some independent philosophical interest (Yoshimi 2010).

Given that Husserl endorses only partial supervenience, he is open to a wider range of possibilities than most contemporary philosophers are. In particular, he is open to such possibilities as downward causation and temporal slippage, and is unconcerned about causal exclusion and related physicalist worries.

Downward causation occurs when mental phenomena directly cause changes in physical phenomena (Kim 1992). We could imagine, for example, a diagonal arrow from M to P* in Fig. 1. Physicalists typically deny that this type of causation is possible. However Husserl claims that it is phenomenologically coherent; we can imagine experiencing a scenario of "reverse dependency" where sensations are produced at the mental level, and the physical level changes accordingly. In such a scenario the mind has "its own causality", and physical changes in the body (indexed by a variable B) are dependent on it:

> [in such a case] we assume that the mind has its own causality, an inner empirical lawfulness, in the production of sensations; i.e., a causality that can first of all unfold in itself and lead to a sensation, to which the state of B would then be linked as dependent on it.
> (Husserl 1989, 309)

As an example, Husserl refers to "the voluntary production of hallucinations" (309) where, presumably, we first imagine something, and the brain then enters an appropriate state to support that imagination.

Husserl also considers the possibility of temporal drift between brain states and the mental states they give rise to, describing it as unclear "whether or not the Objective temporal point of the cerebral stimulation, corresponding to the movement of the hand, must be taken as the same identical temporal point of the sensation" (310). He goes on to locate the source of this unclarity in the more fundamental problem of determining what the time of conscious states is: "Everything depends here on the way of defining the temporal point of a determinate state of consciousness" (309–310). Husserl's instincts were right: the timing of conscious events has emerged as a difficult but important topic, in the wake of Libet's pioneering work on the neuroscience of free will, and in particular his controversial method for measuring the time of conscious intentions (Joordens et al. 2002; Libet 2009).

Although downward causation and temporal drift are unpopular today, they have been endorsed by proponents of strong emergence. Emergence in the philosophy of mind is a family of relations (O'Connor and Wong 2012).[27] The strongest forms of emergence treat the mind as having some genuine autonomy from the physical level, and allow for temporal drift, downward causation, and robust mental causation (O'Connor and Wong 2005).

Figure 1.2 depicts a simplified version of strong emergence, based primarily on (O'Connor and Wong 2005). Physical processes unfold just as they do in physicalism. In addition to causing each other, physical states also cause other emergent mental states to occur. Since the upwards mental-to-physical relation is "dynamic and causal" (664), some temporal drift can occur. Mental states can have causal effects of their own, both in terms of downward causation, and in terms of causation of other mental states. Their "effects . . . include directly determining aspects of the microphysical structure of the object as well as generating other emergent states" (665). There is no problem of causal exclusion in this framework: mental causation is alive and well, alongside physical-to-physical and physical-to-mental

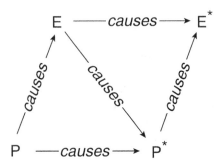

Figure 1.2 A version of strong emergence, between physical states P and emergent states E. Here the emergent states are mental states. Genuine mental causation is allowed via agent causation (upper horizontal arrow). Regular physical causation remains (lower horizontal arrow). Supervenience is replaced by upward causation from physical to mental. Downward causation from mental to physical is allowed.

causation. The view naturally couples with property dualism and agent causal views of the will. An agent's free choices have a direct causal impact on other mental states *and* on physical states.

So, within the space of possibilities left open by Husserl's analysis of the essences of experienced physical bodies, mental states, and mental-physical interrelationships, existing theories have occupied many of the available spots. Experimental philosophy could supplement Husserl's eidetic analyses with controlled studies of intuitions in these domains. Empirical work measuring mind-brain correlations could further constrain the space of open possibilities. Perhaps these zigzagging analyses will lead us to new, unexplored regions of the space of possible solutions to the mind-body problem.

Conclusion

We have seen that phenomenology and philosophy of mind – understood both as philosophical disciplines and as historical traditions – are interrelated in a complex, dynamic way. As historical traditions, they were at one time joined, later diverged, and are coming back together in a larger swarm-like pattern, characterized by local swirlings of overlap and mutual reinforcement, intermittent skirmishes, and shared new directions. Although it is impossible to detail all the integrative possibilities in a single chapter, we have tried to mark out some promising areas, and to illustrate how further collaborations might unfold.

Notes

1 As of November 2017.
2 Interest in consciousness and other internal processes never completely disappeared, either in philosophy or psychology, even during the behaviorist era. See Baars (1986) and Strawson (2015).
3 Husserl uses terms like "horizon" and "motivation" in multiple ways, and much of the scholarly work in Husserlian phenomenology involves distinguishing and clarifying concepts like these (Walsh 2017). We have marked some but not all of the relevant distinctions here (e.g. we distinguish between an "immanent horizon" and "counterfactual horizon").
4 On Husserl's epistemology see (Willard 1984; D. Kasmier 2003; Sanchez 2010; Hopp 2011). On Husserl's eidetic method see (Sowa 2007; David Kasmier 2010).
5 On the nature and scope of Gurwitsch's influence on Merleau-Ponty, see (Toadvine 2001).
6 The new Landes (2013) translation is both timely for and evidence of this increasing appreciation.
7 In this section, we give a detailed overview of the main areas of overlap between phenomenology and philosophy of mind. It is worth noting that phenomenology overlaps other areas of philosophy in similar ways, including philosophy of math (Tieszen 2011; Hill and Da Silva 1997; Hartimo 2010), philosophy of cognitive science (Petitot et al. 1999; Gallagher and Schmicking 2010), epistemology (Willard 1984; Hopp 2011), feminist philosophy, in particular, feminist phenomenology (Fisher and Embree 2000; Heinämaa 1999), queer phenomenology (Ahmed 2006), and phenomenology of race (Alcoff 1999), among others. In the case of philosophy of math especially the historical

origins overlap. Husserl was close friends with Hilbert and Cantor, had Weyl as his student, and was later read by Gödel (Hill and Da Silva 1997). These overlaps between phenomenology and other areas of philosophy are themselves relevant to philosophy of mind, and merit further study.

8 There is now a fairly extensive literature on these connections; see (Føllesdal 1994; Durfee 1976; Willard 1984; Cobb-Stevens 1990; B. Smith 1994; Mohanty 1982; Simons 1992; D. W. Smith and McIntyre 1982; D. W. Smith 2013).

9 See also Horgan and Tienson (2002), who independently develop a similar idea about phenomenal intentionality and verificationism.

10 In addition to Ryle and Sellars, there have been studies of early phenomenology in relation to Wittgenstein, Austen, and Hare, among others (Durfee 1976).

11 Though Katz has said "it is completely wrong... to speak of unity of purpose between Husserl and Chomsky" (qtd. in Kusch 1989, 63), in light of, among other things, Chomsky's emphasis on the biological basis of the rules he describes, which sharply contrasts with Husserl's *a priori* enterprise.

12 Or "Hussearle", as Beyer (1997) puts it. More specific areas of overlap include the structure of intentionality, the relation of mind to language, Searle's concept of the background, and his more recent work on social ontology (Beyer 1997; McIntyre 1984). Searle has responded to the claim that his work is similar to Husserl's, acknowledging that he read some Husserl and assimilated phenomenological ideas via Dreyfus, but denying substantive influence (Searle 2005).

13 The relationship between phenomenology, functionalism, and artificial intelligence or AI (which is closely related to functionalism) is multi-faceted. There may have been some historical influence via the connections outlined above, and in content there are notable similarities (H. L. Dreyfus and Hall 1982; McIntyre 1986; Mensch 1991; Livingston 2005), e.g. insofar as both emphasize abstract rules and structures (in Husserl's case eidetic structures and horizon structures; in the case of functionalism and AI abstract relations between inputs, outputs, and inner states). In light of these similarities between Husserl and AI, Dreyfus regards Heidegger's critique of Husserl as an implicit critique of AI (H. L. Dreyfus and Hall 1982; Hubert L. Dreyfus 1992). For a critical discussion of the assimilation of Husserl to classical AI see (Yoshimi 2009).

14 At least according to realist interpretations of Husserl (as contrasted with idealist readings). Cf. B. Smith (1995).

15 These ideas can also be understood in terms of Merleau-Ponty's work. On one reading, Merleau-Ponty locates content in a kind of perceptual norm or optimum (cf. Dreyfus 2002; Crowell 2013, ch. 6; Kelly 2005). When you see the table from an oblique angle and it appears elliptical to you, the content of your perception represents it as being round since it would appear round from an optimal view (directly overhead). The normativity of this perceptual optimum is established by facts about how our bodies are structured and how our perceptual systems operate in relation to the world.

16 The concept of uninterpreted sensory or hyletic data has been controversial since Husserl's own lifetime. Gurwitsch (1964), drawing on Gestalt psychology, argued that there were no such things as hyletic data, only interpreted Gestalt forms. Hopp (2010) develops his account of non-conceptual content in a Husserlian framework that rejects hyletic data. On the relation between hyletic data and contemporary debates about phenomenal consciousness also see (Shim 2011; Williford 2013).

17 Cf. Siegel's method of "phenomenal contrast" (Siegel 2007; 2010). This method of phenomenal contrast has played a prominent role in recent arguments about the nature and existence of cognitive phenomenology (Siewert 1998; Pitt 2004; Smithies 2013).

18 Motivations in this sense are similar to what Gurwitsch calls the "thematic field" of an act (Gurwitsch 1964), and what William James called fringes (Mangan 2007). They

are also a kind of horizon structure, an "immanent" horizon, which is distinct from the counterfactual horizons described in the main text.
19 Rojcewicz and Schuwer (1989) recall Merleau-Ponty describing the experience of reading *Ideas II* as "*une expérience presque voluptueuse*" (xvi).
20 In asking how people experience these phenomena, Husserl pursues a form of investigation similar to studies of folk intuition in experimental philosophy. Experimental philosophers have in fact addressed the question of how mind and body are intuitively understood (Knobe 2011). It would be interesting to extend these studies to the question of folk intuitions about mind-body relations, and thereby empirically investigate Husserl's claims.
21 As Husserl puts it in the case of psycho-physical dependencies: "How far [mental-physical relations] actually reach is a matter for psycho-physiological empirical investigation to decide. How far [psycho-physical dependencies] can reach, on the other hand, that is to say, how far questions about "physiological correlates" and corresponding hypothetical constructions can be senseful and guiding for the process of actual research, is a matter for psycho-physical inquiries into essences" (Husserl 1980, 16; for further discussion, see Yoshimi (2010).
22 Assuming we are in the "naturalistic attitude" (*naturalistichen Einstellung*), "the attitude of the subject who intuits and thinks in the natural-scientific way" (Husserl 1989, 3).
23 On the standard definition: A properties supervene on B properties iff objects with the same B properties will also have the same A properties. As it is also put: being B-indiscernible entails being A-indiscernible; B-twins must be A-twins, or B properties determine A properties. Also note that states are taken to be a kind of maximal property: the A-state of a thing is the set of A-properties that apply to it at a time; for example the mental state of an organism is (roughly) the distribution of mental properties that apply to it at that time (Yoshimi 2012).
24 In other works he also gives a phenomenological analysis of indiscernibility, or in his terms "qualitative identity", in terms of series of pairwise comparisons. See D. Kasmier (2003).
25 There are some simplifications involved in this diagram. For example, supervenience is typically construed as a relation between sets of properties, whereas it is shown here as a relation between individual states or property instances.
26 Since on his view these processes have a necessary form that cannot be captured by any contingent physical process (Yoshimi 2010 critiques this argument).
27 Weak or epistemic emergence (what most scientists mean by "emergence") is the view that, though everything is physical, it is necessary for practical reasons to study some complex phenomena using higher-level predicates and laws. It would be too unwieldy to, for example, develop a science of biology that only referred to atoms and atomic bonds. Concepts like "species" and laws applying to species are thus epistemically ineliminable features of our scientific practice, even if species ultimately supervene on micro-features of physical systems. There are other forms of ontological emergence as well, e.g. "fusion" based accounts (which draw on quantum physics), whereby the states of an emergent, compound system can determine the states of their constituents, but not conversely (Humphreys, 1997).

Bibliography

Adorno, T. W. (1982). *Against Epistemology: A Metacritique: Studies in Husserl and the Phenomenological Antinomies*. Cambridge, MA: MIT Press.

Ahmed, S. (2006). *Queer Phenomenology: Orientations, Objects, Others*. Durham, NC: Duke University Press.

Alcoff, L. M. (1999). "Towards a Phenomenology of Racial Embodiment," *Radical Philosophy*, 95: 15–26.
Arvidson, S. (2006). *The Sphere of Attention: Context and Margin*. Dordrecht: Springer.
Atterton, P. (2011). "Levinas and Our Moral Responsibility Toward Other Animals," *Inquiry*, 54: 633–649.
Baars, B.J. (1986). *The Cognitive Revolution in Consciousness*. New York, NY: Guilford Press.
Barber, M.D. (2008). "Holism and Horizon: Husserl and McDowell on Non-Conceptual Content," *Husserl Studies*, 24: 79–97.
Bar-Hillel, Y. (1957). "Husserl's Conception of a Purely Logical Grammar," *Philosophy and Phenomenological Research*, 17: 362–369.
Bayne, T., and Montague, M. (eds.). (2011). *Cognitive Phenomenology*. Oxford: Oxford University Press.
Beauvoir, S. (2011). *The Second Sex*. Trans. C. Borde, and S. Malovany-Chevallier. New York, NY: Vintage Books.
Bennett, K. (2008). "Exclusion Again," in Hohwy, J. and Kallestrup, J. (eds.), *Being Reduced: New Essays on Reduction, Explanation, and Causation*. Oxford: Oxford University Press.
Beyer, C. (1997). "Hussearle's Representationalism and the 'Hypothesis of the Background,'" *Synthese*, 112: 323–352.
Beyer, C. (2013). "Edmund Husserl," in Zalta, E. (ed.), *The Stanford Encyclopedia of Philosophy*. http://plato.stanford.edu/archives/win2013/entries/husserl/.
Block, N. (1980). "Troubles with Functionalism," *Readings in Philosophy of Psychology*, 1: 268–305.
Brewer, B. (1999). *Perception and Reason*. Oxford: Oxford University Press.
Breyer, T., and Gutland, C. (2016). *Phenomenology of Thinking*. Abingdon, UK: Routledge.
Brook, A., and Raymont, P. (2014). "The Unity of Consciousness," in Zalta, E. (ed.), *The Stanford Encyclopedia of Philosophy*. http://plato.stanford.edu/archives/win2014/entries/consciousness-unity/.
Byrne, A. (2001). "Intentionalism Defended," *Philosophical Review*, 110: 199–240.
Carnap, R. (1931). "Überwindung Der Metaphysik Durch Logische Analyse Der Sprache," *Erkenntnis*, 2: 219–241.
Carr, D. (1986). "Cogitamus Ergo Sumus," *The Monist*, 69: 521–533.
Chalmers, D. (1996). *The Conscious Mind: In Search of a Fundamental Theory*. Oxford: Oxford University Press.
Chelstrom, E. (2013). *Social Phenomenology: Husserl, Intersubjectivity, and Collective Intentionality*. Lanham, MD: Lexington Books.
Chudnoff, E. (2015). *Cognitive Phenomenology*. Abingdon, UK: Routledge.
Cobb-Stevens, R. (1990). *Husserl and Analytic Philosophy*. Dordrecht: Springer.
Correia, F. (2008). "Ontological Dependence," *Philosophy Compass*, 3: 1013–1032.
Correia, F., and Schnieder, B. (2012). *Metaphysical Grounding: Understanding the Structure of Reality*. Cambridge: Cambridge University Press.
Crane, T. (1998). "Intentionality as the Mark of the Mental," in Crane, T. (ed.), *Contemporary Issues in the Philosophy of Mind*. Cambridge: Cambridge University Press: 229–251.
Crowell, S. (2013). *Normativity and Phenomenology in Husserl and Heidegger*. Cambridge: Cambridge University Press.

Dahlstrom, D. (2007). "The Intentionality of Passive Experience: Husserl and A Contemporary Debate," *New Yearbook for Phenomenology and Phenomenological Philosophy*, 7: 25–42.

Dainton, B. (2000). *Stream of Consciousness: Unity and Continuity in Conscious Experience*. Abingdon, UK: Routledge.

Derrida, J. (2011). *Voice and Phenomenon: Introduction to the Problem of the Sign in Husserl's Phenomenology*. Northwestern University Press.

De Vignemont, F. (2011). "Bodily Awareness," in Zalta, E. (ed.), *The Stanford Encyclopedia of Philosophy*. http://plato.stanford.edu/archives/fall2011/entries/bodily-awareness/.

Dretske, F. (1995). *Naturalizing the Mind*. Cambridge, MA: MIT Press.

Dreyfus, H. L. (1992). *What Computers Still Can't Do: A Critique of Artificial Reason*. Cambridge, MA: MIT Press.

Dreyfus, H. L. (2002). "Intelligence without Representation – Merleau-Ponty's Critique of Mental Representation the Relevance of Phenomenology to Scientific Explanation," *Phenomenology and the Cognitive Sciences*, 1: 367–383.

Dreyfus, H. L., and Hall, H. (1982). *Husserl, Intentionality and Cognitive Science*. Cambridge, MA: MIT Press.

Dummett, M. (1993). *Origins of Analytical Philosophy*. Cambridge, MA: Harvard University Press.

Durfee, H. (1976). *Analytic Philosophy and Phenomenology*. Dordrecht: Springer.

Edie, J. M. (1977). "Husserl's Conception of 'The Grammatical' and Contemporary Linguistics," in Mohanty, J.N. (ed.), *Readings on Edmund Husserl's Logical Investigations*. Dordrecht: Springer: 137–161.

Embree, L. (1972). "Biographical Sketch of Aron Gurwitsch," in Gurwitsch, A. and Embree, L. (eds.), *Life-World and Consciousness*. Northwestern University Press.

Embree, L. (ed.). (2004). *Gurwitsch's Relevancy for Cognitive Science*. Dordrecht: Springer.

Feigl, H. (1958). "The 'Mental' and The 'Physical'," *Minnesota Studies in the Philosophy of Science*, 2: 370–497.

Fisher, L., and Embree, L. (2000). *Feminist Phenomenology*. Dordrecht: Kluwer Academic Publishers.

Flanagan, O. (1992). *Consciousness Reconsidered*. Cambridge, MA: MIT Press.

Flynn, T. (2014). *Sartre: A Philosophical Biography*. Cambridge: Cambridge University Press.

Fodor, J. (1974). "Special Sciences (or: The Disunity of Science as a Working Hypothesis)," *Synthese*, 28: 97–115.

Føllesdal, D. (1994). *Husserl and Frege: A Contribution to Elucidating the Origins of Phenomenological Philosophy*. Dordrecht: Springer.

Føllesdal, D. (2018). "Husserl and Putnam on Twin Earth," in Frauchiger, M. (ed.), *Themes from Putnam*. Frankfurt: Ontos.

Gallagher, S. (2005). *How the Body Shapes the Mind*. Oxford: Oxford University Press.

Gallagher, S., and Schmicking, D. (2010). *Handbook of Phenomenology and Cognitive Science*. Dordrecht: Springer.

Gallagher, S., and Zahavi, D. (2007). *The Phenomenological Mind: An Introduction to Philosophy of Mind and Cognitive Science*. New York, NY: Routledge.

Gilbert, M. (1989). *On Social Facts*. Abingdon, UK: Routledge.

Goldman, A. (2006). *Simulating Minds: The Philosophy, Psychology, and Neuroscience of Mindreading*. Oxford: Oxford University Press.

Grathoff, R. (ed.). (1989). *Philosophers in Exile: The Correspondence of Alfred Schutz and Aron Gurwitsch, 1939–1959*. Bloomington, IN: Indiana University Press.

Gurwitsch, A. (1964). *The Field of Consciousness*. Pittsburgh, PA: Duquesne University Press.

Haddock, G. (2008). *The Young Carnap's Unknown Master*. Farnham, UK: Ashgate Publishing, Ltd.

Harman, G. (1990). "The Intrinsic Quality of Experience," *Philosophical Perspectives*, 4: 31–52.

Hartimo, M. (2010). *Phenomenology and Mathematics*. Dordrecht: Springer.

Heidegger, M. (1962). *Being and Time*. Trans. J. Macquarrie and E. Robinson. New York: Harper & Row.

Heinämaa, S. (1999). "Simone de Beauvoir's Phenomenology of Sexual Difference," *Hypatia*, 14: 114–132.

Hill, C., and Da Silva, J. (eds.). (1997). *The Road Not Taken. On Husserl's Philosophy of Logic and Mathematics*. London: College Publications.

Hopp, W. (2008). "Husserl on Sensation, Perception, and Interpretation," *Canadian Journal of Philosophy*, 38: 219–245.

Hopp, W. (2010). "How to Think about Nonconceptual Content," *New Yearbook for Phenomenology & Phenomenological Philosophy*, 10: 1–24.

Hopp, W. (2011). *Perception and Knowledge: A Phenomenological Account*. Cambridge: Cambridge University Press.

Horgan, T., and Tienson, J. (2002). "The Intentionality of Phenomenology and the Phenomenology of Intentionality," in Chalmers, D. (ed.), *Philosophy of Mind: Classical and Contemporary Readings*. Oxford: Oxford University Press: 520–533.

Humphreys, P. (1997). "How Properties Emerge," *Philosophy of Science*, 64: 1–17.

Hurley, S. (1998). *Consciousness in Action*. Cambridge, MA: Harvard University Press.

Husserl, E. (1960). *Cartesian Meditations: An Introduction to Phenomenology*. Trans. D. Cairns. The Hague: Martinus Nijhoff.

Husserl, E. (1969). *Formal and Transcendental Logic*. Trans. D. Cairns. The Hague: Martinus Nijhoff.

Husserl, E. (1973). *Experience and Judgment*. Trans. J. Churchill, and K. Ameriks. Northwestern University Press.

Husserl, E. (1980). *Ideas Pertaining to a Pure Phenomenology and to a Phenomenological Philosophy: Third Book: Phenomenology and the Foundation of the Sciences*. Trans. T. Klein and W. E. Pohl. Dordrecht: Springer.

Husserl, E. (1989). *Ideas Pertaining to a Pure Phenomenology and to a Phenomenological Philosophy: Studies in Phenomenology of the Constitution*. Trans. R. Rojcewicz and A. Schuwer. Dordrecht: Springer.

Husserl, E. (1997). *Psychological and Transcendental Phenomenology and the Confrontation with Heidegger (1927–1931): The Encyclopaedia Britannica Article, the Amsterdam Lectures,'Phenomenology and Anthropology', and Husserl's Marginal Notes in Being and Time and Kant and the Problem of Metaphysics*. Trans. T. Sheehan and R. Palmer. Dordrecht: Springer.

Husserl, E. (2001a). *Logical Investigations*, Vol. 2. Trans. J. Findlay. Abingdon, UK: Routledge.

Husserl, E. (2001b). *Logical Investigations*, Vol. 1. Trans. J. Findlay. Abingdon, UK: Routledge.

Husserl, E. (2001c). *Analyses Concerning Passive and Active Synthesis: Lectures on Transcendental Logic*. Trans. A. Steinbock. Dordrecht: Kluwer Academic Publishers.

Husserl, E. (2014). *Ideas for a Pure Phenomenology and Phenomenological Philosophy: First Book: General Introduction to Pure Phenomenology*. Trans. D. Dahlstrom. Hackett Publishing Company, Inc.

Jackson, F. (1982). "Epiphenomenal Qualia," *The Philosophical Quarterly*, 32: 127–136.

Joordens, S., van Duijn, M., and Spalek, T. M. (2002). "When Timing the Mind One Should Also Mind the Timing: Biases in the Measurement of Voluntary Actions," *Consciousness and Cognition*, 11: 231–240.

Kaelin, E. F., and Schrag, C. O. (1989). *American Phenomenology: Origins and Developments*. Dordrecht: Springer.

Kasmier, D. (2003). *Husserl's Theory of a Priori Knowledge: A Response to the Failure of Contemporary Rationalism*. Dissertation. Los Angeles, CA: University of Southern California Press.

Kasmier, D. (2010). "A Defense of Husserl's Method of Free Variation," in Vandevelde, P. and Luft, S. (eds.), *Epistemology, Archaeology, Ethics: Current Investigations of Husserl's Corpus*. Continuum.

Kelly, S. (2005). "Seeing Things in Merleau-Ponty," in Carman, T. and Hansen, M. (eds.), *The Cambridge Companion to Merleau-Ponty*. Cambridge: Cambridge University Press.

Kim, J. (1992). "'Downward Causation' in Emergentism and Nonreductive Physicalism," in Beckerman (ed.), *Emergence or Reduction*. de Gruyter & Co: 119–138.

Kim, J. (2003). "Blocking Causal Drainage and Other Maintenance Chores with Mental Causation," *Philosophy and Phenomenological Research*, 67: 151–176.

Kim, J. (2007). *Physicalism, or Something Near Enough*. Princeton, NJ: Princeton University Press.

Kim, J. (2010). *Philosophy of Mind. Third Edition*. Boulder, CO: Westview Press.

Kind, A. (2010). "Transparency and Representationalist theories of Consciousness," *Philosophy Compass*, 5: 902–913.

Knobe, J. (2011). "Finding the Mind in the Body," in Brockman, M. (ed.), *Future Science: Essays from the Cutting Edge*. Random House: 184–196.

Kriegel, U. (2009). *Subjective Consciousness: A Self-Representational Theory*. Oxford: Oxford University Press.

Kriegel, U. (2011). *The Sources of Intentionality*. Oxford: Oxford University Press.

Kriegel, U. (ed.). (2013). *Phenomenal Intentionality*. Oxford: Oxford University Press.

Kriegel, U., and Williford, K. (eds.). (2006). *Self-Representational Approaches to Consciousness*. Cambridge, MA: MIT Press.

Kusch, M. (1989). *Language as Calculus vs. Language as Universal Medium: A Study in Husserl, Heidegger and Gadamer*. Dordrecht: Springer.

Levin, D. (1998). "Tracework: Myself and Others in the Moral Phenomenology of Merleau-Ponty and Levinas," *International Journal of Philosophical Studies*, 6: 345–392.

Lévinas, E. (1995). *The Theory of Intuition in Husserl's Phenomenology*. Trans. Orianne. Evanston, IL: Northwestern University Press.

Libet, B. (2009). *Mind Time: The Temporal Factor in Consciousness*. Cambridge, MA: Harvard University Press.

Livingston, P. (2002). "Husserl and Schlick on the Logical Form of Experience," *Synthese*, 132: 239–272.

Livingston, P. (2005). "Functionalism and Logical Analysis," in Smith, D.W. and Thomasson, A. (eds.), *Phenomenology and Philosophy of Mind*. Oxford: Clarendon Press: 19–40.
Lübcke, P. (1999). "A Semantic Interpretation of Husserl's Epoché," *Synthese*, 118: 1–12.
Lycan, William (2014). "Representational Theories of Consciousness," in Zalta, E. (ed.), *The Stanford Encyclopedia of Philosophy*. http://plato.stanford.edu/archives/win2014/entries/consciousness-representational/.
McDowell, J. (1994). *Mind and World*. Cambridge, MA: Harvard University Press.
McIntyre, R. (1984). "Searle on Intentionality," *Inquiry*, 27: 468–483.
McIntyre, R. (1986). "Husserl and the Representational Theory of Mind," *Topoi*, 5: 101–113.
Mangan, B. (2007). "Cognition, Fringe Consciousness, and the Legacy of William James," in Schneider and Velmans (eds.), *The Blackwell Companion to Consciousness*. Oxford: Blackwell: 671–685.
Margolis, E., and Laurence, S. (2011). "Concepts," in Zalta, E. (ed.), *The Stanford Encyclopedia of Philosophy*. https://plato.stanford.edu/entries/concepts/.
Mathiesen, K. (2005). "Collective Consciousness," in Smith, D.W. and Thomasson, A. (eds.), *Phenomenology and Philosophy of Mind*. Clarendon Press: 235–252.
Mensch, J. (1991). "Phenomenology and Artificial Intelligence: Husserl Learns Chinese," *Husserl Studies*, 8: 107–127.
Merleau-Ponty, M. (2013). *Phenomenology of Perception*. Trans. D. Landes. Abingdon, UK: Routledge.
Mohanty, J. N. (1982). *Husserl and Frege*. Indiana University Press.
Mulligan, K., and Correia, F. (2013). "Facts," in Zalta, E. (ed.), *The Stanford Encyclopedia of Philosophy*. http://plato.stanford.edu/archives/spr2013/entries/facts/.
Murphy, A. (2009). "Sexuality," in Dreyfus and Wrathall (eds.), *A Companion to Phenomenology and Existentialism*. Blackwell: 489–501.
Nagel, T. (1974). "What Is It like to Be a Bat?" *The Philosophical Review*, 83: 435–450.
Noë, A. (2004). *Action in Perception*. Cambridge, MA: MIT Press.
O'Connor, T., and Wong, H. (2005). "The Metaphysics of Emergence," *Noûs*, 39: 658–678.
O'Connor, T., and Wong, H. (2012). "Emergent Properties," in Zalta, E. (ed.), *The Stanford Encyclopedia of Philosophy*. http://plato.stanford.edu/archives/spr2012/entries/properties-emergent/.
O'Regan, K. (2001). "What It Is Like to See: A Sensorimotor Theory of Perceptual Experience," *Synthese*, 129: 79–103.
Overgaard, S. (2007). *Wittgenstein and Other Minds: Rethinking Subjectivity and Intersubjectivity with Wittgenstein, Levinas, and Husserl*. Abingdon, UK: Routledge.
Overgaard, S. (2013). "Motivating Disjunctivism," *Husserl Studies*, 29: 51–63.
Petitot, J., Varela, F., Pachoud, B., and Roy, J.M. (eds.). (1999). *Naturalizing Phenomenology: Issues in Contemporary Phenomenology and Cognitive Science*. Palo Alto, CA: Stanford University Press.
Pitt, D. (2004). "The Phenomenology of Cognition, Or, What Is It Like to Think That *P*?" *Philosophy and Phenomenological Research*, 69: 1–36.
Place, U.T. (1956). "Is Consciousness a Brain Process?" *British Journal of Psychology*, 47: 44–50.
Putnam, H. (1967). "The Nature of Mental States," *Readings in the Philosophy of Psychology*, 1: 222–231.
Ricœur, P. (1967). *Husserl: An Analysis of His Phenomenology*. Trans. Ballard and Embree. Evanston, IL: Northwestern University Press.

Rojcewicz, R., and Schuwer, A. (1989). "Translators' Introduction," in Husserl, E. (ed.), *Ideas Pertaining to a Pure Phenomenology and to a Phenomenological Philosophy: Second Book*. Dordrecht: Kluwer Academic Publishers: xi–xvi.

Rollinger, R. D. (1999). *Husserl's Position in the School of Brentano*. Dordrecht: Springer.

Rowlands, M. (2010). *The New Science of the Mind: From Extended Mind to Embodied Phenomenology*. Cambridge, MA: MIT Press.

Sanchez, C. (2010). "Epistemic Justification and Husserl's Phenomenology of Reason in *Ideas I*," in Vandevelde, P. and Luft, S. (eds.), *Epistemology, Archaeology, Ethics: Current Investigations of Husserl's Corpus*. New York, NY: Continuum.

Sartre, J. P. (1991). *The Transcendence of the Ego: An Existentialist Theory of Consciousness*. New York, NY: Hill and Wang.

Sartre, J. P. (2003). *Being and Nothingness*. Trans. H. E. Barnes. New York, NY: Washington Square Press.

Schmid, H. B. (2014). "Plural self-awareness," *Phenomenology and the Cognitive Sciences*, 13: 7–24.

Schutz, A. (1967). *The Phenomenology of the Social World*. Evanston, IL: Northwestern University Press.

Schutz, A., and Natanson, M. (eds.) (1970). *Phenomenology and Social Reality*. The Hague: M. Nijhoff.

Searle, J. (1980). "Minds, Brains, and Programs," *Behavioral and Brain Sciences*, 3: 417–424.

Searle, J. (1992). *The Rediscovery of the Mind*. Cambridge, MA: MIT Press.

Searle, J. (2005). "The Phenomenological Illusion," in Reicher and Marek (eds.), *Experience and Analysis: Papers of the 27th International Wittgenstein Symposium*: 317–336.

Shim, M. (2011). "Representationalism and Husserlian Phenomenology," *Husserl Studies*, 27: 197–215.

Siegel, S. (2007). "How Can We Discover the Contents of Experience?" *The Southern Journal of Philosophy*, 45: 127–142.

Siegel, S. (2010). *The Contents of Visual Experience*. Oxford: Oxford University Press.

Siegel, S. (2015). "The Contents of Perception," in Zalta, E. (ed.), *The Stanford Encyclopedia of Philosophy*. http://plato.stanford.edu/archives/spr2015/entries/perception-contents/.

Siewert, C. (1998). *The Significance of Consciousness*. Princeton, NJ: Princeton University Press.

Siewert, C. (2013). "Phenomenality and Self-Consciousness," in Kriegel, U. (ed.), *Phenomenal Intentionality*. Oxford: Oxford University Press: 235–257.

Simons, P. (1987). *Parts: A Study in Ontology*. Oxford: Oxford University Press.

Simons, P. (1992). "The Anglo-Austrian Analytic Axis," in Simons, P. (ed.), *Philosophy and Logic in Central Europe from Bolzano to Tarski*. Dordrecht: Springer: 143–158.

Smart, J.J.C. (1959). "Sensations and Brain Processes," *The Philosophical Review*, 68: 141–156.

Smith, A.D. (2008). "Husserl and Externalism," *Synthese*, 160: 313–333.

Smith, B. (1994). *Austrian Philosophy. The Legacy of Franz Brentano*. Open Court.

Smith, B. (1998). "Basic Concepts of Formal Ontology," in Guarino, N. (ed.), *Formal Ontology in Information Systems*. IOS Press: 19–28.

Smith, B., and Smith, D. W. (eds.). (1995). *The Cambridge Companion to Husserl*. Cambridge: Cambridge University Press.

Smith, D. W. (1986). "The Structure of (Self-) Consciousness," *Topoi*, 5: 149–156.

Smith, D. W. (2007). *Husserl*. Abingdon, UK: Routledge.
Smith, D. W. (2013). "The Role of Phenomenology in Analytic Philosophy," in Beaney, M. (ed.), *The Oxford Handbook of the History of Analytic Philosophy*. Oxford: Oxford University Press: 1495–1527.
Smith, D. W., and McIntyre, R. (1982). *Husserl and Intentionality: A Study of Mind, Meaning, and Language*. Dordrecht: Springer.
Smith, D. W., and Thomasson, A. (eds.). (2005). *Phenomenology and Philosophy of Mind*. Oxford: Oxford University Press.
Smithies, D. (2013). "The Nature of Cognitive Phenomenology," *Philosophy Compass*, 8: 744–754.
Sowa, R. (2007). "Essences and Eidetic Laws in Edmund Husserl's Descriptive Eidetics," *New Yearbook for Phenomenology and Phenomenological Philosophy*, 7: 77–108.
Stein, E. (1989). *On the Problem of Empathy*. Washington D.C.: ICS Publications.
Stoljar, D. (2015). "Physicalism," in Zalta, E. (ed.), *The Stanford Encyclopedia of Philosophy*. http://plato.stanford.edu/archives/spr2015/entries/physicalism/.
Strawson, G. (1994). *Mental Reality*. Cambridge, MA: MIT Press.
Strawson, G. (2009). *Selves: An Essay in Revisionary Metaphysics*. Oxford: Oxford University Press.
Strawson, G. (2015). "Consciousness Myth," *Times Literary Supplement*. Feb 25, 2015.
Stueber, D. (2006). *Rediscovering Empathy: Agency, Folk Psycholgy, and the Human Sciences*. Cambridge, MA: MIT Press.
Thomasson, A. (2002). "Phenomenology and the Development of Analytic Philosophy," *The Southern Journal of Philosophy*, 40: 115–142.
Thomasson, A. (2005). "First-Person Knowledge in Phenomenology," in Smith, D.W. and Thomasson, A. (eds.), *Phenomenology and Philosophy of Mind*. Oxford: Clarendon Press: 115–139.
Thompson, E. (2007). *Mind in Life: Biology, Phenomenology, and the Sciences of Mind*. Cambridge, MA: Harvard University Press.
Tieszen, R. (2011). *After Godel: Platonism and Rationalism in Mathematics and Logic*. Oxford: Oxford University Press.
Toadvine, T. (2001). "Phenomenological Method in Merleau-Ponty's Critique of Gurwitsch," *Husserl Studies*, 17: 195–205.
Tye, M. (1995). *Ten Problems of Consciousness: A Representational Theory of the Phenomenal Mind*. Cambridge, MA: MIT Press.
Tye, M. (2000). *Consciousness, Color, and Content*. Cambridge, MA: MIT Press.
Varzi, A. (2015). "Mereology," in Zalta, E. (ed.), *The Stanford Encyclopedia of Philosophy*. http://plato.stanford.edu/archives/spr2015/entries/mereology/.
Vongehr, T. (2007). "A Short History of the Husserl-Archives Leuven and the Husserliana," in *History of the Husserl-Archives Leuven*. Dordrecht: Springer: 99–126.
Vrahimis, A. (2013). *Encounters Between Analytic and Continental Philosophy*. Dordrecht: Springer.
Walsh, P. J. (2013). "Husserl's Concept of Motivation: The Logical Investigations and Beyond," *Logical Analysis & History of Philosophy*, 16: 70–83.
Walsh, P. J. (2014). "Empathy, Embodiment, and the Unity of Expression," *Topoi*, 33: 215–226.
Walsh, P. J. (2017). "Motivation and Horizon: Phenomenal Intentionality in Husserl," *Grazer Philosophische Studien*, 94: 410–435.

Willard, D. (1984). *Logic and the Objectivity of Knowledge: A Study in Husserl's Early Philosophy*. Ohio University Press.

Williford, K. (2013). "Husserl's Hyletic Data and Phenomenal Consciousness," *Phenomenology and the Cognitive Sciences*, 12: 501–519.

Wilson, J. (2009). "Determination, Realization and Mental Causation," *Philosophical Studies*, 145: 149–169.

Wrathall, M., and Malpas, J. (eds.). (2000). *Heidegger, Coping, and Cognitive Science: Essays in Honor of Hubert L. Dreyfus, Vol. 2*. Cambridge, MA: MIT Press.

Yoshimi, J. (2007). "Mathematizing Phenomenology," *Phenomenology and the Cognitive Sciences*, 6: 271–291.

Yoshimi, J. (2009). "Husserl's Theory of Belief and the Heideggerean Critique," *Husserl Studies*, 25: 121–140.

Yoshimi, J. (2010). "Husserl on Psycho-Physical Laws," *New Yearbook for Phenomenology and Phenomenological Philosophy*, 10: 25–42.

Yoshimi, J. (2012). "Supervenience, Dynamical Systems Theory, and Non-Reductive Physicalism," *British Journal for the Philosophy of Science*, 63: 373–398.

Zahavi, D. (2005). *Subjectivity and Selfhood: Investigating the First-Person Perspective*. Cambridge, MA: MIT Press.

Zahavi, D. (2014). *Self and Other: Exploring Subjectivity, Empathy, and Shame*. Oxford: Oxford University Press.

Zhok, A. (2011). "A Phenomenological Reading of Anomalous Monism," *Husserl Studies*, 27: 227–256.

2

THE MIND-BODY PROBLEM IN 20TH-CENTURY PHILOSOPHY

Amy Kind

What is the nature of the mind? What is its relation to the body? These questions – which jointly constitute *the mind-body problem* – lie at the heart of philosophy of mind. Traditionally, there have been two sorts of approaches to this problem. According to the position known as *dualism*, the mind is an immaterial thing not existing in physical space. Dualists believe that there are two fundamental kinds of things in the world: material things, like trees and tables and chairs, and like our physical bodies, and immaterial things, like minds. The mind, according to the dualist, has a different kind of nature from the body (which includes the brain). In contrast, the position known as *monism* holds that there is only one type of fundamental entity in the world. The most influential form of monism, traditionally known as *materialism* but now more commonly referred to as *physicalism*, claims that all entities – including the mind – are physical in nature.

In the wake of René Descartes' influential 17th-century arguments in favor of dualism, it was long assumed that physicalism was not a tenable position. Such was the general philosophical consensus about the mind-body problem at the close of the 19th century.[1] But this was to change in the 20th century, a period of time in which considerable attention was addressed to the mind-body problem, and also in which considerable progress was made. This essay, which aims to take a historical look at this progress, traces the progression of philosophical thought about the mind-body problem over the course of the 20th century.

Because it would be impossible in an article of this sort to survey all of the important developments on the mind-body problem that occurred in the 20th century, I here focus my attention on several of the key movements and themes that occupied philosophical attention over the course of the last 100 years. The first three sections trace the development of physicalism about the mind from behaviorism to the identity theory to functionalism. In the fourth section, I turn to the qualia-based threat to such theories that arose in the last quarter of the century.

1. Behaviorism

The story of the mind-body problem in 20th-century philosophy begins with behaviorism, a movement that dominated philosophical thinking about the mind for at least the first half of the century. Insofar as behaviorism offered a genuine alternative to both traditional dualism and traditional materialism, each of which had been found wanting, its popularity is perhaps unsurprising. Though behaviorist theories come in several different varieties, they all in some way attempt to understand the mind in terms of bodily behavior. While philosophers prior to the onset of behaviorism had long recognized a tight connection between mind and behavior, this connection had generally been understood to be evidential in nature. My reaching for a drink counts as evidence that I'm thirsty; my moaning and groaning counts as evidence that I'm in pain. In contrast, behaviorists argued that we should view the connection between mental states and bodily behavior not as evidential but as constitutive. For the behaviorist, we should not think of bodily behavior as a mere manifestation of some inner mental state; rather, exhibiting such behavior is simply what it is to be in the relevant mental state.

The behavioristic turn in philosophy at the start of the 20th century mirrored a similar turn in psychology. Dissatisfied with the introspectionist methods that had previously been dominant, psychological behaviorists aimed to reorient psychological study towards more objective methods that would put the discipline on a similar footing with other sciences. According to psychological behaviorists, psychology is best understood not as a science of mind but as a science of behavior. Though our primary interest here concerns behaviorism in philosophy of mind, it will be useful to begin with a brief discussion of psychological behaviorism. Doing so will help us to better understand the philosophical varieties of behaviorism.

1.1 Psychological behaviorism

The term "behaviorism" was coined by John Watson (1913) in "Psychology as the Behaviorist Sees It," an article often referred to as the behaviorist "manifesto." Though there had been some isolated expressions of a behavioristic bent among nineteenth century psychologists, psychology in the late 19th century and the early 20th century was largely a study of inner mental life.[2] Following the work of Wilhelm Wundt, often regarded as the father of modern psychology, this study was conducted by way of rigorous introspective investigation. As William James wrote in his *Principles of Psychology*, "Introspective observation is what we have to rely on first and foremost and always" (James 1890/1981, 185).

In urging that psychology should study behavior rather than the inner causes of behavior, psychological behaviorists were largely concerned with issues of scientific methodology. But many of them were also often tempted by a stronger stance, one that denies the existence of such inner causes altogether. This eliminativist tendency was particularly marked in the late-20th-century work of B. F. Skinner, who referred to his view as *radical behaviorism* and contrasted it with the methodological behaviorism of psychologists like Watson. In *About Behaviorism*, where he dismissed alleged inner causes of behavior as "mental fictions," Skinner explicitly identified human thought with human behavior: "Thinking has the dimensions of behavior, not of a fancied inner process which finds expression in behavior" (Skinner 1974, 18, 117–118). Ultimately, however, Skinner's support for eliminativism was not entirely unequivocal. For example, though he claimed in *Science and Behavior* that statements like "he eats" and "he is hungry" both refer to the same behavioral fact, he also noted that the "objection to inner states is not that they do not exist, but that they are not relevant in a functional analysis" (42). As we turn to philosophical behaviorism, we will see a similar flirtation with eliminative behaviorism – and one that is similarly ambiguous.

1.2 Philosophical behaviorism

While behaviorism was widespread among philosophers in the first half of the 20th century, there were really two distinct versions of the view on offer, each springing from a different motivation. The behaviorism associated with philosophers such as Rudolf Carnap and Carl Hempel was an outgrowth of logical positivism and the verificationist theory of meaning. Based on the supposition that there are close logical connections between statements involving mental vocabulary and statements involving behavioristic vocabulary, this view is typically referred to as *logical behaviorism*. The behaviorism associated with philosophers such as Gilbert Ryle and Ludwig Wittgenstein was an outgrowth of ordinary language philosophy. While this view does not have a standard name in the philosophical literature, I will call it *ordinary language behaviorism*.[3]

Logical behaviorism is a theory about the meaning of statements involving mental expressions – statements like "Diego has a toothache" or "Sofia believes that it will rain." While the meaning of these psychological statements may seem to depend on their reference to inner mental states – to Diego's toothache and to Sofia's belief – the logical behaviorists disagree. Instead, they take the meaning of such statements to consist in behavioral facts about Diego and Sofia, i.e., facts about the behavior that these individuals manifest or that they are disposed to manifest.

Underlying this view is a commitment to the verificationist theory of meaning, a theory that takes the meaning of a statement to be established by the conditions of its verification (see Hempel 1980, 17). Consider a claim about temperature, e.g., the claim that the current temperature in my office is 72 degrees Fahrenheit. For such a statement to be true, it would have to be the case that the mercury level of a properly calibrated glass thermometer currently placed in my office would correspond to the number 72 on a Fahrenheit scale. We could also make analogous claims about an alcohol thermometer or an infrared thermometer, or about various other devices; as Hempel notes, there is a long list of other possibilities that make the statement true. Each of these possibilities can be expressed by what he calls a *physical test sentence*. We need not establish the truth of all of the physical test sentences in evaluating the truth of the original sentence. But the key point is that the original sentence about temperature communicates to us nothing more than the fact that these physical test sentences obtain; the original sentence is simply an "abbreviated formulation" of such sentences (Hempel, 1980, 17).

In identifying the meaning of a statement with the conditions of its verification, the verificationist is in turn committed to the claim that statements lacking verification conditions lack meaning. Though such a statement might be grammatically well-constructed, it lacks any content and is thus only a pseudo-statement (see, e.g., Hempel, 1980, 17; Carnap, 1932, 44). What then of psychological statements? Since there is no way in principle to test for inner states like pains and beliefs, must such statements be dismissed as meaningless? To avoid this result, the logical behaviorist suggests that psychological statements have verification conditions that are directly analogous to those we saw in the temperature example. Psychological statements are verified by facts about behavior. For example, the verification conditions for the claim that Diego has a toothache include physical test sentences like the following:

- Diego grimaces and rubs his mouth
- When asked, "What's wrong," Diego utters the words, "I have a toothache."
- Diego has swollen gums and a tooth with an exposed pulp

and so on. For the logical behaviorist, then, mentalistic vocabulary should not be taken to refer to inner mental states. Rather, the meaning of claims involving such vocabulary consists in facts about behavior.

In contrast to logical behaviorism, ordinary language behaviorism was not motivated by verificationism. Rather, the behaviorism of philosophers like Ryle and Wittgenstein was primarily grounded in worries about the problem of other minds, a problem that is particularly acute if there are inner mental states that are private to each individual. As Wittgenstein suggested in his posthumously published *Philosophical Investigations*:

> The essential thing about private experience is really not that each person possesses his own exemplar, but that nobody knows whether other people also have *this* or something else. The assumption would thus be possible – though unverifiable – that one section of mankind had one sensation of red and another section another.
> (Wittgenstein 1953, §272)

As he went on to suggest in the famous "beetle-in-a-box" passage, problems arise from the assumption that people understand a mental state like pain only from their own case:

> Suppose everyone had a box with something in it: we call it a "beetle." No one can look into anyone else's box, and everyone says he knows what a beetle is only by looking at *his* beetle. – Here it would be quite possible for everyone to have something different in his box."
> (Wittgenstein 1953, §293)

While there is considerable dispute about how best to interpret this passage (as well as the larger argument of which it is a part), we can nonetheless here see Wittgenstein's worries about how we would know anything about other minds if mentalistic vocabulary were to refer to private mental states.

Ryle expressed related worries in *The Concept of Mind*, a book that offered an extended attack on the view that the mind is an immaterial substance distinct from the body. On this Cartesian picture, one that Ryle often referred to derisively as "the Cartesian myth" or as "the dogma of the ghost in the machine," solipsistic worries naturally arise: "I can witness what your body does, but I cannot witness what your mind does, and my pretensions to infer from what your body does to what your mind does all collapse, since the premises for such inferences are either inadequate or unknowable" (Ryle 1949, 60). To overcome such worries, Ryle urged that we see mental vocabulary as functioning to refer to behavioral dispositions: "To find that most people have minds . . . is simply to find that they are able and prone to do certain sorts of things" (Ryle 1949, 61). Likewise, Wittgenstein too argued that once we pay careful attention to the way language is used, we see that it is a mistake to see the grammatical function of mental vocabulary as one of reference to mental states; verbal expressions involving the word "pain," for example, are simply instances of pain-behavior, no different from other instances of pain-behavior like crying. (See Wittgenstein 1953, §244.)

In developing their views, both Wittgenstein and Ryle at times seemed to embrace eliminativism. In the beetle-in-the-box passage, for example, Wittgenstein went on to note that "the thing in the box has no place in the language-game at all; not even as a *something*, for the box might even be empty" (Wittgenstein 1953, §293). Likewise, in dismissing Cartesianism as a myth – in claiming that the postulation of mind as an entity distinct from the body is a "category mistake" – Ryle also seems to be expressing sympathy for an eliminativist view. Ultimately, however, neither of these philosophers came down squarely on the eliminativist side. Wittgenstein explicitly pulled back from eliminativism when he noted that the respect in which mental states are fictions is that they are *grammatical* fictions; a sensation "is not a *something*, but not a *nothing* either!" (Wittgenstein 1953, §304) Similarly, though Ryle's scorn for talk of mentality and minds is apparent, his discussion tended to fall short of showing how, exactly, we can successfully analyze such talk away.[4]

1.3 Criticisms of behaviorism

Despite the dominance of behaviorism in the first half of the century, in the 1950s and 1960s it came under attack from several different directions. A sharply negative review of Skinner's 1957 book *Verbal Behavior* by Noam Chomsky (1959) called psychological behaviorism into question. According to Chomsky, language acquisition and verbal competence cannot be explained simply in terms of stimulus and reinforcement; rather, we must postulate innate mechanisms to achieve an adequate explanation. Around the same time, important criticisms directed at both logical behaviorism and ordinary language behaviorism began to surface in the philosophical literature.

One influential criticism derives from the work of Roderick Chisholm (1957). For the behaviorist, belief consists in behavioral dispositions; for example, we might analyze a gardener's belief that it will rain in terms of his disposition to carry an umbrella with him while he works and to put away his watering can. (See Ryle 1949, 174.) But such behavioral dispositions implicitly presuppose the presence of relevant desires: A gardener who believes that it will rain will carry an umbrella only if he wants to stay dry. Thus, any attempt to provide a behavioral definition of belief would have to make reference to desire and, likewise, any attempt to provide a behavioral definition of desire would have to make reference to belief. That such mental notions are inherently connected – that they form an "intentional circle" – dooms any attempt to define them solely in terms of behavior.[5]

A second influential criticism derives from the work of Hilary Putnam and, in particular, from the article "Brains and Behavior." (Putnam 1963) This criticism is aimed specifically at the logical behaviorists. To make the case that the kinds of analyses they offered were in principle unworkable, Putnam asks us to imagine a community of stoic individuals in which all of the adult members have trained themselves to entirely suppress their involuntary pain behavior. These super-spartans might occasionally verbally admit they are in pain – in a normal, pleasant tone of voice – but they will show no other sign. When they stub their toes or burn their fingers, they don't wince or moan, or flush or break out in a sweat, or grab the affected body part. Yet they still feel pain as we do, and they dislike it. Taking this one step further, Putnam next asks us to imagine a community of super-super-spartans. Having been super-spartans for so long, they no longer even make verbal reports of pain, and they will not admit to being in pain if they are asked. Because we can conceive of this sort of case – a case of pain without any pain-behavior whatsoever and, in fact, without even any disposition to pain-behavior – logical behaviorism must be mistaken.

The criticisms of behaviorism struck many as decisive, and by the late 1960s, behaviorism had largely disappeared from view. Though there are behavioristic elements present in the work of some late 20th-century philosophers – perhaps most notably in the work of Daniel Dennett – the vast majority of contemporary philosophers reject the reduction of mind to behavior.[6] As we will see, however, behaviorism left an important legacy, for the rise of both the identity theory and functionalism in the second half of the 20th century can be traced in large part to the lessons learned in discussions of behaviorism.

2. The identity theory

Even while behaviorism was dominating philosophy of mind in the early part of the 20th century, both the philosophical and the psychological literature contained isolated expressions of a different sort of physicalist view, one that identifies mental states not with behavioral dispositions but instead with physical states of the brain. The philosopher Moritz Schlick, for example, claimed that we should not understand the relationship between our experience and brain processes as one of causality but rather one of simple identity (Schlick 1925/1974). Likewise, the psychologist Edwin G. Boring claimed that "consciousness is a physiological event" (Boring 1933, 14). But it was not until the late 1950s that the identity theory achieved philosophical prominence. The rise of the theory owes almost entirely to the publication of three ground-breaking articles: "Is Consciousness a Brain Process," by U. T. Place (1956), "The 'Mental' and the 'Physical'," by Herbert Feigl (1958), and "Sensations and Brain Processes," by J.J.C. Smart (1959). As summarized by Feigl, the identity theory consists in the claim that "the states of direct experience which conscious human beings 'live through,' and those which we confidently ascribe to some of the higher animals, are identical with certain (presumably configurational) aspects of the neural processes in those organisms" (Feigl 1958, 446).

Feigl's development of the theory – which occurred while he was working at the University of Minnesota – proceeded separately from Place and Smart's development of the theory – which occurred while there were both at the University of Adelaide. There are thus various minor differences between what's sometimes called the *American identity theory* and what's sometimes called the *Australian identity theory*. But these differences won't matter for our purposes here.[7] As Place himself notes, "Although there are certain differences of detail in the positions adopted in these three papers, the area of agreement was sufficiently great for all three of the original protagonists to be able to agree that they were all defending the same basic position" (Place, n.d.).

2.1 The case for the identity theory

Prior to the 20th century, materialists had often identified mental states with various physical states. In antiquity, Democritus understood the soul as a sort of fire, made out of spherical atoms, and he took thought to consist in the physical movement of atoms. In the 17th century, Hobbes claimed that sensations are simply internal motions of the sense organs. But the identity theory of the 20th century departs from these previous theories in at least two key ways. First, in focusing on brain processes, the identity theorists aligned themselves with neuroscience. Given the tremendous advances in neuroscientific research in the 20th century, this alignment gave credibility to their theory. Second, and perhaps more importantly, the identity theorists took the psychophysical identities they posited to be directly analogous to other scientific discoveries. Just as scientists discovered that lightning is identical to a certain kind of electrical discharge or that heat is identical to molecular motion, so too the identification of specific mental states with specific brain states emerges as a scientific discovery. We might discover, for example, that pain is identical to the stimulation of c-fibers.

It is worth pausing a moment over this particular example. Though it is now in widespread use in philosophical discussion, the three papers by Place, Feigl, and Smart that ushered in discussion of the identity theory did not invoke this particular identity claim, nor did they use other specific examples of this sort. Rather, they tended to talk more generally of a sensation being identical to some brain process or other. Reference to the pain/c-fiber identification did not become common in philosophical discussions of the identity theory until the 1960s (see, e.g. Putnam 1960 and Rorty 1965). Importantly, however, the use of "the stimulation of c-fibers" or "c-fiber firing" in such discussions seems best understood as a placeholder term, i.e., as a stand-in for whatever brain process is discovered to be identical with pain (assuming that any is). It should thus not be seen as a threat to the identity theory if it turns out that pain is not c-fiber firing but is some other kind of brain process (see, e.g., Puccetti 1977). The precise identity will be determined by scientific discovery.

In drawing an analogy to scientifically discovered identities, the identity theorists emphasized several related features of such identities, some epistemic and some semantic. For example, the identity theorists stressed that the plausibility of their theory hinges on the recognition that not all identities have the same epistemic status. Many identities – like the claims that "red is a color" and "a square is an equilateral rectangle" – can be known *a priori*. In contrast, an identity like "lightning is electrical discharge" can be known only *a posteriori*; it is an empirical claim that results from scientific inquiry. Psychophysical identities, said the identity theorists, are to be understood analogously to claims like "lightning is electrical discharge" rather than to claims like "a square is an equilateral rectangle." Claims like "pain is c-fiber firing" are also the result of scientific inquiry and thus cannot be known *a priori*.[8]

In making their semantic points, the identity theorists called upon early 20th-century research in philosophy of language. Frege's seminal work on the distinction between sense and reference showed that two expressions that refer to the same object may nonetheless differ in meaning by having different senses. Consider the expressions "the Morning Star" and "the Evening Star." Though they both refer to the same object – the planet Venus – the sense of the former expression is something like "the first heavenly body visible in the morning sky," while the sense of the latter expression is something like "the last heavenly body visible in the evening sky." According to the identity theorists, the distinction between sense and reference comes into play in the case of empirically discovered identities. Though the word "lightning" refers to the same phenomenon as the words "electrical discharge," these two expressions do not have the same sense. Likewise, though the word "pain" refers to the same phenomenon as the words "c-fiber stimulation," these two expressions do not have the same sense. Thus, it's no objection to the identity theory that someone might be perfectly able to discuss his own pains and sensations without knowing anything at all about neuroscience or even about the brain – as Smart noted, "a person may well know that something is an A without knowing that it is a B" even though A is identical to B. Thus: "An illiterate peasant might well be able to talk about his sensations without knowing about his brain processes, just as he can talk about lightning though he knows nothing of electricity" (Smart 1959, 147).[9]

More generally, the identity theorists persuasively showed that many potential objections to the identity theory stem from similar confusions about the nature of psychophysical identities. Here it will be worthwhile for us to explore one other specific implementation of this general strategy, since this will also help to illuminate why the identity theory is often referred to as *the topic-neutral theory*. Consider after-images and, more specifically, the fact that we typically refer to them as being colored. For example, after staring at a bright green colored patch, a viewer who turns her attention to a white surface might plausibly describe her experience by saying something like, "I have a magenta afterimage." Call this claim *M*. Claims like M seem to pose a problem for the identity theory: Though the after-image is magenta, the correlated brain process is not, so how can the after-image be identical to the brain-process? In response to this worry, the identity theorist argues that, once claims like M are properly understood, they can be seen to be consistent with physicalism. Though the general line of argumentation owes to Place, the point was more forcefully developed by Smart. As he argued, rather than taking M to commit us to the existence of something magenta-colored, we should best understand it as having the (rough) meaning: *There is something going on that is like what goes on when (for example) I see a corncockle flower*. Understood this way, M contains only "quasi-logical" or "topic-neutral" words and does not presuppose that the after-image is immaterial (Smart 1959, 150). In this way, the identity theorists argued that much of our purportedly mentalistic vocabulary – and indeed, our very experience of our own mentality – is actually non-committal between dualism and physicalism.[10] This insight proves critical to establishing the viability of the identity theory, and more generally, the viability of physicalism.

As our discussion thus far suggests, the initial case put forth for the identity theory was in many ways a defensive one. Feigl, Place, and Smart were typically more concerned to answer or forestall objections than to mount positive arguments for their view. Smart, for example, noted that the object of his paper was "to show that there are no philosophical arguments which compel us to be dualists" (Smart 1959, 143). Insofar as these early identity theorists put forth a positive case for the theory, it rested largely on considerations of Ockham's razor: Given theories of equal explanatory power, we have reason to adopt the one that is ontologically more parsimonious. As Smart put the point:

> If it be agreed that there are no cogent philosophical arguments which force us into accepting dualism, and if the brain process theory and dualism are equally consistent with the facts, then the principles of parsimony and simplicity seem to me to decide overwhelmingly in favor of the brain process theory.[11]

Seeds of a further positive argument lie in a worry originally expressed by Feigl. Immaterial mental states, were they to exist, would have to be "nomological danglers" (Feigl 1958, 428), i.e., they would remain entirely outside the system of physical laws. Later identity theorists further developed this argument, relying heavily on the thesis that physics is thought to be *causally closed*, or *complete*, i.e., the causal history of any physical event can be wholly given in physical terms (see, e.g., Papineau 2002). This thesis, which seems immensely plausible in light of the scientific advances of the 19th and 20th centuries, deprives opponents of the identity theory of a plausible account of mental causation.[12] Intuitively speaking, mental causes play a crucial role in the causal histories of human actions: my desire for a drink causes me to get up from where I'm sitting and walk to the kitchen, my fear causes me to back up when I encounter a rattlesnake on the hiking trail, my toothache causes me to make an appointment with the dentist. If we accept the completeness of physics, however, then someone who denies the identity theory can account for mental causation only by accepting one of the following two unpalatable alternatives:

(1) Human actions are always overdetermined, wholly and completely caused by mental events and also wholly and completely caused by physical events. Thus, even if I didn't have a desire for a drink, I would still have taken the same action.
(2) The appearance of mental causation is an illusion. In reality, mental events are epiphenomenal, i.e., they have no causal power.

In contrast, the identity theorist's account of mental causation is perfectly in line with the completeness of physics. Since the identity theorists claim that mental events are identical to physical events, they can explain human action in terms of mental causes without denying that a physical event's causal history can be given wholly in physical terms.

Generally speaking, then, the positive case for the identity theory can be seen as one of inference to the best explanation. According to the identity theorists, the best way to account for mental causation is to see mental causes as themselves physical. More generally, the best way to account for all of the undeniable psychophysical correlations that we observe is in terms of identity. There are not two distinct things whose correlation needs explanation; rather there is only one thing. As we saw earlier, a similar strategy of inference to the best explanation was employed by the behaviorists. But the identity theorists have a plausible reason to claim that the explanation they offer is better than the one offered by the behaviorists. In reducing mental states to behavior, the behaviorists had to deny that mental-state talk serves a reporting function. For the behaviorist, my claim that I am in pain does not serve to report my pain but rather is part of what constitutes it; consider Wittgenstein's remark that "The verbal expression of pain replaces crying and does not describe it" (Wittgenstein 1953, §244). As the identity theorists pointed out, this seems implausible. But unlike the dualist, who views such a claim as a report of an "irreducibly psychical something" (Smart 1959, 142), the identity theory can view the claim as a report that refers to a brain process (albeit perhaps unknowingly to the one who makes the report).

Though the identity theory in this way makes a considerable advance over behaviorism, the early identity theorists did not fully abandon the behaviorist leanings of the early 20th century. As originally developed, the identity theory was meant to apply only to experiential mental states, states like mental images and pains. With respect to other mental states like beliefs and desires, the early identity theorists thought that behaviorist analyses were largely correct. Place, for example, noted explicitly that for cognitive and volitional concepts "there can be little doubt . . . that an analysis in terms of dispositions to behave is fundamentally sound" (Place 1956, 44). Later identity theorists like David Armstrong and David Lewis explicitly rejected the restriction of the theory to experiential states. Putting emphasis on the virtue of theoretical economy, these later theorists thought that it would be preferable to give a unified account of all mental phenomena (see, e.g., Armstrong 1968, 80). In further developing the identity theory, Armstrong and Lewis also emphasized the causal nature of mental states, thereby paving the way for the functionalist theories of mind that became prominent in the late 1960s and that continue to be prominent today.

2.2 Multiple realizability

To understand the rise of functionalism, however, we must first understand an influential criticism directed against the identity theory in the late 1960s, namely, what we might call the *multiple realizability argument*. Forcefully developed by Hilary Putnam and Jerry Fodor among others, the argument rests on the claim that creatures with very different neural mechanisms might all feel pain, i.e., that pain might be multiply realizable in many different kinds of physical structures. As Putnam puts the point, the truth of the identity theory requires the existence of some type of state such that any creature whatsoever who is in pain is in that physical state. But creatures as diverse as mammals, reptiles, and molluscs all seem unquestionably to experience pain, despite having very different neural structures. And can't we conceive of extraterrestrial life forms who also experience pain? (Putnam 1967, 436) Here we might consider Lewis's example of a hydraulically powered Martian. Martian pain feels just like human pain, though the Martian has a physical constitution quite different from that of humans:

> His hydraulic mind contains nothing like our neurons. Rather, there are varying amounts of fluid in many inflatable cavities, and the inflation of any one of these cavities opens some valves and closes others. His mental plumbing pervades most of his body – in fact, all but the heat exchanger inside his head. When you pinch his skin you cause no firing of C-fibers – he has none – but, rather, you cause the inflation of smallish

cavities in his feet. When these cavities are inflated, he is in pain. And the effects of his pain are fitting: his thought and activity are disrupted, he groans and writhes, he is strongly motivated to stop you from pinching him and to see to it that you never do again.

(Lewis 1980, 216)

In brief, the identity theory postulates an identity between *types* of states, with each type of mental state identified with a type of brain state. (For this reason, the theory is often referred to as *type physicalism*). My pain and your pain are both tokens of the type *pain*, but so too are the pain of an octopus and the pain of a Martian. For the identity theory to be true, all tokens of the type pain must also be tokens of the same type of physical state (be it the state of c-fiber firing or some other state). But just as two token mousetraps (or two token clocks, or two token engines) might be made of – or *realized* by – very different physical materials, so too it seems that two tokens of the type pain might be realized by very different physical states.

The multiple realizability argument came to be seen as a significant threat to the identity theory. Importantly, however, that is not to say that the identity theory has been discarded. Unlike behaviorism, the identity theory continued to attract support through the final decades of the 20th century, and versions of the theory continue to be defended in these early days of the 21st century. Among the various strategies available for responding to the multiple realizability argument, one promising line retreats to species-specific reduction and concedes that human pain is a distinct type of mental state from, e.g., octopus pain. (For discussion, see Kim 1992.)

At this point, it's also worth noting that the threat posed to the identity theory by the multiple realizability argument is not a threat to physicalism in general. Nothing in the argument shows that pain is non-physical, i.e., it is compatible with the argument that all token pains are realized by some physical state or other, even if those physical states are not all of the same type. Thus, for all we've said so far, *token physicalism* remains a viable theory.[13] Other objections that have been raised to the identity theory, particularly those concerning qualia, the phenomenal aspects of our mental states, do count against physicalism more broadly. But since such objections are best understood against the backdrop of both the identity theory and functionalism, we will postpone discussion of them until the final section of this paper.

3. Functionalism

Behaviorism was threatened by the possibility that an organism might be in a mental state without exhibiting any of the characteristic behavior associated with that mental state, i.e., an organism might be in pain without exhibiting any pain behavior. The identity theory was threatened by the possibility that an organism might be in a mental state without being in the characteristic brain state associated with that mental state, i.e., an organism might be in the state of pain without being in the state of c-fiber firing. Functionalism manages to block both of these threats by treating mental states as functional states. For the functionalist, a mental state like pain is identified by the functional role that it plays in the life of the organism. While historical antecedents to functionalism can be found in the work of Aristotle and Hobbes, the view received its first detailed development in the second half of the 20th century.[14] Its rise coincides with important developments in computer science and particularly in artificial intelligence, and functionalists have often drawn on computational analogies in spelling out their position. On the functionalist view, mentality is better thought of at the level of software than at the level of hardware.

3.1 Mental states as functional states

Above we noted that a device like a mousetrap can be realized in multiple different physical structures. For something to be a mousetrap, what matters is not what it is made of but what it does, i.e., the function it performs. The notion *mousetrap* must thus be specified not physically but functionally. In this way mousetraps are different from, say, nuggets of gold. For something to be a gold nugget, it must have a specific physical constitution, i.e., it must be composed of atoms with atomic number 79 – hence the truth of the expression, "All that glitters is not gold." Compare pyrite, or fool's gold, which has a similarly brilliant yellow luster but is a compound of iron sulfide.

Mousetraps are not the only things that are specified functionally. A similar point applies to many other artifact concepts – engines, clocks, pencil sharpeners – and even biological concepts. As Jaegwon Kim notes,

> What makes an organ a heart is the fact that it pumps blood. The human heart may be physically very unlike hearts in, say, reptiles or birds, but they all count as hearts because of the job they do in the organisms in which they are found, not on account of their similarity in shape, size, or material constitution.
>
> (Kim 2011, 131)

The functionalist claims that mental states are better understood on the model of the mousetrap than on the model of gold nuggets. Consider again the mental state pain. This state plays a certain role in the life of an organism. It typically comes about because of bodily damage, and it typically results in wincing, moaning, avoidance behavior, fear, a desire for relief, and so on. Or consider the mental state thirst. It typically comes about because of lack of adequate hydration, and it typically results in dry mouth, liquid-seeking behavior, a desire for liquids, and so on.

As this suggests, the functionalist's characterization of mental states is strikingly reminiscent of the behaviorist characterizations of mental states. In particular, both the functionalist and the behaviorist define mental states in terms of a relation between inputs and outputs. But despite this similarity, there are nonetheless several important differences between the two kinds of characterizations. Unlike the behaviorist, the functionalist does not deny that mental states are internal states of the organism. For the functionalist, a statement like "I am in pain" does not count as just pain behavior along the lines of wincing and moaning but serves as a genuine report. This leads to a related difference between functionalism and behaviorism. By accepting that mental states are internal states of organisms, the functionalist can make reference to such states in the specification of inputs and outputs. Pain produces not only certain characteristic behaviors but also certain mental states; as indicated above, it typically leads to a desire for relief.

Our discussion thus far highlights two important tenets of the functionalist view. First, mental states are interdefined. Second, mental states are multiply realizable. The first point protects functionalism from many of the objections that threatened behaviorism; the second point protects functionalism from many of the objections that threatened the identity theory. While these two tenets underlie functionalism in general, the view comes in several varieties that differ from one another in various important respects.

As originally articulated by Putnam, functionalism was formulated in terms of a Turing machine, a hypothetical device proposed in 1936 by mathematician Alan Turing. (For this reason, Putnam's version of functionalism is often referred to as *machine functionalism.*) In brief, the operations of a Turing machine can be wholly characterized by a set of instructions given in what's often called a *machine table.* For each internal state of the computer, the instructions specify the output that will result from a given input. An example drawn from Fodor (1981) helps to elucidate the concept.[15] Consider a simple gumball machine that sells gumballs for a dime, takes both nickels and dimes, and is capable of dispensing change. The operations of the machine can be wholly described by the following table:

	Dime input	*Nickel Input*
S1	Dispenses a gumball and remains in S1	Proceeds to S2
S2	Dispenses a gumball and a nickel and proceeds to S1	Dispenses a gumball and proceeds to S1

As this table indicates, the machine has two possible states. Metaphorically speaking, we can think of S1 as the state *waiting for a dime* and S2 as the state *waiting for a nickel.*[16] The machine is waiting for a dime when it has received no money since last dispensing a gumball; the machine is waiting for a nickel when it has received a nickel since last dispensing a gumball. If the machine is waiting for a dime and it gets a dime, then it dispenses a gumball and continues to wait for a dime. If the machine is waiting for a dime and it gets a nickel, then it switches to waiting for a nickel. If the machine is waiting for a nickel and it gets a dime, then it dispenses a gumball and a nickel and switches to waiting for a dime. If the machine is waiting for a nickel and it gets a nickel, then it dispenses a gumball and switches to waiting for a dime.

For the machine functionalist, the mind can be thought of as a Turing machine, i.e., the operations of the mind can be completely described by way of a machine table. Each mental state corresponds to one line – perhaps a very long line – in the machine table. Though coming up with the appropriate machine table will undoubtedly be quite difficult, Putnam notes that the project of doing so – that is, the project of coming up with "'mechanical' models of organisms" – is an "inevitable part of the program of psychology" (Putnam 1967, 435).

Returning to the machine table above, note that while it gives a complete specification of the operation of the gumball machine it says nothing about its physical constitution. The gumball machine might be made of plastic, of metal, of wood, and so on. In fact, it might even be made of non-physical stuff. Consider Fodor's claim that: "As far as functionalism is concerned a [gumball] machine with states S1 and S2 could be made of ectoplasm, if there is such stuff and if its states have the right causal properties" (Fodor 1981, 129). Machine functionalists like Putnam tended to think the same could be true of the mind and hence took their view to be compatible with dualism (Putnam 1967, 436).

As functionalism has developed, however, it has tended to be classified as a physicalist view, and reasonably so: Most functionalists see themselves as committed to physicalism. The commitment underlying the physicalist version of functionalism might be captured as follows: While mental states may be realized in many different physical substances, they must all be realized in some physical substance or other. As this suggests, however, the physicalist version of functionalism – and hereafter it should be assumed that I am talking about this version of the view unless I explicitly note otherwise – is not a version of *type* physicalism. Rather, it is a version of *token* physicalism. For the functionalist, every token pain is realized in some physical state, but those physical states might be tokens of different physical types – perhaps c-fiber firing in humans while something altogether different in a hydraulic Martian.

In the wake of Putnam's work, various versions of functionalism have been developed in the philosophical literature. These subsequent versions retain the core commitment of functionalism – that mental states should be understood as functional states – while dropping the commitment to understanding functional states in terms of machine states. Some functionalists endorse *psychofunctionalism*, the view that mental states are defined by the functional roles they play in an empirical theory, specifically, that of cognitive psychology (see, e.g., Fodor 1968). Other functionalists endorse *analytic* or *conceptual functionalism*, the view that mental states are defined by the functional roles they play in our ordinary or "folk" theory (see, e.g., Lewis 1966; Armstrong 1968). This version of functionalism emerges from logical behaviorism and shares its underlying motivation of providing analyses of our ordinary mental state concepts. Yet other functionalists endorse *teleological functionalism*. What's distinctive to teleological functionalism is the claim that that the notion of 'function' must be understood teleologically, i.e., in terms of biological purpose.[17]

3.2 Criticisms of functionalism

By the 1970s, functionalism had become the dominant view in philosophy of mind, and, in fact, even now at the beginning of the 21st century, it continues to enjoy widespread acceptance. But despite its popularity, the view has nonetheless faced significant criticisms. One key strand of attack, emerging from the work of John Searle, claims that functionalism is unable adequately to capture the intentional nature of our mental states. In this context, intentionality doesn't have to do with intention but with *aboutness* or *directedness*. Consider my belief that Albert Pujols is a baseball player. This belief, which is about Albert Pujols, has intentional content. When I hope that Pujols will hit a lot of home runs next season, or when I desire his autograph, these mental states too have intentional content – they too are directed at Albert Pujols. Importantly, mental states can have intentional content even if they are directed at things that do not exist. Someone who has mistaken Conan Doyle's stories for nonfiction might admire Sherlock Holmes and desire his autograph. Though Sherlock Holmes does not exist, these mental states are intentional nonetheless.[18]

Searle's famous Chinese Room thought experiment aims to show that computers cannot achieve understanding and, correspondingly, that functionalism cannot provide an adequate account of mentality. Consider a computer that is programmed to speak Chinese. If the program were good enough – if, say, the program were to put the computer in the same functional states as a native speaker of Chinese – then the computer would produce outputs that were indistinguishable from such a speaker. The computer would appear to understand Chinese. But, says Searle, this appearance would be mistaken, for the mere instantiation of a program cannot endow a computer with understanding. To defend this point, Searle imagines that he is inside a room with a very sophisticated rulebook equivalent to the computer's program. When Searle enters the room, he does not understand Chinese, and has no idea what the different Chinese characters mean – they look to him like mere squiggles. The instructions in the rule book tell him what squiggles to output upon receiving certain other squiggles as input. But now suppose he gets very good at following the rulebook, so good that from outside the room it appears that there is a native Chinese speaker on the inside. This, Searle suggests, gives us a system that is analogous to a computer instantiating a program, a system that passes through the same functional states as a native Chinese speaker does when understanding Chinese. But, says Searle, no matter how good he gets at manipulating the squiggles, he does not understand Chinese. His outputs don't mean anything to him; they lack intentionality. Thus, functionalism fails to account for the intentionality of mental states and hence fails to be an adequate theory of mind.

Functionalists have various responses to this argument. One prominent response charges that Searle is looking for understanding in the wrong place. He is just a cog in the machine while it's the overall system of which he is a part that achieves understanding (see, e.g., Boden 1988). But even if functionalism is able to account for intentional states like beliefs and desires – and many philosophers think that, despite Searle's objections, the theory is especially well suited in this regard – it has faced intense criticism regarding its ability to handle qualitative states.

Consider the experience of seeing a ripe banana, or smelling a skunk's spray, or feeling a dull ache in your lower back. Each of these experiences has *phenomenal* or *qualitative* character – to use a phrase associated with the work of Thomas Nagel, there is *something it is like* to have such experiences. The experience of seeing a ripe banana has a different qualitative character from seeing an unripe banana, and the experience of feeling a dull ache in your lower back has a different qualitative character from the experience of feeling a sharp twinge in your lower back.

Two different arguments have been offered to show that functionalism cannot adequately account for the qualitative character of our mental states. The first such argument – typically referred to as the *absent qualia argument* – owes primarily to the work of Ned Block (1978). Block proposed a thought experiment involving a homunculi-headed robot, i.e., a robot whose body is powered by a system consisting of a billion homunculi.[19] Supposing we're able to map out the functions of the human brain in a machine table, we could assign each homunculus a simple task corresponding to one square of that table, e.g., pushing a certain output button upon receiving a certain input. In this way, the billion homunculi together would constitute a system that is functionally equivalent to the human brain. According to Block, however, it seems implausible that such a system would really feel pain or have the qualitative experience associated with seeing a ripe banana. To demonstrate this implausibility, Block proposes that we recruit one billion humans and have each of them substitute for one of the homunculi. When thinking about a robot powered in this way, most people have the strong intuition that it would lack qualia. But since having qualitative character is essential to the mental state of pain, and to the mental state of seeing a ripe banana, functionalism does not provide an adequate account of these states.

The second qualia-based argument directed at functionalism is what's typically referred to as the *inverted qualia argument*. Underlying the argument is the intuition, first articulated in the 17th century by John Locke, that inversion of the visible spectrum might be behaviorally undetectable, i.e., that two people might have quite different – even inverted – qualitative experiences without this difference showing up in their behavior. Starting in the 1970s, several philosophers began employing the possibility of spectrum inversion in arguments against functionalism (see, e.g., Block and Fodor 1972; Shoemaker 1975). The argument goes roughly as follows. Consider two individuals, Ruby and Kelly, who are functionally identical to one another with respect to their color experiences. Both will refer to red tomatoes as ripe and to green tomatoes as unripe; both stop at red lights and go at green lights; both note that a stop sign has the same color as a Coke can, and that grass has the same color as Kermit the frog. But it seems possible that their qualitative experiences are very different from one another. The experience that Ruby has when looking at a ripe tomato might be different from the experience that Kelly has when looking at a ripe tomato. In particular, Kelly's experience when looking at the ripe tomato might be the experience that Ruby has when looking at Kermit the frog, while the experience that Kelly has when looking at Kermit the frog might be the experience that Ruby has when looking at a ripe tomato. In this case, though Ruby and Kelly have experiences that are inverted from one another, there will be no functional difference. But since the qualitative aspect of a mental state seems central to its being the mental state that it is, functionalism seems inadequate.

Granted, many philosophers have questioned the coherence of spectrum inversion (see, e.g., Dennett 1988). But accounting for qualia has continued to prove problematic for functionalism and, in fact, for physicalism more generally. In the last quarter of the 20th century, debates about qualia emerged to play a key role in the mind-body problem. We turn to these debates in the next section.

4. The age of qualia

With respect to the mind-body problem, the end of the 20th century can in many ways be thought of as the age of qualia. Although the majority of philosophers in the 21st century still consider themselves to be physicalists of one sort or another (see Bourget and Chalmers 2014), since the 1970s there has been significant philosophical attention devoted to qualia and, in particular, to the apparent difficulty in accounting for qualia within a physicalist treatment of mind.[20] If 20th-century discussion of the mind-problem began with the Age of Behaviorism, and subsequently passed through Age of the Identity Theory and the Age of Functionalism, it would not be much of an overstatement to characterize the end of the century (and indeed, the beginning of the 21st century) as the Age of Qualia.

In addition to the qualia-based arguments against functionalism that we considered in the previous section, two related arguments that emerged in the 1970s and 80s brought qualia to the forefront of discussion. The first of these arguments has become known as *the bat argument*; the second has become known as *the knowledge argument*. In the 1990s, a third qualia-based argument – *the zombie argument* – entered the fray.[21] All three of these arguments aim to show that physicalism cannot adequately account for qualia and thus cannot be an adequate theory of mind. At the same time, they have also had the effect of rejuvenating the dualist position that had been dormant for most of the century. In what follows we consider each of these arguments in turn.

4.1 The bat argument

Thomas Nagel introduced the bat argument in his seminal article "What Is It Like to Be a Bat?" (1974). Given that bats are mammals, they are surely conscious – there is surely something that there's like to be a bat. But bats navigate the world very differently from the way that we humans do. While we use our senses of sight, sound, and touch to make our way about the world, bats do so by way of echolocation. Thus, their conscious experience is very different from ours – so different, in fact, that it's claimed that we cannot even imagine what it's like for a bat when it is using its sonar. What it's like to be a bat is thus fundamentally a subjective phenomenon, understood only from a single point a view (namely, the bat's). Since physicalism takes the objective point of view, it cannot capture what it is like to be a bat. Moreover, this failure of physicalism is not a minor one, since the fact that experience is subjective is an essential fact about experience, i.e., the subjectivity of what it is like to be a bat is an essential fact about it. So, concluded Nagel, physicalism cannot capture all the essential facts about experiences.

Even though our own conscious experience is very different from that of the bat, one might question whether Nagel was right to conclude that we can't even imagine it. In an attempt to forestall this kind of objection, Nagel noted that it wouldn't be enough for us to imagine that we have webbing on our arms, that we spend the day in caves hanging upside down by our feet, that we eat insects, and so on. It won't even help to imagine that one has extremely poor vision and that one uses high-frequency signals to perceive the world. As Nagel argued:

> In so far as I can imagine this (which is not very far), it tells me only what it would be like for *me* to behave as a bat behaves. But that is not the question. I want to know what it is like for a *bat* to be a bat. Yet if I try to imagine this, I am restricted to the resources of my own mind, and these resources are inadequate to the task. I cannot perform it either by imagining additions to my present experience, or by imagining segments gradually subtracted from it, or by imagining some combination of additions, subtractions, and modifications.
>
> (Nagel 1974, 439)

Since the time Nagel wrote his article, developments in virtual reality have made possible human experience of something like echolocation. But presumably Nagel would extend the reasoning from the above quotation to deny that even this experience would be enough to enable us to imagine what it is like to be a bat: All that we could learn from such an experience would be what it is like for a human to have some bat-like qualities.

4.2 The knowledge argument

The knowledge argument was introduced by Frank Jackson in the 1980s in a pair of articles: "Epiphenomenal Qualia" (1982) and "What Mary Didn't Know" (1986). The argument centers around a thought experiment involving Mary, a brilliant color scientist.[22] We are asked to imagine that Mary has lived her entire life enclosed in a black and white room and that she has never been exposed to color. She wears black and white gloves, she never presses on her eyeball to have a phosphene experience, and so on. While in the room, however, she has been given black and white textbooks, a black and white television, a computer with a black and white monitor, and other black and white research tools. Moreover,

Mary lives at a future time at which researchers have developed a completed color science. While in her black and white room, Mary masters this color science. Through careful study, that is, she learns the entire physical story of color. She knows exactly how the human eye and the human brain process color, she knows exactly how humans categorize objects by color, and she knows about the similarity relations among colors. Now suppose that one day Mary is released from her black and white environment. Immediately upon her release, Mary sees a ripe tomato. According to Jackson, it seems overwhelmingly plausible that this experience provides Mary with an "aha" moment: Once she sees color for the first time, she learns something new. In particular, she learns what seeing red is like. But since she already knew all of the physical facts about color, since she already knows the entire physical story, that story must not be the whole story. For this reason, physicalism cannot provide an adequate account of our mental states.

Physicalist responses to the argument tend to divide into two broad categories. First, some physicalists have denied Jackson's intuition about Mary, what we might call the *"aha" intuition*. According to Daniel Dennett, who has persistently pushed this line in response to Jackson, the reason that we mistakenly have the "aha" intuition is that we've merely managed to imagine that Mary has lots and lots of physical information, not that she has *all* the physical information. If we were to imagine the situation correctly – if we were really to imagine that Mary has *all* the physical information – we would see that there is nothing left for Mary to learn (Dennett 1991, 398).

This strategy has not been widely pursued, presumably because even most physicalists find the "aha" intuition very hard to deny. Most physicalists instead pursue a second strategy, one that concedes that Mary learns something new upon leaving the room. Such philosophers deny that this concession threatens physicalism, because they deny that what Mary learns consists of a new fact. This second kind of response to the Mary case itself divides into two broad classes. The first group of philosophers deny that Mary's newfound knowledge is factual. Rather, it is a different kind of knowledge – perhaps know-how (Lewis 1990; Nemirow 1990), or perhaps acquaintance knowledge (Conee 1985). A second group of philosophers accept that Mary's knowledge is indeed factual, but they deny that it's knowledge of a new fact. Rather she comes to recognize an old fact in a new way, under a new guise or via new concepts (Loar 1990). Despite such responses, however, the knowledge argument has continued to have considerable traction in philosophy of mind.[23]

4.3 The zombie argument

The zombie argument came to prominence in the mid-1990s through the work of David Chalmers.[24] The philosopher's zombie is importantly different from the brain-eating creatures that populate Hollywood horror movies. As described by Chalmers in *The Conscious Mind* (1996), zombies are understood to be creatures who are physically identical to human beings but who completely lack phenomenal consciousness, i.e., they are completely lacking in qualia. Your zombie twin, for example, is molecule-for-molecule identical to you and likewise identical to you functionally: She processes information just as you do, reports on her mental states just as you do, focuses her attention on the world just as you do, and so on. But, as Chalmers said, "none of this functioning will be accompanied by any real conscious experience. There will be no phenomenal feel. There is nothing it is like to be a zombie" (Chalmers 1996, 95).

Chalmers then argued from the conceivability of zombies to the falsity of physicalism. If we can conceive of a zombie world – a world that is physically identical to ours yet in which there is a complete absence of phenomenal consciousness – then such a world is metaphysically possible. But if a zombie world is metaphysically possible, then facts about consciousness are facts over and above the physical facts. Since the truth of physicalism requires that there be no facts about consciousness that are over and above the physical facts, physicalism must be false.

The zombie argument is often referred to as a *conceivability argument*. It moves from facts about what's conceivable to facts about what's possible. In this regard it resembles Descartes' famous argument for substance dualism, presented in his *Meditations on First Philosophy* (1642). Descartes rested his argument on the claim that he could conceive of the mind existing without the body; from this he concluded that it is possible for the mind to exist without the body and hence that the mind and the body are two separate substances. Chalmers's conceivability argument does not aim to establish substance dualism but rather the falsity of physicalism. His own positive view, developed subsequently in *The Conscious Mind*, is a naturalistic version of property dualism.

Conceivability arguments typically face two different kinds of objections. First, it might be questioned whether the proposed scenario is really conceivable. Second, it might be questioned whether conceivability is really a good guide to metaphysical possibility, i.e., it might be questioned whether the conceivability of a given scenario really shows that such a scenario is logically possible. (See Gendler and Hawthorne 2002.) In addition to criticisms of these sorts, the zombie argument also faces a third kind of criticism. Many physicalists question whether the metaphysical possibility of zombies counts against physicalism, and this in turn leads to questions about how exactly physicalism should be construed. Twenty years after its articulation, the zombie argument continues to be heavily debated.

Conclusion

From the vantage point of these early years of the 21st century, it is still too soon to assess whether we've reached the end of the age of qualia, and, if so, what new age will be ushered in to replace it. It seems clear, however, that phenomenal consciousness continues to pose a threat to physicalist theories of mind. This threat has led some to argue that the mind-body problem is in principle insoluble (see, e.g., McGinn 1989). It also seems to account for the recent resurgence of interest in theories of mentality that in various ways aspire to transcend the traditional dualism-physicalism divide. In particular, many philosophers of mind have begun to explore the coherence of positions like panpsychism and Russellian monism, both of which try to find a place for consciousness at the fundamental level of reality.[25]

But despite the threat of phenomenal consciousness, traditional versions of physicalism continue to enjoy considerable support. In the view of many physicalists, the tremendous neuroscientific progress of the 20th century suggests that it is just a matter of time before we are able to understand mentality entirely in terms of neural mechanisms. Perhaps this will require us to abandon some of our common mental state vocabulary; it might be that our folk psychological concepts like "belief" and "desire" do not map very well unto neuroscientific states. Such is the prediction made by eliminative materialists such as Paul Churchland (see, e.g., his 1981). It might be that we will be able to understand the truth of physicalism only by way of a conceptual revolution of sorts.[26] Alternatively, perhaps, future developments in neuroscience, in conjunction with philosophical theorizing, might enable us better to grasp how a physical reduction of mentality is possible.[27]

Ultimately, however, it remains the case at the start of the 21st century that the nature of mentality is still very much in dispute. Granted, there are some points of widespread agreement. Substance dualism, which had dominated philosophy prior to the 20th century since the time of Descartes, is no longer considered viable. Likewise, behaviorism has been dismissed as a failed experiment. But despite these important points of agreement and the corresponding philosophical progress involved, it is clear that the 20th century did not provide a widely accepted solution to the mind-body problem. It remains to be seen whether such a solution will be found in the century ahead.[28]

Notes

1 See, e.g., the assessment by U. T. Place: "[E]ver since the debate between Hobbes and Descartes ended in apparent victory for the latter, it was taken more or less for granted that whatever answer to the mind-body problem is true, materialism must be false" (Place 2002, 36).
2 See Titchener 1914 for a discussion of 19th century antecedents to behaviorism in psychology.
3 In discussions of behaviorism, philosophers often adopt different classificatory schemes. See, e.g., Byrne (1994) and Graham (2010).
4 In the second half of the 20th century philosophy, non-behaviorist versions of eliminativism were developed by various philosophers. This kind of view, which seems to have its roots in the work of Wilfred Sellars, is notably found in W.V.O. Quine (1960), Paul Feyerabend (1963), Richard Rorty (1965), and Paul Churchland (1981).
5 Chisholm (1957, 173–185). See also Geach (1957, esp. 7–9).
6 See Dennett 1987 for essays in which his behavioristic tendencies are in evidence.
7 See, e.g., Crawford 2013 for discussion of the differences.
8 The early identity theorists also claimed that such scientific discoveries were contingent. In the wake of Saul Kripke's *Naming and Necessity* (1980), this claim is now largely thought to be mistaken.

9 Place (2002, 37) takes this feature of the identity theory to be central in distinguishing it from earlier versions of materialism.
10 For a useful discussion of topic-neutrality, see Armstrong (1999, 75–79).
11 Smart does not work out this argument in any detail, but see Christopher Hill (1991, ch. 2) for a more comprehensive attempt to show that considerations of simplicity favor the identity theory over its dualistic rivals.
12 See Chapter 7 for a detailed discussion of the problem of mental causation.
13 Donald Davidson's anomalous monism is one particularly prominent version of token physicalism. See, e.g., Davidson (1970).
14 See Levin 2013 for a discussion of historical antecedents to functionalism.
15 I have amended this example slightly.
16 In describing the gumball machine's states this way, I do not mean to suggest that the gumball machine should be thought of as having mental states. To reemphasize, the description is meant to be metaphorical.
17 Ruth Millikan's work has been especially important in the development of the teleological notion of function (see, e.g., Millikan 1993).
18 For further discussion of intentionality, see Chapter 8.
19 Block supposed that a billion homunculi would be sufficient to realize the functional organization of the human brain since, at the time that he was writing, that corresponded to the best estimate for the number of neurons in the brain. It is now believed that there are upwards of 85 billion neurons in the brain. Block can of course accommodate this development by increasing the number of homunculi needed to power the robot system.
20 This debate has been accompanied by a corresponding surge of interest in the notion of consciousness more generally. For further discussion of consciousness, see Chapter 3.
21 An additional influential critique of physicalism related to qualia-based considerations was developed in Kripke (1980).
22 Jackson 1982 also included a second thought experiment involving a man named Fred who's able to discriminate more colors than normal human beings. Subsequent discussion, however, has tended to focus almost exclusively on the Mary case.
23 Jackson himself, however, eventually recanted; he no longer believes that the knowledge argument disproves physicalism. See Jackson (2003).
24 A similar argument was previously introduced in Kirk (1974).
25 See, e.g., the collection of papers in Alter and Nagasawa (2015).
26 This point has recently been argued by Nagel: "Our inability to come up with an intelligible conception of the relation between mind and body is a sign of the inadequacy of our present concepts" (1998).
27 For a more detailed discussion of what lies ahead for philosophical theorizing about mentality, see Chapter 12.
28 Thanks to Frank Menetrez and Julie Yoo for comments on a previous draft.

Bibliography

Alter, Torin and Nagasawa, Yujin (2015). *Consciousness in the Physical World: Perspectives on Russellian Monism*. Oxford: Oxford University Press.
Armstrong, David M. (1968). *A Materialist Theory of Mind*. New York: Humanities Press.
Armstrong, David M. (1999). *The Mind-Body Problem: An Opinionated Introduction*. Boulder, CO: Westview Press.
Block, Ned and Fodor, Jerry A. (1972). "What Psychological States Are Not." *Philosophical Review*, 81 (April): 159–181.

Boden, Margaret (1988). *Computer Models of the Mind*. Cambridge: Cambridge University Press.
Boring, Edwin G. (1933). *The Physical Dimensions of Consciousness*. New York: The Century Co.
Bourget, David and Chalmers, David J. (2014). "What Do Philosophers Believe?" *Philosophical Studies*, 170: 465–500.
Byrne, Alex (1994). "Behaviorism," in Guttenplan, Samuel (ed.), *A Companion to the Philosophy of Mind*. Oxford: Blackwell.
Carnap, Rudolf (1932). "Psychology in Physical Language," *Erkenntnis*, 3: 107–142.
Chalmers, David J. (1996). *The Conscious Mind: In Search of a Fundamental Theory*. Oxford: Oxford University Press.
Chisholm, Roderick (1957). *Perceiving: A Philosophical Study*. Ithaca, NY: Cornell University Press.
Churchland, Paul (1981). "Eliminative Materialism and the Propositional Attitudes," *Journal of Philosophy*, 78: 67–90.
Conee, Earl (1985). "Physicalism and Phenomenal Properties," *Philosophical Quarterly*, 35: 296–302.
Crawford, Sean (2013). "The Myth of Logical Behaviourism and the Origins of the Identity Theory," in Beaney, Michael (ed.), *The Oxford Handbook of the History of Analytic Philosophy*. Oxford: Oxford University Press.
Davidson, Donald (1970). "Mental Events," in Foster, Lawrence and Swanson, J. W. (eds.), *Experience and Theory*. London: Duckworth.
Dennett, Daniel (1987). *The Intentional Stance*. Cambridge, MA: MIT Press.
Dennett, Daniel (1988). "Quining Qualia," in Marcel, A. and Bisiach, E. (eds.), *Consciousness in Modern Science*. Oxford: Oxford University Press.
Dennett, Daniel (1991). *Consciousness Explained*. Boston: Little, Brown and Company.
Feigl, Herbert (1958). "The 'Mental' and the 'Physical'," *Minnesota Studies in the Philosophy of Science*, 2: 370–497.
Feyerabend, Paul (1963). "Mental Events and the Brain," *Journal of Philosophy*, 40: 295–296.
Geach, P. T. (1957). *Mental Acts*. London: Routledge and Kegan Paul.
Gendler, Tamar and Hawthorne, John (2002). "Introduction: Conceivability and Possibility," in Gendler, Tamar and Hawthorne, John (eds.), *Conceivability and Possibility*. New York: Oxford University Press.
Graham, George (2010). "Behaviorism," in Zalta, Edward N. (ed.), *The Stanford Encyclopedia of Philosophy* (Spring 2015 edition). http://plato.stanford.edu/archives/spr2015/entries/behaviorism/.
Fodor, Jerry (1968). *Psychological Explanation*. New York: Random House.
Fodor, Jerry (1981). "The Mind-Body Problem," *Scientific American*, 244: 114–125.
Hempel, Carl G. (1980). "The Logical Analysis of Psychology," in Block, Ned (ed.), *Readings in the Philosophy of Psychology*, Volume 1. Cambridge, MA: Harvard University Press: 1–14.
Hill, Christopher S. (1991). *Sensations: A Defense of Type Materialism*. Cambridge: Cambridge University Press.
Jackson, Frank (1982). "Epiphenomenal Qualia," *Philosophical Quarterly*, 32: 127–136.
Jackson, Frank (1986). "What Mary Didn't Know," *Journal of Philosophy*, 83: 291–295.

Jackson, Frank (2003). "Mind and Illusion," in O'Hear, Anthony (ed.), *Minds and Persons*. Cambridge: Cambridge University Press: 421–442.

James, William (1890/1981). *The Principles of Psychology*. Cambridge, MA: Harvard University Press.

Kim, Jaegwon (1992). "Multiple Realization and the Metaphysics of Reduction," *Philosophy and Phenomenological Research*, 52: 1–26.

Kim, Jaegwon (2011). *Philosophy of Mind* (third edition). Boulder, CO: Westview Press.

Kirk, Robert (1974). "Zombies Vs Materialists," *Proceedings of the Aristotelian Society*, 48: 135–152.

Kripke, Saul A. (1980). *Naming and Necessity*. Cambridge, MA: Harvard University Press.

Levin, Janet (2013). "Functionalism," in Zalta, Edward N. (ed.), *The Stanford Encyclopedia of Philosophy* (Fall 2013 edition). http://plato.stanford.edu/archives/fall2013/entries/functionalism/.

Lewis, David (1966). "An Argument for the Identity Theory," *Journal of Philosophy*, 63: 17–25.

Lewis, David (1980). "Mad Pain and Martian Pain," in Block, Ned (ed.), *Readings in the Philosophy of Psychology*, Volume 1. Cambridge, MA: Harvard University Press: 216–222.

Lewis, David (1990). "What Experience Teaches," in Lycan, William G. (ed.), *Mind and Cognition*. Oxford: Blackwell: 29–57.

Loar, Brian (1990). "Phenomenal states," *Philosophical Perspectives*, 4: 81–108.

McGinn, Colin (1989). "Can We Solve the Mind-Body Problem?" *Mind*, 98: 349–366.

Millikan, Ruth (1993). *White Queen Psychology and Other Essays for Alice*. Cambridge, MA: MIT Press.

Nagel, Thomas (1974). "What Is It Like To Be a Bat?" *Philosophical Review*, 83: 435–450.

Nagel, Thomas (1998). "Conceiving the Impossible and the Mind-Body Problem," *Philosophy*, 73: 337–352.

Nemirow, Laurence (1990). "Physicalism and the Cognitive Role of Acquaintance," in Lycan, William G. (ed.), *Mind and Cognition*. Oxford: Blackwell.

Papineau, David (2002). *Thinking About Consciousness*. Oxford: Oxford University Press.

Place, Ullin T. (n.d.). "Identity Theories," *A Field Guide to the Philosophy of Mind*. http://host.uniroma3.it/progetti/kant/field/mbit.htm.

Place, Ullin T. (1956). "Is Consciousness a Brain Process," *British Journal of Psychology*, 47: 44–50.

Place, Ullin T. (2002). "A Pilgrim's Progress? From Mystical Experience to Biological Consciousness," *Journal of Consciousness Studies*, 9: 34–52.

Puccetti, Roland (1977). "The Great C-Fiber Myth: A Critical Note," *Philosophy of Science*, 44: 303–305.

Putnam, Hilary (1960). "Minds and machines." In Hook, S. (ed.) *Dimensions of Mind*. New York: New York University Press. Reprinted in Putnam 1975: 362–385. Page references are to the reprinted edition.

Putnam, Hilary (1963). "Brains and Behavior," in Butler, R. (ed.), *Analytical Philosophy Second Series*. Oxford: Basil Blackwell. Reprinted in Putnam 1975: 325–341. Page references to reprinted edition.

Putnam, Hilary (1967). "The Nature of Mental States," Originally published as "Psychological Predicates," in Capitain and Merrill (eds.), *Art, Mind, and Religion*. Pittsburgh:

University of Pittsburgh Press. Reprinted in Putnam 1975: 429–440. Page references to reprinted edition.

Putnam, Hilary (1975). *Mind, Language and Reality: Philosophical Papers, Volume 2*. Cambridge: Cambridge University Press.

Quine, Willard van Orman (1960). *Word and Object*. Cambridge, MA: MIT Press.

Gilbert Ryle (1949). *The Concept of Mind*. Chicago: University of Chicago Press.

Rorty, Richard (1965). "Mind-Body Identity, Privacy, and Categories," *Review of Metaphysics*, 19: 24–54.

Schlick, Moritz (1925/1974). *General Theory of Knowledge*. Trans. Alfred E. Blumberg. New York: Springer-Verlag.

Shoemaker, Sydney (1975). "Functionalism and Qualia." *Philosophical Studies* 27 (May): 291–315.

Skinner, B. F. (1974). *About Behaviorism*. New York: Alfred A. Knopf, Inc.

Smart, J.J.C. (1959). "Sensations and Brain Processes," *Philosophical Review*, 68: 141–156.

Titchener, E. B. (1914). "On 'Psychology as the Behaviorist Views It,'" *Proceedings of the American Philosophical Society*, 53: 1–17.

Watson, John B. (1913). "Psychology as the Behaviorist Views It," *Psychological Review*, 20: 158–177.

Wittgenstein, Ludwig (1953). *Philosophical Investigations*, translated by G.E.M. Anscombe, New York: Macmillan Publishing Company.

3

A SHORT HISTORY OF PHILOSOPHICAL THEORIES OF CONSCIOUSNESS IN THE 20TH CENTURY

Tim Crane

1. Introduction

Philosophy in the 20th century began and ended with an obsession with the problems of consciousness. But the specific problems discussed at each end of the century were very different, and reflection on how these differences developed will illuminate not just our understanding of the history of philosophy of consciousness, but also our understanding of consciousness itself.

An interest in the problems of consciousness can be found in at least three movements in early 20th-century philosophy: in the discussions of perception and realism by G. E. Moore and Bertrand Russell; in the related discussions of realism and pragmatism in America, in the period between William James and C. I. Lewis; and in the phenomenological movement started by Edmund Husserl. Two common themes in all these movements are: (i) that consciousness is a central or defining feature of the mind, and (ii) consciousness and thought (or intentionality) are interrelated phenomena not to be discussed in isolation from one another. The problem of consciousness in those days was the problem of the nature of our access to the mind-independent world.

By the end of the century, the central concern of theories of consciousness in analytic philosophy was the question of physicalism, and the problem of consciousness had become the problem of explaining how any physical thing could be conscious. Moreover, consciousness was not considered to be the essential feature of the mental, and thought (or intentionality) and consciousness were typically treated as distinct, separable phenomena. Both this conception of consciousness and its perceived relation to the rest of the mind are very different from the conception to be found at the beginning of the century. The aim of this chapter is to explain how this change came about.

2. Thought, perception and the "given"

It is a truism of the history of 20th century philosophy that what came to be called analytic philosophy began in Cambridge with the "revolt against idealism" by Bertrand Russell and G. E. Moore. At the heart of this revolt was the insistence on the mind-independence of the objects of thought. But this insistence was also intertwined with assumptions about consciousness. In one of the seminal texts of early analytic philosophy, "The Refutation of Idealism", Moore argued that thought and sensation "are both forms of consciousness, or to use a term that seems to be more in fashion just now, they are both ways of experiencing" (1903, 437). He then went on to derive anti-idealist conclusions from what he took to be manifest facts about experience.

Moore considers an experience of green and an experience of blue, and asks how they differ and how they resemble each other. He calls the respect in which they differ, the "object" of the experience and the respect in which they are the same, "consciousness" ("without yet attempting to say what the thing I so call is" 1903, 444). He acknowledges that consciousness itself is hard to identify by introspection. In a famous passage, he writes:

> that which makes the sensation of blue a mental fact seems to escape us; it seems, if I may use a metaphor, to be transparent – we look through it and see nothing but the blue; we may be convinced that there is something, but what it is no philosopher, I think, has yet clearly recognised.
> (1903, 446)

But the fact that we find consciousness itself so hard to identify should not make us dismiss it. Philosophers miss this relation because:

> the moment we try to fix our attention upon consciousness and to see what distinctly, it is, it seems to vanish: it seems as we had before us a mere emptiness. When we try to introspect the sensation of blue, all we can see is the blue: the other element is as if it were diaphanous. Yet it can be distinguished if we look attentively enough, and if we know that there is something to look for.
> (1903, 450)

The view Moore is opposed to is what he calls "the content theory", which conceives of the experience of blue on the model of substance and quality (alternatively: object and property). On this theory, perceived blue is conceived of as a "quality of a thing" (1903, 448). For contemporary readers, it is important to bear in mind that this use of the word "content" is entirely different from today's use: from at least the 1980s onwards, the word "content" has been standardly used to refer to representational features of experience. Moore's use of the word makes "content" mean something closer to what we now know today as "qualia": the intrinsic conscious properties of the experience. The content theory, in Moore's sense, implies that if an episode of awareness is an awareness of blue, there has to be a "blue awareness" (1903, 450). Moore thinks this is absurd, and one of the sources of the errors of idealism. Moore seems to think that once we reject the absurd "content theory" and recognise the distinctness of the experience and its object, then we see what is wrong with idealism: "there is, therefore, no question of how we are to 'get outside the circle of our own ideas and sensations'. Merely to have a sensation is already to be outside that circle. It is to know something which is as truly and really not a part of my experience" (1903, 451).

As Thomas Baldwin points out, Moore soon realised that "more needs to be said to handle cases in which something which is not in fact blue looks blue" (Baldwin 2010). This led to Moore's lengthy investigation of whether the objects of experience – which he called "sense data" – are mind-independent or mind-dependent. This question became a preoccupation of the philosophy of perception for some decades, until the whole "sense data" way of thinking was widely abandoned in the 1950s. What lay behind this whole sense-data tradition was not, as some have supposed, a foundationalist epistemology or a concern with refuting scepticism, but a particular conception of consciousness: the "act-object" conception. According to this conception, conscious states and episodes are essentially relations: an "act" relating the subject of the state to its "object" (see Martin 2000). What is "given" in experience (the *datum*, plural: *data*) is the object or objects.

For present purposes, two points about Moore's discussion are especially important. First, for Moore, sensing is a form of consciousness, but thought is a form of consciousness too: his "true analysis of a sensation" applies to thought as well as to sense experience. Moore therefore believed in something like what is now called "cognitive phenomenology": apprehending a proposition is an "act of consciousness which may be called the understanding of meaning" (Moore 1953, 57–59; cf. Tennant 2006). Second, Moore held that "a sensation is, in reality, a case of 'knowing'". The relation we call "being aware of" or "experiencing something" is "just that which we mean in every case by 'knowing'" (1903, 449). As we will see, both these claims about consciousness came to be rejected later in the 20th century.

Moore's emphasis on both the centrality of consciousness was shared both by the emerging science of psychology and by the early phenomenologists. Wilhelm Wundt, whose *Principles of Physiological Psychology* (1904) was one of the founding texts of the discipline, assumed that consciousness was the principal subject-matter of psychology. George Trumbull Ladd, who founded the Psychological Laboratory at Yale in 1892, defined psychology as the "description and explanation of states of consciousness *as such*". William James is reported to have agreed with this definition (Güzeldere 1997). The British psychologist and philosopher G. F. Stout defined psychology as "the science of the processes whereby an individual becomes aware of a world of objects and adjusts his actions accordingly" (1899, 4). Awareness is consciousness, and psychological processes are those that make awareness possible. Stout therefore distinguishes between the psychological – everything that is relevant to the processes whereby an individual becomes aware of the world – and the psychical, or the facts of consciousness themselves (1899, 7).

The psychological is whatever *contributes* to the creation of mental life; so much of the psychological is unconscious. The psychical in "the proper sense" is that which in some way enters into consciousness (1898, 9). In this, Stout registers his agreement with the American psychologist and editor of the famous *Dictionary of Philosophy and Psychology*, J. M. Baldwin, that consciousness is "the common and necessary form of all mental states . . . it is the point of division between mind and not-mind" (Stout 1899, 8). However, like Moore, Stout argued that no definition of consciousness is possible. "What is consciousness?" he asks, and in a striking non-sequitur, answers: "Properly speaking, definition is impossible. Everybody knows what consciousness is because everybody is conscious" (Stout 1899, 7).

Edmund Husserl shared the view that consciousness was a fundamental feature of all mental phenomena (Husserl 1900–1901; 1913). The phenomenological movement he initiated often claimed its inspiration in Franz Brentano's classification of all mental phenomena as intentional (Brentano 1874). Brentano, like Wundt and other psychologists of the day, had assumed that all mental phenomena are conscious – in his terminology, they all involve "presentation" (*Vorstellung*). For Husserl, the "the comprehensive task of constitutive phenomenology" is the task of "elucidating in their entirety the interwoven achievements of consciousness which lead to the constitution of a possible world" (*Experience and Judgement* 1948, 50). Husserl's concern was with the ("transcendental") conditions that make it possible for there to be a world for the subject; and for him, there being a world for the subject is the same as things being present to consciousness (see Poellner 2007, §2). The fundamentality of consciousness was a persistent commitment of the phenomenological tradition (see, for example, Jean-Paul Sartre's (1943) critique of the idea of unconscious intentionality).

As well as the claim that consciousness is definitive of all mental phenomena, these early 20th-century thinkers held that consciousness involves objects (however they are to be ultimately understood) appearing or being present or "given" to consciousness. Moore claimed that every experience "from the merest sensation to the most developed perception of reflexion" involves "that peculiar relation which I have called 'awareness of anything' . . . this is in fact the only essential element in an experience" (1903, 453). H. H. Price, who had studied with Moore, also called the relation of "being given" a "peculiar and ultimate manner of being present to consciousness" (Price 1932, 3). As the term "sense-data" suggests, then, consciousness is givenness (Crane 2000).

This is not to say, of course, that all philosophers of the era thought of givenness in the same way. The Harvard philosopher C. I. Lewis, in his influential work *Mind and the World Order* (1929) argued for a distinction between the given and its properties or qualities (which he called "qualia") on the one hand, and the way the given is interpreted or conceptualised by the mind on the other. We are conscious of the qualia that are given to us, but we have no *knowledge* of them, according to Lewis, because "knowledge always transcends the immediately given" (Lewis 1929, 132). Whenever we attempt to describe a quale we must necessarily conceptualise it, and this inevitably changes what we are aware of. Qualia can be identified only indirectly by describing their place in a relational structure, which allows the possibility of inverted qualia: intrinsically different qualia could play the same role in the network of relations (1929, 124). The given is, in this sense, ineffable. As M.G.F. Martin (2003) has pointed out, this is significantly different from the sense-datum theory, which emphasised the non-conceptual, non-intellectual confrontation with an object in sense experience, the sense-datum. According to the sense-datum theory, perceptual consciousness consists in the relation to this object and is itself a form of knowledge. But in denying that awareness of the given (and its qualia) is a form of knowledge, Lewis "rejects a key element of the sense-datum tradition: sensing as an example of a simple, primitive, or unanalysable state of knowing which relates the knower to something independent of the mind, where the subject's grasp of what is known is pre-conceptual" (Martin 2003, 529). Martin also notes that this aspect of the sense-datum view is also rejected by Husserl's Phenomenology. Husserl thought there was a kind of sensory "matter" (*hyle*) in sense-experience, but he did not think that this matter was something that is perceived: "although Husserl allows a role for the matter of episodes of perceiving, such aspects are not given to a subject as objects of awareness – they are not candidates for knowledge in the way that sense-data are supposed to be" (Martin 2003, 529). Both Husserl and Lewis, then, rejected the idea that the sensory matter of consciousness was an object of awareness.

Whereas Moore and Husserl saw consciousness and thought (intentionality) as intertwined, it is tempting to see Lewis's creation of his conception of qualia as a first step in the separation of consciousness from intentionality which became orthodox in late 20th-century analytic philosophy. The idea that consciousness is something inexpressible, indefinable, inefficacious, additional and separable from the rest of mental life – from judgements, concepts, beliefs, thoughts and so on – came to be the central theme of later discussions of consciousness. I will call this the "phenomenal residue" conception of consciousness. As I will now argue, the conception was not eliminated by the behaviourist revolution in psychology and philosophy; on the contrary, the main legacy of the behaviourist movement was to reinforce this conception.

3. The disappearance of consciousness: behaviourism and "raw feels"

In its early days, as we saw, scientific psychology was unequivocally the science of conscious phenomena. Early 20th-century psychologists traced their origins back to the associationism of James Mill and Alexander Bain, and "association" was supposed to relate ideas, conceived of as conscious occurrences. The introspectionist school of Edward B. Titchener (who had studied with Wundt in Leipzig) attempted to use the detailed description of experience to describe its structure. There was a broad consensus that introspection was the correct method for psychology, and as William James commented, "everyone agrees that we there [i.e. in introspection] discover states of consciousness" (James 1890, 185).

James himself went on to reject the importance of consciousness in a famous paper published in 1904 called "Does 'Consciousness' Exist?": "I believe that 'consciousness', when once it has evaporated to this estate of pure diaphaneity, is on the point of disappearing altogether. It is the name of a nonentity, and has no right to a place among first principles" (James 1904, 477). His actual point is less radical than it initially seems: he rejects consciousness as an "entity" but argues instead that it is a "function", the function of knowing (1904, 478). But nonetheless, James's rejection of any non-epistemic sense of "consciousness" is striking; in some ways it prefigures the rise of behaviourism (see Güzeldere 1997, 13).

Even during the heyday of consciousness in early 20th-century psychology, there was a feeling that consciousness was mysterious, elusive and hard to understand or define. Titchener quoted Bain and the Cambridge psychologist and philosopher James Ward: "'Consciousness' says Professor Ward, 'is the vaguest, most protean, and most treacherous of psychological terms'; and Bain, writing in 1880, distinguished no less than thirteen meanings of the word; he could find more today" (1915, 323–324). Introspectionism did not live long past Titchener's death in 1927, collapsing partly under the weight of the unwieldy complexity of Titchener's results – in his *Outline of Psychology* (1896), he had claimed that there were 44,000 elements in conscious experience – and partly because of the unclarity of the introspective method itself.

Psychology at this time (and indeed throughout the whole century) was very much preoccupied with its scientific status, and behaviourism seemed to grant it the scientific respectability it sought. The behaviourist phase in psychology lasted for at least three decades from the 1920s until the 1950s, and in the hands of Edward Thorndike, John B. Watson, Ivan Pavlov, B. F. Skinner, Clark Hull, E. C. Tolman (and others), it emphasised strict, "objective" measurement of behaviour as the only properly scientific method. Indeed, behaviour itself ultimately became the only serious subject-matter of scientific psychology. Watson was adamant that behaviourism would have nothing to do with consciousness: "Behaviorism claims that 'consciousness' is neither a definable nor a usable concept; that it is merely another word for the 'soul' of more ancient times" (Watson 1930, 3).

In standard introductions to the philosophy of mind, a distinction is typically made between "methodological" behaviourism and "analytical" behaviourism (see e.g. Maslin 2001, ch. 4). Methodological behaviourism is the psychological view that the scientific study of the mind can proceed only through the study of behaviour and its stimulus conditions; this view is of course compatible with there being aspects of the mind that science cannot study. Analytical behaviourism is the view that mental states are constituted by behaviour alone, or by dispositions to behave; this is a constitutive or metaphysical claim about the nature of mental states themselves, or perhaps a conceptual claim about mental concepts.

There are at least two difficulties with this way of classifying positions: first, the analytical behaviourist position, as described, is incredibly implausible. C. D. Broad classified such a behaviourism as a "silly" theory (1925, 6): "one which may be held at the time when one is talking or writing professionally, but which only an inmate of a lunatic asylum would think of carrying into daily life" (1925, 5). Second, and relatedly, it's really not obvious that there have been any philosophical behaviourists in this sense. Watson's remarks about consciousness might suggest that this was his view, but these remarks are better understood as a rhetorical flourish targeted against the dead-end of introspectionism, rather than as a substantive doctrine. (For a different perspective on behaviourism, see Amy Kind's essay in the present volume.)

Sometimes Gilbert Ryle (1949) and Ludwig Wittgenstein (1953) are classified as analytical behaviourists. Certainly Ryle and Wittgenstein had in common their opposition to a picture of the mind which treats mental occurrences as private and "hidden" behind behaviour. Ryle himself explicitly opposed what he called the "official doctrine" that

> when someone is described as knowing, believing or guessing something, as hoping, dreading, intending or shirking something, as designing this or being amused at that, these verbs are supposed to denote the occurrence of specific modifications in his (to us) occult stream of consciousness.
>
> (Ryle 1949, 17)

It is worth noting here that Ryle himself uses the word "consciousness" mostly for reflection on or knowledge about experience, rather than for experience itself; his references to the "stream of consciousness" are largely disparaging (see Ryle 1949, 155ff.).

Ryle's alternative to the "official doctrine" was to focus philosophical attention on the ways in which we actually apply mental terms, and the standards employed or presupposed in these applications. These standards, he claimed, often require public and observable evidence for a mental ascription. But as Julia Tanney points out, "in focussing on what is observable, he does not commit himself to reducing what is observable itself to sequences of 'muscular behaviour'" (Tanney 2014). Moreover, Ryle explicitly denied that he was a behaviourist, and a careful reading of his texts does not support the "philosophical behaviourist" reading. As his later work *On Thinking* made explicit, his declared aim was to steer a course between the "Category-howler of Behaviourism or the Category-howler of Cartesianism" (1979, 17).

Wittgenstein too was concerned to return to the "rough ground" (1953, §107) of real psychological ascriptions, and argued that claims made about so-called "inner" processes "stand in need of outward criteria" (1953, §580). Like Ryle, he tried to undermine what he saw as a mistaken picture of the mind which treats mental occurrences as essentially private and only contingently connected with their behavioural manifestations. Wittgenstein's concept of a "criterion" was supposed to describe the conceptual (or "grammatical") connection between mind and behaviour that was more intimate than mere evidence or causal connection. Mental states may be *expressed* in behaviour, just as (e.g.) an interpretation of a piece of music finds its expression in the musical performance itself. But this is not the same thing as these states being identified with behaviour. Wittgenstein's view is no more "analytical behaviourism" than Ryle's is; and, like Ryle, Wittgenstein himself explicitly denied that he was a behaviourist.

The real influence of behaviourism on later philosophy of mind was felt at first in the work of the logical positivists (or logical empiricists), the philosophers of the Vienna Circle who attempted to develop a "scientific philosophy". The most influential of the logical positivists was Rudolf Carnap, whose influence was particularly strong on W. V. Quine, himself arguably one of the most influential analytic philosophers of the 20th century. Quine explicitly advocated some form of behaviourism in various writings. One way in which this expressed itself was in his explicit rejection of ideas like "sense-data", the "given" and "things before the mind" – ideas which, as we saw above, had dominated discussions of consciousness in the first few decades of the century in epistemology and the philosophy of mind (cf. also Sellars 1956). However, Quine's behaviourism was not an attempt to reduce mental states to behaviour – he was happy to acknowledge the reality of what he called the "heady luxuriance of experience" (Quine 1981, 185). Rather, he rejected mental states as unscientific posits of a pre-scientific age. So Quine should not be classified as an "analytical" behaviourist in the usual sense.

Although the distinction between "methodological" and "analytical" behaviourism is difficult to sustain, it is related to a tension in actual behaviourist writings, between those that are prepared to acknowledge something like consciousness, but deny that it can be scientifically studied, and those that declare there to be no such thing. This distinction does not line up exactly with the distinction between methodological and analytic behaviourism, since those who declare there is no such thing as consciousness do not make any specific proposal about how conscious mentality is related to behaviour (as analytical behaviourists were supposed to have done). All they do is dismiss talk of consciousness as meaningless, unverifiable and unscientific. This does not amount to any genuine philosophical doctrine.

However, scientific resistance to the study of consciousness outlived the official decline and collapse of behaviourism. As Daniel Dennett pointed out as late as 1978,

> one of philosophy's favorite faces of mentality has received scant attention from cognitive psychologists, and that is consciousness itself: full-blown, introspective, inner-world, phenomenological consciousness ... one finds not so much a lack of interest as a deliberate and adroit avoidance of the issue.
>
> (1978, 149)

This was not obviously because all psychologists were still behaviourists, or that the behaviourists actually *denied* the existence of consciousness: "off the printed page" Julian Jaynes commented, "behaviourism was only a refusal to talk about consciousness" (Jaynes 1976, 15). Rather, the dominant view seems to be that one could concede that there is *something* to all this talk about consciousness, but it is not a subject-matter for grown-up scientific psychologists.

This is the view we find in the work of E. C. Tolman, who famously argued that "everything important in psychology ... can be investigated in essence through the continued experimental and theoretical analysis of the determiners of rat behavior at a choice point in a maze" (Tolman 1938, 34). In his 1932 book *Purposive Behaviour in Animals and Men*, Tolman introduced the term "raw feels" as a name for what therefore lies outside the scope of scientific psychology:

> sensations, says the orthodox mentalist, are more than discriminanda-expectations, whether indicated by verbal introspection or by discrimination-box experiments, They are in addition immediate mental givens, "raw feels". They are unique subjective suffusions in the mind.
> (Tolman 1932, 250–251; see also Farrell 1950, 174)

Given Tolman's rejection of mentalism, this sounds as if he is rejecting raw feels; but in fact his view was that science cannot settle the question of whether they exist:

> we never learn whether it feels like our red or our green or our gray, or whether indeed, its "feel" is perhaps sui generis and unlike any of our own.... Whether your raw feels are or are not like mine, you and I shall never discover.... If there be raw feels correlated with such discriminanda expectations, these raw feels are by very definition "private" and not capable of scientific treatment. And we may leave the question as to whether they exist, and what to do about them, if they do exist, to other disciplines than psychology – for example, to logic, epistemology and metaphysics. And whatever the answers of these other disciplines, we, as mere psychologists, need not be concerned.
> (Tolman 1932, 252–253)

The idea that consciousness might consist in ineffable qualities which are inaccessible to science and whose nature is undetectable by others is an idea which we first found in the work of C. I. Lewis (*cf.* his "qualia") and one which permeates philosophical discussions of consciousness later in the century, as we shall see.

The significance of behaviourism for the philosophy of consciousness in the 20th century does not lie in any plausibility that the doctrine might have had as a substantial thesis about the nature of mind and consciousness. Rather, its significance lies in the fact that it generated and helped to sustain a conception of most of mental life as *not essentially involving consciousness at all*. And this conception came to be accepted even by behaviourism's most severe critics. Here is Jerry Fodor, for example, writing in 1991:

> It used to be universally taken for granted that the problem about consciousness and the problem about intentionality are intrinsically linked:

that thought is ipso facto conscious, and that consciousness is ipso facto consciousness of some or other intentional object . . . Freud changed all that. He made it seem plausible that explaining behaviour might require the postulation of intentional but unconscious states. Over the last century, and most especially in Chomskian linguistics and in cognitive psychology, Freud's idea appears to have been amply vindicated. . . . Dividing and conquering – concentrating on intentionality and ignoring consciousness – has proved a remarkably successful research strategy so far.

(1991, 12)

The reference to Freud is largely rhetorical, and may simply be due to the journalistic context in which these remarks appeared. Although it is often claimed that Freud changed our conception of the mental with his discovery of unconscious mentality, Freud's specific impact on analytic philosophy has been minimal. (In fact, the attribution to Freud of the discovery of the unconscious is itself very misleading: see e.g. Whyte 1960; Manson 2000.) A more plausible hypothesis, to my mind, is that what Fodor calls the divide and conquer strategy is a result of the conception of consciousness which was introduced by behaviourism. If this is right, then there is an irony in the fact that the officially anti-behaviourist movements in cognitive psychology and Chomskian linguistics should have embraced a conception of consciousness which "while granting the reality of consciousness, maintains it to be quite inessential to mind, psychology or cognition – and at most, of some peripheral or derivative status or interest" as Charles Siewert puts it (Siewert 1998, 3; see also Siewert 2011). As we will see, this tendency is also central to the physicalist or materialist rejection of behaviourism.

4. Physicalism and the explanatory gap

The main preoccupation of the philosophy of mind in the second half of the 20th century was the question of materialism or physicalism. Materialism was not a 20th century invention, of course: in the early modern era, its origins are recognisable in Hobbes and Cartesians like La Mettrie, and materialist doctrines were popular in 19th century Germany (see Gregory 1977). The logical positivists had formulated a doctrine that they called 'physicalism' (see Carnap 1932, 1955) as a doctrine about the language of science: it says that all truths can be expressed in physical language (that is, in the language of physics). But in keeping with Carnap's general attitude to ontology, this was supposed to be a doctrine purely about a choice of linguistic framework, and not about the world.

W. V. Quine's (1951) rejection of the analytic/synthetic distinction, which he took to lie behind Carnap's philosophy, led to a more direct approach to ontological questions (see Hookway 1988). Quine's view was that ontological questions could be considered on all fours with scientific questions about what there is. Another influential doctrine of Quine's was his naturalism: his belief that philosophy was not just "continuous" with science, but that all ontological questions are really questions for science. Although Quine himself remained a methodological behaviourist in linguistics and in psychology (1990, 37), it is worth pointing out that the combination of naturalism and the straightforward attitude to ontology does not entail behaviourism. Indeed, this combination of views led to a hugely popular non-behaviourist (or "mentalist") version of physicalism in the later decades of the 20th century.

A crucial movement here was the version of materialism which emerged in Australia in the 1950s (often known as "the identity theory"). In a pair of very influential papers, J.J.C. Smart (1959) and U. T. Place (1956) proposed that mental states and processes should be identified with states and processes in the brain. This form of materialism was put forward as an empirical hypothesis, akin to the hypothesis that lightning is an electrical discharge, or that heat is the motion of molecules.

Smart's paper is standardly cited as a revolutionary moment in this history of the mind-body problem, freeing those with scientific or materialist tendencies from the twin strangleholds of behaviourism and Wittgensteinian obscurantism. Of course, originality in philosophy rarely takes this form. The idea that mental states and neural states (or processes or events) are literally identical was not invented by Smart, but had been in the air for a while. Smart himself always gave credit to Place (1956) and Feigl (1958) for explicit formulations, and he identified related views in Carnap and Reichenbach. Some have taken the Australian-British metaphysician Samuel Alexander to have defended the identity theory in the early part of the century, though it is hard to see how this is compatible with his defence of the "emergence" of the mental (see Thomas 2013). And as Place pointed out, the psychologist E. G. Boring, a follower of Titchener, had claimed explicitly in 1946 that "neural process and sensation are identical" (see Place 1990).

Smart was concerned in the 1959 paper with sensations, and said little or nothing about thoughts or other conscious episodes. He considered various objections to the identity theory, the most powerful of which he credited to Max Black. This is the objection that even if the identity theory does identify sensations with brain processes, how can it deal with the "phenomenal qualities" of those processes? For example, even if having an orange after-image is a brain process, where does this leave the qualitative "feel" of this after-image – its "orangey-ness", as it were? Smart responded with what he called his "topic-neutral" analysis of attributions of phenomenal properties. It is "topic-neutral" because the truth of the analysing claim is neutral on whether the property itself is physical or irreducibly "psychical". This is Smart's proposed analysis:

> When a person says, "I see a yellowish-orange after-image" he is saying something like this: "There is something going on which is like what is going on when I have my eyes open, am awake, and there is an orange illuminated in good light in front of me, that is, when I really see an orange."
>
> (Smart 1959,149)

From the point of view of the present investigation, the interesting thing about Smart's analysis is that he thinks this account explains

> the singular elusiveness of "raw feels" – why no one seems to be able to pin any properties on them. Raw feels, in my view, are colorless for the very same reason that *something* is colorless. This does not mean that sensations do not have properties, for if they are brain-processes they certainly have properties. It only means that in speaking of them as being like or unlike one another we need not know or mention these properties.
> (Smart 1959, 150)

These "phenomenal properties" of experience are elusive and ineffable, like Lewis's qualia and Tolman's raw feels. Smart's conception of consciousness, therefore, has a close connection with the behaviourist's "phenomenal residue" conception, despite the fact that he thinks (unlike the behaviourists) that a scientific account of consciousness can be given, by using the topic-neutral analysis. (Feigl (1958, section V) has a similar view of raw feels, which he equates with "qualia".)

Smart's topic-neutral analysis of mental concepts can be seen as an early attempt to develop the functionalist theory of mind, which treats mental states as characterised in terms of their typical causes and effects (cf. Armstrong 1968; Lewis 1966; 1972). Sometimes known as the "causal theory of mind", functionalism became the dominant approach in the philosophy of mind in the 1970s and 1980s.

The most persistent objection to functionalism, posed famously by Ned Block and Jerry Fodor (1972) and then developed by Block (1980), is that it cannot handle the essence of consciousness, the familiar "qualitative feel". Block and Fodor argued, with the use of a number of thought experiments, that a functionalist account of conscious states could be true of different creatures even if they had very different conscious experiences ("inverted qualia") or no consciousness at all ("absent qualia"). Here the essence of consciousness is thought of as something that in its very nature eludes functionalist analysis: this is the phenomenal residue conception of consciousness, which we saw was epitomised in the notion of a raw feel. Indeed, Sydney Shoemaker, in a famous defence of functionalism against Block and Fodor's attack, explicitly links Block's objection to the view that functionalism "cannot account for the 'raw feel' component of mental states, or for their 'internal' or 'phenomenological' character" (Shoemaker 1975, 185).

Taking a broader view, Block's criticism can be seen to belong to a kind whose most general form is found in Thomas Nagel's classic paper "What Is It Like to Be a Bat?" (1974). Nagel begins with the statement that "consciousness is what makes the mind-body problem really intractable" (1974, 435). He then offers a famous definition of consciousness: "fundamentally an organism has conscious mental states if and only if there is something that it is like to *be* that organism – something it is like *for* the organism" and adds, "we may call this the subjective character of experience" (1974, 436). All reductive accounts of consciousness fail, Nagel argues, because "all of them are logically compatible with its absence"

(1974, 436). Nagel illustrates his conclusion with the thought experiment that no matter what one knew about the mental life of a bat from an objective, scientific point of view, one would not thereby know what it was like to be a bat: facts about the bat's consciousness.

Nagel's description of consciousness in terms of the idea of "what it's like" is vivid and compelling. (The idea had originally been proposed by B. A. Farrell (1950, 177) and T.L.S. Sprigge (1971, 167–168), as Nagel willingly acknowledged.) But it is important to emphasise that this idea does not by itself imply the phenomenal residue conception of consciousness. And nor does it imply what Lewis, Feigl and others meant by "qualia" (indeed, the words "quale" and "qualia" do not occur in Nagel's article). This is worth stressing, because many standard introductions to the problem of consciousness equate "phenomenal consciousness" with "subjective experience" with "what it's like" and with "qualia". But there is nothing in the idea of subjective experience as such that requires that we think of it in terms of a phenomenal residue, as I characterised that idea in section 1 above.

Nagel did not argue against the truth of physicalism in his 1974 paper. Rather, he argued that although we have good reasons to think it is true, we cannot understand how it can be true. Frank Jackson, by contrast, used similar considerations to Nagel's to argue that physicalism is false. Jackson's famous "knowledge argument" used the now famous example of an omniscient scientist, Mary, who knows all the physical information about seeing red – information expressible by physical science – but has never seen red (Jackson 1982). When she sees red for the first time, she comes to learn something new; therefore not all information is physical information. (Essentially the same argument was published in the same year by Howard Robinson (1982), and precursors of the argument can be found in Broad 1925, Russell 1927 and Feigl 1958.)

By the last decades of the century, physicalist theories of consciousness could be divided into the optimistic and the pessimistic. Among the pessimists were Nagel, who defended materialism at least until *Mind and Cosmos* (2012), although he insisted that the doctrine is unintelligible. Colin McGinn (1989) took inspiration from Nagel and from Noam Chomsky in defending his "mysterian" view that we are constitutionally incapable of solving the mind-body problem. From Nagel he took the idea that solving the problem requires explaining the "subjective" in "objective" terms. From Chomsky he took the idea that there might be contingent limits on our cognitive capacities, such that we are "cognitively closed" to some problems or what Chomsky calls "mysteries": just as a dog is constitutionally incapable of understanding quantum mechanics, so we may be incapable of understanding the mind-brain relation (which on independent grounds, we know to obtain). Another pessimist is Joseph Levine, who coined the phrase "the explanatory gap" to describe the problem consciousness poses for materialism (Levine 1983; 2001). Levine argues that although we have good reason to think that some kind of materialism thesis is true, we do not have an explanation of the necessary connection that holds between the facts about consciousness and their underlying material bases. Levine's conception of explanation is Hempel's deductive-nomological conception: to explain a phenomenon X is to derive propositions about X from other propositions about the explaining facts and about the laws of nature. Levine argues that Nagel's considerations show that there can be no such deduction. He attempts to close the explanatory gap in Levine (2001).

Among the optimists, Frank Jackson, whose conversion to materialism happened at some time before the mid-1990s, addressed head-on the problem set in Levine's terms. Jackson (1998) follows Lewis in taking the essence of physicalism to be a global supervenience thesis: any possible world which is a minimal physical duplicate of the actual world is a duplicate *simpliciter* (cf. Lewis 1983). He also agrees with Levine that the materialist must explain why this necessary supervenience relation holds: it cannot be a brute fact, since there are no unexplained necessities in nature, on Jackson's view. He proposes explaining supervenience in terms of a functionalist conceptual analysis of mental concepts, in the style of Lewis (1972). By contrast, Robert Kirk (1994) skips the conceptual analysis step, arguing that strict implication alone between the physical and the phenomenal truths is sufficient to close the explanatory gap. Others like David Papineau (2002) argue that physicalism does not need to close the explanatory gap, it only needs to explain why the gap *seems* to imply a metaphysical gap, when in reality there is no such metaphysical gap.

John Searle is a different kind of optimist. He thinks of the mind-body problem as a scientific problem, like the "stomach-digestion" problem (Searle 1992). There is no deep and mysterious metaphysical puzzle about how the stomach manages to digest food; and we should think in the same way about the brain and its mental activity. The analogy suggests that mind is the activity of the brain; but Searle does not pursue the analogy in that direction. Rather, his claim is that mental states are "caused and constituted" by what goes on in the brain. Consciousness is a basic biological fact about us and other conscious organisms; it should be part of the scientific worldview that there is "subjective ontology" (i.e. the ontology of consciousness) as well as "objective ontology". Searle denies that he is a materialist, because he wants to reject the mental/physical contrast, on the grounds that "mental" connotes "mental-as-opposed-to-physical", which he thinks loads the dice somewhat against a properly scientific understanding of consciousness. However, since no plausible version of materialism will accept that "mental" has this connotation, we can safely ignore Searle's claim that he is not a materialist.

For both optimists and pessimists, the central question for physicalism is how to account for consciousness. This question and a wide range of answers to it were summarised and systematised in *The Conscious Mind* by David Chalmers (1996). An expansive and synoptic work, this book set the agenda for discussions of consciousness up to the end of the century and in the first decade of the 21st century. Three things about Chalmers's book are worth noting here: first, his conception of the problem of consciousness; second, his endorsement of the antiphysicalist arguments pioneered by Jackson; and third, his positive speculative theory of consciousness.

On the first point: Chalmers divides the study of consciousness into "easy" problems and the "hard" problem. Easy problems are, for example, those of explaining "the ability to discriminate, categorize, and react to environmental stimuli; the integration of information by a cognitive system; the ability of a system to access its own internal states; the focus of attention; the deliberate control of behavior" and others (Chalmers 1995, 200). We should not dwell on whether "easy" is the right word for these problems, many of which are very difficult indeed; the point is rather the contrast between these scientific questions and what Chalmers calls the "hard" problem of consciousness: the problem of explaining, for any conscious state, why it is conscious at all.

Second, Chalmers thinks that there is no physicalist solution to the hard problem. As Nagel had emphasised, the conditions specified by all current materialist theories of consciousness are logically consistent with the absence of consciousness. If this is right, there can be no deduction from the facts about the physical basis of consciousness to the facts about consciousness. Following Kirk (1974), Chalmers dramatises this with the image of a "zombie": a creature who is a physical replica of a conscious creature, but who lacks consciousness. The easy problems could be solved for the zombie; but having solved these we would still be in the dark about what makes us differ from zombies.

Third, there is Chalmers's positive conception of consciousness. Chalmers thinks of consciousness as metaphysically or logically independent of its functional or physical basis, in a certain sense. He thinks that the facts about consciousness supervene on the physical facts as a matter of lawlike necessity, rather than metaphysical necessity. But later in the book he flirts with a version of panpsychism that he calls "panprotopsychism" – the idea that all matter is endowed with some kind of simple consciousness, whose coming together in organisms produces the conscious phenomena we experience. This seems to have the consequence that consciousness does supervene on the physical after all, since any physical duplicate of our world would be a mental duplicate too; and zombies would be impossible. Paradoxically, then, this kind of panpsychism turns out to be a form of physicalism. (This may not be a problem on the version of panpsychism defended by Galen Strawson (2006); and for a contrasting view of panpsychism see Goff (2017).)

My interest here is not in the truth of physicalism, nor in the arguments for and against it, but the various ways in which consciousness has been conceived. The different conceptions cluster around the different understandings of the invented term "qualia". Literally the plural of the Latin word for quality (singular: "quale"), the word "qualia" came to dominate discussions of consciounsess in the second half of the century. Jackson described himself in his 1982 paper as a "qualia freak", and intended by this to express his anti-physicalist sentiments. He clearly did not mean by "qualia" exactly what C. I. Lewis meant (the ineffable properties of the immediately given), so what did he mean?

Broadly speaking, the term "qualia" came to mean two things in the philosophy of mind of the late 20th century. In one use of the term, to believe in qualia is just to believe in consciousness itself; the use of the term does not imply any particular theory of consciousness. To deny qualia, in this sense then, is to deny consciousness; and what sense can be made of this? But in another use, qualia are properties that are, in Michael Tye's words, "intrinsic, consciously accessible features that are non-representational and that are solely responsible for [the] phenomenal character" of sensory experiences. In itself, this does not imply that qualia are non-physical, as Tye himself acknowledges (Tye 2013). What matters is that qualia are intrinsic properties of *sensory* experiences, they are non-representational (they do not represent anything outside themselves) and available to consciousness. Ned Block adds to this definition the claim that qualia "go beyond" the functional properties of mental states; so the existence of qualia is incompatible with functionalism. Indeed, Block claims that the existence of qualia is of great significance:

> The greatest chasm in the philosophy of mind – maybe even all of philosophy – divides two perspectives on consciousness. The two perspectives differ on whether there is anything in the phenomenal character of conscious experience that goes beyond the intentional, the cognitive and the functional. A convenient terminological handle on the dispute is whether there are "qualia", or qualitative properties of conscious experience. Those who think that the phenomenal character of conscious experience goes beyond the intentional, the cognitive and the functional believe in qualia.
>
> (Block 2003)

It should be clear, I hope, that this conception of qualia is the heir of the phenomenal residue conception of consciousness whose presence I have traced from C. I. Lewis, via the behaviourists, to Smart and Feigl. Consciousness conceived in terms of qualia is non-functional, non-intentional and intrinsic. Often qualia are purely sensory too, though Block does not say this explicitly here. The qualitative nature of experience, on this view, is explained by the instantiation of properties which Block vividly describes as "mental paint" properties. In this he employs an image first mooted and then rejected by William James in 1904: "experience . . . would be much like a paint of which the world pictures were made".

However, the essence of the late 20th-century debates about materialism and consciousness do not presuppose this substantial notion of qualia. Nagel's 1974 argument does not presuppose any specific conception of consciousness, and *a fortiori* it does not presuppose qualia in Block's sense. The same is true of the Jackson-Robinson knowledge arguments. All that these arguments presuppose is that there is such a thing as conscious experience (the experience of an alien creature like a bat, for example, or the experience of seeing red for the first time). They do not presuppose that conscious experience involves qualia in the substantial sense. So if consciousness poses a problem for materialism, this problem cannot be avoided by rejecting this controversial assumption about qualia.

Where the substantial notion of qualia gets a grip is in its application in the objections to functionalism. If qualia are essentially non-functional, as Block says, then obviously sameness of functional role will not suffice for sameness of qualia; and this is exactly what the inverted qualia thought-experiments are supposed to show. Sydney Shoemaker once observed that "belief in qualia often goes with belief in the possibility of 'inverted qualia'" (Shoemaker 2007). It is clear that what he must mean by "qualia" is Block's substantial notion, not the innocuous one. But does this substantial notion of qualia, and the phenomenal residue conception of consciousness which it implies, have any independent plausibility? In other words, what reasons are there, independently of suspicion of functionalism, for thinking that consciousness should be conceived in this way? In the last section of this paper, I will address this question.

5. Consciousness, cognition and intentionality

Any theory of the ontological basis of consciousness – whether dualist, materialist or some other kind – must begin with some idea of what the phenomenon of consciousness is, and how it should be initially characterised. As we saw above, many early 20th-century philosophers thought of consciousness in terms of the idea of "givenness": the presentation to the subject of a special kind of object – e.g. sense-data or qualia. And over the course of the century, consciousness in the analytic tradition became conceived of as a primarily sensory phenomenon, with the sensory element itself conceived of as something inexpressible, indefinable, inefficacious and separable from the rest of mental life. This is what I am calling the "phenomenal residue" conception of consciousness. By the end of the century, it became common to think of states of mind as divided into two categories: the essentially unconscious "propositional attitudes" and the phenomenal residue of sensory qualia (see Crane 2003 for discussion).

One upshot of this picture is that conscious thought becomes very hard to make sense of. If consciousness is essentially a sensory phenomenon, to be thought of in terms of the instantiation of simple sensory properties, then conscious thinking, reasoning, imagining, day-dreaming and other intentional phenomena must be understood in terms of these properties. This is standardly done by conceiving of conscious intentionality in a composite way, as some kind of hybrid of unconscious intentional states and conscious qualia. (As we have seen, the phenomenological tradition, by contrast, connected consciousness and thought at the outset.) But is this the right account of conscious thinking, or of conscious intentionality in general?

In considering the relationship between consciousness and intentionality, there are two questions we need to address: first, can consciousness in general be understood in terms of intentionality at all? And second, how should we understand conscious intentionality itself (e.g. conscious thinking)?

Taking the first question first, there have been two broad approaches which have attempted to understand consciousness in terms of intentionality. One treats consciousness in terms of the representation of mental states: to be a conscious state is to be the object of another (intentional) mental state. This is the *higher-order representation* or *higher-order thought* ("HOT") approach (see Mellor 1977–1978; Carruthers 2000, 2011; Rosenthal 1988; 2005; for reasons of space I ignore here the "same-order" or "self-representation" views, e.g. Hossack 2002; Kriegel 2009).

The other treats consciousness itself as a form of intentionality. Conscious states belong to a sub-category of intentional states; they are conscious in themselves, and not because they are the objects of higher-order states. This is *intentionalism* or *representationalism* (Tye 1995; Dretske 1995; Byrne 2001; Chalmers 2006; Crane 2009). I will consider these views in turn.

The HOT approach has been most fully developed by David Rosenthal (1988; 2005) but it has obvious affinities with earlier views: for example, Ryle's conception of consciousness as introspection, and Armstrong's idea of consciousness as a monitoring mechanism ("consciousness ... is simple awareness of our own state of mind" Armstrong 1968: 95). There are different versions of HOT theory. Some versions say that a first-order state is conscious only when one is actually thinking about it (Rosenthal 2005). Others say that one only has to have the disposition to think about the first order state (Carruthers 2003). Still others think of what is higher-order as a "perception" rather than a thought (Armstrong 1968; Lycan 1996).

Sometimes it is said that the appeal of the HOT theory derives from the idea that being conscious is always being conscious of something (see Lycan 2001). This is debatable. For it is natural to say that being aware of an object in one's perceived environment (say) is an instance of "being conscious of something". But according to the HOT theory, this is not so. For the only application of the notion of being "consciousness of" something which it allows is when one is conscious of one's own mental state. As Rosenthal says, "the first-order state can contribute nothing to phenomenology apart from the way we're conscious of it" (Rosenthal 2005; 32). So it is best not to let too much turn on the interpretation of the intuitive idea of "being conscious of" something.

Criticism of the HOT theory is not normally based on the rejection of the very idea of higher-order thought, or even of the idea that having a higher-order thought about a mental state could be a way of making that state conscious. Rather, the criticism normally comes from the idea that higher-order representation is not necessary for consciousness. (Peacocke 1993 argues that it is not sufficient either; but here I will focus on the objection to the necessity claim.) Many philosophers have argued strongly that some mental states (sensations, for example) are conscious in themselves and not simply because they are the objects of higher-order thought. For example, when one is paying close attention to some intellectual task, one may not be paying attention to, or thinking about, the lingering pain in one's lower back. But that pain is in your consciousness nonetheless. Although HOT theorists have responded to these kinds of complaint, they do linger persistently.

Ned Block has argued influentially that there is a fundamental distinction between two concepts of consciousness: access and phenomenal consciousness

(Block 1995; 2007). A representation is "access conscious" when one can access it in thought, or it is available for being "broadcast" among other representations; and a state of mind is "phenomenally conscious" when there is something it is like to be in this state. One of the ways in which the HOT theory fails, on Block's view, is that it fails to take account of phenomenal consciousness in his sense. Since on Block's view, phenomenal consciousness can occur without access consciousness, and HOT theories in effect say that all consciousness is access consciousness, he claims to have some clear counter-examples to the HOT theory.

Block's distinction is certainly real, in the sense that every theory (with the exception of the HOT theory) attempts to account for the difference between a simple conscious state and thinking about one's conscious states. This is not the same as the distinction between consciousness and attention, since attention is normally conceived in terms of focussing on the objects of conscious experience, and not only on one's mental states. The distinction between consciousness and attention has been explored by philosophers as a way of making sense of the different ways in which one may be said to be conscious of something (see Mole et al. 2011; O'Shaughnessy 2000; Wu 2014; for the view that consciousness is attention, see Prinz 2013).

The mere idea that there are different kinds of consciousness, and that thinking about (or accessing) a state of mind is a different thing from that state's being conscious, is not (*pace* Carruthers 2011) a discovery of the late 20th century, but something which has been around for a while. We find it in G. F. Stout for example:

> consciousness has manifold modes and degrees . . . consciousness includes not only awareness of our own states, but these states themselves, whether we have cognisance of them or not. If a man is angry, that is a state of consciousness, even though he does not know that he is angry. If he does know that he is angry, that is another modification of consciousness, and not the same.
>
> (Stout 1899, 7–8)

Notice too that to make a distinction between access and phenomenal consciousness is not, in itself, to commit to Block's conception of phenomenal consciousness in terms of qualia, understood as "mental paint" properties. So Block's phenomenal/access distinction in itself does not imply the phenomenal residue conception of phenomenal consciousness, even though he has that conception too.

The second way in which consciousness is understood in terms of intentionality is provided by the intentionalist or representationalist theory of consciousness. Intentionalist theories of perception, in particular, had been proposed by Anscombe (1965) and Armstrong (1968). In the following decade, Daniel Dennett (1978) proposed a "cognitive theory" of consciousness, and developed it in his major work, *Consciousness Explained* (Dennett 1991). Other intentionalist theories of consciousness began to develop over the turn of the century, in the work of Harman (1990), Tye (1995), Crane (1998), Byrne (2001) and Chalmers (2004; 2006).

Unlike the HOT theory, the intentionalist theory of consciousness does not explain consciousness in terms of the representation of one's own mental states, but rather explains it in terms of the nature of the state itself. For the HOT theory, states are conscious only when they fall under the "searchlight" of another mental state; for intentionalism, some states are conscious in and of themselves, in virtue of their intentionality. One kind of intentionalism (called "pure" by Chalmers 2004) says that the phenomenal character of a state of mind is identical with or supervenes upon its intentional content (Tye 1995). Another (called "impure" by Chalmers 2004) says that the phenomenal character of a mental state is determined by its whole intentional character: i.e. attitude or mode as well as content (Crane 2001; 2003; 2009).

Sometimes intentionalism is presented as being motivated by physicalism: the thought is that if we can reduce consciousness to intentionality, and intentionality to functional role, then this will facilitate a physicalist solution to the mind-body problem. But even if this is the actual motivation of some intentionalists, it is not essential to the intentionalist programme (see Chalmers 2006). Intentionalism can be motivated by purely phenomenological considerations (Byrne 2001). For example, intentionalism can be motivated by arguing that it is the best way to understand the mind as involving a 'perspective' or a 'point of view' (Crane 2001; 2009), or the best way to elaborate the idea that all mental facts are representational facts (Dretske 1995).

By contrast, Block (1990) has argued that phenomenological considerations, plus some assumptions about intentionality, can be used to refute intentionalism. If Block's arguments are going to be dialectically effective, the phenomenal residue conception of consciousness cannot be an *assumption* of the argument, as an obvious phenomenological fact; rather, it must be the argument's conclusion. For if the phenomenal residue conception were the starting point, then intentionalism would be doomed from the outset, and no further argument would be needed. The fact that Block and others think that argument is needed suggests that they do not really think that the phenomenal residue conception can be assumed.

So far in this section, we have been discussing the attempts to understand consciousness in terms of intentionality. The other large question about the relationship between consciousness and intentionality relates to conscious intentionality *itself*, and how it should be understood. More specifically, the question is about the existence and nature of conscious thinking, or the "phenomenology of thinking". Regardless of what a theory of consciousness says about the intentionality of perception or sensation, thinking is a paradigm of intentionality, and thinking can arguably be unconscious as well as conscious. So what should a theory of consciousness say about this?

Two broad approaches to this question had arisen by the early years of the 21st century. The first is to say that the phenomenology of thinking should be explained in terms of other, independently understood, phenomenological features (e.g. sensation, imagery etc.). We can call this the "reductionist" approach to the phenomenology of thinking. The second is to say that conscious thinking has its own distinctive (or "proprietary") phenomenology, which is not reducible to the phenomenology of other mental episodes. This second view is sometimes called the doctrine of "cognitive phenomenology" (Bayne and Montague 2011), though this term is a little misleading: strictly speaking, it ought to be a name for the phenomenon to be explained itself as opposed to a specific explanation of it.

Those who defend proprietary cognitive phenomenology appeal to phenomena like the distinctive experience of coming to understand a sentence one did not previously understand (Strawson 1994) or the role of phenomenology in coming to know what you believe (Pitt 2004). Those who take the reductionist approach argue that all these phenomena can be accommodated by appealing to phenomenology of other mental episodes (see Lormand 1996; Tye and Wright 2011). A distinct idea, but related to the doctrine of cognitive phenomenology, is the doctrine of phenomenal intentionality (Farkas 2008; Kriegel 2013). This holds that some kinds of intentional phenomena have their intentionality in virtue of their phenomenal properties, as opposed to in virtue of their causal relations to the world or teleological properties. This doctrine requires an independent conception of phenomenal properties which can then be used to explain conscious thought or perception (for example). Strictly speaking, phenomenal intentionality does not entail cognitive phenomenology, since it is possible to hold that the former doctrine applies only to perception (say); and nor does cognitive phenomenology entail phenomenal intentionality, because it is possible to say that there is proprietary phenomenology of cognition without thinking that its intentionality is explained by some previously understood phenomenal properties. But many of the leading thinkers in this area hold both versions (e.g. Pitt 2004).

These debates about cognitive phenomenology and phenomenal intentionality, which arose at the end of the 20th century, illustrate the importance of starting discussions of consciousness with an adequate account of the phenomena. And once again, we find that an obstacle to progress in the debate on cognitive phenomenology is the lingering influence of the "phenomenal residue" conception of consciousness, and the associated distinction between two kinds of mental states (crudely, sensations and propositional attitudes). If we begin with such a conception of consciousness, then it is very hard to make sense of the doctrines of phenomenal intentionality and cognitive phenomenology. But the aim of these doctrines is to explain conscious thought, and what merit can there be in a conception of consciousness which makes the obvious fact of conscious thought impossible to understand?

Conclusion

I have argued that the late 20th-century conception of consciousness in analytic philosophy emerged ultimately from the idea of consciousness as givenness, via the behaviourist idea of "raw feels". In the post-behaviourist period in philosophy, this resulted in the division of states of mind into essentially unconscious propositional attitudes ("beliefs and desires") plus the phenomenal residue of qualia: intrinsic, ineffable and inefficacious sensory states. It is striking how little in the important questions about consciousness depends on this conception, or on this particular division of mental states. So accepting this division and its associated conceptions of intentionality and consciousness is not an obligatory starting point for the philosophy of mind. A historical investigation of how these ideas came to be seen as inevitable can also help us see how we might reasonably reject them.[1]

Note

1 I have been helped in writing this chapter by: very helpful comments on earlier drafts from Amy Kind, Hanoch Ben-Yami, Nico Orlandi and Galen Strawson; conversations with Katalin Farkas, David Pitt and Howard Robinson; and the writings of Charles Siewert.

Bibliography

Anscombe, G.E.M. (1965). "The Intentionality of Sensation: A Grammatical Feature" in Butler, R.J. (ed.), *Analytical Philosophy: Second Series*. Oxford: Blackwell: 156–180.
Armstrong, D. M. (1968). *A Materialist Theory of the Mind*. London: Routledge and Kegan Paul.
Baldwin, Tom (2010). "George Edward Moore," in Zalta, Edward N. (ed.), *The Stanford Encyclopedia of Philosophy* Summer 2010 Edition. http //plato stanford edu/archives/sum2010/entries/moore/.
Bayne, Tim and Montague, Michelle (eds.). (2013). *Cognitive Phenomenology*. Oxford: Oxford University Press.
Block, Ned (1980). "Troubles with Functionalism," in Block, Ned (ed.), *Readings in the Philosophy of Psychology*, Vol. I. London: Methuen: 268–301.
Block, Ned (1990). "Inverted Earth," in Tomberlin, James (ed.), *Philosophical Perspectives, 4 Action Theory and Philosophy of Mind*. Atascadero: Ridgeview: 53–79. Reprinted in Block, N., Flanagan, O. and Güzeldere, G. (eds.), *The Nature of Consciousness*. Cambridge, MA: MIT Press 1997: 677–694.
Block, Ned (1995). "On a Confusion about a Function of Consciousness," *Behavioral and Brain Sciences*, 18: 227–247. Reprinted in Block, N., Flanagan, O., and Güzeldere, G. (eds.). (1997). *The Nature of Consciousness*. Cambridge, MA: MIT Press: 375–416.
Block, Ned (2003). "Mental Paint," in Hahn, M. and Ramberg, B. (eds.). *Reflections and Replies: Essays on the Philosophy of Tyler Burge*. Cambridge, MA: MIT Press: 165–200.
Block, Ned (2007). "Consciousness, Accessibility and the Mesh between Psychology and Neuroscience," *Behavioral and Brain Sciences*, 30: 481–548.
Block, Ned and Fodor, Jerry A. (1972). "What Psychological States are Not," *Philosophical Review*, 81: 159–181.
Boring, E. G. (1946). "Mind and Mechanism," *The American Journal of Psychology*, April.
Brentano, Franz (1874). *Psychology from an Empirical Standpoint*. Edited by L.L. McAlister. Trans. A. Rancurello, D. B. Terrell, and L. L. McAlister. London: Routledge and Kegan Paul (1973) reprinted with an introduction by Peter Simons. London: Routledge 1995. Originally published as *Psychologie vom empirischen Standpunkt*, Leipzig: Duncker and Humblot (1874).

Broad, C.D. (1925). *The Mind and Its Place in Nature*. London: Routledge and Kegan Paul.
Byrne, Alex (2001). "Intentionalism Defended," *Philosophical Review*, 110: 199–240.
Carnap, Rudolf (1932). "Psychology in Physical Language," *Erkenntnis*, 3: 107–142 (1932/3).
Carnap, Rudolf (1955). *Logical Syntax of Language*. Berkeley: University of California Press.
Carruthers, Peter (2003). *Phenomenal Consciousness: A Naturalistic Theory*. Cambridge: Cambridge University Press.
Carruthers, Peter (2011). "Higher-Order Theories of Consciousness," *The Stanford Encyclopedia of Philosophy* Fall 2011 Edition in Zalta, Edward N. (ed.). https://plato.stanford.edu/entries/consciousness-higher/.
Chalmers, David (1995). "Facing Up to the Problem of Consciousness," *Journal of Consciousness Studies*, 2: 200–219.
Chalmers, David (1996). *The Conscious Mind*. Oxford: Oxford University Press.
Chalmers, David (2004). "The Representational Character of Experience," in Leiter, B. (ed.), *The Future for Philosophy*. Oxford: Oxford University Press: 153–181.
Chalmers, David (2006). "Perception and the Fall from Eden," in Gendler, Tamar Szabó and Hawthorne, John (eds.), *Perceptual Experience*. Oxford: Oxford University Press.
Crane, Tim (1998). "Intentionality as the Mark of the Mental," in O'Hear, A. (ed.), *Contemporary Issues in the Philosophy of Mind*. Cambridge: Cambridge University Press: 229–251.
Crane, Tim (2000). "The Origins of Qualia," in Crane, Tim and Patterson, Sarah (eds.), *History of the Mind-Body Problem*. London: Routledge: 169–194.
Crane, Tim (2001). *Elements of Mind*. Oxford: Oxford University Press.
Crane, Tim (2003). "The Intentional Structure of Consciousness," in Jokic, A. and Smith, Q. (eds.), *Consciousness: New Philosophical Perspectives*. Oxford: Oxford University Press: 33–56.
Crane, Tim (2009). "Intentionalism," in Beckermann, Ansgar, McLaughlin, Brian and Walter, Sven (eds.), *Oxford Handbook to the Philosophy of Mind*. Oxford: Oxford University Press: 474–493.
Dennett, Daniel C. (1978). "Toward a Cognitive Theory of Consciousness," *Minnesota Studies in the Philosophy of Science*, 9(1978).
Dennett, Daniel C. (1991). *Consciousness Explained*. London: Allen Lane.
Dretske, Fred I. (1995). *Naturalizing the Mind*. Cambridge, MA: MIT Press.
Farkas, Katalin (2008). "Phenomenal Intentionality without Compromise," *The Monist*, 91: 273–293.
Farrell, B. A. (1950). "Experiences," *Mind* 59: 170–198.
Feigl, Herbert (1958). "The 'Mental' and the 'Physical,'" in Feigl, H., Scriven, M. and Maxwell, G. (eds.), *Minnesota Studies in the Philosophy of Science*. Minneapolis: University of Minnesota Press: 370–497.
Fodor, Jerry A. (1991). "Too Hard for Our Kind of Mind," *London Review of Books*, 13 June: 27.
Goff, Philip (2017). *Consciousness and Fundamental Reality*. New York: Oxford University Press.
Gregory, Frederick (1977). *Scientific Materialism in Nineteenth Century Germany* Studies in the History of Modern Science vol I. Dordrecht: D Reidel.
Güzeldere, Güven (1997). "The Many Faces of Consciousness: A Field Guide," in Block, N., Flanagan, O. and Güzeldere, G. (eds.), *The Nature of Consciousness*. Cambridge, MA: MIT Press: 1–68.

Harman, Gilbert (1990). "The Intrinsic Quality of Experience," in Tomberlin, J. (ed.), *Philosophical Perspectives* 4 (Atascadero: Ridgeview); reprinted in Block, N., Flanagan, O. and Guzeldere, G. (eds.). (1997). *The Nature of Consciousness*. Cambridge, MA: MIT Press: 663–676.

Hookway, Christopher (1988). *Quine: Language Experience and Reality*. Cambridge: Polity Press.

Horgan, Terence and Tienson, John (2002). "The Intentionality of Phenomenology and the Phenomenology of Intentionality," in Chalmers, David (ed.), *Philosophy of Mind: Classical and Contemporary Readings*. Oxford: Oxford University Press: 520–533.

Hossack, Keith (2002). "Self-knowledge and Consciousness," *Proceedings of the Aristotelian Society*. 102: 163–181.

Husserl, Edmund (1900–1901). *Logische Untersuchungen*. Tübingen: Max Niemeyer, 1980. English edition *Logical Investigations*. Trans. J N Findlay 2 vols. London Routledge, 2001.

Husserl, Edmund (1913). *Ideen zu einer reinen Phänomenologie und phänomenologischen Philosophie Erstes Buch*. Tübingen: Max Niemeyer, 1980. English edition *Ideas Pertaining to a Pure Phenomenology and a Phenomenological Philosophy First Book*. Trans. F Kersten Dordrecht: Kluwer, 1982.

Husserl, Edmund (1948). *Erfahrung und Urteil*, ed L Landgrebe. Hamburg: Felix Meiner 1985. English edition *Experience and Judgement*. Trans. J. S. Churchill and K. Ameriks. Evanston: Northwestern University Press, 1973.

Jackson, Frank (1982). "Epiphenomenal Qualia," *Philosophical Quarterly*, 32: 127–136.

Jackson, Frank (1998). *From Metaphysics to Ethics* Oxford: Oxford University Press.

James, William (1890). *Principles of Psychology*. New York: Holt.

James, William (1904). "Does Consciousness Exist?" *Journal of Philosophy, Psychology and Scientific Method*, 1: 477–491.

Jaynes, Julian (1976). *Origins of Consciousness in the Breakdown of the Bicameral Mind*. Boston: Houghton Mifflin.

Kirk, Robert (1974). "Zombies v. Materialists," *Proceedings of the Aristotelian Society Supplementary Volume*, 48: 135–152.

Kirk, Robert (1994). *Raw Feeling: A Philosophical Account of the Essence of Consciousness*. Oxford: Oxford University Press.

Kriegel, Uriah (2007). "Intentional Inexistence and Phenomenal Intentionality," *Philosophical Perspectives*, 21: 307–340.

Kriegel, Uriah (2009). *Subjective Consciousness: A Self-Representational Theory*. Oxford: Oxford University Press.

Kriegel, Uriah (ed.). (2013). *Phenomenal Intentionality*. Oxford: Oxford University Press.

Levine, Joseph (1983) "Materialism and Qualia: The Explanatory Gap," *Pacific Philosophical Quarterly*, 64: 354–361.

Levine, Joseph (2001) *Purple Haze*. Oxford: Oxford University Press.

Lewis, C.I. (1929). *Mind and the World Order*. London: Constable.

Lewis, David (1966). "An Argument for the Identity Theory," *Journal of Philosophy*, 63: 17–25.

Lewis, David (1972). "Psychophysical and Theoretical Identifications." *Australasian Journal of Philosophy*, 50: 249–258.

Lewis, David (1983). "New Work for a Theory of Universals." *Australasian Journal of Philosophy* 61: 343–377.

Lormand, Eric (1996). "Nonphenomenal Consciousness," *Noûs*, 30: 242–261.

Lycan, W.G. (1996). *Consciousness and Experience*. Cambridge, MA: MIT Press.

Lycan, W.G. (2001). "A Simple Argument for a Higher-Order Representation Theory of Consciousness," *Analysis*, 61: 3–4.

McGinn, Colin (1989). "Can we solve the mind-body problem?" *Mind* 98: 349–66.

Manson, Neil (2000) "'A Tumbling-ground for Whimsies'? The History and Contemporary Role of the Conscious/Unconscious Contrast," in Crane, Tim and Patterson, Sarah A. (eds.), *History of the Mind-Body Problem*. London: Routledge.

Martin, M.G.F. (2000). "Beyond Dispute: Sense-Data, Intentionality and the Mind-Body Problem," in Crane, Tim and Patterson, Sarah (eds.), *History of the Mind-Body Problem*. London: Routledge: 195–231.

Martin, M.G.F. (2003). "Sensible Appearances," in Baldwin, Thomas (ed.), *The Cambridge History of Philosophy 1870–1945*. Cambridge: Cambridge University Press.

Maslin, Keith (2001). *An Introduction to the Philosophy of Mind*. Cambridge: Polity Press.

Mellor, D. H. (1977–1978). "Conscious Belief," *Proceedings of the Aristotelian Society*, 78: 87–101.

Mole, Christopher, Smithies, Declan and Wu, Wayne (eds.). (2011). *Attention: Philosophical and Psychological Essays*. Oxford: Oxford University Press.

Moore, G. E. (1903). "The Refutation of Idealism," *Mind*, 12: 433–453.

Moore, G. E. (1953). "Propositions," in *Some Main Problems of Philosophy*. London: George Allen and Unwin: 57–59.

Nagel, Thomas (1974). "What Is It Like to Be a Bat?" *Philosophical Review*, 83: 435–450.

O'Shaughnessy, Brian (2000). *Consciousness and the World*. Oxford: Oxford University Press.

Papineau, David (2002). *Thinking About Consciousness*. Oxford: Oxford University Press.

Peacocke, Christopher (1993). *A Study of Concepts*. Cambridge, MA: MIT Press.

Pitt, David (2004). "The Phenomenology of Cognition or What Is It Like to Think That P?" *Philosophy and Phenomenological Research*, 69: 1–36.

Place U.T. (1990). "E G Boring and the Mind-Brain Identity Theory," *British Psychological Society History and Philosophy of Science Newsletter*, 11: 20–31.

Poellner, Peter (2007). "Consciousness in the World Husserlian Phenomenology and Externalism," in Leiter, Brian and Rosen, Michael (ed.), *Oxford Handbook to Continental Philosophy*. Oxford: Oxford University.

Price, H. H. (1932). *Perception*. London: Methuen.

Prinz, Jesse (2013). *The Conscious Brain*. New York: Oxford Unversity Press.

Quine, W.v.O. (1951). "Two Dogmas of Empiricism," *The Philosophical Review*, 60: 20–43.

Quine, W.v.O. (1981). *Theories and Things*. Cambridge, MA: Harvard University Press.

Robinson, Howard (1982). *Matter and Sense*. Cambridge: Cambridge University Press.

Rosenthal, David (1986). "Two Concepts of Consciousness," *Philosophical Studies*, 49: 329–359.

Rosenthal, David (2005). *Consciousness and Mind*. Oxford: Oxford University Press.

Russell, Bertrand (1927). *The Analysis of Matter*. London: George Allen and Unwin.

Ryle, Gilbert (1949). *The Concept of Mind*. London: Hutchinson.

Ryle, Gilbert (1979). *On Thinking*. Oxford: Blackwell.

Sartre, Jean-Paul (1958). *Being and Nothingness*. London: Methuen; originally published 1943.

Searle, John (1992). *The Rediscovery of the Mind*. Cambridge, MA: MIT Press.

Sellars, Wilfrid (1956). *Empiricism and the Philosophy of Mind*. Cambridge, MA: Harvard University Press 1997.

Shoemaker, Sydney (1975). "Functionalism and Qualia," *Philosophical Studies*, 27: 291–315.
Shoemaker, Sydney (2007). "A Case for Qualia," in McLaughlin, Brian P. and Cohen, Jonathan D. (eds.), *Contemporary Debates in Philosophy of Mind*. Oxford: Blackwell.
Siewert, Charles (1998). *The Significance of Consciousness*. Princeton, NJ: Princeton University Press.
Siewert, C. (2011). "Phenomenal Thought," in Bayne, T. and Montague, M. (eds.), *Cognitive Phenomenology*. Oxford: Oxford University Press, 236–267.
Smart J. J. C. (1959). "Sensations and Brain Processes," *The Philosophical Review*, 68: 141–156.
Sprigge, T.L.S. (1971). "Final Causes," *Proceedings of the Aristotelian Society Supplementary Volume*, 45: 149–192.
Stout, G.F. (1899). *A Manual of Psychology*. London: University Correspondence College Press.
Strawson, Galen (1994). *Mental Reality*. Cambridge, MA: MIT Press.
Strawson, Galen (2006). "Realistic Monism – Why Physicalism Entails Panpsychism," *Journal of Consciousness Studies*, 13: 3–31.
Tanney, Julia (2014). "Gilbert Ryle," *The Stanford Encyclopedia of Philosophy* Winter 2014 Edition in Zalta, Edward N. (ed.). http //plato stanford edu/archives/win2014/entries/ryle/.
Tennant, Neil (2006). "Cognitive Phenomenology Semantic Qualia and Luminous Knowledge," in Greenough, P. and Pritchard, D. (eds.), *Williamson on Knowledge*. Oxford: Oxford University Press.
Thomas, Emily (2013). "Space, Time and Samuel Alexander," *British Journal for the History of Philosophy*, 21: 549–569.
Tolman, E. C. (1932). *Purposive Behaviour in Animals and Men*. New York: Century.
Tolman, E. C. (1938). "The Determiners of Behavior at a Choice Point," *Psychological Review*, 45: 1–14.
Tye, Michael (1995). *Ten Problems of Consciousness*. Cambridge, MA: MIT Press.
Tye, Michael (2013). "Qualia," *The Stanford Encyclopedia of Philosophy* Fall 2013 Edition in Zalta, Edward N. (ed.). http //plato stanford edu/archives/fall2013/entries/qualia/.
Tye, Michael and Wright, Briggs (2013). "Is there a Phenomenolgoy of Thought?" in Bayne and Montague (eds.), *Cognitive Phenomenology*. Oxford: Oxford University Press.
Watson, J. B. (1930). *Behaviorism* (Revised edition). New York: W W Norton & Co.
Whyte, L. L. (1960). *The Unconscious Before Freud*. New York: Basic Books.
Wittgenstein, Ludwig (1953). *Philosophical Investigations*. Edited by G.E.M. Anscombe and Rush Rhees and Trans. G.E.M. Anscombe. Oxford: Blackwell.
Wu, Wayne (2014). *Attention*. London: Routledge.
Wundt, Wilhelm (1874). *Grundzüge der physiologischen Psychologie* (Principles of Physiological Psychology) Leipzig: W. Engelmann.

4

20TH-CENTURY THEORIES OF PERCEPTION[1]

Nico Orlandi

To give a glimpse of theories of perception in the 20th century, I propose to consider perception under two guises. First, we can think of perception as a conscious *relation*. Perceiving is intuitively a basic way of getting acquainted with a mind-independent and material world. We may call this intuitive position 'realism'. We can call the further idea that everything (including perception and its objects) is physical, 'physicalism'. The 20th century in philosophy can be seen as a prolonged attempt to defend realism, and, to a lesser extent, to defend physicalism.[2]

Second, perception can be seen as a *process* that happens subconsciously. It is whatever process gets us to perceive the world as we do. The last century produced a number of models of this process, stemming from the emerging collaboration between philosophy and psychology. Constructivism and ecological approaches are the two main present contenders, while Gestalt theory was popular in the first half of the century.

Before we proceed, I should point out that there is no presumption here that the two topics under consideration, although presented separately, are unrelated. Work in one field influenced work in the other and vice-versa. When possible, the relevant influences will be noted.

1. The perceptual relation and the objects of perception

Sense perception seems to be a form of awareness of a mind-independent reality. When we see a table, hear a doorbell, touch a shirt, taste a pineapple, or smell a flower we seem capable of entering into direct contact with ordinary objects and events. Such objects and events exist independently of perceiving agents.

Defending this realist approach was one of the preoccupations of philosophers based in Cambridge in the first half of the 20th century. 'Sense-data' theory – the dominant strand of philosophical theorizing about perception in this period – originated in the attempt to rescue a realist viewpoint from the British idealism of the late 19th century. Notable British idealists – known as 'neo-Hegelians' – include J.M.E. McTaggart, F. H. Bradley, Edward Caird, Bernard Bosanquet, T. H. Green and Harold Joachim.

Idealism is a complex metaphysical and epistemological position. British idealists held some variation of Berkeley's idea that *esse est percipi*, or that reality is spiritual or mental. Berkeley reached this conclusion by supposing that the only things that are perceived are ideas. Since ideas are mental, he concluded that the world is also mental (Bradley 1899).[3] Early sense-data theorists were reacting to this approach or, more specifically, to the notion that the objects of perception are not ordinary objects, but mind-dependent entities.

1.1 Sense-data theory

Although initially attracted to idealism, G. E. Moore later attempted to refute it (Moore 1903). In presenting his account of perception, Moore introduced the concept of sense-data to British audiences. This concept referred generally to the *immediate* objects of perception (Moore 1910/2014), and Bertrand Russell later popularized it in the *Problems of Philosophy* in 1912.[4] Important in the sense-data tradition are C. D. Broad – one of Russell's students – and H. H. Price – one of Moore's students – who later went on to teach Wilfrid Sellars (Broad 1914; Price 1932). A. J. Ayer is also usually counted among sense-data theorists, but some interpreters argue that his position is harder to classify (Ayer 1956; Martin 2003).

Initially, 'sense-data' was just a term of art to refer to what is immediately and directly given in perception (Huemer 2011). 'Immediate' and 'direct', in this context, mean that the perceptual awareness of sense-data does not depend on the awareness of anything else. Sense-data are simply *given* in sense perception, and sense perception is an unmediated relation to its objects. Importantly, the term 'sense-data' was supposed to be neutral as to the nature of the sense-data themselves. It was an open question whether the objects of perception were physical or mental, mind-dependent or mind-independent, and parts of the surfaces of material objects or not (Russell 1912, 12; Moore 1953, 30).

Moore had hoped to contrast idealism by arguing that sense-data are identical with ordinary entities, but his position encountered difficulties that are now known as 'the problem of perception' (Smith 2002). The problem can be illustrated by reference to perceptual illusion, hallucination, perspectival variation, and the time lag between events in the world and our perceptions of it.[5]

For brevity's sake we can focus on perceptual illusion. In illusions, an item is experienced, but it appears other than it really is. A straight stick may appear bent when placed in water. A soft fabric may feel rough when touched after touching something softer. In these instances, we are perceptually aware of something that has certain properties – something bent or rough – when no corresponding thing has those properties. Because no corresponding entity has the properties perceived, the temptation is to suppose that what we perceive is not the stick itself. We perceive the appearance of the stick. In the visual case, sense-data theorists often talked of the immediate objects of perception as patches of color. We may be aware of ordinary objects in perception, but only indirectly – that is, only *in virtue* of perceiving the objects' appearances.

Further, the argument goes, because there is no relevant phenomenological difference between cases of illusion of this kind and cases of ordinary perception, the reasoning can be extended to apply to every instance of perceiving. In everyday perception, like in illusion, we are directly aware of appearances. Appearances change with perspective. Sense-data theorists took this to suggest that appearances are mind-dependent. Our access to the world is mediated by awareness of these appearances.

Although formulations of the argument from illusion tend to use the visual case, the argument is supposed to work for other modalities as well. It is just not always clear how this works. One may take the objects of audition to be sounds, not ordinary objects (O'Callaghan 2007). We perceive objects *by* perceiving the sounds they produce. So the argument from illusion does not seem to straightforwardly apply to audition. The argument would seem to require, first, that we think of sounds as, in some sense, ordinary and mind-independent; and, second, that we think of sounds as having properties – for example, loudness – that we can misperceive.

But regardless of these difficulties, considerations of illusion lead sense-data theorists to enrich the neutral conception of sense-data. Sense-data are not just the immediate objects of perception. They are also (a) dependent on the mind, and (b) having the properties that they perceptually appear to us to have.

Thesis (a) is peculiar given the original anti-idealism of proponents of sense-data theory, but the theory is supposed to be compatible with realism about the world (Moore 1925). Sense-data theorists, like Moore, tend to also be realists, but without endorsing the original Moorian idea that sense-data are identical with ordinary objects. Sense-data theorists tend to be *indirect* realists, believing that perception puts us in contact with a physical reality, even if only *indirectly*. Perception is not, as pre-theoretically supposed, an *unmediated* form of acquaintance with the world. It is mediated by our contact with entities variably described as 'sense-data', 'mental images', 'impressions' and 'appearances'.

The notable exception to the realist bent of sense-data theory is Bertrand Russell who flirted with both phenomenalism – the thesis that the physical world is a construction out of sensory elements – and with neutral monism – the thesis that the mind and the world are constructions out of a common basis of sensory acts (Russell 1914).

Because sense-data theory conceives of the immediate objects of perception as appearances rather than ordinary objects, it differs from naïve or direct realism of the kind defended by Thomas Reid and by J. L. Austin (Austin 1946; 1962; Reid 1764). Austin argued forcibly that the arguments used against a direct realist position are unconvincing. One of Austin's strategies is to claim that such arguments trade on a misunderstanding of the common-sense expressions 'look', 'appear' and 'seem'. To say that a straight stick appears bent in water, for example, is not to say that we are acquainted only with its looks.

Austin's work belongs to a tradition of Oxford direct realism whose predecessor is most notably Prichard, and whose successors are some contemporary proponents of 'disjunctivism', a position that we will briefly survey in section 1.4 (Hinton 1973; Martin 2003; Prichard 1906; Snowdon 1979; Travis 2004).

Reflection on whether mind-independent objects are the objects of perception is also present in the phenomenological tradition. According to both Edmund Husserl and Maurice Merleau-Ponty, what we perceive appears to exist independently of our own existence. In a line of reasoning that resembles considerations of perspectival variation, but that reaches different conclusions, Husserl and Merleau-Ponty argue that the mind-independence of the objects of perception is given by the fact that we can take multiple perspectives on the objects. It is evident in the fact that taking different perspectives changes the way the objects look (Husserl 1900/1; Merleau-Ponty 1945).

A similar conclusion concerning mind-independence is reached by more recent work on the phenomenology of other modalities. Tactile experience, for example, delivers an appearance of something 'external' and mind-independent insofar as in touching something we experience the limit of our own body (Condillac 1947; Smith 2002; Strawson 1958).

Thesis (b) of sense-data theory, according to which sense-data have the properties that they appear to us to have, is, like thesis (a), a problematic thesis, and it is sometimes credited with the introduction in philosophy of *qualia* – or qualitative properties present in experience. This is not quite right, however. American philosophers had already introduced the term 'qualia' somewhat independently of sense-data theory. Charles Peirce used the term in relation to sense perception in 1866, and C. I. Lewis later used it in discussing the conceptual status of perception (Crane 2000; Lewis 1929; Peirce 1866/1931).

Thesis (b) is a tacit presupposition of the argument from illusion. According to the argument, when one perceptually experiences something, there must be something that one stands in the relation of perceiving to, and this something must have the properties which it seems to the perceiver to have. For example, if it now looks to me as though there is a white expanse before me as I look at a wall, then an actual white expanse must exist, be sensed by me and have the properties I perceive it to have. This is true even if I am misperceiving or hallucinating a wall. And the property of being white, the reasoning goes, must be a non-physical property in this case. This is because nothing in the environment, or in my head, is white when I am hallucinating a white wall.

Experienced properties like 'being white' are examples of qualia. Although there are different senses of the term 'qualia' in contemporary philosophy, we can work with the idea that a quale is a qualitative property present in perceptual experience (Crane 2000 and this volume, Tye 2013). Some take qualia to be properties of the objects of experience. Some take them to be properties of the experiences themselves.

Typical examples of qualia are the color of something seen, the pitch of a heard sound and the smell of an odor. Because qualia can be present in experiences when no property corresponds to them in the environment (or in one's head), they are thought to pose a threat to physicalist accounts of the mind.

Due to its metaphysics of mysterious objects and properties, sense-data theory was mostly abandoned in the second half of the 20th century, when physicalism dominated the philosophy of mind. Indeed, with some notable exceptions (Bermudez 2000; Jackson 1977; O'Shaughnessy 2003), most contemporary philosophers of perception reject sense-data theory.

Two alternative theories of perception emerged: adverbialism and representationalism or intentionalism. The latter continues to be influential today (Armstrong 1961; Burge 2005; 2009; Dretske 1969; Harman 1990; Lycan 1996; Peacocke 1983; Searle 1983; Tye 1992). The former enjoyed popularity in the mid-20th century (Chisholm 1957; Ducasse 1942; Sellars 1975). We should look at each in turn.

1.2 Representationalism or intentionalism

Representationalists point out that the ontological commitments of sense-data theory are peculiar when we recognize that perceiving is a psychological state and, like other psychological states, it can have objects that do not exist. When I think of a unicorn, I am in a psychological state that is about an entity that does not exist. It is hard to see why the mere fact that I can think of a unicorn would imply both that the unicorn exists, and that its perceived properties are present in the world. Similarly, it is not clear why we would want to suppose that perceiving something means that the object perceived exists, and that we should discover properties corresponding to the perceived properties in the natural environment.

The fact that psychological states are about objects (that may not exist) is labeled their 'intentionality'. The fact that such states tell us something about the objects they are about is called their intentional 'content'. Sense-data theory has been charged with ignoring the intentionality of perception, for instance by G.E.M. Anscombe (Anscombe 1965; Searle 1983). Anscombe argues against both sense-data theory and direct realist positions by pointing out that what she calls 'sensation' – and what I have been calling 'perception' – is similar to other mental attitudes in relating us to intentional objects.[6]

Prior to Anscombe, the emphasis on intentionality is present in authors such as Chisholm, Husserl, Merleau-Ponty and Brentano, who reintroduced the very concept of intentionality from Scholastic philosophy (Brentano 1874; Chisholm 1957; Husserl 1900/01; 1913; Merleau-Ponty 1945; Montague this volume). Husserl distinguishes the psychological act of perceiving – the *noesis* – from its content – the *noema*, which directs itself to an object. A perceptual act with a given content can occur in the absence of its object while still aiming at it.

Representationalists about perception tend to also be representationalists about qualia (Anscombe 1965; Byrne 2001; Dretske 1995; Harman 1990; Lycan 1987; Shoemaker 1994; Tye 1994). There are different versions of representationalism about qualia, but the general idea is that qualia are represented properties of represented objects. Some express this view by saying that qualia are 'representational properties'. They are properties of what is represented in perceptual experience. When I am hallucinating a white wall, for example, I am representing a wall as having the property of being white. The wall does not need to be present in my immediate environment, and its whiteness is not an immaterial property of my experience. It is a represented property of a represented (or intentional) object.

This type of position is often coupled with the claim that perception is phenomenologically 'transparent'. When we perceive, we see 'right through' perceptual states to the world (Crane 2003; Harman 1990; Moore 1903). The properties that we are aware of in perception are properties that we attribute to external objects, not to our experiences of them.[7]

J.J.C. Smart's 'topic neutral translation' from the mid twentieth century is an example of representationalism of this kind (Smart 1959). According to Smart, "I see a yellowish-orange after-image" means, roughly, that "there is something going on in me which is like what is going on when I have my eyes open, am awake, and there is an orange illuminated in good light conditions in front of me." This type of translation aims to replace talk of qualia and of other purely mental entities with talk of entities that are presumably more acceptable – that is, with talk of intentional objects and their properties – although it is still a burden of intentionalism to explain what intentional objects ultimately are.

In addition to avoiding a dubious ontology, representationalism is thought to be an improvement over sense-data theory because it better accounts for the epistemic role of perception. Perception is not only what puts us in contact with the world. It is also seemingly capable of grounding our beliefs and judgments concerning the world. Sense-data theorists typically held the position that the perception of sense-data is indubitable, and not influenced by one's concepts or categories – where concepts are roughly ideas that come with certain abilities (Machery 2009; Martin 2003; Price 1932). Although, according to some proponents of sense-data theory, one could be wrong about how things are – and judgments concerning how things are depend on the concepts one has – one could not be wrong about how things appear. One could be wrong that a stick in water is bent – or that it is even a stick. But one couldn't be wrong about its *looks* – that is, about the existence of something that appears bent.

This immunity to error in sense-data theory raises questions concerning the ability of perception, so conceived, to inform about the world in a way that can justify belief. How does an infallible appearance of a color patch justify a belief in worldly objects and events that are presumably different from color patches?[8]

Both Anscombe and members of the phenomenological tradition, such as Husserl, emphasized that perception and belief are similar in the fact that they relate us to intentional objects and in the fact that they have content. Because they have content. Because they have content, perceptual states, just like beliefs, are about items in the environment – they can have a common subject matter – and they can stand in justificatory relations to one another.

One strand of philosophical literature has, then, been interested in spelling out what features perceptual content must have in order to play its epistemic role. A particularly active debate centers on the notion of non-conceptual content. C. I. Lewis discusses themes related to this issue early in the 20th century (Lewis 1929). But it is not until Gareth Evans that the notion of non-conceptual content is introduced in philosophy (Evans 1982).

Proponents of non-conceptual content hold that some mental states have content – representing the world to be a certain way – even when the bearer of those states lacks the concepts that specify the content (Bermudez and Cahen 2012). One can see a white wall – and usefully describe it as such – even if one lacks the concept of a wall and the concept of white.[9] Deniers of non-conceptual content hold that perception needs to have a similar content to beliefs in order to properly relate to them. Since belief is taken to have conceptual content, perception is taken to have this type of content too (Brewer 1999; Byrne 2005; Speaks 2005). The challenge for proponents of non-conceptual content – similar to the challenge that sense-data theory faced – is to account for the rational role of perception.

The popularity of intentionalism in the second half of the 20th century also prompted a reformulation of the debate on the objects of perception in terms of whether perception has rich or poor content.[10] This debate ceased to focus exclusively on ordinary objects. Contemporary philosophers are interested in what kind of properties perceptual content includes. In some conservative views, much like in sense-data theory, perception puts us in contact with the surface properties of objects – so-called 'low-level properties' (Clark 2000). Less conservative positions hold that perception has richer content, including, for example, causation and kind properties (Siegel 2006; 2010). One type of argument in favor of this less conservative view appeals to the effects that expertise has on perceptual experience – a topic on which we will return in section 2.2.

Representationalism aimed to avoid the problematic ontology of sense-data theory. The same is true of adverbialism.

1.3 Adverbialism

Adverbialism holds that when we perceive, we are in a certain kind of mental state of which we can be aware but this mental state does not possess the properties that it appears to us to have.

Consider, again, the example of my experience of a white wall. According to the adverbial theory, my experience involves no thing, either actual or non-actual, that is white. Rather, when I experience a white wall, I sense or perceive 'whitely'. Whitely sensing is just a type of visual sensing. To ask for the location of the white thing I am sensing betrays a false presupposition. Analogously, instead of talking about smiles, we can talk of manners of smiling (Jackson 1975, 128).

Adverbialism is an attempt to get rid of mysterious mental objects and properties by appeal to *manners* of perceiving. In so doing, adverbialism seems to deny altogether that perception is a relation. Perception emerges in this theory as a subjective act that can be done in different manners, rather than as a relation to an outside world. Thus, adverbialism seems to react to sense-data theory by denying something that most other theories accept: the relational status of perception. This feature of adverbialism can be seen as what is most problematic about it.

One of the main problems with adverbialism has come to be known as the 'many properties problem', which, as the name suggests, arises from the fact that experiences seem to be relations to objects that can have multiple properties (Jackson 1975). How do we understand, for example, having a red and round after-image in the adverbial theory? One may be inclined to suppose that we can understand it in terms of seeing redly and roundly. But things get complicated when we think of experiences that involve more than one object with different properties. How do we distinguish experiencing a red, round after-image and a green, square after-image from experiencing a red, square after-image and a green, round after-image? These experiences seem different, but they involve seeing redly, roundly, greenly and squarely in a way that makes them indistinguishable in the adverbial theory. Perhaps, there is a way to respond to these worries by appeal to different acts of seeing that are differently located in space (Sellars 1975). In general, however, the adverbial theory has been unable to survive this type of criticism.

Both representationalists and adverbialists wanted to distance themselves from sense-data theory. It is a further question whether representationalists are akin to sense-data theorists in the form of realism that they accept. As we saw earlier, sense-data theorists tend to be indirect realists. If, by contrast, contemporary intentionalists aspire to hold direct realism, they need to explain how perception can be a relation to intentional objects (and contents) while also putting us in unmediated contact with the world.

A concern with rescuing direct or naive realism is part of the motivation for an alternative view about perception called *disjunctivism* – a position that gained popularity in the second half of the 20th century.

1.4 Disjunctivism

Despite the contrast between sense-data theory and intentionalism, the two theories share an assumption that *disjunctivism* denies. This is the 'common factor' or 'common kind' principle. According to this principle, veridical perceptions, illusions and hallucinations are all states that belong to the same psychological kind. They are all forms of perceptual experience that differ only in accuracy. Disjunctivism denies this principle (Hinton 1973, 71; Martin 2003; McDowell 1987; Snowdon 1979).

According to disjunctivism, the objects of perception are mind-independent, ordinary entities. Illusions and hallucinations are possible, but they are not mental states of the same psychological kind as regular perceptions. One cannot move, as it is done in the argument from illusion, from a conclusion about illusory cases, to a conclusion about perception at large. In veridical perception we are directly acquainted with real entities.

Interestingly, disjunctivists do not deny that perception and hallucination have something in common. Each of these states is an experience that is subjectively indistinguishable from the other. What they have in common, however, is the mere fact that they are subjectively indistinguishable. An experience is *either* a genuine perception *or* a hallucination – hence the theory's name.

While hallucinations are experiences of some kind, perceptions are relational states that are partly *constituted* by their objects. When the objects are not present, perception does not occur. Thus, while the representationalist thinks of perception as essentially a relation to representations, the disjunctivist thinks of perception as being fundamentally a relation to objects (Campbell 2002).[11]

For this and other reasons, John McDowell has argued that disjunctivism is the only theory that explains how perceiving agents are in genuine contact with the world. Other theories, according to McDowell, are all too friendly to skepticism. M.G.F. Martin has similarly argued that disjunctivism is the only theory that accords with our common sense view of perception. Disjunctivism respects the common sense idea that perception is a type of 'openness to the world'.

In sum, if we conceive of perception as a relation, we can see the 20th century in philosophy as a struggle to defend realism and physicalism. Overall, indirect realism is more common in the first half of the century, while direct realism is preferred in the second half, with theories battling over which does a better job at rescuing direct realism. Physicalism is also a constant concern, especially in the second part of the century. In the next section, we consider perception as a type of unconscious process.

2. The perceptual process

The philosophy of perception in the last century has been shaped by cooperation with the developing field of psychology. Psychological theories have in turn been influenced by work in philosophy. The interplay between these and other disciplines eventually developed into what is now known as 'cognitive science'. Cognitive science is a collaboration of academic disciplines geared at understanding mental states and processes. It is controversial whether this is a unified field, but it includes psychology, philosophy, computer science, linguistics and neuroscience.

Cognitive scientists tend to be interested in perception as a process, and to focus on the problem of understanding how it is that we come to perceive the world as we do (Palmer 1999). Perception starts with the stimulation of sensory receptors by environmental elements – for example, by light hitting the retina or by sound waves affecting the ears' membranes. The question is how, from this sensory basis, we come to perceive distal objects and events.

The major psychological theories of perception in the 20th century that address this question are either reactions to, or continuations of what happened in the century before. The second half of the 1800 saw two important developments in the new field of perceptual psychology. First, Wilhelm Wundt proposed structuralism, a position inspired by the British Empiricists. Structuralism was later popularized in the United States by one of Wundt's students, Edward Titchener and, as we will see, it is the psychological counterpart of sense-data theory (Titchener 1902; Wundt 1874).

Second, Hermann von Helmholtz – a German physicist, mathematician and physiologist, who also supervised Wundt in Heidelberg in 1858 – proposed what was later called 'constructivism', a view that became prominent in the second half of the twentieth century and that remains popular today (Helmholtz 1867).

Gestalt psychology – which was particularly influential in the first half of the 1900s – and ecological optics – which gained momentum at mid-century – are reactions to structuralism and to constructivism respectively. The sections that follow outline these theories with an eye to how they influenced – and how they were influenced by – the philosophical theories discussed so far.

2.1 Structuralism and Gestalt psychology

A central thesis of structuralism is 'atomism', the idea that perception arises from a process in which simple, indivisible, and modality specific sensory atoms, not unlike sense-data, are combined. The process of combining was thought to be *associative*. The sensory atoms, or basic sensations, are associated or linked together as a result of prior exposure. In the case of vision, visual sensations of color in each region are concatenated to produce a perception of the color of a whole visual scene based on past encounters.

Because structuralism thought of the atoms of sensation as modality-specific, it had the problem of explaining how sensations from different modalities are integrated into a single percept. This problem will be later called 'the binding problem' and a section of contemporary cognitive science is dedicated to studying it (O'Callaghan 2014; Treisman 1996).

Structuralists thought that visual sensations trigger memories from other senses – for example, how a wall looks triggers memories of how it feels – allowing atoms specific to other senses to be added to the percept. Perception, in structuralism, occurs by a process of unconscious association that makes use of memory. Objects and scenes appear as they do because the perceptual system adds atomic appearances as in a mosaic.

Structuralists held this view together with a preference for the method of introspection. They claimed that, through trained introspection, one could discover the elementary units of perception. This aspect of structuralism was retained in Gestalt Psychology, which thought of consciousness as central to the study of the mind, but it was questioned by both behaviorism and by competing perceptual theories (James 1904; Skinner 1938; Gibson 1979). Later in the century, psychologists decidedly moved away from introspective methods and from the study of consciousness more generally. It was believed that perception could be understood in isolation from consciousness.

Although popular in the second half of the 1800s, the 20th century opened with a publication that put structuralism into question. In 1912, Max Wertheimer published an experiment on phi motion, or apparent motion that is considered the beginning of Gestalt Psychology. Wertheimer's study is taken to show that percepts cannot always be decomposed into basic sensory parts (Wagemans et al. 2012; Wertheimer 1912). Perceived movement, for example, does not depend on seeing an object in two positions – the starting and the end positions.

Motion is a structured whole or 'Gestalten' with its own ontological status and phenomenology.

Wertheimer extended this theory to the perception of shape and rhythm. His model was then developed by his colleagues in Berlin, Wolfang Köhler and Kurt Koffka (Koffka 1935; Köhler 1920). According to Gestalt theory, a perceptual scene has properties that the parts – even when considered together – do not have. Gestaltists were interested not in how the parts compose a whole, but rather in how the structure of a whole affects its subparts. They contrasted structural atomism, with holism.

This holistic thesis had an effect in philosophy, prompting some theorists to question whether appearances are simple and unadulterated in the way in which sense-data theory and structuralism thought they were (Hanson 1958). According to holism, no appearance is what it is independently of how it is situated in a whole. The way an item looks is affected by the way other items in the perceptual field look. Thus Gestalt psychology influenced views that questioned the *neutrality* of perception, a topic on which we will return in the next section (2.2).

Gestalt theorists took themselves to be discovering principles of perceptual organization that are not acquired through experience, or association, and that organize whole appearances.

Although Gestaltists were primarily concerned with rejecting the atomistic convictions of structuralism, they also held views about the physiology of perceiving. Köhler proposed two related ideas. One was that the brain was a dynamic, physical system that converged towards an equilibrium of minimum energy. This idea predates contemporary accounts of the brain based on dynamics and predictive coding (Clark 2013). A second proposal was that the causal mechanism underlying perception was given by a 'physical Gestalt' or an electromagnetic field generated by events in neurons.[12]

Some of these ideas were later shown to be problematic. The notion of a physical Gestalt, for example, was in trouble when it was found that disrupting electrical brain fields did not seriously affect perceptual abilities (Lashley et al. 1951).

These physiological findings may have contributed to Gestalt psychology losing its appeal in the second half of the 20th century. The development of computer science, of cognitive science and of neuroscience may also have offered better theoretical frameworks. Work on perceptual principles of organization and on the emergent structure of perceptual experience, however, continues to this day (Wagemans et al. 2012).

2.2 Constructivism

Another powerful idea that shaped work on perception in the 20th century is the constructivist view that perception involves a type of unconscious inference. Constructivists stress that sensory stimulation is inadequate in perception. In the case of vision, what is projected on the retina consists of light intensities that can be caused by a number of environmental elements. How do we get to see an object when all that is projected on the retina is light?

A similar problem is supposed to arise in the other modalities, but although this is true of audition, it is not clear that the same applies to the rest of the senses (Burge 2010).

In the case of seeing, the question of how we derive a rich view of objects from what is projected on the retina is answered in different ways. Structuralism points to associations based on past experience. Gestalt psychologists hypothesize a number of principles of organization, focusing mostly on how the principles regulate conscious appearances. Constructivism, not unlike Gestalt psychology, centers on some principles of organization and views them as part of an unconscious process that not only organizes, but also adds information to what is contained in sensory stimulation (Helmholtz 1867).[13]

According to constructivism, the perceptual process supplements the initial stimulation by performing a type of inference. In vision, the retinal 'image' is processed by using hidden 'assumptions' to reach perceptual 'conclusions' about the environment. A given discontinuity in light intensity, for example, may be taken to be an edge based on the assumption that discontinuities of a certain kind are typically edges in our world. The perceptual conclusions are 'guesses' as to what is the most likely cause of the stimulation. In this view, the world appears as it does because we construct it to appear as it does.

In constructivism, the internal states of perceptual processing that encode information about the world are typically called 'representations'. Representations are not themselves objects to the experiencing subject. Generally, in cognitive science, representations are subconscious states that carry information about the world, where carrying information is spelled out in different ways (Dretske 1981). The conscious subject is not aware of representations, and she has little or no control over them. A representation, in this context, is a theoretical notion introduced to do explanatory work. It is not clear how representations, understood in this way, relate to the intentional entities postulated by representationalism (see section 1.3.).

Because the inferential view conceives of perception as mediated by representational states, it also conceives of perception as *indirect*, a term reminiscent of indirect realism. The sense in which perception is indirect in the inferential framework, however, is different from the sense employed in sense-data theory (see section 1.1). According to the latter, sense-data are the immediate objects of awareness, and everything else is perceived *by* or *in virtue of* perceiving sense-data. This is not the case in inferential accounts of perception. Percepts are built out of sensory states that carry information, but the sensory states are not *perceived* or *given* to the individual. In this respect, constructivism also differs from structuralism, according to which the atoms of sensation are introspectively available.

Another important difference with both the sense-data tradition and the basic elements of structuralism is that sensory states in constructivism need not be modality specific. Although inferential views typically take vision to be their paradigm example, and some proponents think of the senses as distinct (Fodor 1983), some constructivists have been open to the idea that much of sensation and of perception are multimodal. This is true of recent Bayesian accounts to which I return later.[14]

Interestingly, and despite the dissimilarities between indirect realism and constructivism, some of the considerations that are sometimes brought up in support of the inferential idea are parallel to some of the considerations introduced to suppose that our perceptual access to ordinary objects is mediated. The ability to explain illusion and misperception, for example, is mentioned as one advantage of constructivism in a way that is reminiscent of the argument from illusion (Fodor and Pylyshyn 1981; McClamrock 1995).

Because of its use of the notion of representation, constructivism has a Kantian flavor and, although introduced by Helmholtz in the 19th century, it gained popularity only in the second half of the 20th century (Gregory 1970; Hochberg 1964; Rock 1983). This was partly due to two important, and related, developments. One was the introduction of computers as models and simulators of mental processes (Newell and Simon 1963; Turing 1950). The other was the idea that the brain is an information processing system (Broadbent 1958; Neisser 1967; von Neumann 1951). Both developments shaped the progress of perceptual science and have been influential in philosophy of mind.

Constructivism weds well with a computational and information-processing model of mental activity because computations are traditionally understood as operations on symbols in virtue of rules or algorithms (Fodor 1975; Ullman 1980). If we recognize symbols as information-carrying structures, and algorithms as containing assumptions and rules to process the symbols, then viewing the perceptual process as computational pretty much amounts to viewing it the way the constructivist does – as an inference from some informational states to others.

Partly because of its fit with computer science, constructivism has been widely accepted in philosophy since the 1950s (Marr 1982; Rock 1983; 1997; Ullman 1980; Palmer 1999; Pylyshyn 1984; Fodor 1984; Churchland 1988). Philosophers who do not agree on much else – for example, Jerry Fodor and Paul Churchland – tend to accept it. Derivatively, the notions of representation, computation and information have received extensive scrutiny in philosophy.[15]

The most current version of constructivism is the Bayesian model of perception (Brainard 2009; Clark 2013; Maloney and Mamassian 2009; Mamassian et al. 2002; Rescorla forthcoming). According to such model, the visual system performs inductive inferences on some hypotheses about the environment. These hypotheses are initially selected based on prior experience. The hypotheses are tested in real time given sensory stimulation and either confirmed or changed.

Like Gestalt psychology, constructivism prompted reflection on the neutrality of perceptual appearances. According to constructivism, what we perceive depends on unconscious inferences that employ assumptions about the world. If the assumptions change – through, for example, the acquisition of new knowledge – then it seems that what we perceive should correspondingly change.

Following these developments in psychology, a number of philosophers of science from the middle of the 20th century started questioning the status of observation in scientific theories (Hanson 1958; Kuhn 1962). The idea was that, contrary to common belief, observation is *theory-laden* and scientists working in different paradigms literally perceive different worlds. The opposing view is that observation is *theory-neutral* and it can serve as an impartial tribunal to adjudicate clashes of opinion.

In philosophy of mind, this disagreement later generated two versions of constructivism. Reacting to the idea that observation is theory-laden, Jerry Fodor published an influential work that denied that perceptual inferences are affected by other mental states (Fodor 1983; 1984). Fodor proposed *modularity*. The modular thesis includes a number of claims, but one of the central claims is that perceiving is importantly isolated from thinking and believing. Perceptual processes are largely immune to influence from outside of perception, such that what we perceive is pretty constant through time and across world-views.

Deniers of modularity claim that perception is 'cognitively penetrable' (Churchland 1988). Perception is influenced by background knowledge and expertise such that the same subject may perceive the world differently at different times as a function of a change in beliefs. Along similar lines, different subjects may perceive the world differently as a function of their differing theoretical convictions.

Work on cognitive penetrability and on the modularity of perception is ongoing with philosophers interested in understanding the epistemic consequences of thinking of perception as cognitively penetrable (Raftopoulos 2009; Siegel 2012).

Despite the popularity of constructivism in the second half of the 20th century and the beginning of the 21st century, an alternative position – reminiscent of work in the continental tradition in philosophy – emerged and is now popular in embedded and embodied approaches to mental activity. This is the ecological view of perception that I briefly discuss in the next subsection.

2.3 Ecological perception

The major alternative position to constructivism rejects the computation- and representation-heavy approach to perception in favor of a more 'ecological' way of understanding the perceptual process. In explaining why we see the world as we do, the ecological view says that we should focus on the way the world is.

The main precursor of this type of position in psychology is J. J. Gibson (Gibson 1950; 1966; 1979). Initially influenced by Gestalt Psychology, Gibson's work is primarily a reaction to Helmholtz's ideas. Gibson stressed two elements of the perceptual act. First, that perception happens over time, and in a moving and exploring, body. Second, that the information available in the natural environment and in sensation is rich and not inadequate as supposed by constructivism.

In vision, the information is present in what Gibson calls the 'ambient optic array' which is available to, and picked up by, our eyes. The ambient optic array contains a number of invariants that allow the perceptual system to figure out the distal layout. Slanted surfaces of various kinds, for example, project images on the retina that have characteristic texture gradients (Gibson 1950). Perceivers can use such gradients to see the slant and depth of surfaces in the world.

The richness of environmental stimuli and the embodiment and time extension of perception help Gibson understand how perceiving subjects deal with sensory data without invoking internal inferential and representational structures. Such structures are needed, according to Gibson, only if we conceive of perception as a static process, where the visual system needs to continuously store and add information to an impoverished stimulus. By contrast, Gibson thinks that the perceptual act is an active engagement with the world.

Proponents of this kind of position tend to liken perceiving to the type of engagement present in the tactual modality (Noë 2004). Learning the shape of something by touch requires continuously exploring the object as opposed to trying to form a model of the shape based on a single encounter. Accordingly, perceiving requires the *direct* 'pick-up' of information in a rich biological context in which perceivers can move and explore.

Gibson admitted that the brain needs to somehow attune, and respond to the environment it encounters. But he tried to explain this attunement by using a resonance metaphor. The information in the stimulus simply causes the appropriate neural structures in the brain to fire and resonate (Gibson 1966; 1979).

The metaphor of resonance – which was perhaps influenced by the work of Köhler – remained underdescribed in Gibson, and it was later at the center of criticism. David Marr, for example, while accepting many Gibsonian insights, remarked that ignoring the details of how the brain attunes to the world amounts to oversimplifying the perceptual task (Marr 1982). Marr and other constructivists can be read as trying to supplement what Gibson left unexplained: the internal computational basis of perception.

More recent developments in computer science, such as connectionism, may supplement what Gibson and Köhler had in mind without committing to constructivism (Churchland 1990; Feldman 1981; Grossberg 1982; McClelland and Rumelhart 1986; Rosenblatt 1962). Connectionist networks are nets of connected units that spread information, and attune to the world, by spreading levels of activation – simulating a biological brain. It is open to debate whether such networks make use of representations and perform inferential operations (Ramsey et al. 1991).

Gibson's work inspired a number of philosophers and psychologists in the second half of the 20th century and his influence continues today. His ideas have been borrowed in various ways in the literature on so-called 'embodied and embedded cognition' in philosophy and in psychology. This literature puts into question the need to appeal to representations in the study of mental processes (Clark 1997; Geisler 2008; Hurley 2002; O'Regan and Noë 2001; Orlandi 2014; Wilson 2004).

Although contemporary philosophers of perception often refer back to Gibson, it should be noted that the stress on understanding perceptual processes as embodied and ecologically situated is present in the continental tradition in the first half of the twentieth century – in particular, in Maurice Merleau-Ponty (Merleau-Ponty 1945). According to Merleau-Ponty, there is a type of 'readiness' on the part of the subject in perception that makes an object available for discovery. Rather than postulating internal states that represent information, Merleau-Ponty thought that such representations are *implicit* in the subject's own dispositions to move.

In sum, when considering perception as a process, the 20th century saw the emergence of three theories of perception. Gestalt psychology was prominent in the first half of the century, while constructivism dominated the second half, with ecological approaches serving as a plausible competitor. The century also saw the emergence of intense cooperation between philosophy and disciplines such as psychology, computer science and linguistics.

Conclusion

In this chapter, I traced the history of theories of perception in the 20th century by considering perception under two guises. If we focus on perception as a relation, then I suggested that the 20th century has been preoccupied with defending realism and physicalism.

If we regard perception as a process, then the century was dominated by interaction between philosophy and the emerging cognitive sciences. The first half of the century saw the rise of Gestalt Psychology, while the second half saw the emergence of two views, one centering on internal procedures, and one focusing on environmental interactions.

Notes

1. For help and advice with this chapter, I thank Tim Crane, JJ Dinishak, Jon Ellis, Dan Guevara, Rasmus Grønfeldt Winther, Amy Kind and Samantha Matherne, whose knowledge of history helped a great deal.
2. Although widely used, the term 'physical' is hardly ever spelled out in philosophy of mind. Some contrast 'physical' with 'mental' (which seems unfortunate since the mental would then be non-physical by definition). Often 'physical' is synonymous with 'mind-independent', 'material', 'non-spiritual' and occasionally with 'causally efficacious'. Physicalism was initially a doctrine about the language of science (see Crane, this volume).
3. Thanks to Samantha Matherne for this reference.
4. Martin (2003) notes that the concept of sense-data had already been used in the late 19th century, in the United States by Royce and James.
5. For the argument from illusion, see Ayer (1963: pp. 3–11), and Hume (1748). For perspectival variation and time lag of the kind that occurs when we perceive no longer existing stars, see Russell (1912).
6. Martin (2003) points out that whether this charge against sense-data theory is on point can be questioned. Martin argues that both Broad and Price were aware of the intentionality of perception.
7. G. E. Moore (1903) is an early precursor of transparency. Thanks to Amy Kind for this pointer. For deniers of transparency in some of its formulations, see Block (2000) and Kind (2003).
8. I think that this type of problematic for sense-data theory is raised in Sellars 1956 and it is also a point pressed by Wittgenstein 1953.

9 Paul Crowther (2006) rightly points out that this is only one conception of non-conceptual content in the literature. Indeed, Crowther and Richard Heck disagree on whether this dispute is consistently about a single notion (Heck 2007). For more on this dispute see Evans (1982), Peacocke (1983), Heck (2000), Roskies (2008), McDowell (1994).
10 See Burge 1979 for the idea of mental states having content. See Siegal (2010) for the idea that perception has content.
11 To be fair, representationalists also think of perception as directed at objects. Representations are, by definition, states that stand for something else. But, as I mentioned, representationalists face the challenge of explaining how perception can be a relation to intentional contents while also being a direct acquaintance with objects.
12 A central Gestaltist thesis was also 'psychophysical isomorphism' according to which perceptual experiences are structurally isomorphic to physiological, brain events (Wertheimer 1912; Köhler 1920/1950 and 1947).
13 For a comparison between some of the principles of organization of Gestalt psychology and those of constructivism, see Pomerantz and Kubovy (1986).
14 This is also true of the major competitor of constructivism, the ecological approach that I discuss in section 2.3.
15 The list of references includes Dretske 1981; Fodor 1975; 1983; Haugeland 1991; Millikan 1984; Piccinini 2008.

Bibliography

Anscombe, G.E.M. (1965). "The Intentionality of Sensation: A Grammatical Feature," in Butler, R. J. (ed.) *Analytical Philosophy: First Series.* Oxford: Blackwell: 143–158. [Reprinted in her *Metaphysics and the Philosophy of Mind: Collected Papers, Vol. II.* Oxford: Blackwell; also in Noë and Thompson (eds.) 2002.]

Armstrong, D. (1961). *Perception and the Physical World.* London: Routledge & Kegan Paul.

Austin, J. L. (1946). "Other Minds," *Proceedings of the Aristotelian Society,* Supplementary Volume 20: 148–187.

Austin, J.L. (1962). *Sense and Sensibilia,* reconstructed from the manuscript notes by Warnock, G. J., Oxford: Oxford University Press.

Ayer, A. J. (1956). *The Problem of Knowledge.* London: Macmillan.

Ayer, A. J. (1963). The *Foundations of Empirical Knowledge.* London, MacMillan. *SML edition*: 183–199.

Bermúdez, José Luis (2000). "Naturalized Sense Data," *Philosophy and Phenomenological Research,* 61: 353–374.

Bermudez, J., and Cahen, A. (2012). "Nonconceptual Mental Content," *The Stanford Encyclopedia of Philosophy,* (Spring 2012 edition), Zalta, Edward N. (ed.). http://plato.stanford.edu/archives/spr2012/entries/content-nonconceptual/.

Block, N. (2000). "Mental Paint," in Hahn, M. and Ramberg, B. (eds.), *Essays in Honor of Tyler Burge.* Cambridge, MA: MIT Press.

Bradley, F. H. (1899). *Appearance and Reality: A Metaphysical Essay.* London: Palgrave Macmillan.

Brainard, D. H. (2009). "Bayesian Approaches to Color Vision," *The Visual Neurosciences,* 4. http://color.psych.upenn.edu/brainard/papers/BayesColorReview.pdf.

Brentano, F. (1874). *Psychology from an Empirical Standpoint.* Abingdon, UK: Routledge, Taylor and Francis, 2009.

Brewer, B. (1999). *Perception and Reason.* Oxford: Oxford University Press.

Broad, C. D. (1914). *Perception, Physics, and Reality: An Enquiry into the Information That Physical Science Can Supply about the Real.* Cambridge: Cambridge University Press.

Broadbent, D. E. (1958). *Perception and Communication.* New York: Pergamon Press.

Burge, T. (1979). "Individualism and the Mental," in Rosenthal, David M. (ed.), *The Nature of Mind.* New York: Oxford University Press: 536–567.

Burge, T. (2005). "Disjunctivism and Perceptual Psychology," *Philosophical Topics,* 33(1): 1–78.

Burge, T. (2009). "Perceptual Objectivity," *Philosophical Review,* 118(3): 285–324.

Burge, T. (2010). *Origins of Objectivity,* Vol. 10. Oxford: Oxford University Press.

Byrne, A. (2001). "Intentionalism Defended," *Philosophical Review,* 110: 199–239.

Byrne, A. (2005). "Perception and Conceptual Content," in Sosa, E. and Steup, M. (eds.), *Contemporary Debates in Epistemology,* Oxford: Blackwell.

Campbell, J. (2002). *Reference and Consciousness.* Oxford: Oxford University Press.

Chisholm, Roderick (1957). *Perceiving.* Ithaca, NY: Cornell University Press.

Churchland, P. (1988). "Perceptual Plasticity and Theoretical Neutrality: A Reply to Jerry Fodor," *Philosophy of Science,* 55: 167–187.

Churchland, P. (1990). "Cognitive Activity in Artificial Neural Networks," in Osherson, D. and Smith, E. (eds.), *Thinking: An Invitation to Cognitive Science.* Cambridge, MA: MIT Press: 372–381.

Clark, Andy (1997). *Being There: Putting Brain, Body, and World Together Again.* Cambridge, MA: MIT Press.

Clark, Andy (2013). "Whatever Next? Predictive Brains, Situated Agents, and the Future of Cognitive Science," *Behavioral and Brain Science*: 1–86.

Clark, Austin (2000). *A Theory of Sentience,* Oxford: Oxford University Press.

Condillac, E. (1947). *Traite des sensations, Oeuvres Philosophiques de Condillac,* Volume 1. Paris: Presses Universitaires de France: 219–314.

Crane, T. (2000). The Origins of Qualia. http://sas-space.sas.ac.uk/220/1/The%20origins%20of%20qualia.pdf.

Crane, T. (2003). "The Intentional Structure of Consciousness," in Smith and Jokic (eds.), *Consciousness: New Philosophical Perspectives.* Oxford and New York: Oxford University Press.

Crowther, T. M. (2006). "Two Conceptions of Conceptualism and Nonconceptualism," *Erkenntnis,* 65(2): 245–276.

Dretske, F. (1969). *Seeing and Knowing.* Chicago: University of Chicago Press.

Dretske, F. (1981). *Knowledge and the Flow of Information.* Cambridge MA: MIT Press.

Dretske, F. (1995). *Naturalizing the Mind.* Cambridge, MA: Bradford Books/MIT Press.

Ducasse, C.J. (1942). "Moore's Refutation of Idealism," in Schilpp, Paul Arthur (ed.), *The Philosophy of G. E. Moore.* La Salle, IL: Open Court, 232–233.

Evans, G. (1982). *The Varieties of Reference.* Oxford: Oxford University Press.

Feldman, J.A. (1981). "A Connectionist Model of Visual Memory," in Hinton, G. E. and Anderson, J. A. (eds.), *Parallel Models of Associative Memory.* Hillsdale, NJ: Erlbaum: 49–81.

Fodor, J.A. (1975). *The Language of Thought.* Cambridge, MA: Harvard University Press.

Fodor, Jerry A. (1983). *The Modularity of Mind: An Essay on Faculty Psychology.* Cambridge, MA: MIT Press.

Fodor, J. A. (1984/1990). "Observation Reconsidered," *Philosophy of Science,* 51: 23–43. Reprinted in Fodor (1990): 231–251.

Fodor, J. A., and Pylyshyn, Zenon W. (1981). "How Direct Is Visual Perception?: Some Reflections on Gibson's 'Ecological Approach'," *Cognition*, 9(2): 139–196.

Geisler, W. S. (2008). "Visual Perception and the Statistical Properties of Natural Scenes." *Annual Review of Psychology*, 59, 167–192.

Gibson, J. J. (1950). *The Perception of the Visual World*. Boston: Houghton Mifflin.

Gibson, J. J. (1966). *The Senses Considered as Perceptual Systems*. Boston: Houghton Mifflin.

Gibson, J. J. (1979). *The Ecological Approach to Visual Perception*. Boston: Houghton Mifflin.

Gregory, R. L. (1970). *The Intelligent Eye*. New York: McGraw-Hill.

Grossberg, S. (1982). "Studies of Mind and Brain." *Reidel, Boston*: 5–213.

Hanson, N. R. (1958). *Patterns of Discovery*. Cambridge: Cambridge University Press.

Harman, G. (1990). "The Intrinsic Quality of Experience," in Tomberlin, J. (ed.), *Philosophical Perspectives*. Atascadero: Ridgeview: 31–52, 4, reprinted in Block, Ned, Flanagan, Owen and Guzeldere, Guven (eds.). (1997). *The Nature of Consciousness*. Cambridge, MA: MIT Press: 663–676.

Haugeland, J. (1991). "Representational Genera," *Philosophy and Connectionist Theory*: 61.

Heck, R. G. (2000). "Nonconceptual Content and the Space of Reasons," *Philosophical Review*, 109: 483–523.

Heck, R. G. (2007). "Are there Different Kinds of Content?" In Cohen, J. and McLaughlin, B. (eds.), *Contemporary Debates in the Philosophy of Mind*, Oxford: Blackwell.

Helmholtz von, H, (1867/1925). *Treatise on Psychological Optics* (from 3rd German edition, Trans.) New York: Dover Publications.

Hinton, J. M. (1973). *Experiences*. Oxford: Clarendon Press.

Hochberg, J. (1964). *Perception*. Englewood Cliffs, NJ: Prentice-Hall.

Huemer, Michael (2011). "Sense-data," *The Stanford Encyclopedia of Philosophy* (Spring 2011 Edition), in Zalta, Edward N. (ed.). http://plato.stanford.edu/archives/spr2011/entries/sense-data/.

Hume, David (1748). "Enquiry Concerning HUMAN Understanding," in Selby-Bigge, L. A. (ed.), *Enquiries Concerning Human Understanding and Concerning the Principles of Morals*, 3rd edition revised by P. H. Nidditch, Oxford: Clarendon Press, 1975.

Hurley, S. L. (2002). *Consciousness in Action*. Cambridge, MA: Harvard University Press.

Husserl, E. (1900/1) [2nd, revised edition 1913], *Logical Investigations*. Trans. J. N. Findlay. London: Routledge, 1973.

Husserl, E. (1913). *Ideas Pertaining to a Pure Phenomenology and to a Phenomenological Philosophy – First Book: General Introduction to a Pure Phenomenology*, Trans. F. Kersten. The Hague: Martinus Nijhoff, 1982.

Jackson, F. (1975). "On the Adverbial Analysis of Visual Experience," *Metaphilosophy*, 6: 127–135.

Jackson, F. (1977). *Perception: A Representative Theory*. Cambridge: Cambridge University Press.

James, William (1904). "Does Consciousness Exist?" *Journal of Philosophy, Psychology and Scientific Method*, 1: 477–491.

Kind, A. (2003). "What's so Transparent about Transparency?" *Philosophical Studies*, 115(3): 225–244.

Koffka, K. (1935). *Principles of Gestalt Psychology*. New York: Harcourt, Brace.

Köhler, W. (1920/1950). "Physical Gestalten," in Ellis, W. D. (ed.), *A Sourcebook of Gestalt Psychology*. New York: the Humanities Press: 17–54.

Köhler, W. (1947). *Gestalt Psychology: An Introduction to New Concepts in Modern Psychology*. New York: Liveright.

Kuhn, T. (1962). *The Structure of Scientific Revolutions*. Chicago: University of Chicago Press (1970), 2nd edition, with postscript.

Lashley, K. S., Chow, K. L., and Semmes, J. (1951). "An Examination of the Electrical Field Theory of Cerebral Integration," *Psychological Review*, 58(2): 123.

Lewis, C. I. (1929). *Mind and the World Order: Outline of a Theory of Knowledge*. Dover reprint, 1956.

Lycan, W. G. (1987). *Consciousness*. Cambridge, MA: Bradford Books/MIT Press.

Lycan, W. G. (1996). *Consciousness and Experience*. Cambridge, MA: MIT Press.

McClamrock, R. (1995). *Existential Cognition: Computational Minds in the World*. Chicago: University of Chicago Press.

McClelland, J. L., Rumelhart, D. E., and PDP Research Group (1986). "Parallel Distributed Processing," *Explorations in the Microstructure of Cognition*, 2: 216–271.

McDowell, J. (1987). "Singular Thought and the Extent of Inner Space." In John McDowell & Philip Pettit (eds.), *Subject, Thought, and Context*. Oxford: Clarendon Press.

McDowell, J. (1994). *Mind and World*. Cambridge, MA: Harvard University Press.

Machery, E. (2009). *Doing Without Concepts*. Oxford: Oxford University Press.

Maloney, L. T., and Mamassian, P. (2009). "Bayesian Decision Theory as a Model of Human Visual Perception: Testing Bayesian Transfer," *Visual Neuroscience*, 26(1): 147–155.

Mamassian, P., Landy, M. S., Maloney, L. T., Rao, R., Olshausen, B., and Lewicki, M. (2002). "Bayesian Modelling of Visual Perception." *Probabilistic Models of the Brain: Perception and Neural Function*. Boston: MIT Press, 13–36.

Marr, D. (1982). *Vision: A Computational Investigation into the Human Representation and Processing of Visual Information*. New York, NY: Henry Holt and Co. Inc.

Martin, M. (2003). "Sensible Appearances," in *Cambridge History of 20th Century Philosophy*, edited by Thomas Baldwin.

Merleau-Ponty, M. (1945). *The Phenomenology of Perception*. Trans. Colin Smith, London: Rooutledge 2002.

Millikan, R. G. (1984). *Language, Thought, and Other Biological Categories: New Foundations for Realism*. Cambridge, MA: MIT Press.

Moore, G. E. (1903). "The Refutation of Idealism." *Mind*: 433–453.

Moore, G. E. (1910/2014). *Some Main Problems in Philosophy*. Abingdon, UK: Routledge.

Moore, G. E. (1925). "A Defence of Common Sense," in Muirhead, J. H. (ed.), *Contemporary British Philosophy* (2nd series), London: Allen and Unwin: 193–223. Reprinted in *Philosophical Papers* and in *G. E. Moore: Selected Writings*: 106–133.

Moore, G. E. (1953). *Some Main Problems of Philosophy*. London: George, Allen and Unwin.

Neisser, U. (1967). *Cognitive Psychology*. Englewood Cliffs, NJ: Prentice Hall.

Newell, A., and Simon, Herbert A. (1963). "GPS, a Program that Simulates Human Thought," in Feigenbaum, E. A. and Feldman, J. (eds.), *Computers and Thought*. New York: McGraw-Hill.

Noë, Alva (2004). *Action in Perception*. Cambridge, MA: MIT Press.

O'Callaghan, C. (2007). *Sounds: A Philosophical Theory*. Oxford: Oxford University Press.

O'Callaghan, C. (2014). "Intermodal Binding Awareness," in Bennett, David and Hill, Christopher (eds.), *Sensory Integration and the Unity of Consciousness*. Cambridge, MA: MIT Press.

O'Regan, J. K. and Noë, Alva (2001). "A Sensorimotor Account of Vision and Visual Consciousness," *Behavioral and Brain Sciences* 24(05): 939–973.

Orlandi, N. (2014). *The Innocent Eye: Why Vision is Not a Cognitive Process*. Oxford: Oxford University Press.

O'Shaughnessy, B. (2003). "Sense Data," in Smith, Barry (ed.), *John Searle*. Cambridge: Cambridge University Press: 169–188.

Palmer, S. E. (1999). *Vision Science: Photons to Phenomenology*, Volume 1. Cambridge, MA: MIT Press.

Peacocke, C. (1983). *Sense and Content*. Oxford: Oxford University Press.

Peirce, C. S. (1931). Collected Papers of Charles Sanders Peirce: Vols. 1–6 (C. Hartshorne & P. Weiss, eds.).

Piccinini, G. (2008). "Computation Without Representation," *Philosophical Studies*, 137(2): 205–241.

Pomerantz, J. R., and Kubovy, Michael (1986). "Theoretical Approaches to Perceptual Organization: Simplicity and Likelihood Principles," *Organization*, 36: 3.

Price, H. H. (1932). *Perception*. London: Methuen & Co.

Prichard, H. A. (1906). "Appearances and Reality I," *Mind*, 15(58): 223–229, April.

Pylyshyn, Z. (1984). *Computation and Cognition*. Cambridge: Cambridge University Press.

Raftopoulos, A. (2009). *Cognition and Perception: How Do Psychology and Neural Science Inform Philosophy?* Cambridge, MA: MIT Press.

Ramsey, W., Stich, S., and Garon, J. (1991). "Connectionism, Eliminativism, and the Future of Folk Psychology," in *Philosophy and Connectionist Theory*. Hillsdale, NJ: Lawrence Erlbaum: 199–228.

Rescorla, M. (forthcoming). "Bayesian Perceptual Psychology," *The Oxford Handbook of the Philosophy of Perception*. Oxford University Press.

Reid, T. (1764). *An Inquiry into the Human Mind on the Principles of Common Sense*, Brookes, Derek R. (ed.), University Park: Pennsylvania State University Press, 1997.

Rock, I. (1983). *The Logic of Perception*. Cambridge, MA: MIT Press.

Rock, I. (1997). *Indirect Perception*. Cambridge, MA: MIT Press.

Rosenblatt, F. (1962). *Principles of Neurodynamics: Perceptrons and the Theory of Brain Mechanisms*. Washington, DC: Spartan Books.

Roskies, A. L. (2008). "A New Argument for Nonconceptual Content," *Philosophy and Phenomenological Research*, 76: 633–659.

Russell, B. (1912). *The Problems of Philosophy*. London: Home University Library.

Russell, B (1914). *Our Knowledge of the External World as a Field for Scientific Method in philosophy*. Chicago and London: Open Court Publishing.

Searle, J. (1983). *Intentionality: An Essay in the Philosophy of Mind*. Cambridge: Cambridge University Press.

Sellars, W. (1956). "Empiricism and the Philosophy of Mind," *Minnesota Studies in the Philosophy of Science*, 1(19): 253–329.

Sellars, W. (1975). "The Adverbial Theory of the Objects of Sensation," *Metaphilosophy*, 6(2): 144–160.

Shoemaker, S. (1994). "Phenomenal Character," *Noûs*, 28: 21–38.

Siegel, S. (2006). "Which Properties are Represented in Perception?" in Szabo, T. Gendler and Hawthorne, J. (eds.), *In Perceptual Experience*. Oxford: Oxford University Press: 481–503.

Siegel, S. (2010). *The Contents of Visual Experience*. New York: Oxford University Press.
Siegel, S. (2012). "Cognitive Penetrability and Perceptual Justification," *Nous*, 46(2): 201–222.
Skinner, B. F. (1938). *The Behavior of Organisms: An Experimental Analysis*. Century Psychology Series, edited by Richard M. Elliott. New York: Appleton-Century- Crofts.
Smart, J.J.C. (1959). "Sensations and Brain Processes," *Philosophical Review*, 68: 141–156.
Smith, A. D. (2002). *The Problem of Perception*. Cambridge, MA: Harvard University Press.
Snowdon, P. F. (1979). "Perception, Vision and Causation," *Proceedings of the Aristotelian Society* 81: 175–192.
Speaks, J. (2005). "Is There a Problem about Nonconceptual Content?" *The Philosophical Review*: 359–398.
Strawson, P. F. (1958). *Individuals*. London: Methuen.
Titchener, E. B. (1902). *Experimental Psychology: A Manual of Laboratory Practice*. (Vol. 1) New York, NY: Palgrave MacMillan.
Travis, C. (2004). "The Silence of the Senses," *Mind*, 113(449): 57–94.
Treisman, A. (1996). "The Binding Problem," *Current Opinion in Neurobiology*, 6(2):171–178.
Turing, Alan M. (1950). "Computing Machinery and Intelligence," *Mind*: 433–460.
Tye, M. (1992). "Visual Qualia and Visual Content," in Crane (ed.): 158–716.
Tye, M. (1994). "Qualia, Content, and the Inverted Spectrum," *Noûs*, 28: 159–183.
Tye, M. (2013). "Qualia", *The Stanford Encyclopedia of Philosophy* (Fall 2013 Edition), Zalta, Edward N. (ed.). http://plato.stanford.edu/archives/fall2013/entries/qualia/.
Ullman, S. (1980). *Against Direct Perception*. Cambridge: Cambridge University Press.
Von Neumann, J. (1951). "The General and Logical Theory of Automata," *Cerebral Mechanisms in Behavior*: 1–41.
Wagemans, J., Elder, J. H., Kubovy, M., Palmer, S. E., Peterson, M. A., Singh, M., & von der Heydt, R. (2012). "A Century of Gestalt Psychology in Visual Perception: I. Perceptual Grouping and Figure – Ground Organization," *Psychological Bulletin*, 138(6): 1172.
Wertheimer, M. (1912). "Über das Sehen von Scheinbewegungen und Scheinkorporen," *Zeitschrift für Psychologie*, 61: 463–465.
Wilson, R. A. (2004). *Boundaries of the Mind: The Individual in the Fragile Sciences*. Cognition. Cambridge: Cambridge University Press.
Wittgenstein, L. (1953). *Philosophical Investigations*. Trans. G.E.M. Anscombe, Oxford: Blackwell, 3rd edition, 1967.
Wundt, W. (1874). *Grundzüge der physiologischen Psychologie (Principles of Physiological Psychology)*, Leipzig: Engelmann.

5
20TH-CENTURY THEORIES OF PERSONAL IDENTITY

Jens Johansson

1. Introduction

Three questions have dominated 20th- and early 21st-century thinking about personal identity:

(a) What does it take for us to persist? More precisely, by virtue of what is someone existing at a certain time numerically identical to a certain individual existing at an earlier or later time? Tomorrow I am going to be in the dentist's chair; what makes it the case that that patient is *me* rather than someone else? Is it because he stands in some mental relation to me, or because he has my soul, or because he has my body, or because some other relation holds between him and me?

(b) What matters in survival? Each person seems to have a reason to care about his own future in a special way. For instance, I am bound to feel intense pain during tomorrow's visit to the dentist. Like everyone else, perhaps, I have a reason to dislike these future experiences; but unlike everyone else, I also seem to have a reason to have *prudential* concern about it – to anticipate the experiences "from the inside" with unease and fear. Is this *because* these experiences are experiences of mine – that is, is it because I am numerically identical with the future experiencer – or is it because of something else? Or do I not have such a reason after all?

(c) What are we? This question concerns what kind of thing a human person is. The dentist is going to find a human organism in her chair tomorrow. Am I identical to this organism? If not, how am I related to it: am I a part of it (e.g. a brain), or is it a part of me, or am I a soul associated with it, or am I "constituted" by it (so that we are composed of the same particles without being identical), or are we related in some other way?

Our primary focus in this chapter will be on one particular answer to question (a): personal identity over time holds by virtue of *psychological continuity* (e.g. Lewis 1976; Noonan 2003; Nozick 1981; Parfit 1971, 1984; Perry 1972; Shoemaker 1970; 1984; Unger 1990). This focus is motivated in part by the fact that the psychological-continuity view is the single most discussed theory of personal identity during the past century, and in part by the fact that exploration of the historical development of this view will naturally lead us to some of the most significant aspects of the debates on questions (b) and (c) as well.[1]

2. The psychological-continuity view

20th- and 21st-century versions of the psychological-continuity view can be regarded as refinements of a theory sometimes ascribed to John Locke: personal identity over time obtains by virtue of direct memory links (Locke [1690] 1975). More precisely, someone existing at time t is identical to someone existing at a later time t^* if and only if the latter individual can at t^* remember something the former person experienced at t.

While this account has the virtue of simplicity, it also has the vice of incoherence (Reid [1785] 2003, 52). Suppose that, thirty years from now, A remembers some of my present experiences, and I now remember some of the experiences B had thirty years ago, but A cannot, thirty years from now, remember any of the experiences B had thirty years before now. The present view then entails that, although I am A and I am B, A is not B. But this is out of the question, for two numerically distinct things cannot be identical to one and the same thing.

Philosophers were largely silent on personal identity during the first decades of the 20th century, but in 1941 H. P. Grice proposed a modified and highly sophisticated version of the Lockean view, a version that avoids the above objection (Grice 1941). Grice's complete account is too complex to summarize here, but one of its most crucial components is its appeal to indirect memory links. Personal identity is preserved just in case there is *continuity* of memory: a *chain* of direct memory connections. Because, in our example, A remembers experiences that I have at a time at which I remember B's experiences, Grice's view yields that A is identical with B (and I am A and I am B).

Bishop Butler ([1736] 1975, 100) had accused Locke's theory of being viciously circular: personal identity over time cannot be understood in terms of memory, for memory conceptually presupposes personal identity over time; we simply do not count someone as remembering an earlier experience unless he himself did have the experience. Appealing to indirect memory connections is of no help in answering this objection. However, something that does seem to help is the notion of *quasi-memory* (Shoemaker 1970). Quasi-memory is just like memory except that it does not conceptually presuppose (although it allows) identity between the quasi-rememberer of an experience and the individual who had the experience. Just as my remembering a certain experience conceptually entails that the experience actually occurred, and caused my memory, so my quasi-remembering a certain experience conceptually entails that the experience actually occurred, and caused my quasi-memory; by contrast, whereas my remembering a certain experience conceptually entails that *I* had the experience, my quasi-remembering a certain experience does *not* conceptually entail that I had it. There is thus no circularity in saying that personal identity over time should be understood in terms of (continuity of) quasi-memory.

As suggested by the above, for a long time memory-involving relations outshined other psychological relations on the personal identity scene. This focus can perhaps be partly explained by the fact that the debate long involved a somewhat confusing mixture of metaphysical and epistemological considerations: participants often did not distinguish clearly between the question of what personal identity over time holds in virtue of and the question of what constitutes *evidence* for personal identity over time. (This conflation is facilitated by the frequent use of the term "criterion of personal identity," which has both a metaphysical and epistemological reading.) Memory, or quasi-memory, seems particularly relevant to the latter, epistemological question: having what appears to be a quasi-memory of an earlier experience normally provides me with an excellent reason to believe that I myself did have that experience. For quasi-memory gives us a special kind of access to – a sort of "inside information" of – our own past experiences that we lack to the past experiences of others (that is, we do so *in fact*, though not as a matter of conceptual necessity). Another partial explanation of the focus on memory relations might be that an object's persistence through time is, plausibly, to a large extent a matter of its states at any one time being caused by its states at earlier times. The appeal to memory is obviously congenial to this idea, for as just noted, nothing is a memory (or even a quasi-memory) of an experience unless it is caused by that experience. Many other ordinary mental relations, such as "x believes the same things as y" and "x has the same character traits as y," lack such a causal requirement.

Of course, however, we can still appeal to nearby notions that do involve such a requirement: for instance, "x's beliefs are direct effects of y's beliefs" and "x's character traits are direct effects of y's character traits." And that is precisely what participants in the debate have gradually come to do: they have gradually come to regard personal identity over time as depending on chains of these and countless other mental connections, with quasi-memory as just one relevant psychological connection among others.[2] In other words, what is necessary and sufficient for personal identity over time is the holding of the more general relation of *psychological* continuity.

In addition to these fairly conservative modifications of the simple Lockean view – replacing direct memory links with indirect memory links, replacing memory with quasi-memory, and supplementing quasi-memory with other mental relations – a more drastic revision is apparently called for, in light of the so-called "fission" problem (sections 4–7). But first it will be useful to consider why we should be drawn to the psychological-continuity view in the first place.

3. Reasons to accept the psychological-continuity view

Historically, one important motivation behind the psychological-continuity view has been its strong empiricist credentials. What makes it the case that a certain *present* experience belongs to the same person as a certain other *present* experience?

One possible answer is that these experiences are somehow held together by the same substance: perhaps an immaterial substance, a soul. David Hume ([1739] 1978, 252) famously stated, however, that no such entity can be observed: what one finds by looking into one's own mind (arguably the natural place to look) are just numerous perceptions; one does not find, in addition to these perceptions, a bearer of them, let alone an immaterial bearer. For an empiricist, it would be ideal to instead be able to answer the question by appeal to some mental relation. And Grice (1941) offers just such an answer: these two experiences, he suggests, are had by the same person because they can be known by introspection to be simultaneous. If you are now in pain, your pain is of course simultaneous with my present experiences, but this is not something that can be known by introspection; by contrast, the simultaneity of your pain and your other present experiences can be so known. On Grice's view, this is not because they are all yours; rather, they are all yours because they can be so known. The psychological-continuity view is a natural development of this suggestion. What makes it the case that a certain *present* experience belongs to the same person as a certain *past* or *future* experience? Not, friends of the view insist, their being tied to the same substance (let alone the same immaterial substance), but simply their being elements of the same chain of mental events. They do not belong to this chain because one and the same person has them; rather, they are had by the same person because they belong to this chain.

Another consideration often thought, at least at first sight, to support the psychological-continuity view, is that it is, after all, an account of *personal* identity; and the concept of a person is evidently a psychological one. According to Locke's influential account, for instance, a person is "a thinking intelligent being, that has reason and reflection, and can consider itself as itself, the same thinking thing, in different times and places" ([1690] 1975, 335). As a result, it may be charged that non-psychological approaches to personal identity over time – such as the "bodily" view that sameness of body is necessary and sufficient for personal identity over time – must be based on some kind of conceptual confusion. In fact, however, the confusion lies in this very charge (Olson 1997, 29–30). For even if the concept of a person is a psychological one, this does not mean that psychological features are relevant to a person's persistence. The fact that an individual satisfies a certain concept does not entail that the concept is involved in his identity conditions; after all, a pianist can stop being a pianist without ceasing to exist, and a child can continue to live to old age. Of course, advocates of the psychological-continuity view will hold that the concept of a person is special: it is a "substance concept" – a concept that provides the identity conditions for all things falling under it. But appealing to this claim would be question-begging against opponents of the view; it ought not to persuade anyone not already inclined to believe that psychology is relevant to personal identity over time.

The primary reason to accept the psychological-continuity view is that it gives the intuitively correct verdicts in cases in which a person's psychology is transferred to another body, whereas competing views – most obviously the bodily approach – have the opposite implications. Anthony Quinton's influential 1962 article "The Soul" contains the following case, whose details will likely secure it from oblivion:

> I know two men B and C. B is a dark, tall, thin, puritanical Scotsman of sardonic temperament with whom I have gone on bird-watching expeditions. C is a fair, short, plump, apolaustic Pole of indestructible enterprise and optimism with whom I have made a number of more urban outings. One day I come into a room where both appear to be, and the dark, thin man suggests that he and I pursue tonight some acquaintances I made with C, though he says it was with him, a couple of nights ago. The short, fair, plump, cheerful-looking man reminds me in a Polish accent of a promise I had made to B, though he says it was to him, and which I had forgotten about, to go in search of owls this very night. At first I suspect a conspiracy, but the thing continues far beyond any sort of joke, for good perhaps, and is accompanied by suitable amazement on their part at each other's appearance, their own reflections in the mirror, and so forth.
> (Quinton 1962, 401)

If the bodily view is right, B has gotten C's former mental features, and vice versa. If the psychological-continuity view is right, B has gotten C's former body, and vice versa. As Quinton emphasizes, it is the latter judgment that is intuitively correct.[3]

More exactly, the latter judgment is the intuitively correct one, and what the psychological-continuity view yields, provided that the resulting persons' mental states have been suitably caused by B and C's respective former mental states – that the case really involves psychological *continuity* and not mere psychological similarity.[4] One year after the publication of Quinton's essay, Shoemaker presented a similar case where this requirement is satisfied:

> Two men, a Mr. Brown and a Mr. Robinson, had been operated on for brain tumors, and brain extractions had been performed on both of them. At the end of the operations, however, the assistant inadvertently put Brown's brain in Robinson's head, and Robinson's brain in Brown's head. One of these men immediately dies, but the other, the one with Robinson's head and Brown's brain, eventually regains consciousness. Let us call the latter 'Brownson' . . . When asked his name he automatically replies 'Brown.' He recognizes Brown's wife and family . . . and is able to describe in detail events in Brown's life . . . of Robinson's past life he evidences no knowledge at all.
> (Shoemaker 1963, 23–24)

Again, the intuitively attractive thing to say of this "surgical blunder (of rather staggering proportions!)," as Shoemaker would later describe it (1984, 78), is that it results in *Brown* regaining consciousness: Brownson is identical to Brown.[5] This judgment is incompatible with the bodily view but entailed by the psychological-continuity view (as Brownson has Robinson's body but is psychologically continuous with Brown).

According to a popular line of thought, this verdict can be further boosted by considerations of what prudentially matters (see question (b) in section 1). Suppose that Brown learns, before the operation, that the surgical blunder will occur and that Brownson will enjoy a delicious brownie afterwards. Intuitively, whereas everyone might have a reason to welcome this future experience, Brown has a reason to have *prudential* concern about it – to delightfully anticipate the experience "from the inside." On a common view, this shows that Brownson is Brown, since a person has reason for this kind of prudential concern about a future experience only if he himself is going to have the experience. Arguments such as these need to be treated with some caution, however. It is not clear to what extent the pertinent judgment – that Brown has reason for prudential concern about Brownson's future experience – provides independent *support* for the thesis that Brownson is Brown. It may be that we make it only because we are already disposed to judge that Brownson is Brown (and already believe that personal identity over time is what prudentially matters).

4. The fission problem

The most discussed problem for the psychological-continuity view during the 20th century – especially during the 1970s and 1980s – is the "fission" problem. It is based on the observation that one person can be psychologically continuous with two (or more) future individuals. Although the problem appears to have been originally formulated by Samuel Clarke ([1738] 1978, 844–845), and the modern discussion of it was primarily set in motion by a fantastic case presented by Bernard Williams (1957), most writers have focused on a variant of Shoemaker's Brownson case, due to David Wiggins (1967, 53) and formulated by Derek Parfit as follows:

> *My Division.* My body is fatally injured, as are the brains of my two brothers. My brain is divided, and each half is successfully transplanted into the body of one of my brothers. Each of the resulting people believes that he is me, seems to remember living my life, has my character, and is in every other way psychologically continuous with me. And he has a body that is very like mine.
>
> (Parfit 1984, 254–255)

Call the original person (the "me" in Parfit's story) "Henry," the post-fission person with Henry's left hemisphere, "Lefty," and the post-fission person with Henry's right hemisphere, "Righty." As both Lefty and Righty are psychologically continuous with Henry, the psychological-continuity view, as construed thus far, entails that Henry is identical to each of them. This in turn entails that Lefty and

Righty are identical to each other. But they aren't: they are two, not one.[6] Consequently, psychological continuity cannot be sufficient – and hence not necessary and sufficient – for personal identity over time.

5. The non-branching approach

On the most popular revision of the psychological-continuity view in light of this problem, what is necessary and sufficient for personal identity over time is psychological continuity *that has not taken a branching form* (Shoemaker 1984, 85; cf. Parfit 1984, 263). Thus a person existing at t is identical to an individual existing at a future time t^* only if the latter individual is the *only* one who is at t^* psychologically continuous with the former as he is at t.[7] This clause is not satisfied in the fission case: upon fission, no one is uniquely psychologically continuous with Henry as he is before fission. So, on this non-branching version of the psychological-continuity view, Henry is identical with neither Lefty nor Righty (nor with anyone else existing after fission).

One objection to the non-branching approach is that, precisely because it implies that fission is the end of Henry, it makes fission as bad as ordinary death. This, many think, is not a sensible result: ordinary death seems far worse than fission. Whereas it seems prudentially reasonable for Henry to make great sacrifices in order to prevent his own death, many believe that it would be prudentially irrational for him to do so in order to prevent fission – for instance, by seeing to it that one of his hemispheres is destroyed.

Another objection is that the non-branching approach violates an attractive "intrinsicality" requirement. My identity with an individual seems to be wholly a matter between him and me; after all, numerical identity is arguably the most intimate relation of all. Thus while, for instance, my being the only one who is equally tall as a certain individual does not solely depend on the intrinsic features of the relation between us, my being identical with a future individual seems to do so (Noonan 1985). On the non-branching approach, however, it depends in part on extrinsic features, namely, on whether there are future individuals *other* than him who are psychologically continuous with me.

In Parfit's view, however, such objections draw the wrong lessons from the fission case (1984, 261–270). They derive their force from the assumption that identity is what prudentially matters in survival, but what the fission case reveals is precisely that this assumption is mistaken. After all, Parfit suggests, we should all agree that if Henry's left hemisphere had been placed in a new body and the right one had been destroyed, then he would survive as the person ending up with his left hemisphere – call him "Only" – and his relation to Only would contain what matters.[8] Because Henry's relation to Lefty is intrinsically just like his relation to Only, it too must contain what matters. The fact that, in the fission case, Henry also bears this kind of relation to yet another future person – Righty – does not mean that anything that matters is *missing* from his relation to Lefty. Indeed, since the parallel claims can be made about Henry's relation to Righty, fission is a "double success"; far from depriving Henry of what matters, it gives him what matters twice over. Furthermore, while the non-branching approach does violate the above intrinsicality requirement, this is a serious drawback only if it implies violation of an analogous and more important requirement: namely, that whether *what prudentially matters* obtains between a future individual and me, is something that solely depends on the intrinsic features of the relation between him and me. However, once we separate personal identity from what matters, violation of the former requirement does not imply violation of the latter requirement.

Parfit's treatment of fission has been so influential that fission is often seen primarily as a challenge for the thesis that identity is what matters, rather than a challenge for the psychological-continuity view itself. As Eric Olson (1997, 52–57) has pointed out, however, the Parfitian strategy seems to undercut one of the main reasons to accept the psychological-continuity view. Recall the case where Brownson ends up with Brown's psychology (sect. 4): the claim that Brownson *is* Brown since Brown has reason for prudential concern about Brownson's future experiences, presupposes precisely that one has such a reason only if one is identical to the future experiencer.[9]

6. The plurality of worms

Because the thesis that personal identity is what prudentially matters has considerable intuitive appeal, after all, many proponents of the psychological-continuity view have tried to deal with the fission case in a way that does not require its abandonment. The most popular such strategy is the "cohabitation" approach (Lewis 1976; Noonan 2003; Perry 1972; Robinson 1985). The basic idea is that Lefty and Righty existed even before fission, sharing the same body and psychological features. Up to fission, the only differences between Lefty and Righty concern what is going to happen to them later; in all other respects they are exactly alike. Thus, the idea is not that, even before fission, Lefty has only Henry's left hemisphere, and Righty only his right hemisphere: before fission each of them has the entire brain. Hence whatever one of them thinks and feels and does, the other one also thinks and feels and does: they speak with one voice.

On the non-branching approach, the fission story involves three persons: Lefty, Righty, and Henry. On the simplest and most well-known versions of the cohabitation approach (such as David Lewis's), it involves two: Lefty and Righty. Where does that leave Henry, then: does he not exist at all on this approach? That is a misunderstanding; instead, before fission "Henry" refers ambiguously to Lefty and Righty. So long as what is said is true on both disambiguations, it is true; and before fission, this condition is clearly satisfied by "Henry exists" (for Lefty exists and Righty exists).

It may seem obviously false that there is more than one person associated with Henry's body before fission. As we shall see later (sects. 9 and 10), however, it is arguable that friends of the psychological-continuity view are committed to something very similar to this even in perfectly ordinary, non-fission cases – and so they, at least, are hardly in a position to lightly dismiss the cohabitation approach.

How does the cohabitation approach reconcile the psychological-continuity view with the thesis that identity is what matters in survival? The idea is easiest to explain from the perspective of "four-dimensionalism": the general account of persistence espoused by virtually all cohabitation theorists. According to four-dimensionalism, things persist by having temporal parts, or "stages," located at different times; the persisting object itself is a space-time "worm," composed of its various stages.[10] Conjoined with the psychological-continuity view, this theory yields that two stages belong to the same person in virtue of being related by psychological continuity. In ordinary cases, of course, no stage belongs to more than one person. In the fission case, however, Lefty and Righty share the same pre-fission stages (though no post-fission stages). Now consider such a shared pre-fission stage S1, a post-fission stage S2 of Lefty, and a post-fission stage S3 of Righty. The relation between S1 and S2 seems to contain what matters, and so does the relation between S1 and S3. Crucially, in each of these cases, there is also a single person of which the relevant stages are parts: both S1 and S2 are parts of Lefty, and both S1 and S3 are parts of Righty. It is not the case, then, that we have what matters between two stages in the absence of personal identity over time.

It has been protested, however, that while this approach accommodates some ideas in the vicinity of the intuition that personal identity is what matters, it does not accommodate that intuition itself (Parfit 1976; Sider 1996; 2001, 202–203). For instance, perhaps it accommodates the thesis that, for stages, belonging to the same person is what matters. Moreover, perhaps it accommodates the thesis that, if what matters obtains between a person, as he is at time t, and a person, as he is at time t^*, then the former person exists at t^*. However, according to the critics, what the relevant intuition requires is that, if what matters obtains between a person, as he is at t, and a person, as he is at t^*, then the former person is identical to the latter person. And the fact remains that the relation between Lefty, as he is prior to fission, and Righty, as he is after fission, seems to contain what matters; and the fact remains that Lefty is not identical to Righty.

7. The stage view

A more recent proposal also deserves a mention here. According to another version of four-dimensionalism, the "stage view" (Hawley 2001; Sider 1996; 2001), although there *are* all those temporally extended objects that the "worm" theorist identifies us with, these objects are not what we refer to with ordinary names and predicates (such as "Henry" and "person"). Instead, every ordinary object is an instantaneous stage: thus, you and I and other persons – as well as chairs, doghouses, etc. – exist strictly speaking only for a moment.

The stage theorist does not thereby hold that I have never been asleep, or will never eat lunch. Instead, she handles temporal predication analogously with how Lewis analyses modal predication (Lewis 1986). According to Lewis, claims about how I could have been should be understood in terms of properties of modal counterparts of me: individuals located in other possible worlds who are suitably similar to me. I could have been F just in case there is a modal counterpart of me who is F. Note that the counterpart is not the one who *could* have been F; *I* have that modal property. Similarly, on the stage view, claims about what I have been and will be like (as well as "tenseless" claims about what I am like at various times) should be understood in terms of properties of *temporal* counterparts of me: stages located at other times who are related to me in a suitable way. I was or will be F just in case there is a temporal counterpart of me who is F. Thus I really am going to eat lunch, so long as there is a future temporal counterpart of me who eats lunch. Note that the lunch-eating stage is not the one who *is going to* eat lunch; *I* have that temporal property.

Different theorists can of course disagree on which is the "suitable way" required for a stage to be a temporal counterpart of me. But one obvious candidate is psychological continuity. Given this proposal, the stage theorist has a neat solution to the fission problem (Sider 1996; 2001, 201–202).

Like the cohabitation theorist, and unlike the non-branching theorist, the stage theorist can say that there is a pre-fission person who is going to have Henry's left hemisphere after fission and a pre-fission person who is going to have Henry's right hemisphere after fission. Unlike the cohabitation theorist, the stage theorist can say that the former person is identical to the latter person. For it is open to her to hold that something (in this case, Henry) can have two temporal counterparts located at the same time (in this case, a post-fission time). Moreover, she does not thereby commit herself to the absurdity that, after fission, Henry will (for instance) both have and lack his left hemisphere. For none of Henry's post-fission counterparts (and, of course, no other object) both has and lacks his left hemisphere.

It is arguable that this approach preserves the intuition that personal identity is what matters. Again, what matters seems to obtain between Henry and Lefty, and between Henry and Righty: if we were to torture Lefty and give Righty a present, Henry would have prudential reason for fearful anticipation of the torture and for delightful anticipation of the gift. On the stage view, *Henry himself* would be going to experience the torture, and *Henry himself* would be going to receive the present. It is not obvious that the intuition that personal identity is what matters requires more than this.

In any event, if it does, then this is presumably because persistence over time, or having properties at different times, requires more than the stage view offers. In other words, the stage theorist's solution to the fission problem probably stands and falls with the stage view itself. By contrast, as we saw, the cohabitation theorist's solution to the fission problem is problematic even on the assumption that the cohabitation approach is true.

8. Reductionism

Before we turn to further problems for the psychological-continuity view, we shall briefly consider a related, but more obscure issue of which there was quite a lot of discussion in the years that followed the publication of Parfit's *Reasons and Persons* in 1984. One of Parfit's main theses in this book is what he calls "reductionism" about personal identity. According to reductionism, "the fact of a person's identity over time just consists in the holding of certain more particular facts" (1984, 210) – such as the fact that a future individual is (uniquely) psychologically continuous with me as I am now, or that a future individual has the same body as the one I have now. Non-reductionism, by contrast, asserts that personal identity over time is a "further fact"; it is something "over and above" the obtaining of such psychological or bodily continuities.[11] Although Parfit seems to recognize the conceptual possibility of a non-reductionist view that merely says, for instance, that whereas personal identity holds *if and only if* there is (non-branching) psychological continuity, it does not *consist* in such continuity, he takes the main non-reductionist view to hold that personal identity over time involves the sharing of an immaterial, Cartesian soul.[12]

According to Parfit, though we may be largely unaware of this, large portions of our thinking about ourselves rely on non-reductionism. For example, he contends, we tend to believe – or believe things that presuppose – that it can never be indeterminate whether I am identical to certain past or future individual, an assumption that, he says, is reasonable only on non-reductionism. More dramatically, lots of our most fundamental beliefs about morality and prudence presuppose non-reductionism. For instance, while a common complaint against utilitarianism is that it fails to "take seriously the distinction between persons" (Rawls 1971, 27), Parfit holds that reductionism reveals that that distinction does not deserve to be taken seriously. Moreover, he expresses sympathy for the claim that reductionism, unlike non-reductionism, leaves prudential concern for one's own future unjustified. Since the fact that a future pain, for instance, is mine just consists in mundane facts about certain continuities, and lacks the splendor and star quality of facts about an immaterial soul, it is unreasonable for me to get worked up about it.[13]

It is important to distinguish the thesis that prudential concern for one's own future is unjustified from the thesis that identity is not what justifies prudential concern (sect. 5). For one thing, Parfit's main support for the latter thesis – the fission argument – would be undermined if it were to be shown that Henry would not be justified in having prudential concern for Lefty's (or Righty's) experiences. This would do nothing to undermine the former thesis. For another, even if identity is not what prudentially matters, something else may justify prudential concern – psychological continuity, for instance. After all, in every ordinary case, if a person is going to have a certain future experience, then she is psychologically continuous with the future experiencer. (Indeed, on the psychological-continuity view, this will hold in any possible case, ordinary or not – even the non-branching version takes psychological continuity to be *necessary* for personal identity over time.)

In section 5 we noted Olson's remark that if identity is not what prudentially matters, then the claim that Brown has reason for prudential concern about Brownson's experiences fails to support the psychological-continuity view. A similar point can be made here. If reductionism shows that we do not have reason for prudential concern about our future experiences, then we cannot say that Brownson must be Brown because Brown has reason for prudential concern about Brownson's future experiences.

During the past two decades, the interest in reductionism and its practical significance has waned considerably. It is easy to suspect that this has largely to do with the elusiveness of the issue. One unclarity concerns the content of reductionism and non-reductionism. One might have thought that, when Parfit says that on reductionism, facts about a person's identity over time "consist" in facts about certain continuities, whereas on non-reductionism, facts about a person's identity over time are "further facts," he simply means that reductionism *identifies* these facts, whereas non-reductionism regards them as numerically distinct (so that "further facts" simply means "other facts"). But this is evidently not what he means, for he emphasizes that, on his preferred version of reductionism, facts about personal identity stand to facts about the relevant continuities in the way that a bronze statue stands to the *numerically distinct* lump of bronze with which it coincides. He says:

> If we melt down a bronze statue, we destroy this statue, but we do not destroy this lump of bronze. So, though the statue just consists in the lump of bronze, these cannot be one and the same thing.
>
> (1995, 295)

This analogy is not very helpful, however. The lump may be able to exist without the statue, but if the "reduction base" for personal identity obtains, then so does personal identity over time. After all, the "reduction base" must be a (necessary and) sufficient condition for personal identity over time – for example, non-branching psychological continuity.

Moreover, if we do not identify facts about personal identity with facts about certain continuities, it is hard to see why the former should be taken to inherit the supposed unimportance of the latter (Merricks 1999; see also Johnston 1997). Surely something can depend in very intimate ways on something else while still meriting very different attitudes than it (think of non-natural moral facts versus the natural facts on which they depend, for instance). Yet another obscurity concerns Parfit's idea that *non*-reductionism does *not* leave prudential concern unjustified. It is difficult to see exactly what it is about my sharing an immaterial soul with a future individual that is supposed to make it reasonable for me to care about his experiences (Johansson 2007; Whiting 1986, 547; Wolf 1986, 707).

9. The animalist challenge

While many think that the aforementioned problems for the psychological-continuity view (sects. 2, 4) reveal a need for some substantial adjustments to it – such as the inclusion of a non-branching clause – few have seen them as a reason to abandon it altogether. During the past two decades, however, many so-called "animalists" have claimed to offer just such a reason.

According to animalism, human persons are human animals, members of the species *Homo sapiens* (Ayers 1991; Carter 1988; Mackie 1999a; Olson 1997; 2003; Snowdon 1990; 2014; van Inwagen 1990). This view may seem too obvious to be worth stating: who believes that we are plants or dogs or robots? But animalism is not trivial, for it is incompatible with the psychological-continuity view (as well as with various other popular theories). It is not that the two views explicitly give conflicting answers to any of the three questions in section 1: while the psychological-continuity view is an answer to question (a), the question about our persistence conditions, animalism is an answer to question (c), the question of what kind of thing we are. However, psychological continuity – with or without the "non-branching" qualification – is not necessary and sufficient for a human animal's identity over time, and so if *we* are human animals, as animalism says, it is not necessary and sufficient for *our* identity over time, contrary to the psychological-continuity view (Olson 1994; 1997; 2003).

To see that psychological continuity is not necessary for the identity over time of a human animal, note that every human animal was once an embryo, which did not have any psychological features whatsoever, and hence was not psychologically continuous with anything at all. Moreover, if the animal is unlucky, it might enter a permanent vegetative state, in which it is still alive but has no psychological features.[14] To see that psychological continuity is not sufficient for the identity over time of a human animal, return once again to the Brownson case. After the transfer, the "recipient" animal (the one with what was Brown's brain before the transfer) is psychologically continuous with the "donor" animal (the one that started out with Brown's brain) as it was before the transfer. But surely these are two different animals; the surgeons have moved an organ, not an entire human organism.[15]

So if the psychological-continuity view is true, then we are not human animals. This is troublesome for the psychological-continuity view, for there is an influential argument in favor or animalism: the "thinking animal problem," most forcefully put forward by Eric Olson (1997, 80–91, 97–109; 2003; 2007, 29–39). It begins with the simple observation that, whether or not *I* am a human animal, *there is* a human animal where I am. It is the organism that I see when I look in the mirror, and is currently sitting comfortably in my chair. This animal is suspiciously like me: if it is not me, then it is hiding it very well. This comes out most clearly when we consider the animal's mental properties. Because the animal and I have the same brain (or at least exactly similar brains, located in the same place and composed of the same particles), and the same surroundings, it seems that it must be psychologically indiscernible from me. Olson argues that if I am nonetheless not it, then three problems arise. First, there is a problem of *too many thinkers*. If I am not the animal, then

> [t]here are two thinking beings beings wherever we thought there was just one. There are two philosophers, you and an animal, sitting there

and reading this. You are never truly alone: wherever you go, a watchful animal goes with you.

(Olson 2003, 329).

Perhaps we can accept the cohabitation theorist's claim that two individuals share their thoughts in an extraordinary scenario like the fission case (sect. 6). It is much more unattractive to say that this holds even in all normal cases.

Secondly, there is a problem of *too many persons*: since the animal has the same mental features as I do, it too seems to qualify as a person. For instance, it seems to satisfy Locke's account of personhood (sect. 3): that is, it seems to be "a thinking intelligent being, that has reason and reflection, and can consider itself as itself, the same thinking thing, in different times and places." Whether or not we accept the details of Locke's account, there can hardly be non-persons psychologically indiscernible from persons, just as there cannot be non-roses botanically indiscernible from roses. While the "too many persons" problem (like the other two problems) afflicts animalism's rivals in general, it is (unlike the other two problems) particularly embarrassing for advocates of the psychological-continuity view. For not only is it unappealing to say that there are two persons in my chair right now; in addition, if the animal is a person, then the psychological-continuity view is simply wrong to say – as it does in most versions – that all persons persist by virtue of psychological continuity. As we have just seen, the animal in my chair does not. And if billions of persons persist by virtue of something other than psychological continuity, why not all persons?

Thirdly, even if it can be shown that the animal is not a person after all, an epistemic problem remains. For whenever I think, "I am a person, not an animal," the animal thinks, "*I* am a person, not an animal" – and apparently its epistemic position does not differ in any way from mine:

> It will have the same grounds for thinking that it is a person and not an animal as you have for believing that you are. Yet it is mistaken. If you *were* the animal and not the person, you would still think you were the person. So for all you know, you are the one making the mistake. Even if you are a person and not an animal, it is hard to see how you could ever have any reason to believe that you are.
>
> (Olson 2007, 36)

It is not entirely clear exactly what the main point is supposed to be here. On one interpretation, it is that I have a reason to believe that I am a person, but could not have such a reason if I were not identical to the animal; hence, I am identical to the animal. On another interpretation, the point is that I cannot have any reason to believe that I am not the animal. This is of course unwelcome news for an opponent of animalism: she could not have any reason for her belief that she is not an animal. However, this purely epistemic claim does not, all by itself, imply that she *is* an animal: it does not follow that animalism is true. On yet another interpretation, though, the truth of animalism follows in a more indirect way – namely, via the additional and not implausible premise that if a view of someone's nature is true, then she can have reason to believe in it.[16]

In any case, critics of animalism, and particularly friends of the psychological-continuity view, have suggested various solutions to these problems. For instance, Shoemaker (1999) has appealed to his functionalist theory of mental properties in order to show that human animals do not have mental features. Hence there is only one thinker and only one person in my chair: me. According to another line of response (Noonan 2003, 211), the animal in my chair does think – and so there really are more than one thinker where I am – but because it does not have psychological persistence conditions, it is not a person and does not refer to itself with the first-person singular pronoun. When I think, "I am a person, not an animal," the animal does not think, incorrectly, that *it* is a person, not an animal; instead, it thinks, correctly, that *I* am a person, not an animal. So the animal is not mistaken after all.

These proposed solutions are ingenious – perhaps even more so than they are plausible (Olson 2007, 29–39). Yet another line of response does not amount to a solution, but points out that animalism faces an analogous challenge (Zimmerman 2008; see also Olson 2007, 215–216). Consider my brain, for instance. First, if the animal in my chair thinks, why does not my brain do so as well? The fact that the animal has parts that the brain lacks – legs, arms, etc. – and whose job is *not* to give rise to thought, can hardly indicate that the brain does not think. Secondly, since the brain is psychologically indistinguishable from a person, it seems to be a person as well. Thirdly, how could I ever have any reason to believe that I am the animal and not the brain? Moreover, the argument continues, any reason to deny that the brain thinks as I do would presumably also be a reason to deny that the animal thinks as I do (for example, the view that no material thing can think would rule out both thinking brains and thinking animals), leaving the animalist with no advantage over its rivals with respect to this sort of challenge.

While we cannot go into detail here, the standard reply from animalists appeals to a certain view of composition, according to which there are no composite objects except those that are alive: for any non-overlapping objects, there is something they compose just in case their activities constitute a biological life (van Inwagen 1990; cf. Olson 2007, 226–228). There are chairmen, but no chairs – only particles "arranged chair-wise"; there are dogs, but no doghouses – only particles "arranged doghouse-wise." Although this is of course a highly controversial doctrine, it does have considerable independent support; for instance, it is one of few principled ways of avoiding the perhaps overly extreme views "mereological nihilism" (no objects compose anything) and "mereological universalism" (for any non-overlapping objects, there is something they compose; see sect. 10). In any event, this more moderate view of composition would straightforwardly solve the thinking brain problem. Because the activities of particles "arranged brain-wise" do not constitute a biological life – although they are of course among the particles that make up the organism and whose activities *do* constitute a biological life – there are on this view no brains, and hence no thinking brains.

10. The ontological problem

Again, friends of the psychological-continuity view must deny that we are animals. But even more fundamentally, several writers have argued that it is difficult to find *any* sensible view of what we are – any sensible answer to question (c) in section 1 – that sits well with the psychological-continuity view (Olson 1994; 2007; van Inwagen 1997; 2002; see also Merricks 1999).

Suppose first that "three-dimensionalism" is true: things exist at different times by being wholly present at each of those times, not by having temporal parts; as it is often put, things *endure* through time. What kind of enduring thing am I, if the psychological-continuity view is true?

The brain may seem to be a natural candidate (despite the abovementioned attempts to deny its existence), as it is responsible for a person's mental features; again, in the Brownson case, Brown's psychology goes where his brain goes. In fact, however, psychological continuity – even non-branching psychological continuity – is not necessary and sufficient for a brain's identity over time. It is not necessary, for my brain existed before it had any capacity to sustain mental features; and it may lose that capacity without ceasing to exist. Furthermore, consider a so-called "brain-state transfer" case (Shoemaker & Swinburne 1984, 108–111): a machine records information about the total physical state of Brain A, located in Room A, then erases it; it also erases the total physical state of Brain B, located in Room B; then it produces Brain A's state in the brain located in Room B. After this procedure, the brain in Room B is psychologically continuous with Brain A as Brain A was before the transfer (insofar as brains have mental features at all; but that is assumed by the proposal at issue, since *we* have mental features), not with Brain B as it was before the transfer. Crucially, the brain located in Room B after the transfer is manifestly Brain B: its mental features have gone, but *it* has not gone anywhere. Hence, Brain B has persisted through psychological discontinuity. This also shows that psychological continuity is not sufficient for a brain's identity over time. For, obviously, the brain-state transfer does not result in Brain A becoming identical with Brain B. No process can have such a result, for nothing can become identical with anything other than itself. It would not be reasonable to reply that what really happens in this case is that Brain A is in fact transferred to Room B and becomes composed of the particles that a moment earlier composed Brain B (which ceased to exist when its state was erased). Surely no brain can instantaneously change its location without any of its proper parts having moved from the one location to the other.[17]

A popular view is that persons are (enduring entities and) "constituted" by animals (Baker 2000; Shoemaker 1984): I am composed of the same particles as the animal in my chair and occupy the same place as it, but we have different modal properties (for instance, whereas I could become inorganic, the animal could not). Whatever the merits of this doctrine, it too is difficult to reconcile with the psychological-continuity view (van Inwagen 1997; 2002). For example, the conjunction of the two views implies that, in a brain-state transfer case, an enduring human-organism-sized object – the person – either becomes identical to another object or instantaneously changes its location although none of its proper parts has moved from the one location to the other. This seems no more plausible than the corresponding claim about brains.

Nor can we expect any happy marriage between the psychological-continuity view and the view that persons are enduring immaterial souls (van Inwagen 2002, 178–179). For example, it seems possible for a soul – no less than for an organism or brain – to have its current mental features obliterated and replaced by new ones. Then it persists without being psychologically continuous with itself as it was earlier. (Perhaps a soul cannot exist at a time without having mental features then. But this does not imply that it cannot persist through psychological *discontinuity*.) Furthermore, psychological continuity does not seem sufficient for a soul's identity over time: it seems possible for a soul to become psychologically continuous with *another* soul.

Similar remarks apply to other enduring entitites. But a more promising companion to the psychological-continuity view is four-dimensionalism (let us here focus on its standard version, the worm view; see sect. 6). A four-dimensionalist can describe a brain-state transfer case as follows: the person whose brain-state is transferred to a new head is composed of most pre-transfer parts of one animal (the "donor" animal) and most post-transfer parts of another animal (the "recipient" animal). No object becomes identical to something it has until then been numerically distinct from; instead, two different animals share parts – different ones – with the person. Of course, the view still implies that one human-organism-sized object (the person) can instantaneously change its location even if none of the particles that compose it before the transfer – or more precisely, no particle that is a *spatial* part of it before the transfer – moves from the one place to the other. However, this may be easier to swallow if the object is temporally extended, a "worm," rather than being wholly present at each time of its existence. In any case, this is just an instance of something that friends of four-dimensionalism happily accept regardless of considerations of personal identity. For just about all four-dimensionalists endorse mereological universalism (sect. 9): for any non-overlapping objects, there is something they compose. So there is an object composed of, say, your-chair-a-moment-ago and my-chair-right-now, although no particle has moved from your room to mine.

Naturally, four-dimensionalism is highly contested; on the other hand, so are the general metaphysical views that enemies of the psychological-continuity view are committed to (such as the doctrine of composition appealed to by many animalists; see sect. 9). However, two special problems to do with the combination of the psychological-continuity view and four-dimensionalism (particularly when accompanied by mereological universalism) should be noted. First, it gives rise to a radical variant of the "thinking animal" problem (sect. 9; see Olson 1994, 2007, 122–125; Zimmerman 2003). My present stage thinks as I do, and so do all objects of which it is a stage, nearly all of which are not composed by stages related by psychological continuity. Thus my current thought, "I am a person," is shared by all these objects; how do I know that I am the person with the correct belief rather a non-person with a delusion of grandeur? The odds are strongly against me. Secondly, while the view that *all* person-like individuals persist by virtue of psychological continuity has considerable intuitive appeal, one may wonder how much is preserved of that appeal in the view that, although the vast majority of person-like individuals do not persist by virtue of psychological continuity, some of them (the persons) do so.

Conclusion

Since the 1990s, the personal identity debate has been much more concerned than it used to be with the ontological question of what kind of thing we are (question (c) in section 1), as well as with more general and deep metaphysical issues about, for instance, composition and persistence. Although some might look back with nostalgia on the preceding era – with its obsession with fanciful science fiction examples, compared with which the fission case looks boringly realistic – this shift in focus is to be welcomed. For as animalists in particular have emphasized (Olson 1994; 2007; van Inwagen 1997; 2002), it is relatively hopeless to try to answer question (a) – the question about personal identity over time – independently of question (c), and equally hopeless to try to answer question (c) independently of more general metaphysical issues.

As a result of this shift in focus, the psychological-continuity view is no longer *the* main view in the debate: it is not an answer to question (c), and it is difficult to reconcile with most sensible answers to question (c). However, the view of course still has a great many excellent champions; moreover, every rival view faces considerable problems, too. Given the complexity of the issues, it is probably fair to say that no one yet knows the correct answers to the main questions of personal identity. We need one more century to think things over.[18]

Notes

1 Again, the debate has been dominated by questions (a)–(c), but it involves other issues as well. One of these concerns the kind of identity at play when we speak of an "identity crisis"; for an influential account, see Schechtman (1996). In section 8, I will briefly consider yet another question, which concerns the reducibility of personal identity over time to physical or psychological continuity.
2 Some of these other relations will need to be construed as analogous with quasi-memory: "x carries out the quasi-intention of y," for instance.
3 Locke similarly suggested, in support of his version of the psychological-continuity view, that "should the soul of a prince, carrying with it the consciousness of the prince's past life, enter and inform the body of a cobbler, as soon as deserted by his own soul,

every one sees he would be the same person with the prince" ([1690] 1975, 340). Locke's reference to the soul is confusing, however, since souls do not seem to persist by virtue of psychological continuity (see sect. 10). (The title of Quinton's essay is similarly confusing.)

4 Some philosophers would say that, in addition to the causal conditions necessary for psychological continuity, some further ones are necessary for personal identity (e.g. that the psychological continuity has not come about in an abnormal way). I shall ignore this complication in this chapter.

5 In the book from which the case is taken, Shoemaker himself does not assert that Brownson is Brown; however, he does so in his (1970).

6 This is so whether or not there is a single thing – a larger, scattered object with twenty toes – that Lefty and Righty together compose after fission. They would still be *two* parts of that object, not one.

7 "Only if," but not "if and only if," for one fission product may exist at a future time at which the other one no longer does so; the former is not thereby identical to the original person.

8 However, adherents of the "bodily" view do not agree that Henry is Only; nor do "animalists" (sect. 9).

9 This does not mean that considerations about prudence provide no reason to prefer the non-branching view to non-psychological theories. The separation between personal identity and what prudentially matters is probably much more radical given a "bodily" or "animalist" view (Unger 2000).

10 More exactly, this is the "worm" view – by far the most popular *version* of four-dimensionalism (e.g., Heller 1990; Lewis 1976; 1986). For another version, see section 7.

Some writers use "four-dimensionalism" to denote a view of the metaphysics of time: the view that past, present, and future objects all exist ("eternalism" is a more common name). Like many others, I use "four-dimensionalism" only to denote a theory of persistence – the one that appeals to temporal parts.

11 Although reductionism and non-reductionism concern personal identity over time, they are not answers to question (a) in section 1 (or to question (b) or (c)). Instead, they are, of course, answers to the question, "Does the fact of a person's identity over time just consist in the holding of certain more particular facts, such as facts about psychological or physical continuity?"

12 Merricks (1998) defends a non-reductionist view that does not involve immaterial souls.

13 Historically, considerations of this sort have sometimes been regarded as evidence against reductionism and related views. For example, Butler urged that Locke's theory implausibly makes "the inquiry concerning a future life of no consequence at all to us, the persons who are making it" ([1736] 1975, 99). Parfit turns this kind of argument on its head.

14 Similarly, according to some writers (Feldman 2000; Mackie 1999b), a human animal will eventually become a corpse (unless its death is unusually violent); and outside of horror stories, corpses have no psychological features. This argument is more controversial, however (Olson 2004).

15 Similar considerations show that the psychological-continuity view is incompatible with the doctrine that we are our *bodies*. However, this doctrine does not seem to be the same as animalism. For one thing, some hold that human animals are "constituted" by but numerically distinct from human bodies. For another, some animalists claim that it makes no sense to say that a person is identical to his body (van Inwagen 1980, 283).

16 Brueckner and Buford (2009) interpret the argument in this third way (and argue against it).

17 Similar remarks apply to the view that a human person is a proper part of a brain – for instance, the part that is chiefly responsible for the capacity of consciousness (McMahan 2002).
18 My sincere thanks to Amy Kind and an anonymous referee for their very helpful comments.

Bibliography

Ayers, M. (1991). *Locke: Vol. 2: Ontology*. London: Routledge.

Baker, L. R. (2000). *Persons and Bodies: A Constitution View*. Cambridge: Cambridge University Press.

Brueckner, A. L., and Buford, C. (2009). "Thinking Animals and Epistemology," *Pacific Philosophical Quarterly*, 90: 310–314.

Butler, J. ([1736] 1975). "Of Personal Identity," in Perry, J. (ed.), *Personal Identity*. Berkeley: University of California Press: 99–105.

Carter, W. R. (1988). "Our Bodies, Our Selves," *Australasian Journal of Philosophy*, 66: 308–319.

Clarke, S. ([1738] 1978). *The Works of Samuel Clarke*, vol. 3. New York: Garland Publishing.

Feldman, F. (2000). "The Termination Thesis," *Midwest Studies in Philosophy*, 24: 98–115.

Grice, H. P. (1941). "Personal Identity," *Mind*, 50: 330–350.

Hawley, K. (2001). *How Things Persist*. Oxford: Clarendon Press.

Heller, M. 1990. *The Ontology of Physical Objects: Four-Dimensional Hunks of Matter*. Cambridge: Cambridge University Press.

Hume, D. ([1739] 1978). *A Treatise of Human Nature*, Selby-Bigge, L. A. and Nidditch, P. H. (eds.), 2nd edn. Oxford: Oxford University Press.

Johansson, J. (2007). "Non-Reductionism and Special Concern," *Australasian Journal of Philosophy*, 85: 641–657.

Johnston, M. (1997). "Human Concerns Without Superlative Selves," in Dancy, J. (ed.), *Reading Parfit*. Oxford: Blackwell: 149–179.

Lewis, D. (1976). "Survival and Identity," in Rorty, A. (ed.), *The Identities of Persons*. Berkeley: University of California Press: 17–40.

Lewis, D. (1986). *On the Plurality of Worlds*. Oxford: Blackwell.

Locke, J. ([1690] 1975). *An Essay Concerning Human Understanding*, Nidditch, P. H. (ed.) Oxford: Clarendon Press.

Mackie, D. (1999a). "Animalism *versus* Lockeanism: No Contest," *Philosophical Quarterly*, 49: 369–376.

Mackie, D. (1999b). "Personal Identity and Dead People," *Philosophical Studies*, 95: 219–242.

McMahan, J. (2002). *The Ethics of Killing: Problems at the Margins of Life*. Oxford: Oxford University Press.

Merricks, T. (1998). "There Are No Criteria of Personal Identity Over Time," *Noûs*, 32: 106–124.

Merricks, T. (1999). "Endurance, Psychological Continuity, and the Importance of Personal Identity," *Philosophy and Phenomenological Research*, 59: 983–996.

Noonan, H. (1985). "The Only x and y Principle," *Analysis*, 45: 79–83.

Noonan, H. (2003). *Personal Identity*, 2nd edn. London: Routledge.

Nozick, R. (1981). *Philosophical Explanations*. Cambridge, MA: Harvard University Press.
Olson, E. T. (1994). "Is Psychology Relevant to Personal Identity?" *Australasian Journal of Philosophy*, 72: 173–186.
Olson, E. T. (1997). *The Human Animal: Personal Identity without Psychology*. New York and Oxford: Oxford University Press.
Olson, E. T. (2003). "An Argument for Animalism," in Martin, M. and Barresi, J. (eds.), *Personal Identity*. Malden, MA: Blackwell: 318–334.
Olson, E. T. (2004). "Animalism and the Corpse Problem," *Australasian Journal of Philosophy*, 82: 265–274.
Olson, E. T. (2007). *What are We? A Study in Personal Ontology*. Oxford: Oxford University Press.
Parfit, D. (1971). "Personal Identity," *Philosophical Review*, 80: 3–27.
Parfit, D. (1976). "Lewis, Perry, and What Matters," in Rorty, A. (ed.), *The Identities of Persons*. Berkeley: University of California Press: 91–107.
Parfit, D. (1984). *Reasons and Persons*. Oxford: Oxford University Press.
Parfit, D. (1995). "The Unimportance of Identity," in Harris, H. (ed.), *Identity: Essays Based on Herbert Spencer Lectures Given in the University of Oxford*. Oxford: Clarendon Press: 13–45.
Perry, J. (1972). "Can the Self Divide?" *Journal of Philosophy*, 69: 463–488.
Quinton, A. (1962). "The Soul," *Journal of Philosophy*, 59: 393–409.
Rawls, J. (1971). *A Theory of Justice*. Cambridge, MA: Harvard University Press.
Reid, T. ([1785] 2003). "Essays on the Intellectual Powers of Man," relevant passage repr. in Martin, M. and Barresi, J. (eds.), *Personal Identity*. Malden, MA: Blackwell: 48–54.
Robinson, D. (1985). "Can Amoebae Divide without Multiplying?" *Australasian Journal of Philosophy*, 63: 299–319.
Schechtman, M. (1996). *The Constitution of Selves*. Ithaca, NY: Cornell University Press.
Shoemaker, S. (1963). *Self-Knowledge and Self-Identity*. Ithaca, NY: Cornell University Press.
Shoemaker, S. (1970). "Persons and Their Pasts," *American Philosophical Quarterly*, 7: 269–285.
Shoemaker, S., and Swinburne, R. (1984). *Personal Identity*. Oxford: Blackwell.
Shoemaker, S. (1999). "Self, Body, and Coincidence," *Proceedings of the Aristotelian Society*, 73: 287–306.
Sider, T. (1996). "All the World's a Stage," *Australasian Journal of Philosophy*, 74: 433–453.
Sider, T. (2001). *Four-Dimensionalism: An Ontology of Persistence and Time*. Oxford: Clarendon Press.
Snowdon, P. (1990). "Persons, Animals, and Ourselves," in Gill, C. (ed.), *The Person and the Human Mind: Issues in Ancient and Modern Philosophy*. Oxford: Clarendon Press: 83–107.
Snowdon, P. (2014). *Persons, Animals, Ourselves*. Oxford: Oxford University Press.
Unger, P. (1990). *Identity, Consciousness and Value*. New York: Oxford University Press.
Unger, P. (2000). "The Survival of the Sentient," *Philosophical Perspectives*, 11: 325–348.
van Inwagen, P. (1980). "Philosophers and the Words 'Human Body'," in van Inwagen, P. (ed.), *Time and Cause: Essays Presented to Richard Taylor*. Dordrecht: Reidel. I: 283–300.

van Inwagen, P. (1990). *Material Beings*. Ithaca, NY: Cornell University Press.
van Inwagen, P. (1997). "Materialism and the Psychological-Continuity Account of Personal Identity," *Philosophical Perspectives*, 11: 305–319.
van Inwagen, P. (2002). "What Do We Refer to When We Say 'I'?" in Gale, R. (ed.), *Blackwell Guide to Metaphysics*. Oxford: Blackwell: 175–189.
Whiting, J. (1986). "Friends and Future Selves," *Philosophical Review*, 95: 547–580.
Wiggins, D. (1967). *Identity and Spatio-Temporal Continuity*. Oxford: Blackwell.
Williams, B. (1957). "Personal Identity and Individuation," *Proceedings of the Aristotelian Society*, 57: 229–252.
Wolf, S. (1986). "Self-Interest and Interest in Selves," *Ethics*, 96: 704–720.
Zimmerman, D. (2003). "Material People," in Loux, M. and Zimmerman, D. (eds.), *The Oxford Handbook of Metaphysics*. Oxford: Oxford University Press: 491–526.
Zimmerman, D. (2008). "Problems for Animalism," *Abstracta*, Special Issue I: 23–31.

6

INTROSPECTING IN THE 20TH CENTURY

Maja Spener

Introspection in the 20th century is a vast topic. Discussions involving introspection figured in the relatively new discipline of experimental psychology, as well as in various debates in philosophy of mind and epistemology. Introspection has been a focus of interest as a method of investigation and as a psychological and epistemic capacity itself. Over the course of the century, these theoretical interests did not always connect well, although they have intersected and influenced each other at different points. But there is no helpful sense in which one might talk of 'the history' of introspection in the 20th century if by that one means a straight line of development across ten or so decades of psychological and philosophical theorizing with, and about, introspection. Instead, there is a criss-crossing pattern of various storylines and what I shall do here is track a couple of different strands in the overall pattern to the exclusion of many others.[1] In particular, I shall concentrate on philosophers' and psychologists' *use* of introspection, and the discussions surrounding such use.

A story we are often told is that during the late 19th century and the beginning of the 20th century, experimental psychology was synonymous with introspectionism, exemplified by the work of Wilhelm Wundt and E. B. Titchener. According to the story, these early psychologists took the subject-matter of psychology to be conscious states only and their main method of investigation was introspection. The new experimental science aimed to provide data about consciousness via introspection under scientifically controlled conditions. We are told that this approach, while groundbreaking in its aim to make psychology thus conceived scientific, failed because it imploded from within while at the same time being superseded by a different approach to psychology: behaviourism. Behaviourism rejected not only the idea that introspection could be conducted in scientifically respectable ways, but also the central assumption that the subject-matter of psychology concerned conscious states. According to the story, introspectionism, and with it the use of introspection in theorizing about the mind, was pretty much annihilated after the behaviourists were finished with it (see, e.g., Braisby and Gellatlly, 2012). Behaviourists themselves might not have in the end successfully established their own methodological preferences and choice of the *bona fide* subject-matter of psychology, but they are generally credited with putting an end to introspectionism by the late 1920 or early 1930s.

What is curious, if this story were even half-way true, is that throughout much of the 20th century, within certain philosophical debates (e.g., in philosophy of perception and epistemology) philosophers have been happy to appeal to first-person reflections on sensory experiences in their theorizing. This raises questions about the relationship between the apparently scorching critique of the use of introspection within psychology during the first part of the century, and the continued and relatively easygoing use of introspection in philosophical theorizing. One suggestion might be that psychologists and philosophers were engaged in something like parallel play, working in relative ignorance of each other's fields. While there is a kernel of truth to this, there is also plenty of evidence of common interests and interaction between philosophers and psychologists. So the question is not really whether philosophers and psychologists talked to each other and read each other's work – they clearly did. The question is how much they talked and in what way this is reflected in theorizing in their own domains. The answer is, predictably, complex. In this paper, I make a start on it by showing some of the persisting influences psychology and philosophy had on each other when it comes to using introspection in theorizing. Equally, I highlight the lack – or loss – of influence in certain cases, resulting in a more rudimentary conception of the use of introspection towards the end of the century than the often quite sophisticated earlier debates about it would warrant. I begin with discussions involving introspection in the philosophy of perception in the first half of the century that reflect certain pressures felt at the time concerning the use of introspection in theorizing about experience. I then turn to relevant developments within psychology during this period and earlier, which show a more sustained engagement with various worries about introspection giving rise to these pressures. I finish by looking briefly at philosophical discussions about perceptual experience late in the century displaying a mix of lessons absorbed and lessons forgotten with respect to their use of introspection.

1. Introspection in the sense-datum theory debate

In this section, I will look at how early 20th-century philosophers of perception used introspection in their theorizing. I will focus specifically on proponents and critics of the sense-datum theory of perception. Moore's paper 'The Refutation of Idealism' seems a good starting point because it was published right at the beginning of the century in 1903, and also because it bridges different philosophical epochs. On the one hand, it is engaged in a (from our vantage point) backwards-looking debate with the then still more widely defended idealism; on the other hand it constitutes an early contribution to the ensuing lively focus on sense-datum theories of perception.

In his paper, Moore argues for a distinction between sensory experience and its (mind-independent) object, which he thinks is missing from extant accounts of sensory experience. He is also concerned to explain why his opponents failed to posit such a distinction:

> [T]here is a very good reason why they should have supposed so, in the fact that when we refer to introspection and try to discover what the sensation of blue is, it is very easy to suppose that we have before us only a single term. The term "blue" is easy enough to distinguish, but the other element which I have called "consciousness" – that which sensation of blue has in common with sensation of green – is extremely difficult to fix. That many people fail to distinguish it at all is sufficiently shown by the fact that there are materialists. And, in general, that which makes the sensation of blue a mental fact seems to escape us: it seems, if I may use a metaphor, to be transparent – we look through it and see nothing but the blue; we may be convinced that there *is something* but *what* it is no philosopher, I think, has yet clearly recognised.
>
> (Moore 1903, 446)

Moore suggests here that introspective reflection on experience easily leads philosophers astray on this matter. He points out that introspection does not clearly reveal any conscious element in addition to whatever non-conscious objects experience presents. It is then understandable, according to Moore, that philosophers think that experience is monolithic ('a single term') with no distinctive conscious aspect separable from the objects presented by experience.

Further on, though, he tempers both his claim about what introspection reveals, and about how misleading introspection is concerning the nature of sensory experience. While still insisting that introspective reflection is likely to mislead, he explains that this occurs because it is not done carefully enough:

> [T]he moment we try to fix our attention upon consciousness and to see *what*, distinctly, it is, it seems to vanish: it seems as if we had before us a mere emptiness. When we try to introspect the sensation of blue, all we can see is the blue: the other element is as if it were diaphanous. Yet it *can* be distinguished if we look enough, and if we know that there is something to look for. My main object in this paragraph has been to try to make the reader *see* it; but I fear I shall have succeeded very ill. . . . Whether or not, when I have the sensation of blue, my consciousness or awareness is thus blue, my introspection does not enable me to decide with certainty: I only see no reason for thinking that it is. But whether it is or not, the point is unimportant, for introspection *does* enable me to decide that something else is also true: namely that I am aware *of* blue, and by this I mean, that my awareness has to blue a quite different and distinct relation.
>
> (Moore 1903, 450–451)

Thus, introspection is not a poor guide when done right. Moore is happy to use introspective data in theorizing about the nature of conscious experience; indeed, it forms a central plank in defence of his own view. But he makes clear that since introspection is apt to mislead, using it in theorizing is not easy business. He works hard to get the reader to introspectively attend to experience properly. Moore accepts both that introspection is a major source of *bona fide*, theory-relevant information about the mind, but that significant care must be taken in availing oneself of it.

Versions of Moore's attitude to introspection can be traced through the philosophy of perception in the 20th century. It is common among both sense-datum theorists and their critics dominating discussion in the first half of that century. First and foremost, these philosophers took for granted that in providing an account of conscious perceptual experience one must start with an accurate description of its phenomenal character. Further, they assumed that this description is acquired via first-person access to one's experience. Philosophers talked of, e.g., 'introspecting', 'attending to one's own experience' or 'direct inspection of experience' (see, e.g. Lewis 1929, 57; Firth 1949, 523). This basic assumption of first-person access to important data about perceptual consciousness is reflected in the way philosophers typically employ it without much ado, other than occasional emphatic assertions that we have it. It suggests a relatively uncomplicated and natural-seeming first-person way of becoming aware (or being aware) of one's own conscious experience.

C. I. Lewis, for instance, talks about the character of pure sensory experience, i.e. experience which has not had interpretative involvement from thought (Lewis 1929, 36–66).[2] According to him, 'the sensuously given' is that which is unalterable by different interests or levels of knowledge and it has a distinctive 'sensuous feel or quality'. As such, Lewis says, it must always be ineffable, because when one tries to articulate it one applies interpretation of one type or another. Nonetheless, he expects us to have a good grasp of the given:

> It is that which remains untouched and unaltered, however it is construed by thought. Yet no one but a philosopher could for a moment deny this immediate presence in consciousness of that which no activity of thought can create or alter.
>
> (Lewis 1929, 53)

Lewis does not explicitly say how we are aware of the given, but he clearly thinks that it is in some very basic and ordinary way obvious from the first person. It is 'the brute-fact element in perception, illusion and dream' (57), the 'immediate and indubitable' (65).

A similar stress on what seems beyond doubt and obvious from the first-person is evident in others during this era, such as C. D. Broad and H. H. Price. Broad, e.g., observes that

> The fundamental fact is that we constantly make such judgements as: 'This *seems to me* elliptical, or red, or hot' as the case may be, and that

about the truth of these judgements we do not feel the least doubt. (. . .) I may be perfectly certain at one and the same time that I have the peculiar experience expressed by the judgement: 'This looks elliptical to me' and that in fact the object is not elliptical but round. (. . .) I do not suppose that anyone, on reflection, will quarrel with this statement of fact.
(Broad 1923, 236)

And Price, too, relies easily on introspection. In his book *Perception* he investigates the nature of perceptual experience and how they can justify our perceptual beliefs. He insists that his enquiry is squarely philosophical: '[w]e must simply examine seeing and touching for ourselves and do the best we can' (Price 1932, 2). Providing an example, Price describes what he can and cannot doubt when reflecting on how things appear to him as he is undergoing a visual experience as of a tomato:

[T]hat something is red and round then and there I cannot doubt. Whether the something persists even for a moment before and after it is present to my consciousness, whether other minds can be conscious of it as well as I, may be doubted. But that it now *exists*, and that *I* am conscious of it – by me at least who am conscious of it this cannot possibility be doubted.
(3)

'The something' Price isolates via first-person reflection is a sense-datum. Sense-data differ from other kinds of data present to consciousness on two counts. Firstly, they give rise to belief in external-world objects. Secondly,

it seems plain that there is also another characteristic common and peculiar to them, which may be called 'sensuousness'. This is obvious on inspection, but it cannot be described.
(4)

Again, the quote displays the confidence with which Price and others put forward first-person judgements about experience. In sum, early philosophers of perception took the results of first-person inspection to be palpable, unassailable and generalizable. Further, they considered gathering first-person phenomenal descriptions of experience with which to constrain one's account an appropriate method for theorizing about experience.[3]

Yet there exists also a different current in these discussions about conscious experience. Philosophers agreed that harnessing first-person access to experience for use in theorizing requires some care. Moore, we saw, introduced this complication because introspection is the source of a mistaken view about experience as well as the source of crucial information supporting the right view. As the debate about perceptual experience and the sense-datum theory gathered speed, similar issues arose. For example, there were disputes about what sort of qualities are part of what is presented in phenomenal consciousness and what kinds of objects we are immediately phenomenally conscious of, which are the bearers of such qualities. In particular, opponents of sense-datum theorists maintained that experiential character is as of ordinary objects and properties, rather than as of special sensory objects and their relatively sparse properties (e.g. (Barnes 1944–1945; Reichenbach 1938, 163–169).

These disputes put participating philosophers under pressure concerning their shared assumption about the appropriateness of the introspective method. Many felt the need to balance the claim that the kind of supporting evidence delivered by introspection is tremendously forceful with acknowledgement that there is a genuine debate about the phenomenal character of experience. What had to be reconciled was that certain aspects of experience are 'quite plain', 'indubitable', 'obvious' on the basis of introspection and yet that opponents could be so thoroughly introspectively misled.

The pressure typically was relieved in one of two ways. Just as Moore did, some philosophers attempted to diagnose a problem on the part of the opponent which would explain their failure to introspect adequately, consistent with maintaining that conscious experience was properly introspectively available all along. This style of explanation was preferred by opponents of sense-datum theory who held that the phenomenal character of perceptual experience is as of ordinary objects and properties (as opposed to being as of sense-data with a sparser collection of sensory qualities). When Roderick Firth in 1949 reviews the debate between sense-datum theory and what he calls 'percept theory', he notes that sense-datum theorists seem entirely unresponsive to compelling phenomenological criticism from their opponents. But, he adds,

> [i]f this indifference [to such criticism] is not to be attributed to ignorance or perversity, it is likely to suggest that there are certain fallacies or prejudices which prevent many people . . . from examining perceptual consciousness with complete objectivity.
>
> (Firth 1949, 452)

For instance, philosophers might be prevented from introspecting properly if they are in the grip of a particular conception of perceptual experience which weakens their introspective capacity to judge the character of experience.[4]

The second style of explanation involved allowing that there are different ways to access experience via the first person. This tack, which tended to be used by defenders of sense-datum theory, consisted in shifting the goal-posts from thinking of the debate as manifesting straightforwardly conflicting deliverances of introspection to manifesting different ways to introspect. Lewis, Broad and Price, for instance, each concede that there is a sense in which the character of perceptual experience can be described in terms of presenting ordinary objects and properties. Indeed, they all agree that it is how the character of experience would strike the naïve observer: on *casual* inspection, we encounter 'the thick experience of the world of things' (Lewis 1929, 54), which presents all the rich qualities had by ordinary objects. But these philosophers also insist that in casual inspection we fail to notice something that on *careful* inspection we can become aware of.

One then must make sense of this in terms of an introspective method: what do these different ways of inspecting experience amount to and which one ought we to use in theorizing? To illustrate the general strategy, I focus here on Price's view.[5] Ordinary perceptual consciousness, Price agrees, is consciousness as of material objects (objects are *leibhaftig gegeben* in such consciousness, Price remarks, using Husserl's phrase). However, perceptual consciousness in fact involves two different mental events: acquaintance with a sense-datum and an act of perceptual acceptance, i.e. a kind of taking for granted that there is a material object that 'belongs' to the sense-datum with which one is acquainted.

> The two states of mind, the acquaintance with the sense-datum and the perceptual consciousness of [say] the tree, just arise together. The sense-datum is presented to us, and the tree dawns on us, all in one moment. The two modes of 'presence to the mind' utterly different though they are, can only be distinguished by subsequent analysis.
>
> (Price 1932, 141)

Price holds that while awareness of a sense-datum and awareness of a material object in the same experience arise in unison, they constitute different kinds of cognitive acts. The former is factive, i.e. an acquaintance with something actually existing, which Price calls an 'intuitive' cognitive act. The latter is not factive, as experiential awareness as of material objects is consistent with there being no such object present. Perceptual acceptance is not intuitive, then. However, Price says it is 'pseudo-intuitive' because just like acquaintance of sense-data it contrasts with deliberative or discursive cognitive acts, such as inferring and surmising: it is not an activity but 'effortless . . . undoubting and unquestioning' (153). Price bases these claims on introspection:

> That [perceptual acceptance] has this character is just an introspectible fact, however difficult to describe.
>
> (Price 1932, 156)

As Price explains, the source of this character is different for intuitive and pseudo-intuitive acts, constituting their fundamental difference. However, in ordinary perceptual consciousness, we do not seriously reflect on experience and so we miss the difference.

> What happens is not that we identify [the sense-datum and the material object in an experience], but that we *fail to distinguish* between them. Our state is, as it were, a dreamy or half-awake state, in which we are unaware of a difference, which if we reflected would be obvious. Now

> the sense-datum really is intuitive. And since we fail to distinguish it from the remainder of the thing, the whole thing is *as if* it were intuitive, though only the sense datum actually is so.
>
> (Price 1932, 168)

Thus, Price can agree that the character of ordinary perceptual experience involves the presentation of material objects and their properties – this is so when we introspect in a casual manner. For Price, this does not conflict with the view that introspection reveals distinct sense-data. It would conflict if he were to claim that the very same thing presented in experience which opponents hold to be a material object is really a sense-datum. But this is not so on Price's picture. In the casual case – in *everyday introspection* – we are not theorizing about experience and do not attend carefully to it. We do not discriminate between the two kinds of presented objects in such a superficial characterization. When we do introspect perceptual experience with the aim of providing an account of its nature – in *careful introspection* – we make more fine-grained discriminations. We notice that there are distinct kinds of object which are present to the mind very differently, i.e. there are sense-data, which are intuited, and material objects which are pseudo-intuited.

This sort of explanatory approach was challenged in various ways by critics of sense-datum theory. They typically favoured the first type of explanation, insisting that the first-person inspection genuinely relevant to the introspective method is a kind of everyday introspection. Such introspection is immediate, commonplace and non-theoretical and it produces our naive take on experience. Careful inspection, on the other hand, is a more removed, optional take on experience which has no particular claim to priority in an analysis of perceptual consciousness (Firth 1949, 462–463; Wild 1940, 82). In choosing careful introspection, sense-datum theorists were said to elevate an 'attitude of "doubt" or "questioning"', as Firth puts it, to be the central method in analysing experience without any justification. By contrast, everyday introspection – and with it the introspective datum that experience is as of ordinary objects and properties – is not arbitrary as it is ubiquitous and already in use independently of one's theoretical aims.

A further objection to the method of careful introspection is more fundamental. As we saw, careful introspection aims to expose basic elements of phenomenal character to which we are allegedly insensitive in everyday introspection. Opponents argued that rather than helping to uncover the basic sensory structure of experience, careful introspection leads to a misrepresentation of the character of experience. Once the stance of everyday introspection is abandoned and careful introspection, driven by, say, epistemological concerns, is employed, we are in fact destroying, or at least heavily obscuring, the original target of observation.[6]

Both of these objections – and the wider discussion of which kind of first-person access is appropriate in philosophical theorizing about perceptual experience – echo some of the dominant concerns shaping the discussion in experimental psychology around that time. Firth, for instance, frequently mentions that psychologists agree with him about what direct inspection of experience reveals. He particularly cites Gestalt psychologist Wolfgang Köhler's criticism of introspectionist psychology practiced by Wundt and Titchener as one way to understand what has gone wrong with the sense-datum view (Firth 1949, 461).

Overall, it is evident that philosophers of perception during this period assumed that first-person access to experience makes available an apt description of phenomenal experience. Possession of such access was not a matter of grave concern for any of them, some difficulties and disagreements about the relevant type of access notwithstanding. However, when we look more closely at parallel discussions in psychology around the turn of the century and carrying on into the 1940s, the contrast is stark. For the basic worries at the centre of analogous debates in psychology threatened the very use of introspection in psychological theorizing.

2. The scientific role of introspection

In 1865, John Stuart Mill, responded to Auguste Comte's criticism of scientific psychology and of its core method, self-observation, as follows:

> There is little need for an elaborate refutation of a fallacy respecting which the only wonder is that it should impose upon anyone.
> (Mill 1907/1865, 63)

Comte had previously argued that scientific psychology is doomed for practical and conceptual reasons.[7] Self-observation, he said, in the sense of first-person attention to one's own conscious mental states, results in the destruction of the state one seeks to observe. As soon as one attentively reflects on one's conscious visual experience of a horse, say, one ceases to visually attend (at least in the manner one did before) to the horse and this changes one's visual experience. Moreover, the idea of a single self attending to her own attending seems to require that the self splits attention. But such splitting, according to Comte, is conceptually suspect.

Mill offers two quick responses. Concerning the conceptual worry, he points out that splitting attention has been demonstrated to be possible. He refers to William Hamilton's experiments showing that subjects can attend to several things at once ('as many as six'): while attention is weakened by such splitting, it is not impossible. Furthermore, Mill suggests that the conceptual point can be side-stepped in any case because scientific psychology can use a form of self-observation which does not involve attending to a concurrent act of attention. Rather, good scientific practice would use *immediate retrospection,* a technique of reflecting on a conscious experience just after having it 'when its impression in memory is still fresh' (64). But mainly, concerning both the practical and the conceptual point, Mill simply insists that the assumption that we have introspective knowledge of our own thoughts and experiences is not up for debate. Whatever we say about introspection, on Mill's view, we had better be able to explain how

> we could . . . have acquired the knowledge, which nobody denies us to have, of what passes in our minds. M. Comte would scarcely have affirmed that we are not aware of our own intellectual operations. We know of our observings and our reasonings, either at the very time, or by memory the moment after; in either case, by direct knowledge, and not . . . merely by their results. This simple fact destroys the whole of M. Comte's argument. Whatever we are directly aware of, we can directly observe.
>
> (*ibid.* 64)

Thirty-five years on, William James agrees with Mill's assessment on certain points. He attributes to common sense the unshakable belief that we have introspective awareness of our own conscious states and he asserts that this belief is central to psychology ('the most fundamental of all the postulates of Psychology'):

> Introspective Observation is what we have to rely on first and foremost and always. The word introspection need hardly be defined – it means, of course, the looking into our own minds and reporting what we there discover.
>
> (185)

However, James acknowledges concerns about the accuracy of introspective observation. He notes that there are extreme positions on this issue, ranging from Brentano's claim that introspective apprehension of conscious states is infallible, to Comte's rejection of direct introspective knowledge as 'a pure illusion'. James suggests that Mill's view about introspective knowledge by immediate retrospection expresses a 'practical truth about the matter'. He points out that even those who hold that introspective observation is infallible would concede that *in addition* we have access to our conscious states by immediate retrospective reflection, which is fallible due to the involvement of memory.[8] The question is which of these types of first-person access to the mind can serve as the basis for psychological method. James' answer is that it must be retrospective reflection.

> But the psychologist must not only *have* his mental states in their absolute veritableness, he must report them and write about them, name them, classify and compare them and trace their relations to other things. Whilst alive they are their own property; it is only *post-mortem* that they become his prey.
>
> (James 1890/1981, 189)

Indeed – here James agreed with Comte – judging, labelling or classifying our own conscious states cannot be done concurrently. And, just like in any other area, we are fallible in making classifications and generalizations. This is not merely true of introspective classification and judgement within psychology; it is true in ordinary situations, concerning everyday judgements such as that I feel tired. It may seem as if at that moment one is merely expressing the very feeling one is experiencing 'and so to be experiencing and observing the same inner fact at a single stroke'. But in fact, says James, the experience one is having at that moment is that of saying-I-feel-tired. Insofar as the latter involves the feeling of tiredness it is very different from the feeling of tiredness felt just a moment before. 'The act of naming [it] has momentarily detracted from their force.'

Thus, both ordinary introspective judgement and introspective observation in psychology involve immediate retrospection. Retrospection is required when we are going beyond merely feeling, to classifying and labelling. The question about accuracy thus is an empirical question and, says James, we do 'find ourselves in continual error and uncertainty' when engaging in introspection of this type.[9] But equally, for James, that introspection is difficult and fallible is nothing out of the ordinary. All kinds of observation – especially scientific observation – have this feature. We simply have to do the best we can. And, just like in most other areas of investigation by observation, agreement among participating investigators is the ultimate arbiter of adequate theorizing.

> The only safeguard is in the final *consensus* of our farther knowledge about the thing in question, later views correcting earlier ones, until at last the harmony of a consistent system is reached. Such a system, gradually worked out, is the best guarantee the psychologist can give for the soundness of any particular psychologic observation which he may report.
> (191)

In sum, for James, the adequate psychological method is just ordinary introspective reflection, which involves labelling and classifying conscious experiences based on immediate retrospection. Both the involvement of memory and the activity of classification mean that this kind of introspection is fallible.

James contrasted this method with that employed by his contemporaries in psycho-physics and experimental psychology. He was not a fan of the latter, to put it mildly.[10] His main complaint was that experimental introspection is too restricted in scope, concerning both the conditions under which introspective data can be collected and the kinds of phenomena introspective data can be collected about. For James, this literally takes the life out of the subject-matter, trivializing psychological work. To preserve the lived character of perceptual consciousness – for him so essential to the phenomenon – means using more free-flowing first-person retrospective reflection on ordinary experience, constrained mainly by seeking agreement about its best description with other psychologists and subjects engaged in describing it.

2.1 Wundt and restricted introspection

I now turn to the views of these experimentalists, with a less hostile eye than that of James.[11] I shall concentrate on the key figure of Wilhelm Wundt and then contrast his views briefly with those of his students, Edward Bradford Titchener and Oswald Külpe. Collectively, these psychologists are most often associated with so-called 'classical introspectionist psychology'.

A founding figure in experimentalist psychology as it developed from early psycho-physics in the mid- to late-1900s, Wundt is perhaps the most well-known representative of the German tradition of early experimentalist psychology which gave a key role to introspection. Early on, Wundt distinguished between different kinds of first-person access to conscious experience. He, too, was sensitive to Comte's criticism of introspection as having destructive or distorting effects (see, e.g. (Wundt 1896, 25).[12] In response, Wundt accepted Brentano's distinction between two kinds of first-person access to one's own conscious states, namely self-observation (*Selbstbeobachtung*) and inner perception (*innere Wahrnehmung*) (Brentano 1874, 35–42).[13] According to it, self-observation is an active form of direct deliberative attention to one's conscious experiences; inner perception is the fairly automatic and passive awareness one has of one's own conscious experience, as one goes along in the world in an ordinary manner. Wundt thought that both are real psychological phenomena, but that only inner perception constitutes genuine introspective awareness in the sense of being epistemically successful. For pretty much Comte's reasons, he argued that any attempt at deliberately attending to one's conscious states with the aim of observing them would distort or destroy the latter. So, while this does not mean that self-observing in this manner is impossible *qua* mental activity, it does mean that it cannot yield a scientifically valid form of observation, since the cognitive upshot cannot provide accurate data about the conscious phenomenon putatively attended to (Wundt 1888, 296). Wundt is highly critical of psychologists who use self-observation in their work, likening these efforts to Baron Munchhausen's pulling himself out of the bog by his own hair.

Inner perception, on the other hand, was taken to be the source of our firm common sense belief – one that Wundt endorsed – that we can know about our own conscious experiences. In contrast to self-observation, inner perception can supply the essential data for scientific psychology. But it cannot do so on its own, since it is a passive form of introspection not involving a deliberate attempt to attend to one's conscious experiences. Rather, inner perception involves noticing them indirectly, 'out of the corner of one's "mental eye" (Lyons 1986, 4) as one goes along having them. Inner perception is therefore unsystematic and unpremeditated. The trouble is that if one now tries to directly use inner perception to provide introspective data about conscious experience, one thereby turns passive inner perception into destructive active self-observation.

Our capacity for inner perception therefore has to be carefully exploited so as to yield scientifically respectable data. Wundt's experimental method aims to achieve this by inducing inner perception under tightly controlled circumstances (Danziger 1980, 245). In light of this, he placed severe constraints on using introspection in psychology. They are needed to enable scientific investigation because of the fleetingness of the subject-matter of psychology (i.e. conscious experiential events being very unstable), one the one hand, and the difficulties with our first-person access to this subject-matter, on the other. Given that direct observation is not possible, we have to use objective measures and experiments to observe somewhat indirectly as best as we can. For one thing, we have to ensure that we can get the conscious phenomenon reliably to present in subjects, without the latter attempting to self-observe. Wundt's various experimental set-ups are crucial aids to this (*Hülfsmittel*).[14] For another, Wundt maintained that not all conscious phenomena can be investigated in this manner. Thoughts and emotions, for example, are not reliably correlated with external stimuli to the same extent that basic sensations seem to be. Moreover, concerning sensory experiences themselves, we can acquire data only about elementary features, elicited by simple judgements or behavioural responses. Wundt's experiments shun qualitative reports because for him they are products of active self-observation. He therefore restricted experimental introspective investigation to certain basic aspects of sensory experiences. Other types of conscious and non-conscious mental phenomena, e.g. thought and emotions, were to be investigated by different, non-introspective methods (see (Wundt 1896, 24–28) and (Wundt 1888)). Having developed different methods of investigation for different psychological phenomena under the heading of 'social psychology' (*Völkerpsychologie*), he published extensively in this area. Contrary to currently widespread belief, Wundt's conception of psychology thus encompasses vastly more than investigation by introspection (see (Danziger 1980)).[15]

2.2 Titchener, Külpe and systematic introspection

Wundt was gradually superseded by a new generation of introspectionist psychologists within the first decade of the century. Some were students of his, who, although receiving their training in his laboratory, came to reject many of his restrictions on introspection. Two main brands of introspectionist psychology emerged directly out of Wundt's laboratory: Titchener's structuralism and Külpe's Würzburg school. These differed significantly, and they were at times bitter critics of one another. However, they both endorsed the scientific legitimacy of qualitative data collected from subjective introspective reports under experimental conditions. This alone constituted a clear break with Wundt.[16]

Attitudes to introspection had very much changed among these psychologists. Titchener, for instance, confidently claimed that introspection itself can be a perfectly good source of scientific observation:

> But if self-observation means, simply, psychological observation; and if observation in psychology has as its end a knowledge of mind, . . . then,

> just as certainly, introspection may be as impersonal, as objective, as matter-of-fact, as is the observation of the natural sciences.
>
> (Titchener 1912b, 434)

In response to the kind of worries that had led Wundt to regard inner perception as the only source of legitimate data (which still needed to be manipulated appropriately with the help of various experimental set-ups), Titchener took a more sanguine approach. He argued that these worries concern a former use of introspection in psychology, which is 'precritical, pre-comparative and pre-experimental' (435). It involved introspective judgements that were infected by theoretical bias and the aim for metaphysical systematization. However, Titchener maintained, the mature psychology of his day used introspection differently. For example, in the case of introspective disagreement, a regimented and repeated application of the experimental introspective method could be relied upon to eradicate biased and confused reports.

> Psychology is not the only science in which the strict application of the best available methods leads to opposite conclusions. But is there the same hope, in psychology, that differences will presently be resolved? I see no reason for any but an affirmative answer. (...) A more methodical series of observations, with variation of conditions, would either bring two observers into agreement or would give us the key to their disagreement.
>
> (437)

This echoes James's insistence that introspective observation is just like any other form of scientific observation – fallible and subject to disagreement. Titchener also emphasizes the role of agreement about introspective data in ensuring that the introspective data passes scientific muster. More generally, the various ways in which the new generation of introspectionist psychologists conceived of their work constituted a rapprochement of sorts with the non-experimentalist British empiricist tradition and their use of introspection.

One loosening of Wundtian restraint concerned the proper scope of introspective method. Külpe's Würzburg laboratory, for example, specifically aimed to investigate conscious thought, judgement, emotions and thought's relation to action (see the work of e.g. Karl Marbe, Karl Bühler, Otto Selz, and Narziss Kaspar Ach). Titchener, too, endorsed a much larger domain of investigation, including memory and mental processes more generally (Titchener 1912b, 427–428). More importantly, and correlatively, the other substantial loosening of constraint concerned the kind of introspective access harnessed in psychology, i.e. the proper method of investigation. The new generation accepted retrospection as a central introspective method, along the lines of James and Mill (see, e.g., (Bühler 1908, 100–101; Külpe 1920; Müller 1911; Titchener 1912c)). Typically, they accepted both, use of a more direct introspective awareness along the lines of inner perception, as well as immediate retrospective awareness. With that inclusion, the whole nature of the experimental method changed as well. The method of *systematic introspection* (*Ausfrageexperimente*) became dominant. Experiments designed to elicit immediate retrospective judgements about one's conscious experiences moved away from use of objective, performance-related measures to a focus on subjective report and on qualitative description of experience. In particular, we see a striking change in how the experimenter is involved in the experiment: eliciting qualitative data requires the experimenter to ask questions to which the subject responds.

One consequence was that certain theoretical differences were prone to show up in the introspective data itself, rather than in what was taken to be the scientific interpretation of the introspective data (Danziger 1980, 253). The infamous 'imageless thought controversy' between Titchener and the Würzburg school is a case in point. Würzburgers like Külpe claimed that they could introspect non-imagistic and non-sensational awarenesses (*unanschauliche Bewusstheiten*) reflecting higher cognitive activity. Titchener, on the other hand, argued that introspection did not reveal anything non-imagistic or non-sensational and hence that his opponents were simply confused in various ways, either mistaking sensational composites for putatively non-sensational elements of experience or letting their theoretical preferences infect their introspective data.

This episode thus also reflects another aspect of the state of play among experimental introspectionists in the early decades of the 1900s. The debate had become one about competing pictures of the metaphysics of conscious experience, with Titchener defending a structuralist, bottom-up picture, and the Würzburg school defending a richer conception of conscious experience including complex and higher-level cognitive elements. Titchener adhered to the doctrine of sensationalism, the view that conscious experience is composed of sensory elements that combine to produce the overall experience. Sensationalism, endorsed already by Mill and earlier British empiricists (Mill 1843, ch 4), gives introspection a key role in analysing experience into its basic components and in discovering the rules of combination in terms of which complex conscious contents of ordinary experience can be explained. In this capacity, the role of introspection was to overcome the naïve but misleading take on experience, and to discern the real conscious character with its basic sensational structure. In Titchener's hands, then, introspective investigation of conscious experience is a form of analysis, or, as it was sometimes called 'reduction', of experience into its basic sensory components (Titchener 1912c). Külpe and the Würzburgers endorsed a rather different picture of conscious experience. Specifically, they held that, in addition to sensory aspects, conscious experiences included other fundamental aspects, in the form of mental activity. The latter could not be analysed into combinations of the former. This basic outlook drew on Brentano's act psychology and Husserl's phenomenological approach to investigating experience. The Würzburg emphasis on investigating conscious thinking and activity in experience derived from these very different interests.

Both sides of the debate practiced systematic introspection, however. Yet systematic introspection presented several methodological problems (some old, some new) none of which were particularly hidden from practitioners. Central use of immediate retrospection meant that the concern about memory as a potential source of distortions and gaps resurfaced. The reliance on verbal articulation and report of qualitative data about subjects' conscious experience introduced worries about scientific validity of the data, given the inability to independently check for the presence of the experiences in question. In addition, the experiments of systematic introspection, with their active involvement of the experimenter, have a strong demand character, which presents its own danger for infecting the data collected (Müller 1911). Part of the explanation for why systematic introspection was attractive to its proponents despite all these known problems is the pervasive influence of phenomenalism in science and philosophy at that time.[17] Phenomenalism is the view that theories and explanatory terms must be epistemically grounded in what is directly given in experience. It takes for granted that we have access to what we are experientially given. Access to experience is, of course, the bone of contention in the discussions concerning introspective methodology. However, specific worries concerning introspective method might not have appeared fundamentally threatening but just something to be worked around, in light of the truly dominant position of phenomenalism at the time.

The background influence of phenomenalism also sheds light on the two basic pictures of the nature of experience separating the two camps (see (Danziger 1980), (Boring 1953) and (Hatfield 2005) for more details). Titchener was heavily influenced by the positivism of Ernst Mach, which reinforced the atomistic-sensational conception of conscious experience found in the sensationalism inherited from the British empiricists. As mentioned above, Külpe and the Würzburg school, by contrast, were guided by Brentano's act psychology and Husserl's phenomenological approach and they held a far less constructivist view of conscious experience.

By the 1920s, the method of systematic introspection had more or less run its course. In Germany, Gestalt psychology had taken hold, which, although continuing with some of the basic ideas of the Würzburg school, constituted another important shift in methodological outlook. In the US, among other things, the gradual rise of behaviourist psychology, encompassing an outright rejection of the conception of psychology concerned with inner conscious states, led to a fizzling out of Titchener's programme by the time of his death in 1927.[18]

2.3 Gestalt psychology and phenomenological method

Gestalt psychology is said to have been founded by Max Wertheimer, who argued that movement – independently of an object which moves – could be shown to be literally seen. Perceived movement was to be neither reduced to more constituent sensational elements, nor explained in terms of further judgement (Wertheimer 1912). The recognition of perceived moment as an unreducible feature of conscious experience was followed by recognition of other features, providing a very different conceptual framework of the basic organization of experience.

Describing experience in terms of fundamental organizational features, such as object constancy, was a far cry from the sparse features figuring in Wundt's constrained introspective investigation or Titchener's unconstrained systematic introspective analysis.

Two specific changes are relevant from our point of view. The first is a deliberate return to a less liberal introspective experimental method. Gestalt psychologists attempted to avoid or minimize problems associated with the demand character of systematic introspection and the involvement of memory by including checks of overt behaviour in their experimental techniques (Danziger 1980). The second is a full-throated endorsement of the need for a phenomenological description of experience which is naïve or pre-theoretical. In doing this they rejected both, Titchener's introspective analysis and Wundt's restriction on the scope of introspective investigation. Gestalt psychologists thereby manifested their affinity with the Würzburg school and Husserl's work on phenomenology (Koffka 1924, 150). As Kurt Koffka emphasizes, at the centre of their approach to psychology is the 'phenomenological method':

> In reality experimenting and observing must go hand in hand. A good description of a phenomenon may by itself rule out a number of theories and indicate definite features which a true theory must possess. We call this kind of observation 'phenomenology,' a word which has several other meanings which must not be confused with ours. For us phenomenology means as naïve and full a description of direct experience as possible. In America 'introspection' is the only one used for what we mean, but this word has also a very different meaning in that it refers to a special kind of such description, namely the one which analyses direct experience into sensations of attributes, or some other systematic but not experiential ultimates.
>
> (Koffka 1935, 73)

Indeed, Gestalt psychologists saw themselves in a kind of Goldilocks position between (systematic and analytical) introspectionism and behaviourism. Koffka and Köhler took great pains to explain how their approach differed from, overlapped with – and, of course, improved upon – introspectionism, as well as behaviourism (Koffka 1924; Köhler 1930, 1–77). Both types of experimental psychology were accused of 'remoteness from life'. Behaviourism is criticized for leaving our experience altogether:

> In their justified criticism they threw out the baby with the bath, substituting pure achievement experiments and tending to leave out phenomenology altogether. . . . Without describing the [conscious character of experience] we should not know what we had to explain.
>
> (73)

Introspectionism was criticized for using a procedure to isolate certain features of experience (local size, form and brightness) from their ordinary experiential contexts. The result is that

> of all objective experience, as both layman and psychologist enjoy it in the visual field of everyday life, very little is left as pure and genuine sensory fact (...) As long as the introspectionists' attitude prevails, however, psychology will never seriously study those experiences which form the matrix of our whole life. Instead it will observe and discuss the properties of rare and unusual experience which, though they are supposed to be continually present beneath our naïve experiences, seem to be so well hidden most of the time that their existence has nothing to do with life as we actually experience it.
>
> (Köhler 1930, 64–65)

Gestalt psychologists accepted that the introspectionists' data about experiences is genuine in that there really are such pure sensory experiences, discoverable by the introspective methods in question. But they also held that these experiences do not represent mainstream types of perceptual experience that form the starting point of any psychological inquiry. Gestalt psychologists argued that the central focus of psychology is the description and explanation of direct (naïve, immediate, uncritical) experience, i.e. of everyone's normal experiential awareness when they, say, open their eyes and look around. Ordinary experience is typically *of the world*, of objects such as chairs, tables and trees and their ordinary properties. The character is objective in that it is as of external-world, mind-independent stuff (Köhler 1930, 1–25).

According to Gestalt psychologists, the most apt characterization of experience is obtained by just describing one's surroundings in as naïve a manner as possible: '[a]ny description I can give of my surroundings, of this room, the people in it, and so on, are facts for psychology to start from' (Koffka 1924, 153). Koffka's phenomenological method has its origin in Husserl's work and I provide no more than the briefest gloss on it here.[19] The key thought is that we can gain knowledge of experience by directing our attention outwards into the world first and then shifting our attitude from experiencing the world to considering the character of such experiencing. The shift in attitude is something intellectual we do – Husserl calls it 'bracketing' – where we withhold certain kinds of commitment that come with normal experiencing the world. Such bracketing, according to Husserl, does not distort the experience itself but merely disconnects it from performing its normal function, thereby transforming our experiential knowledge of the world into knowledge of the experiential character of the former. *Much* more would need to be said to adequately present and elucidate Husserl's view and its influence on Gestalt psychologists, among others. But it should be clear already that the phenomenological method differs not only from systematic introspection, but from all the other introspective methods discussed so far. The latter all involve kinds of first-person access to experience via fairly basic psychological kinds (observation, memory, attention, feeling). The former does not; the sense in which it constitutes first-person access to experience is quite different, since the route to first-person awareness of experience is via outward experiential attention together with further deliberate and complex intellectual efforts.

Koffka further explains that one can also take an investigative, first-person ('analytic') attitude to experience, i.e. one can introspect one's experience in the more traditional sense. However, taking *that* attitude to one's experience changes one's mental situation, namely the 'subjective conditions' under which the organism is reacting to the environment. Consequently, it is no surprise that there are different experiences ('reactions') in these cases. 'You were looking at this room and were interested in it at the beginning, you were introspecting and interested in psychology afterward' (154). Thus, introspecting involves changing the experience one is having in a way the phenomenological method does not. In light of this, Koffka argues that, while psychology can and does usefully engage in introspective investigation of conscious experience, it has to do so very carefully. Sometimes the changes brought about in the target experience are not destructive, but are in keeping with the dynamic organization of the target experience's content. In that case, the introspectively changed experience amounts to 'a development' of the former. But sometimes the changes result in an entirely different experience altogether.

> This is why it is wrong to attempt to maintain an analytical attitude at all costs as *the* method of psychology. In most cases such an attitude does not develop the [original experience], but destroys many of its original tendencies. The attitude which is legitimate has to be determined by the nature of each separate whole dealt with, and in this appears the art of introspection. Introspection, like every other kind of observation, is an art, and it is not an easy one.
>
> (158)

The criticism here is not that analytic introspectionism *uses* introspection to investigate conscious experience – Gestalt psychology does so, too. Rather, introspectionism uses it irresponsibly and exclusively. Because of this, the fact that introspection inevitably changes the target experience becomes too destructive. The root problem is that introspectionists use introspective data so acquired as the starting point for theorizing, assuming that it offers the most basic and accurate description of conscious sensory experience. But, as we saw, Gestalt psychologists hold that the latter and hence the starting point for psychology is based on the naïve and uncritical take on it derived from simply describing the scene around one, i.e. describing 'the world, as we have it'.

2.4 Varieties of first-person access

In sum, psychologists of this era tended to accept that introspection delivers useful and important data about the conscious mind, but also that there are different kinds of introspection, i.e. different kinds of first-person access and that not all are equally suitable to the task. Moreover, even if suitable such access must be employed carefully because getting scientifically respectable introspective data is difficult under the best circumstances. They agreed that the central difficulty comes from the potentially distorting and destructive effects of deliberate introspective reflection but they disagreed about what to do about this. Their disagreement has many sources, and I have been able to convey only a small part of the overall story. Among the experimental psychologists, the Gestalt psychologists emphasized further that the first point of departure for the scientist must be a description of 'direct experience', by which they meant ordinary, lived experience from the point of view of the naïve experiencer. As we saw, this description is obtained by describing, as uncritically as possible, the world around one as one is experiencing it. Insofar as this method owes to Husserl's phenomenological method, and by the Gestalt psychologists' own insistence, this way of acquiring first-person data about experience is significantly different from any of the other kinds of first-person access classified as introspection.

In section 1, I said that Firth refers to the Gestalt psychologists' naïve take on experience to explain what he means by direct inspection of experience. Moreover, his critique of sense-datum theory mentions the Gestalt psychologists' rejection of Titchener's systematic introspective method. This clearly shows the influence psychological discussion of introspection had on philosophy of perception at that time. This impact was long-lasting. Thirty years later, P. F. Strawson, in critiquing A. J. Ayer's sense-datum view, insisted that when we ask 'a non-philosophical observer gazing idly through a window' to describe his experience to us '[h]e does not start talking about lights and colours, patches and patterns (Strawson 1979, 43)'. Instead, Strawson claims, the world is objectively 'given with the given' (47).

However, just like in the case of the Gestalt psychologists' view about the naïve description of experience, it is not entirely clear what the nature of the first-person access involved is. According to Strawson,

> [the observer will] *use* the perceptual claim – the claim it was natural to make in the circumstance – in order to characterise [his] experience, without actually making the claim. [He] renders the perceptual judgement internal to the characterization of the experience without actually asserting the content of the judgement. And this is really the best possible way of characterising the experience.
>
> (Strawson 1979, 44)

The Husserlian heritage seems plain in this passage. Against the background of the developments in psychology just discussed, this raises interesting questions about whether – and, if so, in what sense – the method employed counts as a first-person access we recognize as a kind of introspection at all.

3. Transparency and introspecting at the end of the 20th century

While earlier philosophical discussions surrounding perception were typically motivated by epistemological concerns, late 20th-century focus shifted to philosophy of mind topics such as physicalism and the mind-body problem. There was an active debate about perceptual experience between representationalism, qualia theories and disjunctivism. Sense-datum theory had largely dropped out of the picture by then. Some of the main reasons for this connect smoothly with the critique Firth made against Price: the view that sense-datum theory severely distorts the character of experience and that a correct description of the latter involves reference to ordinary objects and properties. It is fair to say that the claim that the phenomenal character of experience is as of the objective world was broadly taken as common ground in the 1980s and 1990s and many disputes about the correct description of phenomenal character concerned certain further details.[20] The details of these views are not important here; rather, it's the way in which such descriptions were typically put forward in those discussions. Specifically, the claim that phenomenal character is as of the objective world was often affirmed in the context of the thesis that experience is transparent to first-person reflection. The transparency thesis has played a powerful role in the philosophy of perception at the end of the century, providing a major source of support for arguments in favour of representationalist and disjunctivist views of perceptual experience. Roughly, it says that when one reflects on what (e.g.) visual experience is like for one – when one reflects on the phenomenal character of one's visual experience – one looks through the experience to what it is about, namely to the ordinary objects and their sensible properties presented in experience. As Tye puts it:

> Why is it that perceptual experiences are transparent? When you turn your gaze inward and try to focus your attention on intrinsic features of these experiences, why do you always seem to end up attending what the experiences are of? (. . .) In turning one's mind inward to attend to the experience, one seems to end up scrutinizing external features or properties.
>
> (Tye 1995, 135–136)

Proponents of the transparency thesis thus maintain that first-person reflection on phenomenal character does not lead to awareness of any special experiential object or properties, distinct from those we would refer to in describing the world as we experience it (see also, e.g. (Shoemaker 1996, 100–101; Dretske 1995, 62)). The most apt description of phenomenal character is in terms of ordinary objects and properties.

Interesting for our purposes is what kind of reflection is supposed to be involved in the transparency thesis. The blunt assumption by philosophers in these debates was that it is introspection (see, e,g (Loar 1997, 597; Lycan 1995, 82; Tye 2000, 51). They tended to identify what they (and others) are doing when they reflect on phenomenal character as introspecting and often called the data about experience thus collected 'introspective evidence' (e.g. (Martin 2000, 219; Crane 2000a, 50). Other phrases are also used, such as 'turning one's attention inwards', or 'attending to one's experience', or 'reflecting on what experience is like' and so forth. The impression one forms on the basis of this literature is that there is a fairly straightforward first-person access to one's own conscious states. It was taken for granted that we have introspective access to our experiences and that such access yields appropriate descriptions of phenomenal character for use in theorizing. However, not much is said about what kind of access it is.

Thus, philosophers of perception towards the end of the 20th century took seriously phenomenal adequacy constraints on their theories, and they did not consider them difficult to come by via introspection. This contrasts with both debates discussed previously. The early sense-datum discussion held that introspecting phenomenal character is possible as well as knowledge-conducing, but they also recognized that it must be done with great care. Moreover, we saw that the fact that opponents accepted different introspective verdicts raised a serious question for them about the kind of first-person access at work in their respective theorizing. Firth argued that direct inspection of experience reveals that phenomenal character is best described objectively, but he also acknowledged different kinds of first-person attitudes one might take to one's conscious experiences and that they might be responsible for the different verdicts. In the case of experimental psychology, we saw that psychologists were much preoccupied with the question of which kind of first-person or introspective access was suitable for gathering accurate descriptions of the target experiences. Much of their discussion was driven by worries over the potential of various kinds of introspection to distort or destruct the target experience and this worry was crucial to their choice of introspective method.

In the last two decades of the 20th century, philosophers of perception in the debates mentioned above were not concerned about these issues. They put forward claims about phenomenal character, where these claims were meant to be obvious upon introspection. Insofar as there was sensitivity to the issue of diverging introspective claims about phenomenal character, this is not taken to impugn the first-person access to conscious experience as such in a serious way. For instance, Michael Martin explains the differences between the descriptions of phenomenal character by sense-datum theorists and representationalists as resulting from prioritizing different elements of the naïve introspective description of phenomenal character which forms common ground between them.

> From this perspective, what is notable about each of the main traditions is not what they seek to defend by reference to introspection, but what they are prepared to reject in the face of introspective support. The

sense-datum tradition denies the manifest fact that it seems to us as if we are presented in experience with mind-independent objects and states of affairs in the world around us. The intentional tradition denies the introspective evidence that things apparently sensed must actually be before the mind for one to experience so.

(Martin 2000, 219)

Most surprisingly, though, is the seeming lack of awareness of any connection between the transparency thesis and Husserlian phenomenological method among many mainstream proponents of the transparency thesis. In their hands, the latter tends to be taken to articulate that which is introspectible, namely the thoroughly objective character of experience. But when one looks at accounts of the process involved, they bear significant resemblance to those put forward by psychologists and philosophers more directly inspired by Husserl.[21] The reason why this is important here is that, as we saw above, whether the phenomenological method counts as a kind of introspection at all is a genuine question.

Late 20th-century discussions involving transparency thus display a kind of selective forgetfulness with respect to introspection. On the one hand, there is a clear line running from early critics of sense-datum theory and the experimental psychologists who influenced them, to later proponents of representationalism and disjunctivism endorsing the thought that naïve reflection on experience reveals its character to be objective. On the other hand, though, the earlier long-standing and sophisticated discussions in which this thought was typically embedded – in particular the distinction between types of first-person access at work in theorizing about conscious experience – has almost entirely washed out.

Notes

1 For instance, I will not provide an overview of all the different accounts of the nature of introspection and self-knowledge put forward. For excellent, up-to-date and comprehensive survey articles covering this material, see Gertler 2008; Kind, April 2015; Schwitzgebel, Summer 2014.
2 I am presenting Lewis as a sense-datum theorist here, but see (Crane 2000b, 180–181) for discussion.
3 '[T]he only way to decide a question of this sort is by direct inspection of perceptual consciousness itself' (Firth 1949, 453).
4 According to Firth, sense-datum theorists might hold an over-intellectualised conception of perceptual experience which 'could blind [them] to the very phenomenological facts which would correct it' (455).
5 See (Broad 1923, 247–8; Lewis 1929, 38–66) different versions of this explanatory strategy. See also Firth 1949.
6 See Firth 1949, 460–461. In the preface to the 1954 reprint of *Perception*, Price says that while he still thinks that sense-datum terminology is useful for describing how things strictly look, say, from a painter's perspective, it is not useful in accounting for ordinary perceptual experience. He explains that sensing (acquaintance with sensedata) is not as previously argued a core constituent of ordinary experience, but is rather itself a kind of phenomenal inspection (Price 1932, ix).

7 See the lengthy passage from *Cours de philosophie positive*, cited in (James 1890/1981, 187–188).
8 James notes Brentano's distinction between 'the immediate *feltness* of a feeling' and our awareness of it via retrospective reflection.
9 Especially when introspecting experiences which are complex or not very strong, according to James. See (James 1890/1981, 190–191) for more discussion.
10 'This method taxes patience to the utmost, and could hardly have arisen in a country whose natives could be bored. Such Germans as Weber, Fechner, Vierordt and Wundt obviously cannot.... (...) There is little of the grand style about these new prism pendulum, and chronograph-philosophers. They mean business, not chivalry. What generous divination, and that superiority in virtue which was thought by Cicero to give a man the best insights into nature, have failed to do, their spying and scraping, their deadly tenacity and almost diabolic cunning, will doubtless some day bring about' (192).
11 That hostility is a manifestation of different viewpoints not just about introspection but also about the overarching theoretical conception of psychology, between the British tradition James is ensconced in, and the German experimentalist tradition of Wundt. For the historical origin and background debates surrounding introspectionist psychology, see (Danziger 1980), also (Boring 1953) and (Lyons 1986, p. ch 1).
12 Wundt was also reacting to similar criticism of introspective methods in psychology by his teacher, Friedrich Lange (Lange 1887, 679–690).
13 'Innere Wahrnehmung' is often translated as 'inner perception' and to avoid confusion I will stick with this terminology. But the choice of words is unfortunate in suggesting the perceptual model of introspection, which seems not strictly part of the notion as it was used by Brentano and Wundt.
14 Wundt disagreed with James's choice of retrospection as the key introspective method. For Wundt, retrospection isn't scientific observation at all because the latter requires by definition that the target of observation be present while being observed (Wundt 1888, 294). Retrospection involves merely remembering the relevant conscious experience. However, Wundt did think that it *can* be used to good effect. Some of his experiments employed retrospection, mainly to retrospectively access the upshot of inner perception.
15 For a representative caricature view of Wundt's psychology as confined to investigating conscious experience via introspection, see Braisby and Gellatly 2012, 9. Also Davies 2005, which presents nuanced picture of the complex development of experimental psychology overall, though.
16 See, e.g., Wundt's detailed criticism of the Würzburg experimental approach (Wundt 1907).
17 For detailed accounts of these background influences see Boring 1953, Danziger 1980, Hatfield 2005.
18 For space reasons, I will concentrate on Gestalt psychology in this paper. But the relationship between behaviourist psychology and introspection is fascinating in its own right (Boring 1953; Lyons 1986, 23–44). For classic papers by early behaviourists critiquing introspectionist psychology, see e.g. Watson 1913; Dunlap 1912. For attempts to account for introspective belief in behaviourist terms see, e.g. (Lashley 1923).
19 My (rudimentary) understanding of Husserl's approach is due to (Thomasson 2005). See Walsh and Yoshimi's chapter on the phenomenological tradition in this volume.
20 One key issue concerned whether one needs to appeal to additional non-objective, qualitative properties to adequately describe phenomenal character (e.g. Harman 1990; Tye 1992; Tye 1995; Tye 2000; Searle 1983; Peacocke,1983; Levin 1995; Block 1980, 278). Another issue, e.g., concerned the precise manner of objective givenness, that is, whether it involves particular objects or merely generalized existential reference to them (e.g. Soteriou 2000; Martin 1997; Davies 1992).

21 The issue plays out in different ways in some later discussions concerning the nature of introspection, see, e.g. Sellars 1956/1997; Drestke 1999; Byrne 2005; Tye 2000. The Husserlian origin is hardly ever acknowledged, much less discussed in any detail. See, though, (Thomasson 2005) for an excellent discussion of Husserl's view of self-knowledge and his influence on Sellars's view in particular.

Bibliography

Barnes, W. (1944–1945). "The Myth of Sense-data," *Proceedings of the Aristotelian Society.*

Block, N. (1980). "Troubles with Functionalism," in Block, N. (ed.), *Readings in the Philosophy of Psychology*. London: Methuen.

Boring, E. (1953). "A History of Introspection," *Psychological Bulletin*: 169–189.

Braisby, N., and Gellatly, A. (2012). "Foundations of Cognitive Psychology," in Braisby, N. and Gellatly, A. (eds.), *Cognitive Psychology*. 2nd ed. Oxford: Oxford University Press: 1–28.

Brentano, F. (1874). *Psychologie vom empirischen Standtpunkt Vol 1*. Leipzig: Duncker & Humblot.

Broad, C. (1923). *Scientific Thought*. London: Kegan Paul.

Bühler, K. (1908). "Antwort of die von W. Wundt erhobenen Einwaende gegen die Methode der Selbstbeobachtung an experimentell erzeugten Erlbebnissen," *Archiv fuer die gesamte Psychologie.*

Byrne, A. (2005). "Introspection," *Philosophical Topics*, 33: 79–104.

Crane, T. (2000a). "Introspection, Intentionality and the Transparency of Experience,". *Philosophical Topics*, 28: 49–67.

Crane, T. (2000b). "The Origins of Qualia," in Crane, T. and Patterson, S. (eds.), *History of the mind-body problem*. London: Routledge: 169–194.

Danziger, K. (1980). "The History of Introspection Reconsidered," *Journal of the History of Behavioural Sciences*: 241–262.

Davies, M. (1992). "Perceptual Content and Local Supervenience," *Proceedings of the Aristotelian Society*: 21–45.

Davies, M. (2005). "An Approach to Cognitive Psychology," in Jackson, F. and Smith, M. (eds.), *The Oxford Handbook of Contemporary Philosophy*. Oxford: Oxford University Press.

Drestke, F. (1999). "The Mind's Awareness of Itself," *Philosophical Studies*, 95: 103–124.

Dretske, F. (1995). *Naturalizing the Mind*. Cambridge, MA: MIT Press.

Dunlap, K. (1912). "The Case Against Introspection," *Psychological Review* (19): 404–413.

Firth, R. (1949). "Sense-data and the Percept Theory," *Mind*: 434–465.

Gertler, B. (2008). "Self-knowledge," *The Stanford Encyclopedia of Philosophy.* (Fall 2017 Edition), Edward N. Zalta (ed.), <https://plato.stanford.edu/archives/fall2017/entries/self-knowledge/>.

Harman, G. (1990). "The Intrinsic Quality of Experience," *Philosophical Perspectives*, 4: 31–52.

Hatfield, G. (2005). "Introspective Evidence in Psychology," in Achinstein, P. (ed.), *Scientific Evidence*. Baltimore: Johns Hopkins University Press: 259–286.

James, W. (1890/1981). *The Principles of Psychology*. Cambridge, MA: Harvard University Press.

Kind, A. (2015, April). "Introspection," *Internet Encyclopedia of Philosophy*, ISSN 2161-0002, http://www.iep.utm.edu/.

Koffka, K. (1924). "Introspection and the Method of Psychology," *British Journal of Psychology*, 15: 149–161.

Koffka, K. (1935). *Principles of Gestalt Psychology*. London: Routledge and Kegan Paul Ltd.
Köhler, W. (1930). *Gestalt Psychology*. London: G. Bell and Sons Ltd.
Külpe, O. (1920). *Vorlesungen ueber Psychologie*. Leipzig: Hirzel.
Lange, F. A. (1887). *Geschichte des Materialismus und Kritik seiner Bedeutung in der Gegenwart*. Iserlohn: J. Baedeker.
Lashley, K. S. (1923). "The Behaviorist Interpretation of Consciousness," *Psychological Bulletin* (30): 237–272; 329–353.
Levin, J. (1995). "Qualia: Intrinsic, Relational or What?" in Metzinger, T. (ed.), *Conscious Experience*. Parderborn: Schoeningh: 277–292.
Lewis, C. I. (1929). *Mind and the World Order*. London: Charles Scribner's Sons.
Loar, B. (1997). "Phenomenal States," in Block, N., Flanagan, O. and Guezeldere, G. (eds.), *The Nature of Consciousness*. Cambridge, MA: MIT Press: 97–615.
Lycan, W. (1995). "Layered Perceptual Representation," *Philosophical Issues*, 7, 81–100.
Lyons, W. (1986). *The Disappearance of Introspection*. Cambridge, MA: MIT Press.
Martin, M. (1997). "The Reality of Appearances," in Sainsbury, M. (ed.), *Thought and Ontology*. Milano, Italy: Franco Angeli: 81–106.
Martin, M. (2000). "Beyond Dispute: Sense-data, Intentionality and the Mind-body Problem," in Crane, T. and Patterson, S. (eds.), *History of the Mind-Body Problem*. London: Routledge: 195–231.
Mill, J. S. (1843). *A System of Logic*. s.l.:s.n.
Mill, J. S. (1907/1865). *Auguste Comte and Positivism*. London: Kegan.
Moore, G. E. (1903). "The Refutation of Idealism," *Mind*, 433–453.
Müller, G. E. (1911). "Zur Analyse der Gedaechtnistaetigkeit und des Vorstellungsverlaufes," *Zeitschrift fuer Psychologie*, I(5).
Peacocke, C. (1983). *Sense and Content*. Oxford: Clarendon Press.
Price, H. H. (1932). *Perception*. London: Methuen.
Reichenbach, H. (1938). *Experience and Prediction*. Chicago: Chicago University Press.
Schwitzgebel, E. (2014, Summer). "Introspection," *The Stanford Encyclopedia of Philosophy*. (Winter 2016 Edition), Edward N. Zalta (ed.), <https://plato.stanford.edu/archives/win2016/entries/introspection/>.
Searle, J. (1983). *Intentionality: An Essay in the Philosophy of Mind*. Cambridge: Cambridge University Press.
Sellars, W. (1956/1997). *Empiricism and the Philosophy of Mind*. Cambridge, MA: Harvard University Press.
Shoemaker, S. (1996). "Qualities and Qualia: What's in the Mind?" in *The First-Person Perspective and other Essays*. Cambridge: Cambridge University Press: 97–120.
Soteriou, M. (2000). "The Particularity of Experience," *European Journal of Philosophy*, 173–189.
Strawson, P. (1979). "Perception and its Objects," in: MacDonald, G. (ed.), *Perception and Identity: Essays Presented to A. J. Ayer*. Ithaca, NY: Cornell University Press: 41–60.
Thomasson, A. (2005). "First-Person Knowledge in Phenomenology," in Smith, D. W. and Thomasson, A. (eds.), *Phenomenology and Philosophy of Mind*. Oxford: Oxford University Press.
Titchener, E. B. (1912a). "Description vs Statement of Meaning," *American Journal of Psychology*, (23): 165–182.
Titchener, E. B. (1912b). "Prolegomena to a Study of Introspection," *American Journal of Psychology*, (23): 427–448.

Titchener, E. B. (1912c). "The Schema of Introspection," *American Journal of Psychology*, (23): 485–508.

Tye, M. (1992). "Visual Qualia and Visual Content," in Crane, T. (ed.), *The Contents of Experience*. Cambridge: Cambridge University Press: 158–176.

Tye, M. (1995). *Ten Problems of Consciousness*. Cambridge, MA: MIT Press.

Tye, M. (2000). *Consciousness, Color and Content*. Cambridge, MA: MIT Press.

Watson, John B. (1913). "Psychology as the Behaviorist Views It," *Psychological Review* (20): 158–177.

Wertheimer, M. (1912). "Experimentelle Studien ueber das Sehen von Bewegung," *Zeitschrift fuer Psychology and Physiologie der Sinnesorgane*: 61.

Wild, J. (1940). "The Concept of the Given in Contemporary Philosophy – Its Origin and Limitations," *Philosophy and Phenomenological Research*: 70–82.

Wundt, W. (1888). "Selbstbeobachtung und innere Wahrnehmung," *Philosophische Studien*: 292–309.

Wundt, W. (1896). *Grundriss der Psychologie*. Leipzig: Engelmann.

Wundt, W. (1907). "Ueber Ausfrageexperimente und ueber die Methoden zu Psychologie des Denkens," *Psychologische Studien*, (3): 301–360.

7

THE MENTAL CAUSATION DEBATES IN THE 20TH CENTURY

Julie Yoo

1. Introduction

The 'mind-body problem' covers two distinct but related metaphysical problems. One is synchronic: how to account for the structural relation between mental states and their underlying neural states. The other is diachronic: how to explain the apparent causal relations between a person's environment, her mental states, and her body. The problem of mental causation pertains to the latter.[1]

We can see the problem of mental causation in an illustration. As evening approaches, you notice that it is getting darker. This observation, along with your desire to see better, triggers the urge to seek a light switch. Luckily, you spot one. Your hand moves toward it and flicks it on, illuminating the room and letting you see again. Every part of this story involves the apparent causal interactions among the environment, one's mind, and one's body. One's surroundings seem to cause the mental state of perceiving the dimming ambient light, and this mental state seems to lead to the desire to see better, which then produces a sequence of movements in one's arm. It certainly seems that one's mental states play a critical role – if you wanted to remain in the dark or had some other mental state, the story would have turned out differently.

Explaining how one's mental states figure in as causes and as effects *alongside* the causal activity going on in the body has been notoriously difficult. Ever since Descartes (1596–1650) deemed the mind wholly non-physical and substantially different from the body, mind-body interaction has been deeply baffling.[2] After all, if the mind is wholly non-physical, how can it 'push' against the brain to make it move the arm? Twentieth-century work on mental causation has undergone radical shifts in the very approach to the problem – from returning to the 17th-century debates about the tenability of dualism, to rejecting the problem all together as a pseudo-problem, to finally returning to it again with unparalleled interest. Indeed, the history of the mental causation debates in this century has unfolded with ever greater drama, as the end of the century has brought into focus not just one, but many, distinct problems of mental causation, each posing unique threats to its very possibility.

This essay is divided into three sections. The first covers the early 20th-century writings on mental causation. The second presents the mid-century denial of mental causation as a legitimate problem. And the third and longest section lays out the late 20th-century discoveries of new difficulties for mental causation, along with the most significant strategies proposed in their wake.

2. Early 20th century: "naturalist" approaches to mind-body interaction

Despite three centuries separating the early 20th-century philosophers from Descartes, there is a seamless continuity between them (see Maja Spener's entry in this volume on Descartes and 20th-century approaches to introspection). The virtues and drawbacks of the positions mapped out by the post-Cartesian philosophers of the 17th century, namely, interactionism, parallelism, and epiphenomenalism (see the Appendix for a summary of these positions), were still very much alive in the debates in the early 20th century, fueled, no doubt, by the rapid growth of new scientific approaches to the mind and the materialist metaphysics they naturally insinuated.[3]

In light of these trends, it is understandable why philosophers would have been pressed to re-examine the plausibility of explaining mind-body interaction in broadly naturalistic terms. Roy Wood Sellars summed up the zeitgeist this way:

> Until recently, dualistic theories have been in the ascendant. Whatever form this dualism took, whether parallelistic or interactionistic, it rested upon certain traditional assumptions and inhibitions which have only lately been undermined by the growth of science and the corresponding increase of what may be called a realistic naturalism.
>
> (1918, 155)

Of the naturalist positions, reductive materialism offers the most straightforward account of mental causation, since it is nothing other than plain physical causation that goes by a mental description. Indeed, there simply is no problem of mental causation for reductive materialism since the mind is not placed in a separate ontological category from the body. Despite this Occamite advantage, conceptual difficulties for reductive materialism have made (and continue to make) the option controversial. More attractive were epiphenomenalism, panpsychism, and emergentism, the main positions on mental causation in the early 20th century.

Epiphenomenalism was defended by T. H. Huxley (1874) and George Santayana (1942). On this view, mental states are causal "byproducts" of neural (physical) states but do not themselves cause physical or other mental states. Although epiphenomenalism has the virtue of avoiding some of the problems that beset Cartesian interactionism (see the Appendix), it is admittedly at odds with common sense. We can grant that the sensation of pain is a causal consequence of neural activity, but we also believe that the sensation of pain *qua* sensation can make a person go through great lengths to put a stop to it. Mental states certainly appear to have highly focused efficacy. Moreover, this efficacy seems to have a plausible Darwinian explanation. As argued by William James, were it not for the evolutionary adaptiveness of pains that warn against harm, humans would not be where they are today (1890). James's Darwinian strategy was not sufficiently developed to accommodate the efficacy of representational contents of intentional states, a desideratum for a complete account of mental causation, but it was a solid *a posteriori* strategy to support the efficacy of phenomenal states.

Another view popular at the time was panpsychism, promoted by James (1907 and 1909), Russell (1927), and Whitehead (1929). The idea was developed in different ways. On James's version, the nature of the physical is such that it is "dusted" with mentality, where mentality is an ineliminable aspect of the basic physical structure of the world. On Russell's version, space, time, and matter are "grounded by" a form of mentality. Because the mental was supposed to be a fundamental feature of the world, panpsychists perhaps assumed that the mechanisms of mental causation were obvious. For Whitehead, the world evolves as it does by virtue of participating in the mind's intrinsic "spontaneity and creativity." But this inchoate idea is not obvious. Indeed, for all its popularity, panpsychism faced some large open questions. Was the universe supposed to be "dusted with" or "grounded by" fully conscious minds or only protoconscious minds? And how did the dusting or grounding take place?[4] These gaping holes might explain why there was no official panpsychist account of mental causation.

The most developed view of mental causation to come out of the early 20th century was the emergentist notion of downward causation. Emergentism was embraced on both sides of the Atlantic: by Samuel Alexander (1920), Lloyd Morgan (1923), and C. D. Broad (1925) in the UK and by William James (1890), Roy Wood Sellars (1920 and 1922), and Arthur Lovejoy (1926) in the US. The view was (and still is) appealing because it promises to strike a delicate balance between the austerity of mechanistic views, where the mind is nothing but the aggregate of purely physical parts, and the extravagance of panpsychism and dualism. Unlike the panpsychists who postulated mentality at the most basic level, the emergentists accounted for the ontological status of mentality in terms of the arrangement of "more basic" physical (neural) constituents. Once those constituents were combined in the right way, mental properties were said to *emerge*, not as causal consequence of the lower-level constituents, as a dualist interactionist would construe things in the "bottom-up" direction, and not as a logical consequence of the properties of the lower level, the way the mass and shape of a wall is a logical consequence of the mass and arrangement of the constituent bricks. Instead, emergent properties were said to emerge as brute, novel, products that synchronously non-causally and nonlogically arise out of their underlying constituents.

On the emergentist view, higher-level phenomena such as minds have a distinctive causal capacity over and above the causal powers of the constituents whose arrangements make their emergence possible. These distinctive causal powers enable changes at the higher level (intra-level causation), the lower-level phenomena being insufficient on their own to bring about these changes. The exercise of these distinctive causal powers at this higher level also involves what philosophers call *downward causation* (inter-level causation).

There are two different ways downward causation can be construed. The first is in terms of the "top-down" part of dualist interactionist causation. On this construal, higher-level phenomena bring about changes at the lower level that would not have come about were it not for the presence of the emergent forces doing their thing; the emergent properties bring about changes at the lower level.[5] On the other construal, and one more difficult to pin down, downward causation does *not* bring about changes in the lower level as such. This construal is implicit in Alexander's objection to epiphenomenalism:

> The mental state is [alleged by some dualists as] the epiphenomenon of the neural process. But what neural process? Of its own neural process. But that process possesses the mental character, and there is no evidence to show that it would possess its specific neural character if it were not also mental.
>
> (1920, Vol I, 8)

According to Alexander, a neural process has the properties it has in virtue of being the process for a certain mental state. Had the process been a neural process for a different mental state, the neural processes would have had different physical properties. That is, there is no way to prise the mental apart from its neural correlate. This blocks the mind-body separation necessary to get epiphenomenalism off the ground. On one way of interpreting Alexander's view, higher-level phenomena determine how the lower-level constituents get to behave, not by directly exerting causal powers on the lower level, but by constraining which causal powers the underlying processes may exercise. This would mean that the laws of the special sciences, and thus laws of higher-level kinds, including mental kinds, are irreducible to the laws of fundamental physics. However, the properties that figure in these irreducible laws do not exert causal powers over and above the causal powers of their lower-level physical constituents. Instead, the higher-level laws non-causally constrain the expression of the causal powers of physical properties. This is not interactionist downward causation. It is, one might say, *downward determination*.

The mental causation debate, while lively in the early 20th century, came to a halt in the mid-20th century, when a core assumption shared by rival materialist accounts of mental causation came under close scrutiny. This assumption was realism about the mind.

3. Mid-20th century: questioning reasons as causes

With the rise of behaviorism, ordinary language philosophy, and the influence of the late Wittgenstein, the 1930s to the 1960s witnessed a thorough rejection of the

Cartesian framework, and with it, the very conception of mind as something that can wield causal powers.[6]

The most forceful and notable of these critiques came from Gilbert Ryle (1949). According to Ryle, the Cartesian metaphysics of mind came down to the puerile idea of a ghost in the machine. Thinking of the mind as an entity like a body, except that it is non-physical, involved a "category mistake," Ryle's term for a fundamental error in one's very conceptual grasp of the phenomenon at hand. This error was committed not only by dualists, according to Ryle, but also by materialists according to whom the mind was, again, an object, though thoroughly mechanical in nature (Ch. III, "The Will"). Questions about what caused your hand to turn on the light switch – whether it was the mind or instead the body – were just the wrong questions to ask. Using ordinary language as a guide:

> [W]e say simply 'He did it [the action]' and not 'He did or underwent something else which caused it'.
>
> (1949, 82)

The general lesson people took from Ryle was that reasons are not causes. In short, there is no mental causation in the traditional sense.

Three arguments were given for this negative claim. One, which we can call *the improper category objection*, is that reasons do not belong to the right ontological category to count as causes. This is because they are not *events*: "Motives are not happenings and are not therefore of the right type to be causes" (Ryle 1949, 113). Actions are also not appropriately classifiable as events, according to Elizabeth Anscombe (1957). Neither reasons nor actions are to be modeled on physical change, for physical changes are backed by evidence and support predictions. Nothing like this applies to reasons or actions.[7]

A second argument for the negative claim, which we can call the *necessitation objection*, is that there is a logical or conceptual (*a priori*) tie connecting reports of reasons and reports of actions, violating one of the Humean principles governing causal claims, namely, that the descriptions of causes and their effects must be logically contingent and *a posteriori*. As A. I. Melden 1961 explains in his *Free Action*:

> If the relation were causal, the wanting to do would be, indeed must be, describable independently of any reference to the doing. But it is logically essential to the wanting that it is the wanting to do something of the required sort with the thing one has. Hence the relation between the wanting to do and the doing cannot be a causal one.
>
> (1961, 128)

Reports of practical reasoning, however, seem to display a conceptual tie. When we say things like "She turned on the light switch because she wanted to brighten the room and believed that by turning on the switch, the room would get brighter," there is an air of logical necessity or triviality to the claim; had she believed or desired differently, it seems to follow that she would have done something else a matter of analytic inference. Such is the mark of explanations in terms of reasons, according to Melden. To dispel the air of logical necessity, one could say, "She turned on the light switch because the fast-spiking interneurons were activated by an increase in dopamine in her prefrontal cortex." But then this would not be an explanation of the action in terms of the person's *reasons*.

The third argument, which we can call the *general law objection*, comes from another Humean constraint on causation. If causation is a matter of constant conjunction, then a causal relation obtains in virtue of there being a general law to the effect that causes of a certain kind always lead to effects of this other kind. But, M. F. Cohen tells us:

> [I]n neither first nor third person statements does a motive [reason] explanation of an action rest upon an empirical generalization about what the agent (or others) would do in like circumstances when possessed of such a motive.
>
> (1964, 331)

Indeed, the generalizations of folk psychology are riddled with qualifications and escape clauses: all things being equal, if you fear something, you will avoid it; all things being equal, if you want something, you will seek it; and so on. Without a non-*ex post facto* way way of accounting for when all things are equal, generalizations appealing to an agent's reasons appear unfit to work as empirical law-like generalizations.

These anti-causal arguments about reasons and actions held considerable sway in the mid-20th century until they were overturned dramatically by Carl Hempel (1962), Kim & Brandt (1963), and most notably, Donald Davidson (1963 and 1970), who placed the problem of mental causation once again in the the forefront of philosophy of mind.

4. Late 20th century: the *many* problems for mental causation

We now enter the golden age of the mental causation debates. Not only do we see an array of novel approaches to the traditional Cartesian problem, but we also discover unforeseen problems whose solutions have inspired some impressive feats of creativity and ingenuity. These include:

> *The Anomalism Problem*: If events can be causally related only if there are laws that cover them, the absence of psychological or psychophysical laws jeopardizes mental events as candidates for efficacy.
>
> *The Exclusion Problem*: If the physical domain is causally closed, then your turning on the switch has a fully sufficient physical cause

that "excludes" other possibly mental causes in bringing about the action.

The Externalism Problem: If representational states are individuated broadly as suggested according to content externalism, then short of invoking spooky action at a distance, mental contents do not look like they play a role in causing behavior.

These are independent problems. That is, the solution to one does not yield a solution to the others. This section takes each of these problems in turn.

4.1 The anomalism problem

4.1.1 Davidson's argument for reasons as causes

Davidson (1967 and 1970) takes on all three mid-century objections to treating reasons as causes: the improper category, necessitation, and general law objections. Against the improper category objection, Davidson claims not only that causes are correctly classifiable as reasons, but that, without a causal reading of reasons, there is no way to draw the critical distinction between a *mere* reason and a *motivating* reason for acting. Say that you thought that turning on the light switch would make a delightful clicking noise but that the click was not why you turned it on. If your primary concern was to illuminate the room, hearing the click was not the trigger for your action, even though it might have been *a reason* for it. The trigger for the action is what engages our interests when we explain a person's action, especially when issues of agency, free will, and moral responsibility are at stake. A story in terms of mere reasons tells us only how an action was reasonable in light of the beliefs and desires an agent may have held at the time. What is essential is the reference to the actual causal forces that produced the action.

Against the necessitation objection, Davidson (1967) explains how causal relations obtain no matter how we describe them. Suppose an event c causes an effect e and we decide to label c as "the cause of e." Surely the causal relation does not disappear just because we now utter "the cause of e caused e." The descriptions we choose to pick out the events do nothing to affect their causal workings. A crucial corollary to this reply is the idea that a single event can be picked out by nonequivalent descriptions. This plays a pivotal role in Davidson's handling of the general law objection. Davidson agrees with Melden, Anscombe, and other anti-causalists that there are no general laws relating reasons and actions. But if one endorses the Humean condition where singular causal relations are made possible only by falling under general laws, which Davidson does, a causal relation between reasons and actions means they do fall under general laws, just not laws with mental descriptions.

These replies to the anti-causalist objections make up Davidson's famous argument for anomalous monism (1970), the argument that placed the issue of mental causation front and center up to this very day. The argument draws on three principles:

Mental Causation: At least some mental events interact causally with physical events.
Anomalism of the Mental: There are no strict deterministic laws on the basis of which mental events can be predicted and explained.
Nomological Character of Causality: Events enter into causal relations insofar as they fall under strict laws.

Given the principle of the anomalism of the mental, no mental event m can cause a physical event p (or any other event, for that matter) on account of its governance under a psychological law or psychophysical law, since no such laws exist.[8] But the principle of the nomological character of causality requires that all causal relations be covered by a strict law.[9] So if m is to cause p, there has to be a strict law that makes their causal connection possible. As the only candidates for strict laws are physical laws, this means that m can cause p only if it is covered by a strict *physical* law. An event's being covered by a physical law entails that it is a physical event, so it follows that m is a physical event. That is, every efficacious mental event is token identical with a physical event, and the token identity thesis is established. This establishes monism in the form of token physicalism. Demonstrating the causal efficacy of mental events is now easy: because physical events unproblematically enter into causal relations and mental events simply are physical events, mental events are causally efficacious.

4.1.2 Criticisms of Davidson's argument

Token physicalism is the linchpin of Davidson's theory of anomalous monism, and virtually every philosopher concedes that the theory allows for a mental event to cause other events.[10] But a number of critics have objected that anomalous monism blocks an event's mental *properties* from playing a causal role and thus fails to furnish a solution to the problem of mental causation (Loewer and LePore 1987; Fodor 1989; McLaughlin 1989).

Take any causal relation holding between a reason c and an action e. According to the critics, c causes e in virtue of subsumption under a strict causal law. Laws of this kind relate only *physical* properties because it is only in physics that we get strict laws. So what secures the causal relation between c and e is c's instantiation of a physical property, not its instantiation of a mental property. Therefore, the critics conclude, c *qua* mental makes no causal difference since it is c *qua* physical that accounts for c's efficacy, permitting mental events to enter into the same causal relations even if the content were changed or eliminated as long their physical properties remained intact. Surely, an account of mental causation that is indifferent to thought content is not an account of *mental* causation.

This objection has come to highlight one of the most important 20th-century insights into the problem of mental causation. While establishing the efficacy of a mental *event* may be a step in the right direction, what we really want is an account that demonstrates how the mental *properties* of an event can be causally relevant.[11] This worry, which goes by *type epiphenomenalism* (since the concern is over the relevance of mental properties or types, not token events), drives all contemporary problems of mental causation.[12]

Davidson (1993) has countered that there is a mistake in the very idea that events are causes *in virtue of* certain of their properties or that *c* causes *e qua* some property or other. Reports of causation, according to Davidson (1967), are extensional and should not be conflated with explanations, which are intensional. The mark of an extensional context is its immunity to shifts in truth value under substitution of co-referring expressions. Insisting that "*c qua* physical causes *e*" is true but "*c qua* mental causes *e*" is false, under anomalous monism, conflates causal reports with explanations. As McLaughlin (1993) has shown, however, the critics are not guilty of conflating causation with explanation. Emphasis on the properties certainly alters the truth-value of the causal report, but not because it violates extensionality. To violate extensionality, the "in virtue of" qualification in "*c* causes *e* in virtue of the fact that *c* has F" would have to make the cause of an event essentially description-dependent, but this qualifier does not do this: citing what makes it the case that a pair of particulars is related in a certain way doesn't involve the need to cite what descriptions are true of the particulars. The reason why "*c qua* physical causes *e*" is true, but "*c mental* causes *e*," is false, is that the modifiers specify different properties of the cause *c* in which one of its properties, but not the other, secures the conditions under which the causal relations hold. Since the principle of the nomological character requires strict laws for securing a causal connection among events and since only physical laws are arguably strict, this explains why truth values differ between causal reports that reference a physical property and those that reference a mental property.

4.1.3 Other solutions to the problem of anomalism

Those working on the problem of anomalism have proposed other solutions that purport to credit causal relevance to mental properties. Two accounts stand out.

One is Fodor's proposal, where M and P can appear in the familiar generalizations of folk psychology, but modified by *ceteris paribus* clauses (1991). This approach endorses Davidson's principle of the nomological character of causality, but denies that only strict laws can do the job. The most pressing question for this approach is how the *ceteris paribus* conditions are cashed out (Schiffer 1991). If all things are to be equal in the vocabulary of psychology, then the generalizations will look trivial or *ex post facto*: if the things being equal for someone to do A if she wants to do A comes down to there being no overriding desires or not changing her mind at the last minute, then the generalization looks like an analytic truth, not an empirical one (a problem the mid-century philosophers like Ryle, Anscombe, and Melden had long pointed out). If, on the other hand, they are cashed out in different vocabulary, say, in lower-level vocabulary (this is Fodor's view), then they lose their identity as full-fledged generalizations of folk psychology since they would ultimately have to be framed in physical vocabulary, making Fodor's strategy just collapse into Davidson's original proposal.

The second is LePore and Loewer's proposal (1987), where the relation between M and P is a relation of counterfactual dependence. A mental property M of event c is causally relevant to property P of event e if c causes e, c has M and e has P, M and P are metaphysically independent (satisfying Hume's condition), and e's having P counterfactually depends upon c's having M, that is, if c did not have M, then e would not have had P. The main problem with this approach is that counterfactual dependencies may not be enough (Braun 1995; Kim 1998; McLaughlin 1989). Fires give off both heat and smoke. Only the heat is relevant to warming a room. However, there is a counterfactual dependency of the heating upon the smoke because smoke and heat reliably co-occur when a fire is lit. Thus, there are misleading counterfactual dependencies, and for all we know, the counterfactual dependency of bodily motion upon mental properties is misleading.

One has to wonder whether the approaches by Fodor and LePore and Loewer miss the point of the principle of the anomalism of the mental. Davidson's insistence on there being no laws couched in the vocabulary of folk psychology is not a mere empirical observation that no laws have yet been formalized. It goes back to insights made by Ryle, Wittgenstein, and Anscombe. We make sense of people's minds and actions, not by invoking a universal law and initial conditions, but by appreciating why an action was performed given the agent's distinctive constellation of beliefs and desires set within a unique, non-repeatable, set of circumstances (McDowell 1984; Child 1993). In brief, we gain a better understanding of an agent's reasons in terms of a narrative setting, not a scientific one where individual peculiarities are whitewashed in the interest of capturing (possibly nonexistent) generalities (von Wright 1971).

4.2 The exclusion problem

4.2.1 A formulation of the exclusion problem

Kim is to be credited with introducing the the exclusion problem as it is known today (1984, 1989, 1998, 2005). Kim's formulation is a reworking of a problem raised in by Norman Malcolm (1968), who asked whether it is possible for a segment of behavior to have both a 'mechanistic,' or physicalistic explanation as well as a mentalistic or a 'purposive' one. This raises the question of whether it is possible to give multiple complete explanations for a single *explanandum*. The answer given by Malcolm was 'no'; a complete explanation makes any other superfluous. Thus, once an explanation for an action has been furnished by an appeal to its physiological antecedents, the full explanatory picture has been completed, leaving no room for a further explanation couched in terms of reasons.[13]

With Kim's principle of explanatory realism, Malcolm's problem of explanatory exclusion becomes the problem of *causal* exclusion. According to this principle, certain structural features of the world ('truthmakers') underwrite the correctness and truth of an explanation. Thus, the question of whether we can have distinct explanations for a single *explanans* becomes the question of whether we can have distinct causes of a single effect. This is the principle of causal exclusion:

Exclusion: If a property F is causally sufficient for a property G, then no property F* distinct from F is causally relevant to G.

Epiphenomenalism results from applying this principle to the currently popular metaphysics of non-reductive physicalism, which consists of these two theses:

Causal Completeness of the Physical: For every physical property P, there is a physical property P* that is causally sufficient for P.[14]

Irreducibility of the Mental: For every mental property M and physical property P, M is distinct from P.[15]

According to the irreducibility thesis, your desire to turn on the switch is not reducible to any physical property. The subsequent motion of your arm moving towards the switch has a fully sufficient physical cause, according to the causal completeness thesis. Since no effect requires more than its sufficient cause, your desire is 'excluded' from contributing to your behavior, according to the exclusion principle, rendering your desire epiphenomenal.

The exclusion principle does not rule out the possibility of overdetermination. It is only supposed to cast suspicion on *systematic* overdetermination. For instance, a single case where a person dies because she is both shot in the heart and suffers a brain aneurysm, both of which would have been independently sufficient for her death at exactly the same time is permitted under the principle. What is not permitted is when *every* assassination is also overdetermined by a fatal aneurysm. Without something tying the two types of events together, there is no basis for postulating such a cosmically improbable pairing of outcomes. Likewise, while it would not strain credulity to think that on a certain occasion, one's turning on the light switch is caused by the right neurophysiological processes, and independently of those processes, by one's having the desire to turn on the switch, one certainly would not want to postulate a framework that magically coordinates parallel causation for every instance of mental causation. The point of the principle of exclusion is to rule out extensive parallel causation.

The exclusion problem casts a wide net. Its epiphenomenalist conclusion applies not just to mental properties, but to all properties not strictly reducible to a physical property. This includes the phenomena of the special sciences. Furthermore, the exclusion problem does not require any particular theories of causation; whether we go with the nomic subsumption model, the counterfactual model, process theories, or some other theory, the problem still arises. What follows is a survey of some general strategies for solving the exclusion problem.

4.2.2 Dual explanandum solutions

On this approach, psychological explanations accomplish one thing, while physical or neurobiological explanations accomplish another (see Dretske 1988; Jackson and Pettit 1990; Lowe 2006). The causal relations they track are different and thus do not compete against each another. For this reason, there is no basis for exclusion. Such a view was popular among the mid-century philosophers influenced by Ryle, Anscombe, and the late Wittgenstein. Kim (1989), however, poses a dilemma for this approach. If we insist that a bit of behavior has some causal origin that is irreducibly mental, and therefore non-physical, then this effectively violates the causal completeness of the physical domain. If not, then we are back to the very problem of exclusion that the dual explanandum strategy was designed to avoid.

4.2.3 Partial reduction solutions

The demise of the central state identity theory of U. T. Place (1956) and J.J.C. Smart (1959) has rendered non-reductive physicalism the most plausible metaphysics to hold for those who also reject dualism.[16] There are two notable approaches to mental causation within the framework of non-reductive physicalism. One aims to reduce a mental property M to a single physical kind P *relative to* some species S (Lewis 1966; 1972; 1983). Known as *species-specific* or *local* reductions, we can identify a mental property like pain with a physical property in an organism, for a given species, so that we have human pain, Martian pain, octopus pain, and so on:

$$S \rightarrow (M \leftrightarrow P).$$

The problem with this approach is that it faces the one over the many problem familiar to students of Plato: some F must be common to all instances of F in virtue of which they count as having F. Otherwise, human pain, octopus pain, and Martian pain are pains in name only (Shoemaker 1981; Pereboom and Kornblith 1991).

On the other partial reductionist approach, it is not mental *properties* that are reduced per se, but rather their *instances*. These instances are to be construed as tropes (see Macdonald and Macdonald 1986; Robb 1997).[17] The idea here is that we can reduce a mental trope to a physical trope in the spirit of Davidson's token identity strategy so that the mental trope will get credited with causal relevance as long as the physical trope with which it is identical is efficacious. The trope identity approach, however, may not give us any substantive advantage over Davidson's event identity (Nordhoff 1998). The trope approach must, at a minimum, demonstrate that a mental trope is indeed identical with a physical trope. But on the face of it, they look like different tropes. Tropes are as finely grained as they come; short of analytic equivalence between the terms picking out a trope, there is little support for this strategy since mental and physical terms are notoriously non-equivalent in meaning.[18]

4.2.4 Property dependence approaches: supervenience and realization

Some defenders of mental causation working within non-reductive physicalism aim to preserve the full irreducibility of the mental rather than construing it in partially reductive terms. On this view, the mental is irreducible, but also dependent on the physical in a substantive way so as to be consistent with the doctrine of physicalism. The most developed approach within this view is Yablo's construal of the psychophysical supervenience relation in terms of determinables and determinates (1992). It is a view that is designed to be consistent with the multiple realizability of a mental property by diverse physical properties. The idea is that just as the more general determinable red can be realized by the more specific scarlet and crimson determinates, the various physical realizations – neural, silicon-based, etc. – are to be construed as the determinates of the more general mental determinable. The motivation behind this approach is the modality of the relation between determinates and determinables; determinates supervene upon their determinables with logical or metaphysical necessity.[19,20] The virtue of a relation holding with this modality is that the mental and the physical can 'mutually participate' as *the cause*, a feat they can pull off "since a determinate cannot preempt its own determinable." (Yablo 1992; 250) Consider what goes on when we press our brakes at a red light. The fact that the red is crimson does not exclude or pre-empt the redness. Likewise, when you turn on the light switch, the neurophysiological goings on do not pre-empt your desire to illuminate the room. Both the mental and the physical have a role to play in bringing about behavior.

While this approach has great appeal, it faces possible counterexamples. Consider the even more general determinable of being colored. Among its determinates are red, yellow, and green. The determinable is certainly present when any one of these determinates is present, but in the case of traffic lights, each of the determinates has a different effect: the red causes cars to stop, while the green causes cars to go. With such varying outcomes, the presence of the more general determinable, being colored, is irrelevant. This means that an account of mental properties modeled after determinables will not, without further qualification, be saved from causal exclusion.[21]

Another property dependence approach to the problem of exclusion exploits the nature of realization. Shoemaker (2001) construes the functionalist notion of realization in a way that is meant to get around the counterexample affecting Yablo's determinable/determinate approach. On Shoemaker's view, both realized and realizing properties have "causal powers," sets of actual and possible causes and effects that a property's instantiation can have. The causal powers of the realized (mental) property are said to form a subset of the causal powers of the realizing (physical) property. The benefit of this view is that a subset of causal powers cannot be trumped or overridden by its superset, as the subset is just a *part of* the superset. (An earlier, but less developed, strategy along these lines was suggested by Kim 1993.) Thus, if a 10-pound brick crushes a statue, then the part of the brick that weighs 8 pounds will certainly be involved in the effect, and not excluded by the 10-pound brick it partly constitutes. Likewise, the causal powers of your desire to see better, which form a subset of the the causal powers of the concurrent neurophysiological goings on, are a part of getting your body to turn on the light switch. If the causal powers of your desire form a subset of the causal powers of your body, surely your body will not exclude the causal role of your mental states since the causal powers of the mental state partly constitute the total causal powers of the body. Shoemaker's strategy has enormous intuitive appeal, but, as with Yablo's approach, it also faces potential counterexamples. Gillett and Rives (2005) argue that the subset/superset distinction regarding causal powers does nothing to help the realized mental property play a genuine causal role.

4.3 The externalism problem

4.3.1 A formulation of the externalism problem

We now come to the last of the many contemporary problems of mental causation.[22] The problem applies to mental states having representational or propositional contents – intentional states. According to externalism, we must take into consideration facts physically external to a person's body when individuating contentful mental states. These may include facts about one's physical environment, as well as facts about the linguistic norms of one's speech community (Putnam 1975; Burge 1979; Kripke 1980). Suppose someone used the term 'motorcycle' to refer to cars. Pointing to her four-door sedan, she says "I need to get gas for my motorcycle." Given how 'motorcycle' and 'car' are used in our speech community, we would say that our driver is mistaken in her application of 'motorcycle'. Now suppose that there is a different community, one that uses 'motorcycle' to refer to cars and motorcycles. Had our driver grown up in that community, she would be perfectly correct in her use of 'motorcycle' when referring to her four-door sedan.

Our assessment of which predicate application is correct or incorrect can be carried over to beliefs (Fodor 1987; McGinn 1989). If we place the driver in our speech community, she would be accused of holding false beliefs about cars, but that very same driver placed in the alternative community would be credited with holding true beliefs about cars. Beliefs with different truth conditions cannot be the same belief. This means that our driver has different beliefs depending on which speech community we place her in, even though we keep all her intrinsic physical properties properties the same. That is, externally individuated properties fail to supervene upon an individual's intrinsic (the brain). But then it looks like contents make no causal difference to what the person does.

The problem for mental causation generated by externalism is that causation, intuitively understood, involves only the intrinsic properties of objects and events. Externalist ways of individuating mental properties, however, render them extrinsic to a person's body. Consequently, they appear causally irrelevant to proximal effects. To appreciate this, consider the causal irrelevance of the property of being a genuine dollar bill. If you put a convincing counterfeit dollar into a soda machine, the power of that bill to get the machine to dispense a soda comes only from its intrinsic properties – its size, shape, and design. The fact that the bill is counterfeit (or genuine), an historical and hence extrinsic property of the bill, makes no difference to the causal workings of the machine. Under externalism, our bodies are like the soda machine and our thoughts are like the real or counterfeit dollar. Our bodies respond only to what is proximally going in or around it, not to the contents of our beliefs.

4.3.2 Solutions to the externalism problem

Solutions to the argument from externalism pursue one of two strategies. One is to deny the thesis of externalism for mental content (see Fodor 1980). The other is to deny that only intrinsic features can be causally relevant to proximal causal mechanisms (see Burge 1993). Let us begin with the denial of externalism. The strategy here is to appeal to *narrow content*. Narrow content is the content that intrinsic twins have in common; narrow content, by stipulation, supervenes upon the intrinsic properties of an individual (Fodor 1991). Think about the purely intrinsic features of the dollar bill – features that would be equally shared by a genuine bill and a counterfeit. The intrinsic features are their *narrow* properties. They supervene upon the internal properties of individuals and are thus shared by their physical duplicates. Narrow content is the content one entertains under the Cartesian account of mental representation: as you entertain a thought of water, the content of that thought never 'reaches out' beyond your head. Intentional properties, then, individuated narrowly, will be just as suited to causing behavior as any other internal properties of a person.

The appeal to narrow content certainly gets around the problem of causal irrelevance that faces externally individuated content, but the notion of narrow content is highly contentious. Some have even argued that the notion is incoherent (see Adams et al. 2007). Consider again the counterfeit dollar. Surely we do not value it just because it shares the same intrinsic features as the genuine article. Whether a piece of currency or a work of art is genuine or a fake matters to us. The significance of Putnam's and Burge's insights into the individuation of general terms lies in their observation about our ordinary attributive practices; they conform to the externalist model, not the internalist one.

The alternative solution is that there can be 'broad causation' (see Burge 1993; Yablo 1997). This view requires a little stage setting. On this approach, there is the causation of bodily motion by neural properties, on the one hand, and then there is the causation of intentionally characterized action by broadly individuated mental content. Take, for instance, one's waving to a friend: by doing this, one performs the *action* of greeting a friend, but one *also* engages in a *purely bodily process* that engages one's bones and muscles. On this solution to the problem of externalism, we have two causal processes – one that pertains to the proximal visual stimuli that result in the bodily movement – this would be 'narrow causation' – and a different one that pertains to the appearance of the friend, resulting in the action of greeting – this would be 'broad causation.' The friend one has in mind, of course, is the individual with whom one has had actual causal contact, not some physically similar but distinct individual. To the extent that one has in mind the friend and not the look-alike, one's thought has broad content, which, on this approach, causally results in the action.

The very concept of wide causation, however, goes against our ordinary intuitions about what causation involves. According to our ordinary intuitions, we assume that causes and their effects must be in spatial contact with each other or mediated by things that spatially link them together – that there is no action at a distance. But wide causation asks us to believe exactly this – that things are caused by situations that have no physical contact with them. It would make no difference, it seems, that it was the friend and not the doppelganger that motivated one to wave. For this reason, wide causation is not an easy solution to accept (but see Yablo 1997 for a defense).

Conclusion

As we can see, most of the action on the mental causation debates in the 20th century takes place post 1970, starting with the numerous criticisms of Davidson's influential account of mental causation in his groundbreaking "Mental Events" (1970). Thanks to the momentum generated by that paper, late 20th-century work on the metaphysics of mental causation has made great progress towards clarifying the desiderata for an adequate solution. The first desideratum is crediting a clear causal role to the mental *qua* types, not just to particulars falling under mental types. The second is identifying the scope of one's solution since there are several non-overlapping problems of mental causation. And the third is specifying whether one's solution pertains to phenomenal properties or representational properties, since they face different causal problems.

These achievements, of course, would not have been possible were it not for the work done in the early and mid 20th century. Indeed, current innovative approaches to the mind owe their inspiration to positions proposed during these periods. This is certainly the case for epiphenomenalism, (Walter et al. 2006), emergentism (Bedau and Humphries 2008; Macdonald and Macdonald 2010; Gillett 2016), and panpsychism, (Nagisawa and Alter 2015). Anti-causalism about reasons as well has found new proponents (Hutto 1999; Tanney 2008). The sophistication and richness of the 21st-century debates on mental causation have their roots firmly planted in the impressive work accomplished in the 20th century.

APPENDIX: DUALIST ACCOUNTS OF MENTAL CAUSATION

The three main dualist accounts of mental causation are interactionism, parallelism, and epiphenomenalism. The thick horizontal line represents the division between the mental (above the line) and the physical (below the line); the arrows represent a cause leading to an effect.

Interactionism

Mental events directly cause physical events, and vice versa. Specifically, certain physical events would not occur without the intervention of mental events.

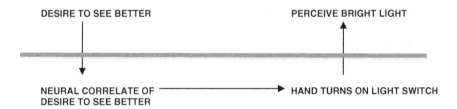

Figure 7.1 Interactionist Causation

This is Descartes' account of how the mind and the body causally interact with each other: there is direct causation from the mental to the physical and from the physical to the mental. The most common objections to interactionism are the problem of spatiality, the problem of energy conservation, and the 'pairing problem.'

According to the problem of spatiality (Princess Elizabeth of Bohemia 1618–1680), all effects need to be in spatial contact with the things that cause the movements. If the mind has no spatial location, it is hard to understand how it can make our bodies move. (Descartes' reply that the interaction takes place in the pineal gland does not address the concern. Surely locating where the mystery takes place does not solve the mystery.) According to the problem of conservation, the total energy of the physical system must be uniform at all times. A mental cause, under a dualist account, would be an outside causal influence upon the brain when the brain is instructed to do the mind's bidding. Any *outside* causal influence would create an energy surplus in the physical system, violating conservation. There is, finally, the 'pairing problem' (Kim 2005), nicely presented by Durant Drake when he asks:

> How does the soul know just where to strike in the brain to produce the brain-events which are the necessary antecedents to the activity of the organism? *We* should not know where to stimulate the brain, or what sort of motions must be produced there. – It is difficult enough to imagine how an immaterial desire or volition could start or steer a brain-process, but the difficulty of imagining how the spaceless desire or volitions knows just which atoms or electrons to move . . . is greater still.
> (1923, 225, Drake's emphasis)

To locate, hit, and maneuver a physical target, there must be a physical means of managing this feat. A non-physical entity cannot pull off this feat without presupposing a physical means of solving the problem.

Parallelism

There is complete causal segregation when it comes to causation in and by the mind and causation in and by the body. Mental events cause and are caused by only other mental events; physical events cause and are caused by only other physical events.

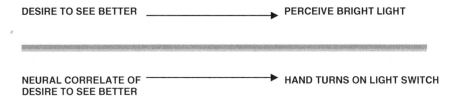

Figure 7.2 Parallelist Causation

Parallelism circumvents some of the problems that trouble interactionism. It certainly would not face the problem of conservation, since the mental and physical realms are never allowed to interact. It also does not face the problem of spatial interaction, since, again, the two realms are causally segregated. However, it does face a version of the pairing problem with a vengeance, which is a part of the larger problem of mind-body coordination: what allows a mental event to *line up* with its appropriate physical correlate? In other words, if you want to greet a friend, how do you end up with a waving arm rather than a hop, skip, and a jump? Why do you perceive an increase in ambient light when the light goes on and not, say, taste pineapple? For two systems that are supposed to have no causal contact with each other, our minds and bodies are remarkably well coordinated.

There are two different accounts of how the coordination is achieved: Gottfried Leibniz's (1646–1716) *pre-established harmony* and Nicolas Malebranche's (1638–1715) *occasionalism*. Both accounts appeal to a *deus ex machina* to explain the coordination. According to Leibniz's pre-established harmony, when God chose to create our world as the best of all possible worlds, that world was one where every mental event was (non-causally) paired with its appropriate bodily event. The pairing is so precise that the mind and the body are like two separate clocks wound up in advance to chime at precisely the same time. On this view, God is fairly 'hands-off' when it comes to coordinating an individual's mind with her body, having done all the work ahead of them when choosing our world's blueprint. Not so on Malebranche's account. According to Malebranche, coordination is achieved by God on an event by event basis; whenever someone wants to greet a friend, God is right there to make her arm wave. God, in his omniscience and omnipresence, is always ready to bring about an appropriate behavior for a given thought. To modern ears, these solutions to the coordination problem probably sound *ad hoc*. Of course, Leibniz and Malenbranche do not appeal to God out of desperation or lazy convenience; previous commitments to constraints on causation and a metaphysics that includes God's existence motivate their solutions. But in the absence of these commitments, the coordination problem goes unsolved, making parallelism implausible.

Epiphenomenalism

This is a view developed by Thomas Huxley (1825–1895) and Santayana (1863–1952). On this view, mental events are caused by physical events but mental events themselves never cause anything (not even other mental events). Durant Drake (1923) illustrates epiphenomenalism with the idea of a cinematic projection of two people fighting. As far as what is happening on the screen, no one is actually hitting anyone. At most, the light emanating from the screen has the power to produce flickering images. The figures on the screen have no causal powers to strike a blow. Analogously, whatever mental states appear to be caused by these images – fear, excitement, expectation – are byproducts of the neural states of the viewer. These mental byproducts, just like the image of the fighter's formidable right hook, have no effects.

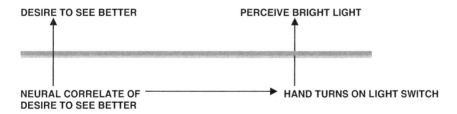

Figure 7.3 Epiphenomenal Causation

Epiphenomenalism does not face the problem of causal coordination, the main sticking point for parallelism. It also does not face the interactionist problems of spatial location, the pairing problem, or the problem of conservation, since no new energy is ever introduced, thanks to a causally impotent mind. However, epiphenomenalism flies in the face of intuition – that what we think makes a causal difference to how we act. Everything being equal, when you feel hungry, you go to the refrigerator, not the garage; when you want to stay dry in the rain, you use an umbrella, not a strainer. Without further qualification to the nature of the relation between the mental and the physical, epiphenomenalism is consistent with the view where the body is doing exactly what it would be doing with the appropriate mental states, except that the mental states are completely absent, or worse, totally antithetical to the mental states that make sense of the body's behavior. If an important constraint on philosophical theories is that they stay close to ordinary appearances, epiphenomenalism strays from it quite a bit.

Notes

1. See the entry by Amy Kind in this volume on the mind-body problem for a discussion of the synchronic problem. As will become apparent, one's position on reduction, the synchronic problem, significantly constrains one's account of mental causation, the diachronic problem.
2. Actually, the problem is ancient. See Caston (1997) for discussion.
3. This was a period when the foundations for modern psychology were being established. Physiologists such as Paul Broca, David Ferrier, and Charles Sherrington were mapping the neural correlates of mental functions. Wilhelm Wundt was creating the very discipline of experimental cognitive psychology in his *Principles of Physiological Psychology* (1904). William James was proposing methods of gathering introspective data in his two-volume *Principles of Psychology* (1890). And John Watson was founding the principles of behaviorism in his *Behavior: An Introduction to Comparative Psychology* (1914). All of this was going on during an immensely fertile time for biology, chemistry, physics, medicine, engineering, and industry.
4. See Nagasawa & Alter (2015) for contemporary approaches to panpsychism.
5. Epiphenomenalism can be construed in partially emergentist terms. The epiphenomenal would certainly have no downward causal powers; but nor would they be ("bottom-up") caused to come into being by the lower-level phenomena. Rather, they would be emergent. This reading is closer to the kind of epiphenomenalism George Santayana proposed (1949). His epiphenomenalism does not involve one-way causation.
6. U. T. Place (1956) and J.J.C. Smart (1959) are notable exceptions, who proposed the full reduction of mental properties and processes to the physical. One should note that the concerns of Place and Smart lay primarily with phenomenal properties, not with intentional ones, which make up the focus of the anti-causalists.
7. Many others agreed with Ryle and Anscombe about this: Flew (1949), Hamlyn (1953), Foot (1957), Winch (1958), and Hart & Honoré (1959).
8. 'Psychophysical law' covers both causal laws relating mental events with behavior (e.g. "pains cause clutching the wounded area") as well as non-causal intertheoretic laws that tie types of mental state with their underlying neurophysiological correlates (e.g. "pain is c-fiber stimulation"). Davidson denies the existence of both kinds of connections.
9. There are two things to keep track of here. One is the nomological requisite for causation. The other is the strictness requirement for these laws. Both are controversial.

There are singularist accounts of causation that reject nomological requisite for causation, defended by Anscombe (1959), Hart and Honoré (1959), and more recently, de Pinedo (2006), who all deny that laws are necessary for events to enter into causal relations. And there are those like Fodor (1980; 1991) and Schiffer (1991) who endorse the nomological requisite for causation, but deny the strictness requirement. Davidson concedes that among the basic laws of physics may be probabilistic laws. But whether a law is determinist or probabilistic is orthogonal to the issue of strictness, which is about the universality of the conditions under which the laws hold. Probabilistic laws would be strict in this sense.

10 Hornsby (1981) and Child (1993) have questioned the soundness of Davidson's argument for token identity.

11 This has nothing to do with realism regarding properties or universals. The point is that causal relevance must be accorded to the mental *qua* types, not just mental particulars *qua* particulars. Realists and nominalists alike share the same burden regarding this desideratum for an account of mental causation.

12 The problem of type epiphenomenalism is not surprising for a coarse-grained account like Davidson's. On his view, events are individuated in terms of their causes and effects. Entities individuated in this way can cover large spatio-temporal chunks having many properties, only some of which may be causally relevant. But the problem of epiphenomenalism does not get fixed with a more fine-grained theory of events. On Kim's fine-grained account (1973 and 1976), an event is an ordered triple, <object, property, time>, where an event is the exemplification of a constitutive property by a constitute object at a time. On this approach, an event e_1 is the same event as e_2 just in case they consist of the same constitutive object, property, and time. Since a physical property and a mental property are arguably distinct properties and thus distinct constitutive properties, mental events would not be token identifiable with physical events. In that case, Kim's theory of events would face the problem of token epiphenomenalism for the class of mental events.

13 Malcolm used this reasoning as a reductio against mechanism, arguing that its very utterance was itself an intentional act, and thus a testament to its falsity in spite of our rhetorical assertion of its truth.

14 The causal completeness principle is one of two central theses of the doctrine of physicalism. The other thesis is that to create the world and the conscious individuals who live therein, all you need are only micro-physical physical ingredients – physical particles, properties, and laws. The doctrine of physicalism is thus best understood as a two-part thesis, a diachronic thesis about the causal completeness of the physical domain, and a synchronic thesis regarding the fundamentality of physical properties in fixing all the other properties. There are, undoubtedly, thorny issues about how 'physical' should be defined. Known as 'Hempel's dilemma,' after Carl Hempel (1969), 'physical' can't be defined in reference to current physics since it is probably wrong or at best incomplete, but it also can't be defined in reference to some open-ended future physics since that would make the thesis vacuous. What we mean by 'physical' in physicalism is probably best captured by Barbara Montero (2009), who says that the usage of self-declared physicalists reflects a commitment to a fundamental ontology including anything non-mental. So were it discovered by future physicists that, say, there is mind-dust at the fundamental level, these self-declared physicalists would proclaim that they wrong all along about the natural world.

15 We need not be talking about irreducibility in a robust sense, as in property dualism, where mental properties are only nomologically and thus metaphysically contingently associated with physical properties. The multiple realizability of mental properties supports irreducibility in only the minimal sense denying the identification of mental types with physical types.

16 Please see the Amy Kind's entry on the mind-body problem in this volume for a discussion of the considerations that led away from the identity theory.
17 Tropes and properties differ in that while a property is repeatable, a trope is not. A realist about properties would say the distance in a marathon is a single property, being 26.2 miles, that is "fully present" in every marathon. A trope theorist, on the other hand, would say that a distinct 26.2-mile trope is instantiated for every marathon that takes place.
18 See also Schneider (2012) who argues that a psychophysical trope identity theorist cannot also maintain her commitment to non-reductive physicalism. This is because the non-reductive aspect of the thesis requires the non-identity of the mental and the physical *qua* types. But when one helps oneself to psychophysical trope identities, then the class of mental tropes that make up the mental type will just consist of physical tropes only and this is reductionism, plain and simple. Mental properties do no work *qua* types under psychophysical trope identity. If this is right, then the appeal to mental tropes to save *mental* causation is a non-starter.
19 Borrowing from Kripke's defense of necessary *a posteriori* identities (1980), Yablo suggests that we treat determinates and their determinables as necessary *a posteriori* one-way conditionals.
20 The difference between supervening with logical or metaphysical necessity, on the one hand, and supervening with physical or nomological necessity, on the other, comes down to whether subvenient duplicates are always or only sometimes accompanied by the supervening properties. Under logical or metaphysical necessity, base duplicates exactly match their supervening properties as a matter of logical necessity; we can no more have base duplicates with differing supervening properties than we can have non-H_2O water. Under physical or nomological necessity, base duplicates match their supervening properties only as a matter of contingent laws of nature. In short, properties tied together by physical supervenience can be fully prised apart; properties tied together by logical supervenience cannot.
21 Yablo is fully aware of this problem in his (1992) and offers an account in terms of "causal proportionality" to solve it. For criticisms, see Crane (2008), Dowe (2010).
22 Well, maybe not the last problem. Under a functionalist approach, mental properties are defined in terms of other mental properties and behaviors. This approach, in effect, forges logical connections between mental states and behaviors, violating Hume's condition that causes and effects must be logically contingent. Rupert (2006) has offered some suggestions for responding to this problem.

Bibliography

Adams, F., Drebushenko, D., Fuller, G., and Stecker, R. (2007). "Narrow Content: Fodor's Folly," *Mind and Language*, 5(3): 213–219.
Alexander, S. (1920). *Space, Time, and Deity*, Volumes I and II. London: Macmillan.
Anscombe, E. (1957). *Intention*. Oxford: Oxford University Press.
Antony, L. (1995). "I'm a Mother, I Worry," *Philosophical Issues*, 6: 160–166.
Bedau, M., and Humphries, P. (2008). *Emergence: Contemporary Readings in Philosophy and Science*. Cambridge, MA: MIT Press.
Braun, D. (1995). "Causally Relevant Properties", *Philosophical Perspectives*, 9: 447–475.
Broad, C. (1925). *The Mind and Its Place in Nature*. London: Routledge & Kegan Paul.
Burge, T. (1979). "Individualism and the Mental," in French, Uehling and Wettstein (eds.), *Midwest Studies in Philosophy*, IV, Minneapolis: University of Minnesota Press: 73–121.

Burge, T. (1993). "Mind-Body Causation and Explanatory Practice," in Heil and Mele (eds.), *Mental Causation*, Oxford: Clarendon Press: 97–120.

Caston, V. (1997). "Epiphenomenalisms, Ancient and Modern," in *The Philosophical Review*, 106(3): 309–363.

Child, W. (1993). "Anomalism, Uncodifiability, and Psychophysical Relations," *Philosophical* Review, 215–245.

Cohen, M. F. (1964). "Motives, Causal Necessity, and Moral Accountability," *Australasian Journal of Philosophy*, 42.

Crane, T. (2008). "Causation and Determinable Properties: On the Efficacy of Color, Shape, and Size," in Hohwy, J. and Kallestrup J. (eds.), *Being Reduced: New Essays on Reduction, Explanation, and Causation*. Oxford: Oxford University Press.

Davidson, D. (1963). "Actions, Reasons and Causes," *Journal of Philosophy*, 60: 685–700.

Davidson, D. (1967). "Causal Relations," *Journal of Philosophy*, 64: 691–703.

Davidson, D. (1970). 'Mental Events," in Foster, L. and Swanson, J. (eds.), *Experience and Theory*. Amherst: University of Massachusetts Press.

Davidson, D. (1993). "Thinking Causes," in Heil, J. and Mele, A. (eds.), *Mental Causation*. Oxford: Clarendon Press.

de Pinedo, M. (2006). "Anomalous Monism: Oscillating Between Dogmas," *Synthese*, 148: 79–97.

Dowe, P. (2010). "Proportionality and Omissions," *Analysis*, 3: 446–451.

Drake, D. (1923). "The Mind-Body Impasse," *The Philosophical Review*, 32(2): 225.

Dretske, F. (1988). *Explaining Behavior*. Cambridge, MA: MIT Press.

Flew, A. (1949). "Psycho-Analytic Explanations," *Analysis*, 10:11.

Fodor, J. (1980). "Special Science," in *Representations: Philosophical Essays on the Foundations of Cognitive Science*, by Fodor, J. Cambridge, MA: MIT Press.

Fodor, J. (1987). *Psychosemantics*. Cambridge, MA: MIT Press.

Fodor, J. (1989). "Making Mind Matter More," *Philosophical Topics*, 17: 59–79.

Fodor, J. (1991). "You Can Fool Some of the People All the Rime, Everything Else Being Equal: Hedged Laws and Psychological Explanations," *Mind*, 100: 19–33.

Foot, P. (1957). "Free Will as Involving Determinism," *Philosophical Review*, 66.

Gillett, C. (2016). *Reduction and Emergence in Science and Philosophy*. Cambridge: Cambridge University Press.

Gillett, C., and Rives, B. (2005). "The Non-existence of Determinables: Or, A World of Absolute Determinates as Default Hypothesis," *Nous*, 39: 483–504.

Hamlyn, D. (1953). "Behavior," *Philosophy*, 28.

Hart, H.L.A., and Honoré, A. M. (1959). *Causation in the Law*. Oxford: Oxford University Press.

Hempel, C. (1962). "Rational Action," *Proceedings and Addresses of the American Philosophical Association*, 35.

Hempel, C. (1969). "Reduction: Ontological and Linguistic Facets," in Morgenbesser, S. et al. (eds.), *Essays in Honor of Ernest Nagel*. New York: St Martin's Press.

Hornsby, J. (1981). "Which Physical Events Are Mental Events?" *Proceedings of the Aristotelian Society*, 81.

Hutto, D. (1999). "Cause for Concern: Reasons, Causes and Explanations," *Philosophy and Phenomenal Review*, 59(2): 381–401.

Huxley, T. (1874). "On the Hypothesis that Animals are Automata and its History," *The Fortnightly Review*, 16(New Series): 555–580.

Jackson, F., and Pettit, P. (1990). "Program Explanation: A General Perspective," *Analysis*, 50 (2): 107–117.

James, W. (1890). *The Principles of Psychology*, Volumes I and II. Cambridge, MA: Harvard University Press.

James, W. (1907). *Pragmatism: A New Name for Some Old Ways of Thinking*. Cambridge, MA: Harvard University Press.

James, W. (1909). *A Pluralistic Universe*. Cambridge, MA: Harvard University Press.

Kim, J. (1973). "Causation, Nomic Subsumption, and the Concept of an Event," *Journal of Philosophy*, 70: 217–236.

Kim, J. (1976). "Events as Property Exemplifications," in Brandt, M. and Walton, D. (eds.), *Action Theory*, Dortrecht: D. Reidel.

Kim, J. (1984). "Epiphenomenal and Supervenient Causation," *Midwest Studies in Philosophy*, 4: 31–49.

Kim, J. (1989). "Mechanism, Purpose, and Explanatory Exclusion," *Philosophical Perspectives*, 3: 77–108.

Kim, J. (1993). "The Non-Reductivist's Troubles with Mental Causation", in Heil, J. and Mele, A. (eds.), *Mental Causation*. Oxford: Clarendon Press.

Kim, J. (1998). *Mind in a Physical World*. Cambridge, MA: MIT Press.

Kim, J. (2005). *Physicalism, or Something Near Enough*. Princeton, NJ: Princeton University Press.

Kim, J., and Brandt, R. (1963). "Wants as Explanations of Actions," *Journal of Philosophy*, 60.

Kripke, S. (1980). *Naming and Necessity*. Cambridge, MA: Harvard University Press.

Lewis, D. (1966). "An Argument for the Identity Theory," *Journal of Philosophy*, 63: 17–25.

Lewis, D. (1972). "Psychophysical and Theoretical Identifications," *Australasian Journal of Philosophy*, 50: 249–258.

Lewis, D. (1983). "'Mad Pain and Martian Pain' and 'Postscript,'" in Lewis, D. (ed.), *Philosophical Papers*, Volume 1. Oxford: Oxford University Press.

Loewer, B., and LePore, E. (1987). "Mind Matters," *Journal of Philosophy*, 84: 630–642.

Lovejoy, A. (1926). "The Meanings of 'Emergence' and Its Modes," *Proceedings of the Sixth International Congress of Philosophy*. London: Longmans, Green, & Co: 20–33.

Lowe, E. (2006). "Non-Cartesian Substance Dualism and the Problem of Mental Causation," *Erkenntnis*, 65(5): 5–23.

Macdonald, C., and Macdonald, G. (1986). "Mental Cause and Explanation of Action," *Philosophical Quarterly*, 36: 145–158.

Macdonald, C., and Macdonald, G. (2010). *Emergence in Mind*. Oxford: Oxford University Press.

McDowell, J. (1984). "Functionalism and Anomalous Monism," in LePore, E. and McLaughlin, B. (eds.), *Actions and Events: Perspectives on the Philosophy of Donald Davidson*. Oxford: Basil Blackwell.

McGinn, C. (1989). *Mental Content*, Oxford: Blackwell.

McLaughlin, B. (1989). "Type Epiphenomenalism, Type Dualism, and the Causal Priority of the Physical," *Philosophical Perspectives*, 3: 109–135.

McLaughlin, B. (1993). "On Davidson's Repose to the Charge of Epiphenomenalism," in Heil, J. and Mele, A. (eds.), *Mental Causation*. Oxford: Clarendon Press.

Malcolm, N. (1968). "The Conceivability of Mechanism," *Philosophical Review*, 77: 45–72.

Melden, A. (1961). *Free Action*. London: Routledge and Kegan Paul.

Montero, B. "What Is the Physical," in McLaughlin, B., Beckermann, A. and Walter, Sven (eds.), *Oxford Handbook in the Philosophy of Mind*. Oxford: Oxford University Press.

Morgan, C. (1923). *Emergent Evolution*. London: Williams and Norgate.

Nagasawa, Y., and Alter, T. (2015). *Consciousness in the Physical World: Perspectives on Russellian Monism*. Oxford: Oxford University Press.

Nordhoff, P (1998). "Do Tropes Resolve the Problem of Mental Causation?" *Pacific Philosophical Quarterly*, 48: 221–226.

Pereboom, D., and Kornblith, H. (1991). "The Metaphysics of Irreducibility," *Philosophical Studies*, 64(2): 125–145.

Place, U. (1956). "Is Consciousness a Brain Process?" *British Journal of Psychology*, 47: 44–50.

Putnam, H. (1975). "The Meaning of 'Meaning,'" *Philosophical Papers, Vol. II: Mind, Language, and Reality*. Cambridge: Cambridge University Press.

Robb, D. (1997). "The Properties of Mental Causation," *Philosophical Quarterly*, 47: 178–194.

Rupert, R. (2006). "Functionaism, Mental Causaiton, and the Problem of Necessary Effects," *Nous* (40)2: 256–283.

Russell, B. (1927). *An Outline of Philosophy*. London: Allen and Unwin.

Ryle, G. (1949). *The Concept of Mind*. Chicago: University of Chicago Press.

Santayana, G. (1942). New York: Charles Scribner's Sons.

Schiffer, S. (1991). "Ceteris Paribus Laws," *Mind*, 100: 1–17.

Schneider, S. (2012). "Non-Reductive Physicalism Cannot Appeal to Token Identity," *Philosophical and Phenomenological Research*, 85(3): 719–728.

Sellars, R. (1918). "An Approach to the Mind-Body Problem," *The Philosophical Review*, 27(2): 150–163.

Sellars, R. (1920). "Evolutionary Naturalism and the Mind-Body Problem," *The Monist*, 30(4): 568–598.

Sellars, R. (1922). "Is Consciousness Physical?" *Journal of Philosophy*, 19(25): 690–694.

Shoemaker, S. (1981). "Some varieties of functionalism *Philosophical Topics*, 12(1): 93–119.

Shoemaker, S. (2001). "Realization and Mental Causation," in Gillett, C. and Loewer, B. (eds.), *Physicalism and Its Discontents*. Cambridge: Cambridge University Press.

Smart, J. (1959). "Sensations and Brain Processes," *Philosophical Review*, 68: 141–156.

Tanney, J. (2008). "Reasons as Non-Causal, Context-Placing Explanations" in Sandis, Constantine (ed.), *New Essays on the Explanation of Action*. Palgrave Macmillan.

Walter, S., Pauen, M., and Staudacher, A. (2006). "*Epiphenomenalism: Dead End or Way Out?*" *Journal of Consciousness Studies*, 13(1–2): 7–19.

Watson, J. (1914). *Behavior: An Introduction to Comparative Psychology*. Henry Holt & Co.

Winch, P. (1958). *The Idea of a Social Science*. London: Routledge & Kegan Paul.

Wundt, W. (1904). *Principles of Physiological Psychology*. Trans. E. B. Titchener. New York: Macmillan.

von Wright, G. (1971). *Explanation and Understanding*. London: Routledge & Kegan Paul.

Whitehead, A. (1929). *Process and Reality*. New York: Macmillan.

Yablo, S. (1992). "Mental Causation," *The Philosophical Review*, 101: 245–280.

Yablo, S. (1997). "Wide Causation," *Philosophical Perspectives*, 11: 251–281.

8

INTENTIONALITY

From Brentano to representationalism

Michelle Montague

1. Introduction

In this chapter, I want to say something about the role played by Franz Brentano (1838–1917) in bringing the topic of intentionality to the forefront of philosophical attention in the twentieth and early twenty-first centuries. The time period this chapter covers is substantial, and I will only be able to discuss a limited number of issues and philosophers. I will only gesture at Brentano's influence on the continental tradition, although one of the most remarkable features of his philosophy is precisely the extent of its influence on both the continental and analytic philosophical traditions.[1] I will focus on three works: the first edition of *Psychology From an Empirical Standpoint*, published in 1874 ('*Psychology*'); the Appendix of supplementary remarks that accompanied the republication of Book Two of *Psychology* in 1911 ('the Appendix'); and certain essays from his *Nachlass* published in 1924. These works are collected in an English translation published in 1973 and 1995 with the title *Psychology From an Empirical Standpoint*.[2]

Brentano's theory of mind is wide reaching and complex. It covers such topics as the unity of consciousness, the fundamental classification of mental phenomena, and the role of emotions in our knowledge of value – in addition to offering theories of intentionality and consciousness. Here I will focus on only two of Brentano's central claims, and I will state them using the term 'intentionality', although Brentano never used this noun himself.

[1] Intentionality is the mark of the mental; all and only mental phenomena are intentional.[3]
[2] Consciousness and intentionality are constitutively related, and cannot be treated in isolation from one another.

[1] is undoubtedly what Brentano is best known for in present-day analytic philosophy. In his *Psychology* he characterized mental phenomena in terms of 'object-directedness', and it is this that we have come to call 'intentionality'. But we need

to consider what motivated this particular characterization in some detail if we are to achieve an adequate understanding of what Brentano meant by [1].

Many analytic philosophers who accept the characterization of intentionality in terms of 'object-directedness' immediately go on to raise as a problem – 'the problem of intentionality' – the fact that we are apparently able to think about non-existent objects. The problem, briefly, is that if we take intentionality to be a relational phenomenon, and accept that relations can only hold between existent things, then we cannot give any account of how we can be intentionally related to non-existent things when we think – as we apparently do – about non-existent things.

I think that Brentano was not particularly concerned with this issue in the 1874 *Psychology*. It is only in the 1911 Appendix that he addresses it directly, and his awareness of it seems to be partly the result of the work of two of his students, Kasimir Twardowski (1866–1938) and Alexius Meinong (1853–1920). Twardowski showed that Brentano's theory could escape certain seemingly implausible consequences by means of the introduction of a distinction between the *content* and the *object* of mental phenomena. Meinong accepted some of Brentano's central psychological insights and extended them in one seemingly natural ontological direction. Brentano then attempted to acknowledge and address these developments in his Appendix by offering a characterization of intentionality that was different from the one he gave in 1874.

The focus on our apparent ability to think about non-existent objects was intensified in the analytic tradition by the work of Roderick Chisholm (1916–1999). He characterized much of Brentano's work on intentionality in terms of it. But although the idea that we can think about non-existent objects raises interesting questions, and may raise problems for a theory of intentionality, I think it is a mistake to approach Brentano's original theory of mental phenomena from this direction. It misrepresents his position, and leads to further misapplications and distortions of his work.

I will focus on two such misrepresentations. The first is the idea that Brentano's theory of intentionality has dualist metaphysical implications. The second is the idea that Brentano was wrong to think that all and only mental phenomena are intentional, because intentionality can be found everywhere in the physical (non-mental) world. These may be interesting ideas in themselves, but to see them as directly tied to Brentano's theory of intentionality is – I claim – to miss the central questions and methodology that drove some of Brentano's most brilliant work in the *Psychology*.

[1] has been much discussed in analytic philosophy. Less attention has been paid to [2]. In fact, for most of the twentieth century (I will speak simply of 'the twentieth century' although the particular position I have in mind is more accurately described as 'the dominant position in analytic philosophy of mind in the later twentieth century'), it was orthodoxy in analytic philosophy of mind to suppose that consciousness or phenomenology and intentionality can exist in the complete absence of the other.[4] The reasons for this are complex, and I will mention only a few. First, twentieth-century theories of intentionality tended to focus on propositional attitudes, which are implicitly or sometimes explicitly assumed

to involve no phenomenology. Second, and connectedly, many theorists accepted the claim that there are unconscious mental states with unconscious mental content – from which it immediately follows that there are intentional states that lack any phenomenology.[5] I will argue that both of these motivations for separating consciousness and intentionality in this way are related to Chisholm's characterization of intentionality. Brentano, by contrast, took consciousness or phenomenology to be a thoroughly intentional phenomenon, and argued directly against the reality of unconscious mental states. Indeed, Brentano's theory of consciousness was partly motivated by this rejection. There is, then, an important respect in which the twentieth-century view of consciousness and intentionality drifted far from Brentano's original view.

In the last two decades of the twentieth century a theory, which its proponents chose to call 'representationalism', became prominent in analytic philosophy of mind. It appeared to accept versions of both [1] and [2].[6] But the appearance of affinity is superficial. Brentano's motivations for asserting [1] and [2] were very different from those of the representationalists. One of the central motivations for representationalism, which I will call the 'transparency thesis', is in direct conflict with Brentano's theory of consciousness. And although both theories appeal to intentionality to account for consciousness, the role intentionality plays in each theory results in very different theories of consciousness.

The plan of the chapter is as follows. In section 2, I try to put Brentano's theories of consciousness and intentionality in the context of his overall aims in 1874. I then briefly describe the shift in his views in the 1911 Appendix. In section 3, I introduce Twardowski and Meinong's developments of Brentano's theory. In section 4, I summarize Chisholm's influential linguistic interpretation of Brentano's 'marks of the mental'. In section 5, I discuss the relation between Brentano's views and the representationalist position. I conclude with a few remarks about some recent theories of consciousness and intentionality that do much better than representationalism in capturing some of the spirit of Brentano's philosophy.

2. Brentano from 1874 to 1911

One of Brentano's main goals in his 1874 masterpiece was to demarcate the field of psychology in a way that showed it to be a distinctive and unified discipline. He had two central motivations. First, he believed that psychology contained the roots of aesthetics, logic, ethics and politics. Logic, he thought, was rooted in 'immediately evident' judgments, ethics was rooted in 'immediately evident' emotions, and these immediately evident judgments and emotions provided us with knowledge of the necessary truths that constitute the foundations of logic and ethics.[7] Second, he believed that a unified discipline could be established only by dispelling the lack of clarity and disagreement among his contemporaries about psychology's subject matter and method. Most of the *Psychology* is dedicated to this second undertaking.[8]

Defining the field of psychology, therefore, involved two essential tasks: articulating its method and marking out its proprietary subject matter. What I hope to make clear in what follows is the central way in which the notions of intentionality and consciousness featured in Brentano's attempt to accomplish both tasks.

Brentano conceived of psychology as a 'Cartesian science' in the sense that it had an epistemologically certain foundation.[9] With Descartes, Brentano argued that we can know truths about our mentality with certainty.[10] His conception of psychology was at the same time fully empirical, not because it was based on experimentation that could be repeated and observed from the third-person standpoint, but because its truths were based on experience itself. Psychology, in short, was a first-person empirical science that provided necessary truths about our mental lives.

Mental phenomena were the proper subject matter of psychology, according to Brentano. The correct definition of the discipline is accordingly 'the science of mental phenomena'. Brentano first argued that this definition was a suitable replacement for the 'Aristotelian' definition of psychology as 'the science of the soul'. The new definition could avoid the controversial metaphysical assumption of the Aristotelian definition, i.e. that there are souls, while retaining the ability to address one of the main concerns of the Aristotelian definition, namely the question of immortality.[11] Secondly, and more arduously, Brentano aimed to give a detailed characterization of what he took mental phenomena to be. Reference to intentionality would be essential to this task.

All the sciences study *phenomena*, according to Brentano, where 'phenomena' is taken in its original meaning of 'appearances'. Physics, chemistry, biology and psychology all study appearances, appearances understood as the 'data of consciousness': what is given to consciousness, what shows up in consciousness. "All the data of our consciousness are divided into two great classes," he says, "the class of physical and the class of mental phenomena" (59/77), and it is in terms of these two great classes that the subject matter of the natural sciences is distinguishable from the subject matter of psychology: the natural sciences study physical phenomena; psychology studies mental phenomena.

What are physical phenomena? What are mental phenomena? And given that both types of phenomena are appearances, what distinguishes them from each other? The first thing to do, perhaps, is to note the fundamental respect in which both physical phenomena and mental phenomena *in Brentano's sense* are mental phenomena *in our sense* (i.e. our standard present-day sense), simply because they are appearances.

Brentano's examples of physical phenomena are color, light, sound, spatial location, and heat, and at first glance this list seems like a familiar starting point for characterizing physical objects and their properties. It seems to connect directly with our ordinary view of things, according to which there is a world of mind-independent physical objects that have various mind-independent physical qualities that are the proper object of study of the natural sciences.

In asserting that physical phenomena are mere appearances, however, Brentano's starting point is very different. On his terms, 'physical phenomena' are not part of any experience-transcending mind-independent reality, but only signs of something that is transcendent in this way. A physical phenomenon is an appearance created by our causal relation to something independent of us. As such, physical phenomena cannot give us knowledge of how things 'really and truly are'. He puts this point variously by saying that

> The phenomena of light, sound, heat, spatial location and locomotion . . . are not things which really and truly exist. They are signs of something real, which, through its causal activity, produces presentations of them. They are not, however, an adequate representation of this reality, and they give us knowledge of it only in a very incomplete sense. We can say that there exists something which, under certain conditions, causes this or that sensation. We can probably also prove that there must be relations among these realities similar to those manifested by spatial phenomena, shapes and sizes. But this is as far as we can go. We have no experience of that which truly exists, in and of itself, and that which we do experience is not true. The truth of physical phenomena is, as they say, only a relative truth.
>
> (14/19)

> we have no right . . . to believe that the objects of so-called external perception really exist as they appear to us. Indeed, they demonstrably do not exist outside of us. In contrast to that which really and truly exists, they are mere phenomena.
>
> (7/10)

> We have nevertheless seen how the expression "physical phenomena" is sometimes erroneously applied to . . . forces themselves.
>
> (76/100)

So the subject matter of the natural sciences, according to Brentano, is physical phenomena, e.g. color, sound, warmth and odor, all of which are appearances. Natural sciences do not directly study 'things in themselves', even though some people mistakenly think they do.

So much for physical phenomena. What about mental phenomena?[12] Brentano's examples include hearing a sound, seeing a colored object, thinking a general concept, loving a dog, and judging that grass is green. Since mental phenomena and physical phenomena are both phenomena, things 'of the mind' so to speak, to fully understand how psychology is distinguished from the natural sciences, Brentano now faces the third question listed above: what distinguishes mental phenomena from physical phenomena? To give a clear definition of the field of psychology is to answer this last question. Examples of physical and mental phenomena may provide a sense of their difference, but Brentano wishes to find a more principled way of distinguishing them.

He considers four main possibilities. I'll briefly introduce the alternatives he found inadequate before turning to his favored and most famous criterion.

1. Mental phenomena are either presentations or are "based upon" (61/82) presentations; all other phenomena are physical phenomena.

By presentation, Brentano does not mean what is presented, but the act of presentation. An act of presentation is required for anything to appear in consciousness. To be presented with something is precisely to have something appear to one in consciousness. "As we use the verb "to present", "to be presented" means the same as "to appear"." (62/81) "We speak of a presentation whenever something appears to us" (153/198).

One of Brentano's main aims in the *Psychology* was to provide a fundamental classification of mental phenomena. To this end, he divided mental phenomena into three fundamental categories: presentation, judgment, and love/hate.[13] But the three categories are not situated on the same level, for in order for anything to be judged or perceived (Brentano counts perceptions as judgments) or loved or hated, it must first appear in consciousness, and this requires an act of presentation. For example, a physical phenomenon, e.g. a color or a sound, is an appearance in the sense that it is what can appear to consciousness, but a presentation is required in order for any physical phenomena to appear at all. Acts of presentation, therefore, form the foundation of every judgment and emotion.

This act of presentation forms the foundation not merely of the act of judging, but also of desiring and of every other mental act. Nothing can be judged, desired, hoped or feared, unless one has a presentation of that thing (61, 80).[14]

Brentano, then, endorses this way of distinguishing mental from physical phenomena.

But even after one has divided mental phenomena into two groups in this way, those which are presentations and those which are based on presentations, and has in this way distinguished them from all physical phenomena, which are neither presentations nor based on presentations, there is still a question about what fundamental feature it is that all appearances that are mental phenomena have in common, what fundamental feature it is that makes them mental and so distinguishes them from all appearances that are physical phenomena. A single diagnostic sufficient and necessary condition of mental phenomena would be preferable.

2. Physical phenomena always appear with spatial location and extension, whereas mental phenomena always appear without extension and spatial location.[15]

Brentano puts this criterion aside for two reasons. First he notes that it is contested from both directions. Some argue that sound and olfactory phenomena are examples of physical phenomena that appear to be non-spatial.[16] Berkeley argues that color is essentially non-spatial, and some of Brentano's contemporaries, e.g. Herbart, Spencer and Lotze, argue that all physical phenomena are essentially non-spatial. In contrast, Aristotle argues that mental phenomena such as sense perceptions are spatially located in our sensory organs, while others claim that sensory appetites are localized. Although Brentano remarks that all of these criticisms may be unjustified, his second reason for rejecting this criterion is that it only provides a negative characterization of mental phenomena. What is wanted is a unified and a positive characterization of mental phenomena.

3. Only mental phenomena are perceived in inner consciousness or inner perception and thus are "those phenomena which alone can be perceived in the strict sense of the word" (70/92).

Brentano distinguishes inner perception from external perception. External perception is always of physical phenomena in Brentano's sense, such as color, sound and spatial location. Inner perception is always of mental phenomena. The German word for perception, "Wahrnehmung", literally means taking something to be true, and since the phenomena of external perception cannot be proved real or true, they cannot reveal the true nature of the external world, there is a sense in which external perception is not perception at all. So, for Brentano, the phrase "external perception" is arguably a misnomer. We do, however, perceive our own mental phenomena in this strict and literal sense. According to Brentano, inner perception is immediate and infallibly self-evident (70/91). We can know that mental phenomena are real and we can know their real nature through inner perception: "The phenomena of inner perception . . . are true in themselves. As they appear to be, so they are in reality, a fact with is attested to by the evidence with which they are perceived" (15/19–20).

It is important to note that by "inner consciousness" and "inner perception", Brentano does not mean what contemporary theorists typically call "introspection", or what Brentano and his contemporaries also call "inner observation" (*Beobachtung*). Introspection or inner observation is one mental act taking a distinct mental act as an object or as the focus of attention. For Brentano, inner consciousness is a self-intimating phenomenon where a mental act takes itself as object, not as the focus of attention, but only 'in passing' or 'by the way' (*nebenbei*), as Aristotle observed. One shouldn't suppose that to say that a mental act takes itself as object only 'in passing' is to suggest that this taking itself as object is unimportant or inessential. For, in fact, its taking itself as object in this way is constitutive of its existence as a conscious mental phenomenon – essential to its existing at all as a conscious mental phenomenon.

The importance of inner perception cannot be underestimated in elucidating Brentano's conception of psychology. Not only is inner perception what makes a conscious mental state conscious at all, it is also our main source of evidence for making psychological distinctions. I'll postpone a more thorough discussion of inner perception to section 5, where I consider Brentano's theory of consciousness in more detail.

Although Brentano accepts this third criterion and doesn't express any explicit dissatisfaction with it, he thinks there is a better way of capturing what is distinctive of mental phenomena, which brings us to what Brentano is most well known for.

4. All and only mental phenomena have intentionality. This is of course based on Brentano's famous passage:

> Every mental phenomenon is characterized by what the Scholastics of the Middle Ages called the intentional (or mental) inexistence of an object, and what we might call, though not wholly unambiguously, reference to a content, direction toward an object (which is not to be understood here as meaning a thing), or immanent objectivity. Every mental phenomenon includes something as object within itself, although they do not all do so in the same way. In presentation, something is presented, in judgment something is affirmed or denied, in love loved, in hate hated, in desire desired and so on. . . . This intentional in-existence is characteristic exclusively of mental phenomena. No physical phenomenon exhibits anything like it. We can, therefore, define mental phenomena by saying that they are those phenomena which contain an object intentionally within themselves.
> (68/88–89)

Although this was Brentano's favored way of distinguishing mental phenomena from physical phenomena – "Nothing distinguishes mental phenomena from physical phenomena more than the fact that something is immanent as an object in them" (152/197) – what it amounts to is 'not wholly unambiguous'. For in this short passage, Brentano provides four ways of characterizing mental phenomena. Mental phenomena essentially involve:

- intentional (or mental) inexistence of an object;
- reference to a content;
- direction to an object (although 'object' is not to be understood here as meaning a thing);[17]
  and
- immanent objectivity.

Later in the same chapter, Brentano adds a fifth by characterizing mental phenomena in terms of "the reference to something as an object" (74/97).

In the end, it is arguable that Brentano means the same thing by all of these expressions. In contemporary philosophy they are all replaced by the term 'intentionality', and intentionality is then typically characterized in terms of 'aboutness', 'of-ness' or 'object directedness'.

The key to seeing the interchangeability of these expressions, perhaps, is to see the relationship between the phrases 'direction to an object' and the 'intentional inexistence of an object'.[18] There has been a great deal of debate about Brentano's use of the term 'intentional inexistence', but I think his meaning can be made sufficiently clear by considering his overall project. Many have argued that what Brentano meant by the intentional inexistence of an object was that all the objects of mental phenomena literally "*exist in*" or "*dwell in*" mental phenomena.[19] Since all phenomena are by definition appearances, that is, 'things of the mind', and phenomena, whether physical or mental, are the objects of mental phenomena, all objects of mental phenomena are literally 'in the mind'. Although I think this interpretation is correct, we can go further in understanding the term 'intentional inexistence' if we consider how Brentano contrasts it with 'real existence' as these phrases apply to mental and physical phenomena.

For Brentano, 'intentional inexistence' signals something about the nature of the objects towards which our mental phenomena are directed. Both mental phenomena and physical phenomena can be the objects of mental phenomena. Physical phenomena, for example, are the objects of presentations of sounds, colors, spatial location, etc. Mental phenomena are the objects of inner perception, but also can be the objects of introspection. Insofar as anything is the object of a mental phenomenon, it has intentional inexistence. So, 'intentional inexistence' is a perfectly general phrase, which applies to any possible object of a mental phenomenon. But only some objects of mental phenomena have 'real existence', and those are mental phenomena only when they are objects of inner perception. That is, only some objects have real existence in addition to intentional inexistence. An object has 'real existence' when it is presented to us as it is in itself. By this criterion, physical phenomena, e.g. sounds, colors, etc. do not have 'real existence', because they do not present us with a transcendent reality as it is in itself. Sound, for example, as an object of a mental act, does not reveal to us the true nature of a mind-independent quality in nature. Mental phenomena, when they are the objects of introspection, i.e. when one mental act is directed at a distinct mental act in a focused fashion, do not have 'real existence', for introspection does not reveal the true nature of mental phenomena. Only when mental phenomena are objects of inner perception is their true nature revealed to us, and so it is only in the case of inner perception that mental phenomena have 'real existence', as well as intentional inexistence.

> We said that mental phenomena are those phenomena which alone can be perceived in the strict sense of the word. We could just as well say that they are those phenomena which alone possess real existence as well as intentional existence. Knowledge, joy and desire really exist. Color, sound and warmth have only a phenomenal and intentional existence.
> (70/92)

> The phenomena of inner perception are a different matter. They are true in themselves. As they appear to be, so they are in reality, a fact which is attested to by the evidence with which they are perceived.
> (15/19)

So, we can now see why intentionality, for Brentano, must be characterized in terms of 'intentional inexistence', because it is the term that applies to *all* possible objects of mental phenomena: The 'intentional inexistence' of an object is what is distinctive of all mental phenomena; only some of the objects of mental acts have 'real existence'.

This interpretation of Brentano's characterization of intentionality is very foreign to our contemporary understanding of intentionality. We tend to begin with the idea that our intentional mental states are typically directed at, or relate us to, a mind-independent reality.[20] In fact, we take the paradigm cases of such intentional mental states to be relations to physical objects. And if this is our starting point, the idea that we can think about objects that do not exist becomes a pressing problem. If intentional mental states are relations, and relations can only have relata that exist, how can we think about non-existent objects? Similarly, if we can only stand in genuine relations to things that exist in space and time and have causal influence, and abstract objects don't exist in space and time and don't have causal influence, how can we think about, and hence become intentionally related to, abstract objects?

Although Brentano later started thinking about intentionality in these terms in the 1911 Appendix, it didn't seem to concern him at all in 1874. The shift is evident in the following remarks. In the very first sentence of the Appendix he writes, "What is characteristic of every mental activity is, as I believe I have shown, the reference to something as an object. In this respect, every mental activity seems to be something relational" (211/ 271). In the Foreword to the 1911 edition, he characterizes his shift in thinking about intentionality as follows: "One of the most important innovations is that I am no longer of the opinion that the mental relation can have something other than a thing [*Reales*] as its object" (xxvi/xxiii). And in the *Nachlass* (*XIV On Objects of Thought*) he writes:

> Anyone who thinks thinks of something. And because this is part of the concept of thinking, this concept cannot be a unitary one unless the little word "something," too, has a single meaning. . . . [I]f the "something" is a univocal concept, it can only be a generic concept under which everything which is supposed to be an object of thought must fall. And consequently it must be maintained that anyone who is thinking must have a thing (*Reales*) as his object and have this as his object in one and the same sense of the word. This is in opposition to Aristotle, . . . and to many moderns who say that we do not always have a thing, but often have a non-thing (*Nicht-Reales*), as our object.

In these passages, we see Brentano move from thinking about intentionality as involving *reference to something as object* to thinking of it explicitly as a *relation*, and as a relation only to *Reales*. It is important to bear in mind Brentano's original distinction between an object and a thing (Reales). He immediately sees the difficulty in thinking of intentionality as a relation to Reales:

> If I take something relative (*ein Relativ*) from among the broad class of comparative relations, something larger or smaller for example, then, if the larger thing exists, the smaller one must exist too. . . . It is entirely different with mental reference. If someone thinks of something, the one who is thinking must certainly exist, but the object of his thinking need not exist at all. In fact, if he is denying something, the existence of the object is precisely what is excluded whenever his denial is correct. So the only thing which is required by mental reference is the person thinking. The terminus of the so-called relation does not need to exist in reality at all. For this reason, one could doubt whether we really are dealing with something relational here, and not, rather, with something somewhat similar to something relational in a certain respect, which might, therefore, better be called "quasi-relational".
> ("*Relativliches*") (*Appendix* 211–12/271–272)

As Crane (2006) points out, calling intentionality 'quasi-relational' doesn't do much more than name the problem of thinking of intentionality in relational terms. So although Brentano started thinking about intentionality in different terms, he didn't produce a sophisticated theory in these new terms.

So what happened between 1874 and 1911, and how do Brentano's 'innovations' relate to current issues in the theory of intentionality? We can begin to answer both of these questions by first considering Twardowski and Meinong's developments of Brentano's views and Brentano's awareness of these developments.

3. Twardowski and Meinong

Both Twardowski and Meinong attempted to improve on aspects of Brentano's 1874 theory of intentionality. In his book *On the Content and Object of Presentations* (1894/1977), Twardowski introduced a distinction between content and object, which provided a possible clarification of Brentano's notion of 'immanent object' and addressed a puzzling issue with Brentano's theory of judgment. In his famous article 'The Theory of Objects' (1904), Meinong developed a theory of objects with Brentano's insight about intentionality as one of its central building blocks.

I'll begin with the puzzle for Brentano's theory of judgment and Twardowski's solution. The puzzle results from two features of Brentano's theory, namely that judgments are 'objectual', and that the object of a particular mental act is an 'immanent object', which has 'intentional inexistence' in the act.

Brentano's objectual theory of judgment stands in contrast to a 'propositional' theory of judgment.[21] Very briefly, according to a propositional theory, judgments are intentional attitudes, which are related to propositions or something proposition-like. A typical example is *Jenny judges that grass is green*, where 'that grass is green' designates a proposition or something proposition-like. According to Brentano's objectual theory, judgment is a *sui generis* mental phenomenon in which we either affirm or deny the existence of an object, but this is not to be understood as predicating existence of an object. Although 'There is an x, such that x is F' does involve predicating F of x, according to Brentano's theory, 'There is an F' involves no predication. For Brentano, all simple judgments have one of two contents: 'There is an F' or 'There is not an F.' Every simple judgment is directed at an individual object – an F – and either affirms or denies the existence of that object. The following are reductions offered by Brentano's theory:

<Every dog is cute> is reducible to <There is no non-cute dog>;
<No dog is cute> is reducible to <There is no cute dog>;
<Some dog is cute> is reducible to <There is a cute dog>;
<Some dog is not cute> is reducible to <There is a non-cute dog>.[22]

Now consider my judgment that the aether does not exist. According to Brentano, the object of this mental act, the aether, is an immanent object, so it does 'exist' inside my consciousness – it appears to my consciousness. So, it seems there is a sense in which I would be wrong in denying its existence. The obvious issue here is that what I wish to deny the existence of is not an immanent object, which intentionally exists in my mental act, but rather something that if it did exist would exist independently of my consciousness. Judging that the aether does not exist means rejecting a physical space-filling substance outside of my consciousness. In other words, the object of this judgment does not seem to be an object that has only 'intentional inexistence'.

Twardowski offers a solution to this problem by attempting to clarify the notion of an 'immanent object'. According to Twardowksi, every mental phenomenon has a content (*Inhalt*) and an object (*Gegenstand*): "One has to distinguish . . . between the object at which our idea "aims, as it were," and the immanent object or the content of the presentation."[23] The *content* of a mental act is wholly "inside" the mind and depends for its existence on the occurrence of a mental act. The *object* of a mental act is that at which the act aims, and typically does not depend on the occurrence of a mental act:

> We shall say of the content that it is thought, presented, *in* the presentation; we shall say of the object that it is presented *through* the content of the presentation (or through the presentation). What is presented *in* a presentation is its content; what is presented *through* a presentation is its object. . . . When one says something is presented, one merely has to add whether it is presented *in* the presentation or *through* the presentation. In the first case, 'the presented' means the content of the presentation; in the second, the object of the presentation.[24]

The notion of an 'immanent object' is identified with the content of the presentation, while the object of a presentation provides us with a more intuitive notion of what it is to be an object of a mental act, namely something that typically exists beyond the mental act itself. Twardowski is abandoning Brentano's restriction to theorizing only about phenomena. With this development, Twardowski can easily solve the puzzle for Brentano's theory of judgment. There is a mental content (immanent object), through which the aether is presented and judged *as non-existing*. That content, present in me, exists. The object of my judgment, the aether itself, does not exist.

The example of the aether has further significance, because although Twardowski's distinction between content and object clarifies certain aspects of Brentano's overall theory of intentionality, and even foreshadows our contemporary way of thinking about intentionality, it leaves a very difficult issue unresolved. Twardowski and Meinong never forsook the idea that every mental phenomenon has an object, in addition to having a content. If every mental phenomenon is object directed, in the sense of object introduced by Twardowski, then what do we say about our thoughts about objects that don't exist, such as thinking of the aether or the golden mountain? It is this consideration, together with the question of how to analyze negative existentials and the ontological status of mathematical entities, that motivated Meinong's theory of objects.

Meinong summarized his own approach to the theory of objects as follows:

> It may sound strange to hear that metaphysics is not universal enough for a science of Objects, and hence cannot take on the task just formulated. . . . Without doubt, metaphysics has to do with everything that exists. However, the totality of what exists, including what has existed and will exist, is infinitely small in comparison with the totality of the Objects of knowledge.[25]

According to Meinong, concrete objects, if they exist, exist in space and time. Abstract objects, such as propositions or mathematical entities 'subsist' outside of space and time, and objects such as the golden mountain or Pegasus neither exist nor 'subsist'; they are 'beyond being or non-being'. This last category of objects, non-existent objects, has been the most controversial, despite its accounting for our seeming ability to think about non-existent objects and our ability to meaningful deny their existence. What is critical for understanding this aspect of Meinong's theory is the independence of an object's Sosein (what an object is, what properties it has) from its Sein (existence).

> The Sosein of an Object is not affected by its Nichtsein . . . neither being nor non-being can belong essentially to the Object in itself . . . the Object as such stands 'beyond being and non-being' . . . The Object is by nature indifferent to being, although at least one of its two Objectives of being, the Object's being or non-being, subsists.[26]

There has been a lot of discussion and criticism of Meinong's theory of objects.[27] My goal here is not to discuss Meinong's approach in detail, but to show how his sophisticated theory of objects was in part motivated by a Brentanian claim about intentionality, namely, that all mental phenomena are object-directed. Once this claim is divorced from Brentano's assertion that the objects of mental phenomena are 'immanent objects', and intentionality is seen as a relational phenomenon, if we accept at face value that we think about non-existent objects, it seems it is no leap at all to postulate non-existent objects!

Although it is not clear what Brentano thought of Twardowski's content/object distinction, he completely rejected a Meinongian development of his main insights. Although he doesn't explicitly mention Meinong, he does say the following in the 1911 Appendix (213–14/274):

> I do not wish to bring this discussion of mental reference to a close without having given a word of consideration to the view that there is a distinction between "being" and "existing." According to this view both are to be taken in a very peculiar sense. Namely, a person might be led to say that if someone is mentally referring to an object, the object really always has being just as much as he does, even if it does not always exist as he does . . . I confess that I am unable to make any sense of this distinction between being and existence.

Twardowski's content/object distinction is very much in line with current conceptions of intentionality, for discussions about intentionality typically focus on the notions of 'intentional content' or 'representational content', and the objects of our intentional states are typically taken to be mind-independent entities.[28] Brentano's resistance to a Meinongian theory of objects is also clearly in sync with present day attitudes towards Meinong and Meinongian-inspired views. But although Brentano may have rejected Meinong's postulation of non-existent objects, theorists have continued to focus on the possibility of thinking about the non-existent in twentieth-century analytic philosophy.

4. From Chisholm's Brentano to contemporary theories of intentionality

More than any other analytic philosopher, Roderick Chisholm (1916–1999) brought Brentano's philosophy to the attention of the analytic tradition.[29] First, he introduced Brentano's theory of intentionality as centrally concerned with our apparent ability to think about non-existent objects. Second, and now putting aside Brentanian exegesis, Chisholm's focus on thinking about the non-existent set the stage for much of the discussion about intentionality in the second half of the twentieth century. I'll consider both of these issues in turn.

After citing Brentano's famous passage, Chisholm summarizes it as follows:

> When Brentano said that these attitudes "intentionally contain an object in themselves," he was referring to the fact that they can truly be said to

have objects even though the objects which they can be said to have do not in fact exist. Diogenes could have looked for an honest man even if there hadn't been any honest man.[30]

Chisholm elucidates this understanding of Brentano in what I will presently introduce as Chisholm's 'three marks of intentionality', although he does so in terms of intentional sentences, thus conducting his discussion of intentionality in linguistic terms. His central idea is that intentional sentences create intensional contexts. An intensional context is a feature of sentences in which existential generalization and the principle of substituting co-referring terms fail. Failures of existential generalization for simple declarative sentences and for sentences with propositional clauses constitute Chisholm's first and second marks of intentionality, and the failure of the principle of substitution of co-referring terms constitutes his third mark of intentionality.

Existential generalization is a rule of inference in first order logic, for example, according to which atomic sentences such as 'Fa' (where 'a' stands for a singular term and 'F' stands for a predicate) entail that there exists an x such that x is F ('∃xFx'). For example, "Bill is an honest man" entails that there exists an honest man. Existential generalization fails in intensional contexts. For example, a sentence such as "Diogenes looked for an honest man" is intensional, because neither it nor its contradictory "Diogenes didn't look for an honest man" implies that there are or there are not honest men. Chisholm extends this point to cover sentences with propositional clauses such as "James believes there are tigers in India". Neither this sentence reporting James's belief nor a sentence reporting its contradictory implies that there are or there are not tigers in India.

According to the principle of substitution of co-referring terms, co-referring names and definite descriptions can be substituted in a sentence while preserving its truth-value. For example, if 'Muhammad Ali' is substituted for 'Cassius Clay' in the sentence "Cassius Clay was a great boxer", then the truth-value of the original sentence is preserved. As already noted, this principle fails for certain intentional sentences. We can't validly infer that "Lois Lane believes that Clark Kent can fly" from the sentence "Lois Lane believes that Superman can fly" despite the fact that 'Superman' and 'Clark Kent' are co-referring terms.

After providing these three marks of intentionality, Chisholm claims that

> we may now re-express Brentano's thesis – or something resembling that of Brentano – by reference to intentional sentences. Let us say (1) that we do not need to use intentional sentences when we describe nonpsychological phenomena; we can express all of our beliefs about what is merely "physical" in sentences which are not intentional. But (2) when we wish to describe perceiving, assuming, believing, knowing, wanting, hoping and other such attitudes, then either (a) we must use sentences which are intentional or (b) we must use terms we do not need to use when we describe nonpsychological phenomena.[31]

Although this 're-expression' of Brentano's view might be correct in letter, Chisholm's 'three marks of intentionality' in terms of which he motived this re-expression are not in the spirit of what motivated Brentano's views in 1874. I argued in section 2 that a concern about our ability to think about non-existent objects wasn't even on the conceptual map for Brentano in 1874.[32] At best, Chisholm's considerations capture some of what started to concern Brentano in the 1911 republication of Book Two of the *Psychology*. Nonetheless, this interpretation of Brentano as focused on thoughts about non-existent objects is the one many contemporary analytic philosophers have accepted, and it has led to further claims and challenges to the idea that intentionality is the mark of the mental.[33] I will consider two.

First, it has led some philosophers to draw metaphysical conclusions about the mind-body problem, namely that certain forms of reductive physicalism are false.[34] Here is a standard summary of this view expressed in the entry on Chisholm in the *Stanford Encyclopedia of Philosophy* (Feldman and Feldman: section 8):

> Brentano's Thesis [is] not entirely clear, but its importance should be obvious. Suppose that every psychological fact somehow involves something with "intentional inexistence" (however precisely this is to be construed). Suppose that no physical fact involves a thing with intentional inexistence. Then it would follow that no psychological fact can be identified with a physical fact; one version of the psycho-physical identity theory would be false; physicalism of some popular varieties would be untenable.

Very roughly, according to reductive physicalism, the physical is something entirely non-mental that can be fully characterized in the term of physics. For Brentano in 1874, both mental and physical phenomena are appearances, "things of the mind", so the possibility of ontologically reducing the mental to the physical, as it is understood by reductive physicalism, does not even arise. Furthermore, Brentano's views in 1911 are too underdeveloped to conjecture about his possible views on reductive physicalism.

Second, the failure to take into account how Brentano understood the notion of physical phenomena has led to a challenge to the idea that intentionality is the mark of the mental in the sense that it is a property that can be possessed only by mental phenomena. This challenge is most vividly expressed by 'naturalistic' theories of intentionality that dominated discussion of intentionality in the second half of the twentieth century.

The initial consensus was that the way to naturalize intentionality was to identify a wholly naturalistically (scientifically) characterizable relation that holds between states of the brain and states of the environment in such a way that the states of the brain can be said to reliably track the states of the environment. Given this tracking, the states of the brain could be said to 'carry information' about the environment, and so be genuinely intentionally about the environment.

Many 'tracking theorists' agreed that a reductive naturalistic explanation of intentionality must begin by accepting the idea that lawful causal correlation between states of the brain and states of the environment is the foundation for the former representing (or carrying information about) the latter. But if intentionality is fundamentally a matter of causal co-variation of this kind, then intentionality can be found amongst non-mental phenomenon such as smoke and fire, tree rings and the age of trees, shadows and objects and indeed anywhere causal co-variation is found.[35] And so intentionality ceases to be the mark – the distinguishing mark – of the mental.

On this view, object-directedness cannot be limited to mental phenomena. After noting the ubiquitiousness of intentionality, Dretske goes on to characterize the mental in terms of our apparent ability to think about the non-existent:

> what we are trying to build is a system that exhibits that peculiar array of intentional properties that characterizes thought. We are, in particular, trying to build systems that exhibit what Chisholm describes as the first mark of intentionality, the power to say that so-and-so is the case when so-and-so is not the case, the power to misrepresent how things stand in the world.[36]

Chisholm's interpretation of Brentano, with its focus on misrepresentation, came to dominate much of the contemporary discussion about intentionality. Philosophers offered various explanations of the possibility of misrepresentation. Dretske, Millikan and Papineau – to name a few – offered teleological accounts, while Fodor appealed to the phenomenon of asymmetric dependence.[37] I don't have the space to give the details of these accounts, but they all endorse the claim that object-directedness as such is not enough to adequately characterize mental phenomena. On this view, it is only by considering the idea that we can think about the non-existent do we get to the heart of what is distinctive of mental intentionality – an idea that will obviously be rejected by those to whom it seems obvious that we can never properly be said to think about things that don't exist. My main point here is that this move beyond object-directedness to adequately characterize the mental only arises if we ignore what Brentano meant by 'physical phenomena'. For Brentano, physical phenomena are appearances, and it is not clear that it makes sense to ask if one appearance 'carries information' about another appearance. Moreover, since physical phenomena are 'things of the mind', the kind of reduction naturalistic theories of intentionality are after cannot be achieved on a Brentanian theory.

5. Consciousness and intentionality: Brentano and representationalism

So far I have focused on the phenomenon of intentionality. I have attempted to characterize Brentano's initial theory of intentionality, with its specific motivations and concerns, and then trace it through his students' attempts to clarify and develop his views, through Chisholm's interpretation of Brentano, with its focus on thoughts about the non-existent, to the focus on the non-existent that has been so influential in contemporary theories of intentionality. I'll now turn to a further way in which Chisholm's approach to intentionality impacted twentieth-century philosophy of mind.

As previously noted, twentieth-century analytic philosophers typically made a sharp theoretical distinction between the intentional properties of mental states, the properties they have in virtue of being about or of something, on the one hand, and the conscious or phenomenological properties of mental states, the properties they have in virtue of there being 'something it is like' to be in them, on the other hand. Intentional properties and phenomenological properties were widely assumed to be metaphysically independent, and were accordingly studied in isolation from each other.[38]

In this section, I'll argue that Chisholm's focus on existential generalization and the principle of substitution led to a focus on 'propositional attitudes', which in turn partly motivated the mistakenly 'separatist' approach to intentionality and phenomenology in contemporary philosophy. I'll then summarize Brentano's unified approach to these phenomena and his rejection of what motivated contemporary philosophers to treat consciousness and intentionality separately. Although it may seem that Brentano's view is hopelessly out of step with contemporary views, I'll consider one contemporary view, representationalism, which looks to have strong affinities with Brentano's views. I'll argue that these affinities are superficial, but that there is another contemporary approach, perhaps what we can call the 'consciousness first approach', that is far closer to the spirit of Brentano's work.

5.1 *The separation of phenomenology and intentionality*

The explanation for the separatist approach to the phenomena of consciousness (phenomenology) and intentionality in recent philosophy is complicated and multifaceted, and I have the space only to gesture at two of its sources. First, recent theories of intentionality have tended to focus on the propositional attitudes, e.g. beliefs and desires, which have been almost universally assumed to lack any phenomenology.[39] Indeed, intentionality was often straightforwardly characterized in terms of propositions.

Here are two typical examples of this approach. First, according to Perry:

> The phenomenon of intentionality suggests that attitudes are essentially relational in nature: they involve relations to the propositions at which they are directed.... An attitude seems to be individuated by the agent, the type of attitude (belief, desire, etc.), and the proposition at which it is directed.[40]

And Stoljar concurs:

> In one formulation, the problem of intentionality is presented as concerning a particular class of properties, intentional properties. Intentional properties are those properties expressed by predicates formed from verbs of propositional attitudes.[41]

Philosophers then took traditional propositional-attitude states to be prime examples of states that did not possess any phenomenology. Braddon-Mitchell and Jackson and Nelkin provide standard statements of this position. According to Braddon-Mitchell and Jackson,

> perceptual experiences are prime examples of states for which there is something it is like to be in them. They have phenomenal feel, a phenomenology. . . . Cognitive states are prime examples of states for which there is *not* something it is like to be in them, of states that lack a phenomenology.
>
> (1996, 129, 295)

And Nelkin states:

> Neither the *believing* nor the *consciousness* that one oneself is believing *feels* like anything, if by 'feels' one means some sort of phenomenal or phenomenological state. It is only because we take sensations and sensation-like states as our paradigms of consciousness that we think that any state about which we are conscious must have phenomenological properties.
>
> (1989, 424; original emphasis)

A second factor that contributed to the separatist treatment of intentionality and phenomenology was a focus on unconscious mental states. A concern with propositional attitudes like beliefs and desires naturally leads to a concern with unconscious mentality, since beliefs and desires are paradigm cases of dispositional or 'sub-personal' states. Furthermore, functionalism – perhaps the dominant theory in analytic philosophy of mind in the second half of the twentieth century – was most successful in accounting for beliefs and desires; so functionalists naturally focused on these sorts of attitudes. More generally, the postulation of unconscious mentality was entirely natural within a functionalist framework, given its analysis of mental states partly in terms of behaviour or behavioural dispositions.[42] One central argument for the existence of unconscious mental states is that it is necessary to explain certain sorts of behaviour.[43] If someone then asks why the relevant behaviour indicates an unconscious mental state, rather than simply indicating that the subject is in a particular neurological state which has certain causal properties, the functionalist has an immediate answer: for if there is a *constitutive* connection between mental states and causal properties related to behaviour or behavioural dispositions, then exhibiting the relevant behaviour will be powerful evidence for – if not proof of – unconscious mental states.[44]

5.2 Brentano's theory of consciousness

All this is very foreign to Brentano, who holds that there is constitutive relationship between consciousness and intentionality, so that one cannot study them in isolation from one another. Indeed Brentano's rejection of unconscious mentality is partly motivated by his theory of consciousness.

To see this, it will be helpful to begin with a general outline of his theory of consciousness. Its central pillar is the idea that conscious intentional episodes are 'of', i.e. *intentionally of*, a whole lot more than just external world objects and properties.[45] The basic idea is simple and ancient – and Aristotelian. It is that in having a visual experience of a tree in leaf (for example), the subject, in addition to being aware of the tree and any other relevant external content, is also aware of the awareness of the tree. In having a particular conscious experience, the subject is always and necessarily also aware of that very experience itself. There is always some sort of awareness of the experience or experiencing: conscious awareness always involves – constitutively involves – some sort of awareness of that very awareness.

What I am here calling 'awareness of awareness' Brentano called "inner consciousness" or "inner perception".[46] As mentioned in section 2, inner perception provides us with a special kind of access to our conscious experiences and should be clearly distinguished from introspection.[47] Brentano does so in the following passage:

> Psychology . . . has its basis in perception and experience. Above all, however, its source is to be found in the *inner perception* of our own mental phenomena. . . . Note, however, that we said that inner *perception* [*Wahrnehmung*] and not introspection, i.e. inner *observation* [*Beobachtung*], constitutes the primary and essential source of psychology. These two concepts must be distinguished from one another. One of the characteristics of inner perception is that it can never become inner observation. We can observe objects which, as they say, are perceived externally. In observation, we direct our full attention to a phenomenon in order to apprehend it accurately. But with objects of inner perception this is absolutely impossible. . . . It is only while our attention is turned toward a different object that we are able to perceive, as it were *in passing*, the mental processes which are directed toward that object.
>
> (22–23/29–30; translation modified)

Brentano agrees with Aristotle's characterization of inner perception: "knowledge and perception and opinion and understanding have always something else as their object, and themselves only *by the way*".[48] Although this awareness is only 'by the way', according to Brentano, inner perception is immediate, infallible and self-evident (70/91).

What role did the rejection of unconscious mentality play in motivating this theory of consciousness? After considering several different definitions of 'consciousness', Brentano offers the following:

> I prefer to use ["consciousness"] as synonymous with "mental phenomenon," or "mental act." For, in the first place, the constant use of these compound designations would be cumbersome, and furthermore, the term "consciousness", since it refers to an object which consciousness is conscious of, seems to be appropriate to characterize mental phenomena precisely in terms of its distinguishing characteristic, i.e., the property of the intentional in-existence of an object, for which we lack a word in common usage.
> (78–79/102)

'Consciousness' refers to an object one is conscious of.[49] Since according to Brentano all mental phenomena refer to an object, all mental phenomena are conscious in the sense that they all have an object. He then asks

> whether there are any mental phenomena which are not objects of consciousness. All mental phenomena are states of consciousness; but are all mental phenomena conscious, or might there also be unconscious mental acts?
> (79/102)

For Brentano, this is the question of whether there can be mental phenomena that are not objects of mental acts themselves. In contemporary terms, can there be unconscious mental acts or states? The contemporary answer to this question is a resounding 'yes'. Brentano disagrees. He spends the whole of Chapter II of Book Two arguing that there are no unconscious mental phenomena.

According to Brentano, a mental state is conscious if and only if it is the object of a mental state, and if all mental states are conscious, then all mental states are the objects of mental states. A mental state can be an object either if it is the object of a higher-order mental state, or if it is the object of the very state which is conscious.[50] Brentano opts for the latter approach: "consciousness of the mental phenomena which exist in us is given in the phenomena themselves" (102/133). In our current terms, Brentano's theory is a same-order theory as opposed to a higher-order theory of consciousness. According to a higher-order theory a mental state is conscious in virtue of having a distinct, unconscious higher-order state directed at it. According to a same-order theory, the awareness of a state that makes that state a conscious state is part of that very state itself.[51]

Brentano considers and rejects four kinds of arguments for the claim that there are unconscious mental phenomena: first, an argument that certain facts of experience require the postulation of unconscious mental acts; second, an argument that certain conscious mental acts must bring about unconscious mental phenomena as their effects; third (and harder to follow), an argument that the relationship of the intensity of a mental act and its concomitant mental act requires that the latter be unconscious in the case of conscious mental phenomena – *the strength of the concomitant consciousness is a function of their own strength,* and that, because of this relationship, in certain cases in which the latter is a positive magnitude, the former must lack a positive value. Finally, an argument that accepting that there are only conscious mental acts leads to a vicious infinite regress of mental acts. He sums up the last argument as follows:

> we could attempt to prove that the hypothesis that each mental phenomenon is an object of a mental phenomenon leads to an infinite complexity of mental states, which is both intrinsically impossible and contrary to experience.
>
> (81/105)

It is in response to this fourth kind of argument that Brentano formulates his 'same-order' view of consciousness. One can summarize the dialectic as follows:

[i] If there are no unconscious mental states, then all mental states are conscious, i.e. all mental states are the objects of mental states. (This follows from Brentano's understanding of the word 'consciousness'.)

[ii] *Prima facie* objection: if all mental states are conscious, then there is a vicious regress of mental states.

Brentano uses hearing, the presentation of a sound, to illustrate the *prima facie* threat of a vicious regress. If no mental phenomenon is possible without a correlative consciousness of it, then, along with the hearing, the presentation of a sound, we have to have a presentation of the hearing, i.e. a presentation of the presentation of the sound. But then it looks as if the presentation of the presentation of the sound must be accompanied by a presentation of it in turn. So now we have three presentations: the presentation of the sound, the presentation of the presentation of the sound, and the presentation of the presentation of the presentation of the sound. Either the series will be infinite or it will terminate in an unconscious presentation. (The higher-order view avoids this regress by accepting unconscious mental states at the second-order.) If one denies that there are unconscious presentations, one seems committed to an infinite number of mental acts even for the simplest act of hearing.

[iii] Same-order response to *prima facie* objection: the consciousness necessary to make a mental phenomenon conscious is built into the mental phenomenon itself.

In a typical perceptual experience, say, awareness of the external object and the awareness of the experience itself are so intimately and intrinsically related that they constitute a single mental state. According to Brentano,

> inner experience seems to prove undeniably that the presentation of the sound is connected with the presentation of the presentation of the sound in such a peculiarly intimate way that its [the presentation of the presentation's] very existence constitutes an intrinsic prerequisite for the existence of this presentation. This suggests that there is a special connection between the object of inner presentation and the presentation itself, and that both belong to one and the same mental act.

> The presentation of the sound and the presentation of the presentation of the sound form a single mental phenomenon; it is only by considering it in its relation to two different objects, one of which is a physical phenomenon and the other a mental phenomenon, that we divide it conceptually into two presentations. In the same mental phenomenon in which the sound is present to our minds we simultaneously apprehend the mental phenomenon itself. What is more, we apprehend it in accordance with its dual nature insofar as it has the sound as content within it, and insofar as it has itself as content at the same time . . . we can say that the sound is the primary object of the act of hearing, and that the act of hearing itself is the secondary object (98–99/179–180).

[iv] So all mental states are conscious, i.e. all mental states are the objects of mental states.

One can certainly hold that all mental states are conscious, and reject the same-order view. Brentano simply argues that one can hold a view of consciousness according to which for a mental state to be conscious is for it to be an object of mental state without a regress resulting and without accepting the reality of unconscious mental acts.

Some have worried that even if Brentano avoids a regress of higher and higher mental states, there may be an internal regress for the same-order view.[52] Brentano asks, "When we have a presentation of a sound or another physical phenomenon and are conscious of this presentation, are we also conscious of this consciousness or not?" (99/129) He believes that we must answer yes, but we can nonetheless avoid any internal regress:

> These results show that the consciousness of the presentation of the sound clearly occurs together with the consciousness of this consciousness, for the consciousness which accompanies the presentation of the sound is a consciousness not so much of this presentation as of the whole mental act in which the sound is presented, and in which the consciousness itself

exists concomitantly. Apart from the fact that it presents the physical phenomenon of sound, the mental act of hearing becomes at the same time its own object and content, taken as a whole.

(100/129)

That is, consciousness of a mental state is self-luminous in the sense that it 'gets a glimpse of itself' because it is 'of' the whole mental state of which it is a constituent or part.

5.3 *Representationalism: back to Brentano?*

At this point, Brentano's views appear to stand in sharp contrast to contemporary theorizing about intentionality and consciousness. Not only does he treat these phenomena as intrinsically – metaphysically – related; he also denies the possibility of unconscious mentality. Interestingly, however, it seems that 'representationalism', a view that rose to prominence in analytic philosophy in the closing decades of the twentieth century, shares certain affinities with the two main Brentanian theses discussed in this chapter (according to which all mental states are intentional, and intentionality and consciousness are constitutively related). At the same time, it seems that representationalism can accept some of the main theses that have motivated more recent non-Brentanian views of intentionality – namely the attempt to naturalize intentionality and the acceptance of unconscious mental states.

Is such a unification really possible? Representationalism is a view about the relationship between the phenomenological properties and the intentional properties of conscious mental states. There have been many variants of the view since its introduction into analytic philosophy,[53] but its proponents have for the most part focused on conscious perceptual states, including bodily sensations such as pain and hunger.[54] One important dimension of variation concerns the modal strength of the relationship that is taken to hold between the phenomenological properties of perceptual states and their intentional properties. According to the 'supervenience' version of the view, the phenomenological character of a conscious perceptual state is (metaphysically) *determined* by the properties that that state represents. A stronger 'identity' version simply *identifies* the two sets of properties. On this view, if two states represent the same properties, e.g. roundness and redness, the phenomenology of those states will be identical; and if two states share the same phenomenology, e.g. the what-it's-likeness of experiencing redness and roundness, then the properties those states represent will be identical.

As stated, the strong (identity) form of representationalism doesn't take a stand on which set of properties is more basic – on whether the phenomenology is more basic in such a way such that intentionality is grounded in phenomenology,[55] or whether intentionality is more basic in such a way that phenomenology is grounded in intentionality. The original proponents of representationalism supported the latter approach, however, and typically combined it with a reductive 'naturalization' approach to intentionality – a combination of views I'll call 'Standard representationalism.'

The Standard representationalist view accepts both the Brentanian claim that all mental phenomena are intentional, and that there is a constitutive relationship between consciousness and intentionality. According to Standard representationalism, all consciousness or phenomenology is accounted for in terms of intentionality, so all mentality is intentional. That is, phenomenological properties just are a certain kind of representational content. It then follows trivially that consciousness and intentionality are constitutively related. At the same time, nothing in Standard representationalism prevents there being unconscious mental states. An unconscious mental state is simply a mental state that has representational content but no phenomenology.

The apparent affinities between Brentano's views and Standard representationalism are, however, superficial. Putting aside their disagreement about unconscious mentality, I'll focus on two other fundamental differences. First, one of the main motivations for Standard representationalism, which I'll call the 'transparency thesis', conflicts directly with Brentano's theory of consciousness. Second, although both views acknowledge a constitutive relationship between intentionality and consciousness, the role that intentionality plays in accounting for the nature of consciousness is very different in the two theories, and their views of the nature of consciousness are equally different.

The transparency thesis is a thesis about what we are aware of and what we can be aware of in having perceptual experiences.[56] In particular, it is a claim about the sense in which we can be aware of the phenomenology of perceptual experiences. Its advocates claim that our only possible access to our experiences is to examine them via introspection,[57] and that when a subject introspects her normal visual experience she only ever finds the properties that objects in her environment appear to have. She does not and cannot become aware *of* her experience or any features of her experience via introspection or indeed in any other way.

Tye (2014, 40) summarizes the key transparency claims as follows:

1) We are not aware of features of our visual experience.
2) We are not aware of the visual experience itself.
3) We cannot attend to features of the visual experience.
4) The only features of which we are aware and to which we can attend are external features (colors and shapes of surfaces, for example).

> As far as awareness goes, the thesis is that when we try to introspect a visual experience occurring in normal perception, we are not aware of the experience or its features (intrinsic or not) *period*.

If we take phenomenology to be an introspectible feature of experience, as most Standard representationalists do, and if all that is introspectible according to the transparency thesis are properties attributed to objects, then it's plausible that *all* there is to the phenomenological content of an experience are the properties attributed to objects, i.e. the representation of properties of objects.[58]

Plainly, then, these "transparentist" claims about what we can and can't be aware of in having conscious experience are in direct conflict with Brentano's theory of consciousness. For, according to Brentano, we are always and essentially aware of experience in the very having of experience. That is, every conscious experience constitutively involves an intentional relation to itself. This feature of Brentano's theory not only directly conflicts with the transparency thesis; it also makes clear that the way in which intentionality and consciousness are constitutively related, according to each theory, is very different. For Standard representationalism, consciousness is accounted for in terms of the representation of the properties of physical objects. For Brentano, consciousness is a matter of an experience being intentionally related to itself.

At first glance, Standard representationalism looks as if it may help to recapture some of Brentano's insights. Further inspection reveals that the two theories have very little in common. There are, however, contemporary views that are much more in tune with Brentano's views. The contemporary same-order and higher-order views of consciousness both accept the claim that a conscious state is one we are aware of being in, although they disagree about how to further explicate this claim. Searle 1992, Siewert 1998 and Strawson 1994 all argue that intentionality requires consciousness, what I earlier called the 'consciousness first approach', and all would claim to be entirely naturalistic in their approach to the mind. Proponents of the still more recent 'phenomenal intentionality approach' (e.g. Horgan and Kriegel) also accept that there is a kind of intentionality, 'phenomenal intentionality', which is essentially grounded in consciousness. It is a burden on all of these views to give an account of unconscious mental content, or else deny its existence, as Brentano does.

Notes

1 See e.g. de Beauvoir 1949, Gurwitsch 1966, Husserl 1900–01, Heidegger 1927/1962, Merleau-Ponty 1945/1963, and Sartre 1948/1956.
2 All of my citations from *Psychology from an Empirical Standpoint* are from the English translation. I cite the page numbers from both the 1973 and 1995 editions, with the 1995 citation coming first.
3 Brentano uses the expressions 'mental phenomenon', 'mental act' and 'experience' interchangeably. I will also sometimes speak of mental states, and intentional or propositional attitudes.
4 Two notes should be made about this use of the term 'phenomenology'. First, I will use the terms 'consciousness' and 'phenomenology' interchangeably. This is controversial, because some contemporary philosophers argue for a non-phenomenological kind of consciousness. See e.g. Dennett 1991, 1993 and Nelkin 1989. Second, the term 'phenomenology' was originally used to designate a method of theorizing, arguably initiated by Brentano and most famously practiced by Husserl 1900/1, Merleau-Ponty 1945/1963, and Sartre 1943, according to which, one studies conscious mental phenomena from the 'first-person perspective'. My use is divorced from this tradition. For contemporary introductions to the phenomenological traditions see e.g. Gallagher and Zahavi 2008 and Moran 2000.

5 Powerful thought experiments such as inverted spectrum and inverted earth thought experiments provide a further motivation for the metaphysical separation of intentionality and phenomenology. I don't have the space to discuss these arguments in this chapter. See e.g. Block 1990, Shoemaker 1982 and Tye 2009.
6 I will use 'representationalism' as a name for this position in what follows although it used to have a very different meaning. It referred to positions like Locke's theory of perception. Dretske 1995, Tye 1995, 2009 and Lycan 1996, 2001 are central proponents of representationalism, and in this chapter I will focus on them. See Armstrong 1968 for an early endorsement of representationalism.
7 It would be a mistake to charge Brentano with 'psychologism', understood as the doctrine that logic (for example) is the study of contingent psychological truths, which was criticized by e.g. Frege 1884 and Husserl 1900–01. I should also note that Brentano doesn't use the term 'evident' to describe the kinds of emotions that can give us evaluative knowledge. I have extended the use of 'evident' for ease of exposition.
8 Brentano summarizes some of these disagreements in Book One, Chapter 1 of the *Psychology*.
9 In his later work, Brentano distinguished between what he called 'descriptive psychology' and 'genetic psychology'. Descriptive psychology is concerned with necessary truths about our psychology based on evidence provided by first-person experience. Genetic psychology is concerned with causal laws, laws governing how mental phenomena arise and the connections between the mental and the physiological. According to Brentano, descriptive psychology is the more fundamental in the sense that we have to adequately describe phenomena before we can go on to give explanations of them.
10 Descartes 1641.
11 I won't discuss Brentano's argument for this claim.
12 Remember that this is a distinction within the class of mental phenomena in our ordinary larger sense of the expression of 'mental phenomena'.
13 He follows Descartes in this tripartite classification, which he expounds and defends in Chapters 5–8 of Book Two of the *Psychology*. The love/hate category covers all emotions.
14 Brentano classified desires, and willing in general, as emotions.
15 Brentano cites Descartes, Spinoza, Kant and Bain as holding this view. Sometimes Brentano drops the word 'appear' and simply speaks of physical phenomena as having extension and spatial location. To avoid confusion here, it is important to always keep in mind that Brentano is concerned only with appearances, whether they are physical appearances or mental appearances.
16 There is still a lively debate about whether sound is inherently spatial. See e.g. P. F. Strawson's 1959 famous discussion of the 'sound world' and O'Callaghan and Nudds's 2009 collection on sound.
17 By 'thing' I take Brentano to mean a particular individual thing, as opposed to something general such as a universal.
18 It is clear through out the *Psychology* that Brentano is using 'content' and 'object' interchangeably.
19 See e.g. Crane 2006, Jacquette 2004, Moran 1996, Mulligan 2004, and Smith 1994.
20 See e.g. Byrne 2006, Crane 2001, Dickie 2010, and Jeshion 2010.
21 For discussion of Brentano's objectual theory see e.g. Chisholm 1982 and Kriegel 2018.
22 Notably absent from these reductions are singular propositions of the form <a is F> and complex judgements involving e.g. conditionals. These are the hardest cases for Brentano's theory, but I do not have the space to discuss them here. See Kriegel 2018 for a spirited defense of Brentano's theory.
23 1894/1977: 2.

24 1894/1977: 16. Although I don't have the space to go into detail here, Twardowski offers three arguments for the content/object distinction, one of which is the familiar idea that we can present the same object in two different ways by having two presentations with the same object but with different contents (1894/1977: 27–33).
25 1904:79.
26 1904: 82/86. Roughly, Meinong uses the term 'objective' to mean abstract proposition or state of affairs.
27 See e.g. Crane 2014, Findlay 1963, Grossman 1974, Parsons 1980, Tichy 1988, and Zalta 1988.
28 Some philosophers, e.g. Byrne 2006 and Searle 1983, argue that the puzzle of thinking about non-existent objects dissolves once we have a content/object distinction. The basic idea is that the thought that the golden mountain is golden has a content, but no object.
29 See e.g. Chisholm 1957 and 1986.
30 1957/2002: 484.
31 1957/2002: 486.
32 See McAlister 1976 for a very clear criticism of Chisholm's interpretation of Brentano.
33 See e.g. Quine's (1960: 220) remark that Brentano's thesis of intentionality is the claim that 'there is no breaking out of the intentional vocabulary by explaining its members in other terms'.
34 Hartry Field claims that Brentano thought it was impossible to give a materialistically adequate account of the relation between a person and a proposition (1978:78).
35 See e.g. Dretske 1994/2002: 493.
36 1994/2002: 493.
37 See e.g. Dretske 1981, Fodor 1987, Millikan 1984, and Papineau 1993.
38 Although Brentano did not use the term 'phenomenological properties' or the 'what it's like' locution to characterize consciousness, in being concerned with how things seem or appear to a subject, Brentano was essentially concerned with experiential or phenomenological features of consciousness.
39 It's arguable that this focus on the propositional attitudes is largely due to Chisholm's influential discussion of intentionality (the failures of existential generalization and the principle of substitution are most evident with respect to sentences reporting propositional attitudes); but Frege's 1892 article 'On Sense and Reference' also contributed to a focus on propositional attitudes.
40 1994: 387–388.
41 1996:161.
42 There are many varieties of functionalism, but for my purposes here I have focused on what is sometimes called 'analytic functionalism'. See e.g. Armstrong 1981 and Lewis 1972.
43 The 'disassociation paradigm' is the standard method for studying unconscious perception. According to it, theorists first establish that the subject does not consciously perceive some stimulus x. Second, if the stimulus x has some effect, whether direct or indirect, on thought, evaluation, memory, recognition or some cognitive process, then the subject is thought to unconsciously perceive the stimulus x.
44 What about conscious perceptual states, which arguably have phenomenological and intentional properties? Even for these states, the metaphysical separation of phenomenology and intentionality was argued for on the basis of inverted spectrum and inverted earth thought experiments.
45 For ease of exposition, I'll speak of external objects and properties, although this departs from Brentano's restriction to physical phenomena in the 1874 publication of the *Psychology*.
46 Inner perception is an aspect of inner consciousness.
47 See Textor 2015 on Brentano's distinction between inner perception and introspection.
48 *Metaphysics* X.9.1074b35–6; my emphasis.

49 Translator's note to the *Psychology*: "von welchem das Bewusstein Bewusstein ist." This linguistic support for the recommended usage of "Bewusstein", depending as it does on the structure of the German word, does not apply to the English word "consciousness" (79/102).

50 Brentano understands acquired or stored knowledge in terms of dispositions: "Naturally philosophers were well familiar with the fact that we can possess a store of acquired knowledge without thinking about it. But they rightly conceived of this knowledge as a disposition toward certain acts of thinking, just as they conceived of acquired character as a disposition toward certain emotions and volitions, but not as cognition and consciousness (79/103).

51 For contemporary higher-order views, see e.g. Carruthers 2005, Gennaro 1996, Lycan 2004, and Rosenthal 2005, 2009. For contemporary same-order views, see e.g. Kriegel 2003, 2009, Montague 2009, Montague 2016, and Williford 2006.

52 See e.g. Gurwitsch 1979 and Zahavi 2006.

53 See e.g. Chalmers 2004, Levine 2003, and Tye 2009 for summaries of the kinds of representationalism.

54 Many have found it counterintuitive to count mental states such as pain and anxiety as intentional. Brentano offers a spirited argument that pain is intentional (63–5/82–5/), which foreshadows the representationalist attempt to deal with this difficulty. See e.g. Crane 2009 and Tye 2015 for a contemporary defense of this view. Although representationalism restricts itself to a discussion of conscious perception, some account of conscious thought and conscious emotion is needed. See e.g. Bayne and Montague 2011 for discussion of the relationship between phenomenology and conscious thought.

55 For versions of this kind of view, see e.g. Farkas 2008, Kriegel 2013, Mendelovici forthcoming, Pautz 2008, 2013, Searle 1992, Siewert 1998, and Strawson 1994.

56 Tye has been a central advocate of the transparency thesis, since Harman expounded it in 1990, and I will focus on Tye's account in what follows. G. E. Moore is sometimes cited as advocating the transparency thesis. Strawson 2015 argues that this is a mistake.

57 This conflicts directly with Brentano's claim that our best access to our experiences is inner perception.

58 There has been a lot of discussion about exactly what the transparency thesis is, and how exactly it supports representationalism. See e.g. Kind 2003, Pautz 2007, Stoljar 2004, and Strawson 2015.

Bibliography

Aristotle (c. 340/1936). *De Anima*. Trans. W. S. Hett. Cambridge, MA: Harvard University Press.

Armstrong, D. M. (1968). *A Materialist Theory of Mind*. London: Routledge and Kegan Paul.

Armstrong, D. M. (1981) *The Nature of Mind*. St. Lucia: University of Queensland Press.

Bayne, T., and Montague, M. (eds.). (2011). *Cognitive Phenomenology*. Oxford: Oxford University Press.

Block, N. (1990). "Inverted Earth," in Tomberlin, J. (ed.), *Philosophical Perspectives, 4: Action Theory and Philosophy of Mind*. Atascadero, CA: Ridgeview: 53–80.

Brentano, F. (1874/1973, 1995). *Psychology from an Empirical Standpoint*. Trans. L. McAlister, A. Rancurello, and D. B. Terrell. London: Routledge and Kegan Paul.

Byrne, A. (2006). "Intentionality," in Pfeifer, J. and Sarkar S. (eds.), *Philosophy of Science: An Encyclopedia*. Abingdon, UK: Routledge.

Carruthers, P. (2005). *Consciousness: Essays from a Higher-order Perspective*. Oxford: Oxford University Press.
Chalmers, D. (2004). "The Representational Character of Experience," in Leiter, B. (ed.), *The Future of Philosophy*. Oxford: Oxford University Press.
Chisholm, R. (1957). *Perceiving: A Philosophical Study*. Ithaca: Cornell University Press.
Chisholm, R. (1982). *The Foundations of Knowing*. Minneapolis: University of Minnesota Press.
Chisholm, R. (1986). *Brentano and Intrinsic Value*. Cambridge and New York: Cambridge University Press.
Crane, T. (2001). *Elements of Mind*. Oxford: Oxford University Press.
Crane, T. (2006). "Brentano's Concept of Intentional Inexistence," in Textor, M. (ed.), *The Austrian Contribution to Philosophy*. London: Routledge.
Crane, T. (2009). 'Is Perception a Propositional Attitude?' *Philosophical Quarterly* 59: 452–469.
Crane, T. (2014). *The Objects of Thought*. Oxford: Oxford University Press.
de Beauvoir, S. (1949/1997). *The Second Sex*. Trans. H. M. Parshley. London: Vintage.
Dennett, D. (1991). *Consciousness Explained*. Boston, MA: Little Brown.
Dennett, D. (1993). "Precis of Consciousness Explained," *Philosophy and Phenomenological Research*, 53(4): 889–892.
Descartes, R. (1641/1985). "Meditations and Objections and Replies," in *The Philosophical Writings of Descartes*, vol. 2. Trans. J. Cottingham et al. Cambridge: Cambridge University Press.
Dretske, F. (1981). *Knowledge and the Flow of Information*. Cambridge, MA: MIT Press.
Dretske, F. (1994/2002). "A Recipe for Thought," in Chalmers, D. (ed.), *Philosophy of Mind: Classical and Contemporary Readings*. Oxford: Oxford University Press.
Dretske, F. (1995). *Naturalizing the Mind*. Cambridge, MA: MIT Press.
Dickie, I. (2010). "We Are Acquainted With Ordinary Things," in Jeshion, R. (ed.), *New Essays on Singular Thought*. Oxford: Oxford University Press.
Farkas, K. (2008). "Phenomenal Intentionality Without Compormise," *The Monist*, 91 (2): 273–293.
Field, H. (1978). "Mental Representation," *Erkenntnis*, 13(1): 9–61.
Findlay, J. N. (1963). *Meinong's Theory of Objects and Values*. Clarendon: Oxford University Press.
Fodor, J. (1987). *Psychosemantics: The Problem of Meaning in Philosophy of Mind*. Cambridge, MA: MIT Press.
Frege, G. (1884/1974). *The Foundations of Arithmetic: A Logico-Mathematical Enquire into the Concept of Number*. Trans. J. L. Austin. Oxford: Blackwell.
Frege, G. (1892/1980). "On Sense and Reference," Trans M. Black, in Geach, P. and Black, M. (eds.), *Translations from the Philosophical Writings of Gottlob Frege*. Oxford: Blackwell.
Gallagher, S., and Zahavi, D. (2008). *The Phenomenological Mind: An Introduction to Philosophy of Mind and Cognitive Science*. London and New York: Routledge.
Gennaro, R. (1996) *Consciousness and Self-Consciousness: A Defense of the Higher-Order Thought Theory of Consciousness*. Amsterdam: John Benjamins.
Grossman, R. (1974). *Meinong*. London: Routledge.
Gurwitsch, A. (1941/1966). "A Non-egological Conception of Consciousness", in *Studies in Phenomenology and Psychology*. Evanston: Northwestern University Press.

Gurwitsch, A. (1979). *Human Encounters in the Social World*. Trans. F. Kersten. Pittsburgh: Duquesne University Press.

Harman, G. (1990). "The Intrinsic Quality of Experience," *Philosophical Perspectives*, 4: 31–52.

Heidegger, M. (1927/1962). *Being and Time*. Trans. J. Macquarrie and E. Robinson. Oxford: Basil Blackwell.

Horgan, T., and Tienson, J. (2002). "The Intentionality of Phenomenology and the Phenomenology of Intentionality," in Chalmers, D. (ed), *Philosophy of Mind: Classical and Contemporary Readings*. Oxford: Oxford University Press.

Husserl, E. (1900–1901/2001). *Logical Investigations* Vols 1 and 2, Trans. J. N. Findlay, with revised Trans. Dermot Moran. London and New York: Routledge.

Jacquette, D. (2004). "Brentano's concept of intentionality," in Jacquette, D. (ed.), *The Cambridge Companion to Brentano*. Cambridge: Cambridge University.

Jeshion, R. (2010). "Singular Thought: Acquaintance, Semantic Instrumentalism, and Cognitivism," in Jeshion, R. (ed.), *New Essays on Singular Thought*. Oxford: Oxford University Press.

Kind, A. (2003). "What's So Transparent about Transparency?" *Philosophical Studies*: 225–244.

Kriegel, U. (2003). "Consciousness as Intransitive Self-consciousness: Two Views and an Argument," *Canadian Journal of Philosophy*, 33(1): 103–132.

Kriegel, U. (2009). *Subjective Consciousness. A Self-Representational Theory*. Oxford and New York: Oxford University Press.

Kriegel, U. (2013). "The Phenomenal Intentionality Research Program," in Kriegel, U. (ed.), *Phenomenal Intentionality*. New York: Oxford University Press.

Kriegel, U. (2018). "Brentano on Judgment as an Objectual Attitude," in Gzrankowski, A. and Montague, M. (eds.), *Non-Propositional Intentionality*. Oxford: Oxford University Press.

Levine, J. (2003). "Experience and Representation," in Smith, Q. and Jokic A. (eds.), *Consciousness: New Essays*. Oxford: Oxford University Press.

Lewis, D. (1972). "Psychophysical and Theoretical Identifications," *Australasian Journal of Philosophy*, 50: 249–258.

Lycan, W. (1996). *Consciousness and Experience*. Cambridge, MA: Bradford Books/MIT Press.

Lycan, W. (2001). "The Case for Phenomenal Externalism," in Tomberlin, J.E. (ed.), *Philosophical Perspectives* 15: *Metaphysics*. Atascadero: Ridgeview Publishing.

Lycan, W. (2004). 'The Superiority of HOP to HOT', in R. Gennaro (ed.) *Higher-Order Theories of Consciousness* (Amsterdam: John Benjamns): 93–114.

McAlister, L. (1976). "Chisholm and Brentano on Intentionality," in McAlister, L. (ed.), *The Philosophy of Brentano*. London: Duckworth.

Meinong, A. (1904). "The Theory of Objects," Trans. I. Levi, D. B. Terrell, and R. Chisholm, in Chisholm, R. (ed.), *Realism and the Background of Phenomenology*. Atascadero, CA: Ridgeview, 1981: 76–117.

Mendelovici, A. (forthcoming). *Phenomenal Intentionality: How to Get Intentionality from Consciousness*.

Merleau-Ponty, M. (1945/1962). *The Phenomenology of Perception*. Trans. Colin Smith. London: Routledge & Kegan Paul.

Millikan, R. (1984). *Language, Thought, and Other Biological Categories*. Cambridge, MA: MIT Press.

Montague, M. (2009). "The Content of Perceptual Experience," in McLaughlin, B. Beckerman, A. and Walter, S. (eds.), *The Oxford Handbook of Philosophy of Mind*. Oxford: Clarendon Press.

Montague, M. (2016). *The Given: Experience and its Content*. Oxford: Oxford University Press.

Moran, D. (1996). "Brentano's Thesis," *Proceedings of the Aristotelian Society*, Supplementary Volume 70: 1–27.

Moran, D. (2000), *Introduction to Phenomenology*. London: Routledge.

Mulligan, K. (2004). "Brentano on the Mind," in Jacquett, D. (ed.), *The Cambridge Companion to Brentano*. Cambridge: Cambridge University Press.

Nelkin, N. (1989). "Propositional Attitudes and Consciousness," *Philosophy and Phenomenological Research*, 49(3): 413–430.

Nudds, M., and O'Callaghan, C. (2009). *Sounds and Perception: New Philosophical Essays*. Oxford: Oxford University Press.

Papineau, D. (1993). *Philosophical Naturalism*. Oxford: Blackwell Publishing.

Pautz, A. (2007). "Intentionalism and Perceptual Presence," *Philosophical Perspectives*, 21: 495–541.

Pautz, A. (2008). "The Interdependence of Phenomenology and Intentionality," *The Monist*, 91(2): 250–272.

Pautz, A. (2013). "Does Phenomenology Ground Mental Content?" in Kriegel, U. (ed.), *Phenomenal Intentionality*. New York: Oxford University Press.

Parsons, T. (1980). *Nonexistent Objects*. New Haven: Yale University Press.

Perry, J. (1994). "Intentionality," in Guttenplan, S. (ed.), *A Companion to the Philosophy of Mind*. Oxford: Blackwell.

Quine, W.V.O. (1960). *Word and Object*. Cambridge, MA: MIT Press.

Rosenthal, D. (2005). *Consciousness and Mind*. Oxford: Oxford University Press.

Rosenthal, D. (2009). "Higher Order Theories of Consciousness," in McLaughlin, B. and Beckermann, A. (eds.), *Oxford Handbook of the Philosophy of Mind*. Oxford: Oxford University Press.

Sartre, J. (1943/1956). *Being and Nothingness*. Trans. H. Barnes. New York: Philosophical Library.

Searle, J. (1983). *Intentionality*. Cambridge: Cambridge University Press.

Searle, J. (1992). *The Rediscovery of the Mind*. Cambridge, MA. MIT Press.

Shoemaker, S. (1982). "The Inverted Spectrum," *Journal of Philosophy*, 79: 357–381.

Siewert, C. (1998). *The Significance of Consciousness*. Princeton, NJ: Princeton University Press.

Smith, B. (1994). *Austrian Philosophy*. LaSalle, Ill. & Chicago: Open Court.

Stoljar, D. (1996). "Nominalism and Intentionality," *Nous*, 30(2): 161–181.

Stoljar, D. (2004). "The Argument from Diaphanousness," in Escurdia, M., Stainton, R. & Viger, C. (eds.), *Language, Mind and World: Special Issue of the Canadian Journal of Philosophy*. University of Alberta Press: 341–390.

Strawson, G. (1994). *Mental Reality*. Cambridge, MA. MIT Press.

Strawson, G. (2015). "Real Direct Realism," in Coates, P. and Coleman, S. (eds.), *Phenomenal Qualities: Sense, Perception and Consciousness*. Oxford: Oxford University Press.

Strawson, P. F. (1959). *Individuals: An Essay in Descriptive Metaphysics*. London: Muthuen.

Textor, M. (2015). "Inner Perception Can Never Become Inner Observation: Brentano on Awareness and Observation," *Philosophers' Imprint*, 15(10): 1–19.

Tichy, P. (1988). *The Foundations of Frege's Logic*. Berlin: Walter and de Gruyter & Co.

Thomasson, A.L. (2000). "After Brentano: a One-Level Theory of Consciousness," *European Journal of Philosophy*, 8: 190–209.

Twardowski, K. (1894/1977). *On the Content and Object of Presentations*. The Hague: Martinus Nijhoff.

Tye, M. (1995). *Ten Problems of Consciousness*. Cambridge, MA: MIT Press.

Tye, M. (2009). "Representationalist Theories of Consciousness," in McLaughlin, B., Beckerman, A. and Walter, S. (eds.), *The Oxford Handbook of Philosophy of Mind*. Oxford: Oxford University Press.

Tye, M. (2014). "Transparency, Qualia Realism, and Representationalism," *Philosophical Studies*: 39–57.

Tye, M. (2015). "The Nature of Pain and the Appearance/Reality Distinction," in Coates, P. and Coleman, S. (eds.), *Phenomenal Qualities: Sense, Perception & Consciousness*. Oxford: Oxford University Press.

Williford, K. (2006). "The Self-Representational Structure of Consciousness," in Kriegel, U. and Williford, K. (eds.), *Self-Representational Approaches to Consciousness*. Cambridge, MA: MIT Press.

Zahavi, D. (2006). *Subjectivity and Selfhood: Investigating the First-person Perspective*. Cambridge, MA: MIT Press.

Zalta, E. 1988. *Intensional Logic and the Metaphysics of Intentionality*. Cambridge: MIT Press.

9

WITTGENSTEIN AND HIS LEGACY

Severin Schroeder

After a brief account of Wittgenstein's conception of philosophy (1.), I shall describe what I call the 'inner-object model' of mental occurrences, i.e. the kind of dualist position that Wittgenstein argued against in different areas of the philosophy of mind (2.). The following sections present his discussion of this prevalent misconception with regard to bodily sensations and other minds (3.), understanding (4.), thinking (5.), and voluntary action (6.). Finally, I shall briefly consider the relation between Wittgenstein's views and functionalism (7.).

1. Wittgenstein's conception of philosophy

As a young man, Wittgenstein had made himself a name as one of the foremost philosophers of his age by the publication of his *Tractatus Logico-Philosophicus* (1921). In this first book, under the influence of the founding fathers of modern formal logic, Gottlob Frege and Bertrand Russell, he offered a unified theory of logic, language, and the metaphysical structure of the world. However, when some ten years later, after having worked for a while as a primary school teacher and then as an architect, he returned to philosophy, Wittgenstein found his earlier views deeply flawed. He began to rethink not only the details of his earlier doctrines, but the whole approach: the whole conception of philosophy underlying them. The result was his second book, the *Philosophical Investigations*, published only after his death. In it he first offers a devastating critique of his earlier theories (not of their technical details, but of their underlying assumptions), then sketches his startlingly new approach to philosophy and, finally, applies this new approach to various problems in the philosophy of mind.

In a famous polemical passage in his *Enquiry*, Hume claimed that an academic discipline that was neither mathematics nor empirical science could result only in 'sophistry and illusion' (Hume 1748, 165). How can philosophy, as a non-mathematical *a priori* discipline avoid this verdict? Wittgenstein's response to Hume's challenge is that philosophy is indeed concerned with sophistry and illusion. However, what Hume failed to realise is that philosophers do not only *produce* sophisms and illusions, but that there is also the perfectly respectable, critical philosophical activity of *dissolving* sophisms and *dispelling* illusions – a philosophy that seeks clarity and understanding of difficult conceptual relations, rather than new knowledge or theories.

Philosophical problems come about when we fail to understand, or are even confused by, our concepts and the ways they relate to each other. We tend to have an overly simplified picture of the workings of language which, when applied to certain concepts, is likely to result in paradox. For example, we naturally expect nouns to be names of (kinds of) objects (*BB* 1), as suggested by words like 'tree', 'house' or 'foot'. Therefore, when trying to understand the meaning of a word such as 'mind', we naively assume that it too must stand for a kind of object or substance, the question being only what kind of object that could be: a material object (say, the brain) or perhaps a mysterious non-spatial soul substance (as envisaged by Descartes). Both alternatives lead to implausible results. The mistake was to construe the word 'mind' as a name of a thing in the first place (cf. *PI* §308). Hence, the very question 'What (kind of thing) is the mind?' should not be answered, but rejected, as it is based on a conceptual misunderstanding. Frequently, a philosophical problem is a confusion 'expressed in the form of a question that doesn't acknowledge the confusion' (*PG* 193).

In order to dissolve such philosophical problems, we need to pay more careful and unprejudiced attention to the actual functioning of the concepts in question. Hence we assemble reminders of common usage (and common sense) (*PI* §127), and we give synoptic representations of the use of the words involved (*PI* §122). The result of such philosophical investigations will be *clarity*: the demolition of illusions (*PI* §118), a better understanding of the relations between certain concepts. It will not, however, lead to any new and surprising insights or theories (*BT* 419). If one wanted to characterise Wittgenstein's philosophy in one sentence, one could say that it is a defence of common sense against some clever forms of nonsense (or patent falsehood) suggested by a misunderstanding of the forms of our language.[1]

2. The inner-object model

The starting point of Wittgenstein's later philosophy, and one of its leitmotifs, is a critique of his own earlier ideas about language, in particular of a view that could be called *referentialism*: the view (already illustrated in the previous section) that 'a word has meaning by referring to something' (*PO* 454), and that 'language consists in naming objects, namely: people, species, colours, pains, moods, numbers, etc.' (*BT* 209v). Later in the *Philosophical Investigations*, having discussed and rejected referentialism in general, Wittgenstein considers various specific instances of referentialism, and further confusions and problems to which it gives rise, in the philosophy of mind. Referentialism applied to psychological terms – such as 'sensation', 'thought', 'understanding', 'willing' – results in a philosophical picture which can be called *the inner-object model*. If words (at least nouns and verbs) stand for objects, then psychological words must presumably stand for inner objects, perceived by one's inner sense inside one's mind, which we tend to think of as a private container to which only its owner has access. (Of course the word 'object' must be taken in the broadest sense to cover any objective phenomena, including states, processes and events.)

'The inner-object model' is basically another name for 'Cartesian dualism'. But whereas the latter label emphasises Descartes's distinction between the mental and the physical, the former indicates the surprising thrust of Wittgenstein's critique: that on Descartes's picture the difference between the mental and the physical, far from being overly pronounced, appears rather too slight! The psychological realm is construed in parallel to the physical realm: thoughts and feelings are regarded as objects like chairs and tables – only located in a private mental space rather than the public physical space. Against this picture, Wittgenstein is going to argue that the differences between psychological and physical concepts are far greater than commonly assumed.

3. Sensations and other minds

In §243 of the *Philosophical Investigations* Wittgenstein presents the idea of a private sensation language: 'The individual words of this language are to refer to what can only be known to the person speaking; to his immediate private sensations. So another person cannot understand the language' (*PI* §243). This passage naively expresses the dualist, or inner-object view (and not, as the following discussion shows, Wittgenstein's own position): It is simply assumed that sensations, feelings, moods, and the rest are private, inner objects, inaccessible to others. Wittgenstein's procedure in §§243–315 of the *Investigations* is to develop the consequences of that view with respect to words for bodily sensations and feelings and then to show how those consequences lead to absurdity or contradiction. Chief among those consequences is the following: as an inner object a bodily sensation – and indeed the mind on the whole – is logically independent of any behavioural manifestations; just as the contents of a box are logically independent of the label on the box. From this follows the problem of other minds: If minds are logically independent of behaviour, how can we ever know for certain what others think or feel, or indeed, whether they think or feel anything at all? There is always the possibility of deception: people can hide their feelings and simulate feelings they do not have. And there is also the deeper worry that the contents of our minds may be, to some extent, incommunicable. How do you know whether what you call your 'pain' is at all like the private experience I call 'pain'? When I give names to my feelings the meanings of these names are, strictly speaking, as inaccessible to you as those private feelings of mine. You may guess what I feel, and hence what my words mean, but you can never be certain about it. Thus the inner-object model of sensations leads to the idea of a strictly private language, one that could not possibly be understood by anybody else.

I shall now reconstruct Wittgenstein's principal objections to the inner-object view of sensations.

(i) A first objection can be called the *idle-wheel argument*. Suppose that when people complain about pains they have experiences that vary dramatically from

person to person, but are so insuperably private that these differences can never be ascertained. Then, these differences can never affect the public use of the word 'pain', for example the way one talks about one's ailments to one's doctor. Hence, where the meaning of our public word 'pain' is concerned, any entirely private occurrence that might accompany the use of that word 'drops out of consideration as irrelevant' (*PI* §293). As Wittgenstein puts it in §271: 'a wheel that can be turned though nothing else moves with it, is not part of the mechanism'.

(ii) Another line of attack against the inner-object model of sensations concerns the Cartesian idea of a privileged knowledge of the contents of one's own mind:

> In what sense are my sensations *private*? – Well, only I can know whether I am really in pain; another person can only surmise it. – In one way this is false, and in another nonsense. If we are using the word "to know" as it is normally used (and how else are we to use it!), then other people very often know when I'm in pain. – Yes, but all the same not with the certainty with which I know it myself! – It can't be said of me at all (except perhaps as a joke) that I *know* I'm in pain.
>
> [*PI* §246]

Of course, by ordinary standards, we often do know when others are in pain. In order to make scepticism about other minds appear at all plausible, some more demanding standard needs to be invoked, and that is what seems to be the infallible knowledge one has of one's own sensations. By comparison with this paradigm of 'real knowledge', it would indeed appear that not much else can be 'known'. Wittgenstein's reply swiftly turns the tables: Far from being a paradigm of knowledge this is not really a case of knowledge at all! Why not? The crucial point is that what we ordinarily call knowledge presupposes the logical possibility of error and ignorance. You can be said to know something only where it would also have been conceivable for you not to know it. Just as you cannot meaningfully be said to be the winner of a game in which nobody can lose, there is no sense in speaking of knowledge where there is, logically, no possibility of ignorance, doubt or error (*PI* p. 221: PPF §311). Hence, since one cannot be mistaken or in doubt about one's own sensations (*PI* §288), one cannot really say that one knows of one's own sensations either. Thus, scepticism about other minds is stopped in its tracks: By ordinary standards, it is undeniably possible often to know what others feel. And this cannot be said to be only an inferior kind of knowledge compared with my knowledge of my own pain, for I do not have *knowledge* of my own pain. The ability to express one's own feelings is not correctly described as knowledge.[2]

(iii) There is yet another objection to the view that one cannot know but only surmise what others feel. Although apparently a consequence of the inner-object assumption, it is in fact inconsistent with that assumption. The claim that I know sensations only from inner experience is incompatible with my attributing sensations, though precariously, to others. It does not even make sense to assume that

something like one's private experience *might* also be had by somebody else. This objection, which goes to the core of the inner-object model, may be called the *ascribability argument*. It is tempting to think: 'If I suppose that someone has a pain, say, then I am simply supposing that he has just the same as *this*' (cf. *PI* §350). Wittgenstein's reply is that the proponent of the inner-object model lacks the conceptual resources for this transition from introspection to talk about the feelings of others:

> If one has to imagine someone else's pain on the model of one's own, this is none too easy a thing to do: for I have to imagine pain which I *don't feel* on the model of the pain which I *do feel*. That is, what I have to do is not simply to make a transition in the imagination from pain in one place to pain in another. As, from pain in the hand to pain in the arm. For it is not as if I had to imagine that I feel pain in some part of his body (which would also be possible).
>
> [*PI* §302]

According to the inner-object view, one learns what pain is by *having* pain. When, for example, I have hurt myself, I concentrate on the feeling and impress it upon myself that *this* is what one calls 'pain'. But, Wittgenstein objects, even *if* that procedure allowed me henceforth to identify my own pains correctly, it would not enable me to understand statements of the form '*NN* is in pain'. Introspection can never teach me how to ascribe a sensation to a particular person – not even to myself. For when I feel pain, I do not feel *my self* having the pain. I only feel pain in a certain place, so the idea that others have pain I could only understand to mean that I feel pain in other bodies.

The difficulty is not how to make the transition from 'I am in pain' to 'He is in pain', but from 'There is pain' to 'He is in pain'. From the point of view of introspective consciousness that is acquainted with pain only as something *felt*, the idea of another person's pain amounts to pain-that-is-not-felt – which must appear as a contradiction in terms. Roughly speaking, feeling pain (my own pain) cannot teach me to understand the idea of pain that is not felt (others' pain).

In fact, in order to make sense of the assumption that someone else is in pain it is not the *experience* of pain I need, but the *concept* of pain. And a grasp of this concept includes an understanding of what it means to ascribe pain to a particular person. I must know, in brief, that 'the subject of pain is the person who gives it expression' (*PI* §302). Of course, a pain need not be expressed: one can in many cases keep one's sensations to oneself. Moreover, an expression of pain may be faked. Still, it is part of our concept of pain that certain patterns of behaviour (crying, moaning, sighing, gnashing one's teeth, holding or protecting the aching part of one's body, etc.) are natural expressions of pain (cf. *PI* §244). They are the typical forms of behaviour of someone in pain who is unrestrained and willing to show his feelings.

Wittgenstein here introduces a useful distinction between two types of evidence: *criteria* and *symptoms*. If it is part of the very meaning of a term '*F*' that some phenomenon is (good, though not infallible) evidence for the presence of *F*, then that phenomenon is a criterion of *F*. If, however, we have discovered only through experience that *F* is usually accompanied by a certain phenomenon, then that phenomenon is only a symptom of *F* (*BB* 24–25, cf. *PI* §354). The upshot of the ascribability argument (*PI* §302) is that, in order to ascribe a sensation to a particular person, we need a *criterion* by which to identify sensations in others (for it must be determined what it *means* for somebody to *have* a sensation). And there is indeed such a criterion, namely appropriate expressive behaviour, which is not just a symptom of sensations, but forms an integral part of the grammar of sensation words. But with that criterion in place, the inner-object picture collapses. As there is a *conceptual* link between pain, for example, and certain forms of expressive behaviour, the idea that in spite of that behaviour – by reference to which the word 'pain' has been given its meaning (*PI* §244) – there might never be any pain becomes inconsistent.

It has to be admitted, of course, that the criterial link between the inner and the outer is not a neat one-to-one correlation. There is the possibility of deception: pain-behaviour may be insincere. However, the sceptical consequences of this qualification are limited, for four reasons.

First, deceit too is a distinctive form of behaviour (*NfL* 241d): there are criteria by which to tell whether someone is sincere or deceitful; otherwise we could not meaningfully speak of sincerity and deception (*LW* 42g). Although we may not always be able to tell whether someone is sincere or not, we can normally say what kind of further evidence would settle the matter.

Secondly, deceit is a rather complicated form of behaviour that can only be attributed to creatures whose behavioural repertoire displays a good deal of intelligence. It requires a motive based on an understanding of what is to be gained by simulation (*RPP I* §824). Thus the idea that a baby may be dishonest is incoherent (*PI* §249).

Thirdly, although for any isolated utterance or piece of behaviour one could imagine a context that would expose it as mere pretence, this is not true of sufficiently long sequences of circumstances and behaviour. If over months you observe someone suffering from an obvious and severe injury, it is ridiculous to insist that this might be a mere pretence.

Finally, that it is logically possible for a proposition to be false is not in itself a reason to doubt its truth. It is simply a trivial grammatical feature of *any* empirical proposition. (This is a general objection to all forms of philosophical scepticism.)

(iv) In one of the most discussed passages of the *Philosophical Investigations*, Wittgenstein illustrates the way sensation language is envisaged by the proponent of the inner-object picture. To highlight the dualist belief that sensations are logically independent of expressive behaviour it is assumed in a thought experiment that I have no natural expression for a given sensation, but only have the sensation (*PI* §256). And now: 'I want to keep a diary about the recurrence of [that]

sensation. To this end I associate it with the sign "S" and write this sign in a diary for every day on which I have the sensation' (*PI* §258).

Wittgenstein continues to object that when trying to keep such a private sensation diary (1) I have no criterion of correctness. Therefore, (2) whatever is going to seem right to me is right. And so, (3) here we can't talk about 'right' (*PI* §258). This is what I call the *no-criterion argument*.

The final conclusion is a little exaggerated. 'Whatever is going to seem right to me is right' is not the same as, 'Anything is right' (which would make the use of the word 'right' pointless). It would still be *wrong* for me to write down 'S' on a day when none of my sensations seemed to be of the same kind as the one I initially called 'S'. What Wittgenstein should have concluded is: (3*) 'And that only means that here we can't talk about an *error*.' This is exactly what he says elsewhere about reporting one's pain (*PI* §288).

Now, what about conclusion (2)? Given that there is no criterion to check whether truthful 'S' inscriptions are *objectively* true or false (i.e. true or false independently of the person's impression), is it not possible nonetheless to wonder whether they are? After all, there are other cases of unverifiable propositions that must nevertheless be objectively true or false. For example, 'Immediately before her death Queen Victoria remembered her wedding day' is presumably a proposition that is either true or false, although as it happens it can never be confirmed or disconfirmed. The question arises whether the private diarist's 'S' inscriptions might not be of the same character: Could they not be objectively true or false, even though it is impossible to check?

There is, however, a crucial difference between those cases. In the case of the conjecture about Queen Victoria's last thoughts, we may insist on truth or falsity because we know perfectly well what it means to say, for example, that someone remembers Prince Albert, etc. That is to say, although stymied in these special circumstances, *we are able in countless other cases to ascertain whether that predicate applies or not*. In contrast, with 'S' the problem is precisely that we cannot draw a distinction between a generally unproblematic predicate and its unverifiable application in only some particular cases. We cannot refer back to other applications of 'S' under more straightforward circumstances. The diarist's entries are, and will remain, the only applications of 'S' available. There is no room in this case for a notion of truth that would not coincide with sincerity, not simply because 'S' inscriptions are found to be uncheckable, but because (unlike in the case of Queen Victoria's last thoughts) there is no predicate involved whose applications would be checkable under *any* circumstances. Hence, the attempt to construe the sign 'S' as the name of objective mental occurrences fails.

It should be emphasised that this conclusion, (2), is not based on the controversial doctrine of verificationism: the view that the sense of a proposition is its method of verification or falsification, and that therefore any un(dis)confirmable statement must be meaningless. For one thing, the issue is about simple *predicates*, not about statements. For another thing, the claim is not that because 'S' inscriptions are unverifiable they are meaningless; the claim is merely that 'S' inscriptions cannot be construed as descriptions of inner objects. After all, that 'S' inscriptions are not based on criteria and therefore unverifiable does not distinguish them from countless ordinary first-person present-tense psychological utterances. I cannot apply any criteria to verify my claim that I have a slight headache (nor can anybody else), and yet one would surely not want to dismiss that statement as meaningless.

The no-criterion argument provides yet another refutation of the inner-object model. If a sensation were an inner object perceived and identified through introspection, it should be possible occasionally to misperceive and misidentify it. One could, for instance, be mistaken in one's belief that one was in pain. That sounds absurd. For we do not identify our sensations by criteria (*PI* §290), and where there is no criterion, there is no possibility of error. But how *do* we identify our (own) sensations? The answer is that we do not identify them at all.

How then do words refer to sensations? Our natural responses to pain are not the result of an identification. Rather, the sensation of pain *makes* us cry. And later verbal expressions are grafted onto natural ones: we are trained until a suitable verbal expression comes as naturally to us as a cry or a moan (although, of course, we also learn to suppress all such reactions) (*PI* §244).

It is part of the very concept of pain that certain forms of behaviour are natural expressions of pain. If someone behaves in such a way, and is truthful – that is what we call 'being in pain'. That is the way the concept of pain is formed. The question whether someone is in pain or not is decided by that person's sincere behaviour. As a consequence, the philosophical query whether people's sincere avowals of pain are correct – whether they are *really* in pain when they truthfully says they are – does not make sense. Sincere avowals are correct 'by definition'; their correctness is built into our concept of pain.

In resolving the philosophical problem of other minds, Wittgenstein draws attention to its connection with another one: the problem of first-person authority. As noted above, Wittgenstein's objection to Cartesian dualism is not (as one might expect) that it exaggerates the distinction between the mental and the physical, but, on the contrary, that it makes it appear too slight. The dualist conception of psychological phenomena is too much shaped after our concept of physical objects or events. Construed as inner objects, sensations and thoughts in others become elusive; but, as Wittgenstein was the first to note, sensations and thoughts in ourselves become problematic too. If expressing one's feelings were a matter of observing and reporting inner occurrences, the special authority we have in expressing what we feel would be puzzling. Error would at least appear to be a possibility. Only when the inner-object model is rejected, can the puzzle of first-person authority be resolved. Our virtual infallibility (linguistic mistakes apart) in expressing our own feelings is not due to our eagle-eyed gaze of introspection, but simply to linguistic meaning. Whatever you find painful *is* painful to you. That is what we mean by 'painful'.[3]

4. Meaning and understanding: the paradox of the instantaneous experience of complex contents

Unlike bodily sensations (such as pain), understanding, thoughts, intentions, and memories have a specific intentional content: they are *about* something else. How is that possible? The most natural, indeed virtually unavoidable, answer is that such mental occurrences must be inner *representations* of whatever their contents are. But this view, Wittgenstein shows, leads to a formidable problem: Understanding, intention, expectation, remembering, and other such mental occurrences, can have remarkably rich and complex contents. It may take very long to spell out completely what exactly someone understood, intended, expected or remembered on a given occasion. And yet it appears that the understanding, intending, expecting, or remembering can occur instantaneously: in a flash. How is that possible? How can so much be experienced in a flash?

Consider, for instance, that it is possible to grasp the meaning of a word in an instance (*PI* §§138–139), although an account of the meaning of a word, of all the details of its use, would have to be extremely long and complicated. How can it be present to my mind all at once? 'What really comes before our mind, when we understand a word?', Wittgenstein asks, and proceeds to consider the Lockean view that it is 'something like a picture' (*PI* §139). However, understanding a word cannot be the same as having a mental image, for any image can be interpreted, or applied, differently. For instance, the perspectival drawing of a cube (as a candidate for giving meaning to the word 'cube') may also be taken as a two-dimensional figure consisting of a square and two trapeziums. Again, the image of a dog may be taken to represent: a particular golden retriever, or any golden retriever, or any dog, or a mammal, or an upright position, or many other things (cf. *PI* §139). Indeed, one cannot even assume that when an image is produced in one's mind by hearing a word this image must represent what one takes the word to mean. The word 'winter' may produce in me the image of an old aunt pouring out tea without my being under the strange misapprehension that that is what the word 'winter' means. Two people hearing a word can have the same mental image and yet a different understanding of the word, manifested in the different ways they apply it and the different explanations they give (cf. *PI* §140). And it is also possible that two people have different mental images when hearing the same word, although they are in perfect agreement about its meaning. These objections are equally applicable to the complementary account of meaning something as having mental images (*PI* §663).

So, we may indeed have a mental image of a cube in our mind when hearing (or uttering) the word 'cube', but that is not what understanding (or meaning) the word consists in, as one can understand without having any mental image and no mental image guarantees understanding. Still, the idea is there, and persistently recurs in the *Investigations*, that a mental state, possibly instantaneous, can have a determinate content, possibly very extensive and complicated. After all, we do mean, understand, remember or intend complicated processes, for example:

> There is no doubt that I now want to play chess, but chess is the game it is in virtue of all its rules (and so on). Don't I know, then, which game I wanted to play until I *have* played it? Or is it rather that all the rules are contained in my act of intending?
>
> <div align="right">[<i>PI</i> §197]</div>

This is what I call the *paradox of the instantaneous experience of complex contents*: The contents must all be there in a flash, for I can correctly avow that at a particular moment I intend (or have understood, or expect, or remember) something. But then again, the contents are not all there in a flash, for I am not really aware of all the details: all possible uses of the word; or all rules of chess; they are not all in front of my mind at the same time.

Consider the example of a pupil taught to write down (the beginning of) the series of even numbers on being given the order '+ 2'. Up to 1000 he does that correctly; we ask him to continue and 'he writes 1000, 1004, 1008, 1012' – :

> We say to him: "Look what you're doing!" – He doesn't understand. We say: "You should have added *two*: look how you began the series!" – He answers: "Yes, isn't it right? I thought that was how I *had* to do it." – Or suppose he pointed to the series and said: "But I did go on in the same way." – It would now be no use to say: "But can't you see. . . . ?" – and go over the old explanations and examples for him again.
>
> <div align="right">[<i>PI</i> §185]</div>

Obviously, the pupil did not understand the order '+ 2' the way his teacher understood it and meant it. The pupil was not meant to write 1004 after 1000. Does that mean that the teacher had thought explicitly of 1002 as the correct number to write after 1000? No, or if he had thought of that particular transition, then not of countless others. He rather thought that the pupil 'should write the next but one number after *every* number that he wrote' (*PI* §186). This is a general rule, or formula, that may have been in the teacher's mind when he gave the shorthand order '+ 2'. Now the question is whether the presence of such a rule in someone's mind can account for his understanding or meaning an infinite series. Obviously not (cf. *PI* §152). The teacher may give the rule to his pupil (instead of the abbreviated signal '+ 2'), make him learn it by heart, and yet there is no guarantee that the pupil will continue correctly. It is conceivable that he misunderstands the explicit rule just as he misunderstood the order '+ 2': taking it as *we* would take the rule: 'Add 2 up to 1000, 4 up to 2000, 6 up to 3000, and so on' (*PI* §185). So, any rule, even the most explicit one, can be misunderstood; and in endless ways, too: whichever way the pupil continues the series, his writing can always be regarded as in accordance with the rule – *on a suitable interpretation* (cf. *PI* §86). And now it is puzzling how it should be at all possible to follow a rule, for 'Whatever I do is, on some interpretation, in accord with the rule' (*PI* §198)!

This line of argument (which Wittgenstein does not endorse, but present for critical discussion) can be put as follows:

1) A series of numbers can be continued in various ways.
2) The way it is meant to be continued is expressed by a rule (or formula).
3) A rule (or formula) can be interpreted in various ways.
4) Therefore, a rule (or formula) cannot determine a continuation.
5) Therefore, our meaning (as expressed by a rule) cannot determine a continuation.

The final conclusion (5) is partly based on (2): That the teacher *meant* the series to be continued in a particular way we tried to explain by saying that he had some general rule or formula in mind. So, if that rule cannot fix a standard of correctness, clearly, his meaning that rule cannot do it either.

The flaw (to which Wittgenstein wants to direct out attention) lies in the step from (3) to (4): That a rule can be interpreted in various ways does not entail that a rule cannot determine a continuation. One might as well argue as follows:

Your bicycle could always be stolen.
Therefore, it can never be used.

It is obviously fallacious to argue from 'It can go wrong' to 'It can't go right'. *If* your bicycle is indeed stolen from you, then of course you cannot use it; but it is well possible, perhaps even likely, that it is not stolen and then you *can* use it. Moreover, even if your bicycle is stolen, it can (and probably will) still be used – though not by you. Similarly: for any given continuation (e.g. 1000, 1002, 1004), a suitable rule (e.g. $x_n = 2n$) can always be interpreted *not* to yield that result – but it need not be so interpreted and normally it isn't. And even if the rule '$x_n = 2n$' is interpreted in a deviant way, it will still determine a continuation of the series, albeit not the one we expected (but perhaps the one written down by the deviant pupil).

There remains the worrying consideration that a rule needs to be interpreted at all. It cannot *by itself* determine a continuation. It seems that in order to understand it in some way, you need to give it an interpretation. And once you accept that an interpretation is necessary, you seem to be launched on an infinite regress: for whatever interpretation you give, it is in no better a position than the rule itself. It, too, needs to be interpreted in a particular way (cf. *PI* §86) – and so on, and so forth.

Wittgenstein's response to that puzzling consideration is that for us to think, even *for a moment*, that on a certain understanding the formula '$y = x^2$', for example, yields 25 for $x = 5$, the infinite regress that seemed to threaten must have been stopped. Our understanding in this case cannot just be an interpretation: that is, another formula to paraphrase the first, of which again it would be an open question how to understand it (*PI* §201). Our understanding of a rule cannot forever be mediated by another rule.

What it amounts to is simply this: we are able to work out that for $x = 5$ the formula '$y = x^2$' yields 25. How? Well, 'I have been trained to react to this sign in a particular way, and now I do so react to it' (*PI* §198). This is the core of the matter: knowing-how (a skill) cannot, ultimately, be explained in terms of knowing-that (a piece of information). For any piece of information, for any formula in the mind, we would again need to *know how* to apply it. It may happen occasionally that our understanding of a formula is based on, or mediated by, our understanding of another formula. But such a translation of one formula into another cannot be the basic case of understanding: or else we would never *begin* to learn the meaning of any formula. Likewise, our basic linguistic understanding, the mastery of our first language, can evidently not be explained in terms of translation into another language.

There is a strong temptation to think that when we have understood in general how to proceed, somehow all the correct applications must be laid down in advance in the mind, so that each step can be justified by reference to that perfect mental instruction manual. But that perfect mental instruction manual is an illusion and (as explained) a logical impossibility. Our basic skills must stand on their own. They are engendered by training, but what they enable us to do is open-ended and cannot be exhaustively listed in training, nor could there be such an exhaustive list in the mind or anywhere else (cf. *Z* §§300–301).

The paradox of the instantaneous experience of complex, or even infinite, contents resulted from a mistaken, but very natural, idea of a mental process or occurrence. It is extremely tempting to envisage mental occurrences as comprehensive representations: that must somehow *contain* everything the mental representation is about or directed at. That kind of mental representation would be astonishing enough where what we have in mind is fairly complex – as with the rules of chess, which appear to be represented in our momentary desire to play chess (*PI* §197); but it becomes patently impossible when we mean or understand an infinite arithmetical series. At first glance it seemed that such infinity could conveniently be represented by a short formula, but then it became clear that our meaning or understanding the formula would have to contain how the formula was to be applied in an infinity of instances (to forestall an infinity of possible misunderstandings) – which again, appears to make such meaning (or understanding) a mind-boggling feat. So, how can the mind perform such a feat? It cannot. The truth is that no such marvellously rich representation occurs; and it is an error to think that it needs to occur for meaning (or understanding) to be possible. That is Wittgenstein's dissolution of the paradox of the immediate experience of complex, or even infinite, contents.

But then: if meaning one thing rather than another is not brought about by a comprehensive and infallible mental representation of that thing, how *is* it brought about? – In response to this question Wittgenstein merely invites us to remember under what circumstances it is correct to say that somebody meant something. There is no such thing as an intricate mental mechanism of meaning that could be investigated and explained (*PI* §689). There is no process of meaning: 'For no *process* could have the consequences of meaning something' (*PI*, p. 218: PPF §291). Any process you might think of can occur without your meaning the thing in question. What makes it true, then, that when I say 'Let's play a game of chess' I mean the game of chess with all its rules, and not some other game? The link is not made by some miraculous mental mechanism, but by the circumstances in which the utterance is made: In English 'chess' is the name of a particular game the rules of which have been listed and widely published; there are clubs and organisations that insist on those rules, and people are taught those rules at home or at school. So when a competent and normally educated English speaker speaks of 'chess' he can be taken to mean what we all call 'chess' (cf. *PI* §197). In other words, there is no doubt that when he speaks of 'chess', he speaks of chess (cf. *PI* §687). – Admittedly, it is conceivable that someone uses the word 'chess', but means backgammon; either because his knowledge of English is less than perfect, or simply through a slip of the tongue. But how would such a person differ from someone who uses the word 'chess' correctly? There need not be any difference in what went through their heads at the time of the utterance: If God had looked into their minds he might not have been able to see *there* which game they wanted to play (*PI*, p. 217: PPF §284). Rather, to say that they meant different games amounts to saying that they will respond differently when, say, the pieces are set up in front of them, or that they *would* have responded differently, had the matter been pursued further (*PI* §§187, 684). Frequently, the difference between different thoughts or intentions is only a conditional one: one that *would* manifest itself (or would have manifested itself) under certain circumstances.

5. Thinking

What is thinking? Again, the most natural answer will be informed by the inner-object model. Thinking appears to take place in our minds, and so in order to get clear about its nature, or about the meaning of the word 'thinking', we watch ourselves, the contents of our minds, while we think, expecting that 'what we observe will be what the word means'. Wittgenstein objects that 'this concept is not used like that' (*PI* §316). What can be observed in my consciousness when, for example, I am thinking that I have to write to my aunt thanking her for a birthday present I didn't like at all? Not a lot. If it is not the first time that I think of this mildly tiresome obligation, the thought will perhaps re-appear in my mind as nothing more than a peculiar feeling of uneasiness. I don't have to repeat to myself what I am uneasy about; I know straightaway what this feeling is about. When I dwell a little longer on the thought, I will perhaps see a mental image of the parcel I received from her together with a vague auditory image of the telephone conversation we had six months ago. Are these images the thought? No, for if I just told someone the images, he would not get the thought (*Z* §239). Even if I add, what is not really part of the mental images, from whom I had the parcel and with whom I had spoken on the telephone, it is impossible to work out that I am thinking of writing her a thank-you letter. Exactly the same mental images might accompany somebody's thought that he would *not* write in response to the parcel, or that he expected soon to receive another parcel from the same sender.

We are inclined to believe that when we think something the content of the thought must somehow be represented in our consciousness, but this is usually not the case. And even when the contents of a thought are fairly comprehensively expressed *in foro interno*, one cannot simply read off the thought from this inner representation. For the fact that the *words* 'I have to write to my aunt to thank her for that awful present' go through my mind does not necessarily mean that I am having that thought. Just now, for example, they went through my mind when I did not have any such thought – merely as an example for this philosophical consideration.

The word 'think' functions rather differently from the word 'write'. When I am *writing* that it will rain tomorrow, this content is completely laid down on the paper and can be read off there; when I am *thinking* that it will rain tomorrow there need not be any such readable representation in my mind. Usually, what can be found there resembles more a private shorthand, for example, a few diagonal lines which *I* take *in this case* as indicating that it will rain tomorrow, although that is not a meaning the lines have for others or in other cases.

> I can see, or understand, a thought complete before my mind's eye in a flash in the same sense in which I can make a note of it in a few words or a few pencilled dashes.
>
> [*PI* §319]

That of course raises the question: 'What makes this note into an epitome of this thought?' (*PI* §319). The answer is: 'The use that I make of it' (MS 124, 218). Should anyone ask me what those pencilled dashes mean, I can explain it; and if I look at the note later it will remind me that I expected rain for the next day. Of course, my mental images cannot be presented to others nor kept for my own later recollection. But the analogy lies in the fact that I can say authoritatively and without being constrained by semantic conventions what the images or words flitting through my mind mean: what thoughts they are illustrating for me. This is the way our concept of thinking functions: What I think is what I can sincerely declare to be my thought, and what can also manifest itself in my further behaviour. The words and images that go through my mind when I am thinking are ultimately quite irrelevant.

In his early philosophy, in the *Tractatus Logico-Philosophicus*, Wittgenstein had taken thinking to be a process accompanying speech and giving it meaning, a process that was itself rather similar to speaking. In the *Investigations* he was to criticise that view:

> When I think in language, there aren't 'meanings' going through my mind in addition to the verbal expressions: language itself is the vehicle of thought.
>
> [*PI* §329]

The idea of thinking as a process that accompanies speech and gives it significance doesn't sit well with the fact that it is possible to think aloud. When I think aloud: 'What do I have to do today? Ah, yes, write to Aunt Agatha to thank her for that awful present she has sent me' – what is it that gives meaning to those words? Are the words accompanied by a process of thinking or meaning them? In that case, the actual thinking would be the accompanying process, not the words. And if one always needed the backing of such a mental process, it wouldn't be possible at all to think aloud. But then it wouldn't be possible to think quietly in words either. For surely, whether the words are uttered aloud or are only articulated quietly in my mind cannot make any difference. But in fact, when I said those words there was nothing else going on in my mind at the time. It *is* possible to think in words, aloud or quietly, without any accompanying mental process.

Having ascertained that thinking can take the form of words uttered aloud, Wittgenstein raises the question whether one can imagine people who could *only* think aloud (*PI* §331). It is not difficult to imagine that everything somebody says to himself he says aloud, like a person on stage whose thinking is thus laid open to the audience. In that case he could not simultaneously speak to others and articulate thoughts to himself. But that is perhaps something most people cannot do anyway. I find my own mental comments are always made between public utterances and not simultaneously with them. So the transition from speaking quietly in one's mind to speaking aloud seems unproblematic. The crucial question, however, is whether it is possible for *all* thinking to be articulated in words.

In that case, our intellectual life would have to slow down considerably. For in fact, our thoughts often occur much faster than we could express them in words. Somebody who could think only in words would take much longer to have a thought in its entirety before he could act accordingly. There are many situations, for example when driving a car, where such a delay in one's thoughts and actions could have serious consequences and be a great handicap.

However, the philosophical concern goes deeper than that. A bit further in the discussion, Wittgenstein raises the following point:

> But didn't I already intend the whole construction of the sentence (for example) at its beginning? So surely it already existed in my mind before I uttered it out loud!
>
> [*PI* §337]

However much a person is inclined to think aloud or soliloquise, it is hardly possible that when uttering a word of his thoughts he never knows what words will come afterwards. If one were to speak the beginning of a sentence without any anticipation of the following words, one could not know why one uttered the first words, which frequently don't make any sense without the sequel. In that case, one would have to speak as in trance. In fact, however, somebody who consciously expresses his thoughts (or thinks aloud) does not need to wait for the end of his sentences to find out himself what he was going to say. In some sense, the thoughts are already in one's mind before they are fully articulated. It follows that, even when one is thinking in words, the thoughts cannot really be identified with their verbal expression. My awareness of my thoughts is not read off, and not entirely simultaneous with, the words that may embody the thoughts.

This is closely connected with the considerations of the previous section, which were triggered by the puzzlement at the fact that I can in a split second have the intention to play chess, for example. How can something as complicated as the game of chess be all in my mind in such a short space of time? The same problem arises when I take the time to formulate the sentence 'I would like to play chess'. For I have to utter these words *with understanding*: that is, I must while I am speaking know what I mean by 'chess'. All the numerous details of what I mean (e.g., that it is a game in which every player has eight pawns that can move only forward) are part of my thought. (For I didn't mean, for example, a game in which every player has nine pawns.) In other words, even when I am thinking in complete sentences, my thoughts comprise more than the mere words. They also comprise a certain understanding of those words: the capacity to explain them and to develop their countless implications.

This is the reason why thinking cannot strictly be identified with any process in the mind: thinking requires an understanding of its contents, a capacity to explain it, apply it, and draw inferences from it. Yet a capacity belongs to a different logical category from a process.

6. Voluntary action

What is a voluntary action? How is it to be distinguished from a mere event? To begin with, a voluntary action is performed by a conscious agent. However, that is not sufficient to characterize voluntariness, for conscious agents can also be passively involved in a mere event. I can jump off a wall, but I can also inadvertently fall off it or be pushed off it against my will. The bodily movements in these cases *need* not be different. Suppose in a given pair of cases they are exactly the same, how then are we to distinguish between the voluntary action and the mere event? It seems that the voluntary action must contain *more* than the mere event: there must be an extra element of willing or intention. So it should be possible to isolate that element of willing by a thought experiment of subtraction: 'what is left over if I subtract the fact that my arm rises from the fact that I raise my arm?' (*PI* §621). What is Wittgenstein's answer to this question? – He does not give an answer. As so often in philosophy, the question is misguided, and instead of answering it we should find out what is wrong with it. It is, in fact, another instance of referentialism inviting us to construct some spurious inner object (event, process, or state). Words used to characterize an action as voluntary (like 'will' and its cognates) are uncritically taken to denote some mental occurrence, some phenomenon that added to the mere bodily movement turns it into a voluntary action.

This is the inner-object model of voluntary action. According to its classical version, going back to Descartes and the British Empiricists, 'what is left over if

I subtract the fact that my arm rises from the fact that I raise my arm' is an *act of will*, or (as Hume called it) a *volition*. For a bodily movement to be voluntary it must be *caused* by an act of will; without such a cause the same movement would be involuntary. Wittgenstein was familiar with similar views held by Bertrand Russell and William James. He offered three objections to this theory:

The *first objection* is very simple: The volitions or acts of will postulated by the theory do not exist. If we take an impartial look at what goes on in our minds whenever we move our body voluntarily, no suitable mental events causing the movements come to light. However, the elusiveness of acts of will tends to be obscured by philosophers' selective attention, when they focus on only a few especially favourable examples, such as this one: 'I deliberate whether to lift a certain heavyish weight, decide to do it, I then apply my force to it and lift it' (*BB* 150). Here we have some occurrences that could, without absurdity, be thought to constitute willing: some anticipatory thinking of the action, an act of resolve, a sensation of bodily effort. And now we take our ideas about voluntary action from this kind of example and assume lightly that those ideas must apply to all cases of willing (*BB* 150). But of course not all cases are like that. We frequently do things without any such preliminaries. Just think of ordinary speech, which is often entirely unpremeditated and effortless, yet not for that matter involuntary.

Second Objection: Willing is thought to be a mental occurrence, but a mental occurrence must be either voluntary or involuntary. That leads to a fatal dilemma: If the mental act of willing is itself subject to the will, in order to be proper willing it would have to be willed. But then we are launched on an infinite regress: For the event of willing to be voluntary it has to be caused by an earlier event of willing; but that earlier event, too, in order to be voluntary would have to be caused by yet an earlier event of willing, and so on *ad infinitum* – which is absurd. So it seems more promising to deny that willing itself could be subject to the will: 'I can't will willing' (*PI* §613). But that sounds odd as well. It would appear that 'willing too is merely an experience . . . It comes when it comes, and I cannot bring it about' (*PI* §611). But now the whole idea of voluntariness, of being in control of one's actions, seems to be lost. That must be wrong too (*PI* §612). The dilemma shows that the whole question (whether or not willing can be willed) is misbegotten. Willing is not the sort of thing of which it makes sense to ask whether it is voluntary or involuntary. 'Willing' is neither the name of an action, nor of a passive experience. It is not the name of a mental occurrence of any kind.

Third Objection: According to the inner-object model, a voluntary bodily action is a bodily movement caused by a mental act. Thus, on this theory I *bring it about* that, say, my arm rises. But in fact, Wittgenstein objects, I don't (*PI* §614). I don't do anything else as a means to effect the rising of my arm. In particular, it cannot be said that I contract certain muscles in order for my arm to go up, for I don't even know which muscles need to be contracted for the arm to go up. (It is rather the other way round: I could raise my arm in order to bring about the contraction of whatever muscles are involved in the process.) Nor do I bring about bodily movements by acts of wishing or deciding. Wishing that something may happen is actually incompatible with doing it voluntarily (*PI* §616). The word 'wish', like 'hope', implies that one is not fully in control of what will happen. If I wish my arm to rise and, lo! it does – it wouldn't be my action and I'd be very surprised (*Z* §586b). A decision to raise my arm, on the other hand, is of course likely to lead to my raising my arm; but it does not just cause my arm to go up. Again, I'd be rather surprised if it did. It would not be my own doing (*PI* §627). A decision to do something may of course lead to a voluntary action, but it occurs *before* the action and cannot be regarded as part of it. Hence it cannot figure in the analysis of the concept of a voluntary action.

Those three objections show that the inner-object model of voluntary action must be rejected. Words like 'voluntary' or 'willing' do not stand for some distinctive mental occurrence that must precede or accompany a movement for it to be voluntary. How, then, is the word 'voluntary' used? Again, we should not expect the answer to be an exciting revelation. The concept is a familiar one, so its philosophical elucidation can only be a reminder of what in practice we are all familiar with. 'Voluntary movement is marked by the absence of surprise' (*PI* §628). I am not a third-person observer to my own behaviour: I cannot look on with interest to see what will happen next, and then perhaps be surprised by it. That is related to the observation that my action's being voluntary is incompatible with my wishing for it to happen (*PI* §616). For one can only have wishes about what is not entirely under one's control, and where something is not under one's control one can doubt whether it will happen (or never have thought of it), and hence be surprised if it does. Of course, that is not to say that all things that happen to us come as a surprise; but with mere events and involuntary actions surprise is at least always logically *possible*, whereas to the extent to which an action is voluntary there is logically no room for surprise.

Why not? It is tempting to think that one is not surprised here because one knows so reliably of one's own voluntary movements. Then naturally the next question is: *how* does one know, and the almost unavoidable answer is that one *feels* one's own voluntary movements, perhaps in one's muscles and joints: ' "How do you know that you have raised your arm?" – "I feel it." ' (*PI* §625). But feelings can be deceptive. Whatever sensations may be characteristic of raising one's arm, it is surely conceivable that in a laboratory they might be produced artificially, by drugs or electric currents. So when now I raise my arm with my eyes shut, whatever sensations I have in my muscles and joints, it should be conceivable that *they* are deceptive. Hence, if my awareness of my voluntary movements were based on such sensations, I should be able in this situation to consider it possible that I am *not* moving my arm (*PI* §624). But I find myself unable to do so; for my certainty that I am moving my arm is not based on the evidence of such sensations. I am just certain that I have raised my arm, and there is no evidence on which my certainty is based (*PI* §625).

The puzzle of first-person authority about one's own agency is not unlike that about one's sensations, and Wittgenstein dissolves it in a similar way. The puzzle is generated by treating the case as one of *knowledge*; which, first, makes it appear strange that there shouldn't be any possibility of error, and which, secondly, makes us look (in vain) for some grounds or evidence on which this extraordinary knowledge could be based. To remove the puzzle we only need to realize that the certainty is the result of our grammar. It is built into our very concept of a voluntary action that the agent is aware of it (cf. *Z* §600) – which is therefore as unsurprising as the fact that bachelors are without exception unmarried.

Consider a related case: You express an intention to go for a walk. Now the question 'How do you know?' makes no sense (or could only be understood as asking: 'How do you know that you will not be prevented?'). An expression of intention is not based on any evidence and cannot be erroneous. In this respect expressions of intention are like declarations that one acted voluntarily: the agent's authority is simply built into our concepts.

7. Wittgenstein's influence

Wittgenstein's anti-Cartesian insistence that there is a conceptual link between mental states and expressive behaviour has often been accused of being a form of behaviourism. But, in fact, he nowhere showed any inclination to try to *reduce* mental states to behaviour (or behavioural dispositions), and it is indeed fairly obvious that, for most mental phenomena, there is no immediate expressive behaviour. Thoughts, for example, manifest themselves in words or deeds only when suitably combined with other mental states or dispositions. Taking this interrelatedness of mental states seriously, while accepting Wittgenstein's valuable insight in the importance of behaviour for the explanation of the mind, led philosophers in the 1970s from behaviourism to a more sophisticated theory: functionalism.

How do Wittgenstein's views on the mind compare and relate to functionalism? Certain similarities are undeniable. When Wittgenstein, in order to clarify our concept of pain, sketches the case of a child who has hurt himself and cries, and is later taught verbal pain-behaviour (*PI* §244), one may be tempted to see that as an anticipation of the functionalist conception of a human being as a mechanism that connects certain inputs (injury) with certain outputs (crying). Teaching may change this input-output function, presumably by affecting the mechanism's inner states that mediate between input and output.

As explained in the first section, for Wittgenstein, the only licit philosophical method was conceptual analysis. Yet conceptual analysis is not likely to yield a simple and yet non-trivial reductive formula about the nature mental states. In particular, conceptual analysis provides no reason to expect that our concepts correspond to the functional states of a determinate input-output mechanism. For example, given my strong desire to eat strawberries, it may be very *likely* that coming to know that there are strawberries for me in the fridge will cause me to go and eat them, but then again, one can easily imagine that I won't: – I may decide to keep them for later; or to offer them to my neighbour; or I may suddenly remember that I need to make an urgent phone call; or I refuse them because I don't want to be under any obligation to the giver; or it may occur to me that

I don't really care for strawberries any more. And even if there is no understandable reason for me not to eat the strawberries, it remains certainly conceivable that I don't. Sometimes people do react in strange ways that they can't fully explain. Although there are conceptual links between our descriptions of beliefs, desires, and actions, they don't normally allow any predictions with logical certainty. All we can say is that a certain desire and a certain belief make a certain action *understandable*; or: under the circumstances a certain belief was a good *reason* to act in a certain way. But other actions would have been equally understandable and justifiable by reasons; and even actions that are not readily or fully understandable would at least be conceivable.

Note also that, with the possible exception of sense perception, our concepts of mental states are virtually open with respect to the causal origin of those states. If my neighbour's ironic smile caused in me the firm conviction that he was a Russian mafia boss, I might well be accused of being irrational; yet this insufficient ground for my belief would not speak against attributing this belief to me if I expressed it with all seriousness. It is not built into our concept of a belief that it has to be caused in certain specific ways. Again, we have of course some empirical knowledge about the likely causes of pain and might be sceptical if somebody complained of pain in the absence of any such likely cause; yet its not a *conceptual* truth that for something to qualify as pain it must be caused in such and such a way. Indeed, we know from experience that occasionally people suffer pain from unidentifiable psychological causes.

So a *specific* functionalist identity claim can certainly not be established *a priori*. Our concepts of mental states do not imply any specific possibilities of origin or causal potential. Is it then perhaps *a priori* plausible to assume that any mental state is identical with *some* specific functional state defined by its possible origin and causal potential, to be discovered by future psychological research? No, for it cannot be ruled out that two instances of the same mental state may differ in their possible origin and causal (or dispositional) potential. Thus, some instances of the belief that p may in a certain surrounding of other mental states cause a feeling s, while other instances of the same belief do not. In fact, since we don't know the specific causal (or dispositional) potential of any mental states it is *a priori* unlikely that our concepts should classify mental states exactly according to their causal (or dispositional) potential. It appears even more unlikely if we bear in mind that it is an essential feature of our most common mental or psychological concepts that they are self-ascribable in a way that is both authoritative and not based on evidence. My sincere avowal of a feeling, a preference, or a belief is, *ipso facto*, an expression *of what I feel, prefer, or believe*, even though it is not based on any observation of my mind, let alone a study of its causal mechanisms. My sincere avowal would, obviously, itself be an effect of the mental state in question; an effect that, under normal circumstances, suffices for us to identify that mental state. So, our concepts of such *mental states* are such that we identify them by *one* telling effect, namely the subject's avowal. But isn't it highly improbable that a *functional state*, defined by a list of *all* its possible causes and possible effects, should be identifiable from only a single one of its effects? Clearly, one should expect that this single effect, the subject's sincere avowal, could be caused by very many different functional states. The concept of a functional state is far more finely grained and sharply defined than that of, say, the belief that Paris is the capital of France, or that of an admiration for Daniel Auteuil.

Functionalism starts out with certain conceptual truths, namely that mental states are affected by perception and sensation; they affect or condition other mental states; and they lead to, and manifest themselves in, certain forms of behaviour. As far as these truisms (and their importance for the philosophy of mind) are concerned, there is agreement between Wittgenstein and functionalism. But, then, functionalists are greatly impressed by the fact that these truisms highlight a certain similarity between a human being and a computer, a so-called Turing machine, with input, distinct functional states, and output. And now functionalism presses this analogy: insisting that it is not merely an analogy, but an identity, that, in fact, a human being *is* a Turing machine, albeit a highly complicated one, and that mental states just *are* functional states. This second step – from an analogy to an identity claim – is where functionalism parts company with Wittgenstein. This second step is neither the result of conceptual analysis, nor supported by empirical evidence. It is a typical philosopher's mistake. One is enthralled by a neat and attractive *picture*.

Here, as in other cases, Wittgensteinian considerations have been taken up by later philosophers of mind, but in a very different spirit, which quickly brings them in conflict with Wittgenstein's approach. His conception of philosophy limiting itself to conceptual clarification has not found many followers. Too strong seems to be the allure of quasi-scientific theory construction in philosophy.[4]

Notes

1 For further discussion and illustration of Wittgenstein's conception of philosophy, see Schroeder 2006, 151–168.
2 Admittedly, it is possible to use the expression 'I know I am in pain' in a meaningful way; but then the word 'know' functions rather differently from its ordinary employment. It may, for example, be used in a bad-tempered request not to be told what one doesn't need to be told.
3 It is important to have a clear understanding of the target of the no-criterion argument. Contrary to what is often maintained in the secondary literature, the argument is not meant to be an objection to the private sensation diary described in §258. Rather, it is an objection to a misconstrual of this or indeed any other sensation language: namely the inner-object conception and its immediate consequence that one *perceives* one's own sensations. Hence, the no-criterion argument is also directed at the view that others can have only an indirect perception of my sensations: For if I do not *perceive* my sensations, others cannot be said to perceive them only indirectly. The point concerns ordinary sensations, such as pain, just as much as the 'private', fictitious scenario in which natural expressions or a familiar use of the sensation word are set to one side. What the argument is *not* supposed to show is that one cannot keep a record of sensations without a natural expression.
4 I am grateful to Amy Kind and an anonymous referee for their helpful comments on an earlier version of this paper.

Further Reading

Budd, M. (1989). *Wittgenstein's Philosophy of Psychology*. London: Routledge; new ed. 2014.
Hacker, P.M.S. (1990). *Wittgenstein: Meaning and Mind. Vol. 3 of an Analytical Commentary on the Philosophical Investigations*. Oxford: Blackwell.
Hacker, P.M.S. (1996). *Wittgenstein's Place in Twentieth-Century Analytic Philosophy*, Oxford: Blackwell.
Hacker, P.M.S. (2010). "The Development of Wittgenstein's Philosophy of Psychology," in Cottingham, J. and Hacker, P.M.S. (eds.), *Mind, Method, and Morality: Essays in Honour of Anthony Kenny*. Oxford: OUP: 275–305.
Malcolm, N. (1970). "Wittgenstein on the Nature of Mind," *American Philosophical Quarterly*, 4: 9–29.
Racine, T. P., & Slaney, K. L. (eds.). (2013). *A Wittgensteinian Perspective on the Use of Conceptual Analysis in Psychology*. Basingstoke: Palgrave Macmillan.
Rundle, B. (1997). *Mind in Action*. Oxford: Clarendon Press.
Schroeder, S. (ed.). (2001). *Wittgenstein and Contemporary Philosophy of Mind*. Basingstoke: Palgrave Macmillan.
Schroeder, S. (2006). *Wittgenstein: The Way Out of the Fly-Bottle*. Cambridge: Polity.

Bibliography

Hume, David (1748). *Enquiry Concerning Human Understanding*, edited by Selby-Bigge, L. A. and P. H. Nidditch (1975). Oxford: OUP.
Schroeder, Severin (2006). *Wittgenstein: The Way Out of the Fly-Bottle*. Cambridge: Polity.

Ludwig Wittgenstein

BB *The Blue and Brown Books*, Oxford: Blackwell, 1958.
BT *The Big Typescript, TS 213*. Edited and translated by C. Grant Luckhardt and Maximilian A. E. Aue. Oxford: Blackwell. (BT)
LW *Last Writings on the Philosophy of Psychology*, eds.: G.H. von Wright, H. Nyman; tr.: C.V. Luckhardt, M.A.E. Aue, Oxford: Blackwell, 1982.
MS Manuscript (numbered in accordance with G.H. von Wright's catalogue, in his 'The Wittgenstein Papers', in his: *Wittgenstein*, Oxford: Blackwell, 1982) from *Wittgenstein's Nachlass: The Bergen Electronic Edition*. Edited by the Wittgenstein Archives at the University of Bergen. Oxford: Oxford University Press, 2000.
NfL *Notes for Lectures on "Private Experience" and "Sense Data"* (1934–1936), in PO, 202–288.
PG *Philosophical Grammar*, ed.: R. Rhees, tr.: A.J.P. Kenny, Oxford: Blackwell, 1974.
PI *Philosophical Investigations*, 4th ed.: P.M.S. Hacker & J. Schulte; trans.: G.E.M. Anscombe, P.M.S. Hacker, J. Schulte, Oxford: Wiley-Blackwell: 2009.
PO *Philosophical Occasions 1912–1951*, eds: J. Klagge & A. Nordmann, Indianapolis: Hackett, 1993.
RFM *Remarks on the Foundations of Mathematics*, eds: G. H. von Wright, R. Rhees, G.E.M. Anscombe; tr.: G.E.M. Anscombe, rev. ed., Oxford: Blackwell, 1978.

RPP *Remarks on the Philosophy of Psychology*, 2 vols, eds.: G.E.M Anscombe, G. H. von Wright, H. Nyman; tr.: G.E.M Anscombe, C. V. Luckhardt, M.A.E. Aue, Oxford: Blackwell, 1980.

TLP *Tractatus Logico-Philosophicus*, trans. D. F. Pears and B. F. McGuinness. London: Routledge & Kegan Paul, 1961.

Z *Zettel*, eds: G.E.M. Anscombe & G. H. von Wright, tr.: G.E.M. Anscombe, Oxford: Blackwell, 1967.

10

THE BOUNDARIES OF THE MIND[1]

Katalin Farkas

1. The Cartesian conception of the mind

The subject of mental processes or mental states is usually assumed to be an individual, and hence the boundaries of mental features – in a strict or metaphorical sense – are naturally regarded as reaching no further than the boundaries of the individual. This chapter addresses various philosophical developments in the 20th and 21st century that questioned this natural assumption. I will frame this discussion by first presenting a historically influential commitment to the individualistic nature of the mental in Descartes' theory. I identify various elements in the Cartesian conception of the mind that were subsequently criticized and rejected by various externalist theories, advocates of the extended mind hypothesis and defenders of embodied cognition. Then I will indicate the main trends in these critiques.

Descartes' work was partly a response to developments in natural science in the 17th century, and one of his goals was to provide a theoretical-philosophical foundation for modern science which rejected Aristotelian natural philosophy. Descartes was not the last philosopher who hoped to make a lasting contribution by providing a theory that integrates philosophy with modern science. Ever since the 17th century, there has been an occasionally reoccurring anxiety in philosophy – famously expressed for example by Kant in the *Critique of Pure Reason* – about the fact that while the sciences appear to make great progress, philosophy in comparison seems to make very little, if any progress. Various remedies have been suggested, for example by offering a methodology or grounding for philosophy that is either imported from the sciences, or is comparable to the objectivity and explanatory power of scientific method. This will be one of the persisting themes in this chapter. In section 2, we will see how the attempt to ground philosophical theories by semantics offers the hope of progress and questions the Cartesian boundaries of the mind at the same time. In section 3, we will see how naturalism about the mind also leads to reconsidering the issue of boundaries.

Descartes' considerations about the nature of the mind in his Second Meditation have had a profound effect on the development of philosophy in the Western tradition.[2] In the First Meditation, Descartes considers the possibility of being deceived by an evil demon. The starting point is the simple observation that things can appear different from the way they are. Extending the gap between appearance and reality to its extreme, it is possible, contends Descartes, that the world I take to be around me does not exist, that even my body does not exist, but all appearances of a world and my body are results of the manipulations of an evil demon. If I were the victim of the demon, things would appear exactly the same as they do now, but in reality, they would be very different. The modern version of this scenario of radical deception is usually known as the "brain-in-a-vat" or "the Matrix" scenario, where the stimuli arriving to our brain from external objects or the rest of our body are replaced by an elaborate machinery of virtual reality.

Even in this case of radical deception, Descartes argues, I would still be a thinking thing; moreover, a thinker who would have exactly the same mental features as I do now. The sky and earth may not exist, but I would still *believe* they do; the light I seem to see and the noise I seem to hear may not be there, but I would still *feel* that they are. Two points are worth emphasizing here. First, even though the demon scenario allows for the non-existence of my body, Descartes explicitly says that, at this point, he is still agnostic about the existence of a mind separable from the body. So the resulting conception is not committed to dualism about mind and body. Second, there is an important epistemic asymmetry between my mind and the rest of the world: namely, the possibility of being deceived by a demon, or being a brain in a vat, threatens, at least prima facie, my knowledge of the rest of the world, but it does not threaten my knowledge of the content of my mental states. This does not necessarily mean that I am omniscient or infallible about the nature of my mind; but it does mean that at least in *this comparison* – i.e. vulnerability to a threat from the demon scenario – the mind fares *better* than the body. The title of the Second Meditation is fittingly "The nature of the human mind, and how it is better known than the body".

Eventually, by the end of the *Meditations*, Descartes arrives at the conclusion that the mind is indeed distinct from the body. At the same time, Descartes was very interested in the body's contribution to our mental life, and his view can be summarized (with some simplification) as follows. There are mental phenomena, most notably, sensory (perceptual and bodily) experiences, and emotions, which are caused by the brain. Nerves from our sense-organs and throughout the body carry stimuli as far as the pineal gland in the brain. The gland has a distinctive state for each type of sensory or affective experience and causes our immaterial mind to undergo that experience. How this causal connection works between two entirely different substances is of course one of the greatest puzzles for a Cartesian dualist, but this is not the topic of this chapter (see Chapters 2 and 7). It is more interesting for our purposes that apparently Descartes thought that non-sensory or non-affective cognition (for example, pure theoretical and practical reasoning) need not, or indeed could not, involve the body in such an intimate way (Farkas 2005). So there is a separation between what we may call "pure" cognition, on the one hand, and sensory and affective mental states, on the other. This separation, in itself, is not Descartes' invention. Aristotle draws a similar distinction between rational and non-rational parts of the soul.

I provide this sketch of Descartes' conception of the mind because much of the following discussion will be usefully understood by the various critiques' deep or superficial disagreement with certain elements of the Cartesian conception. In one way or another, many philosophers in the 20th and 21st century objected to the idea that a solitary mind deceived by an evil demon or evil scientist can have the same mental features as we do; or to the idea that the physical basis of mental phenomena can be restricted to the brain; or to the idea that pure cognition is largely independent of the body. This chapter focuses on developments in the analytic philosophical tradition (for a critique of the Cartesian conception in continental philosophy, see, for example, Hubert Dreyfus's commentary on Heidegger's *Being and Time* (Dreyfus 1991). I will not attempt to reconstruct all pros and cons in the debates I mention; for state-of-the-art summaries of these issues, it is worth consulting, for example, Lau and Deutsch (2014) and Wilson and Foglia (2011). Instead, I shall try to trace some broad historical tendencies that influenced philosophical thinking on the boundaries of the mind.

2. "Externalism" or "anti-individualism"

2.1 The semantic tradition

Gottlob Frege is often identified as one of the first and most influential figures in the history of analytic philosophy.[3] Frege proposed the first systematic modern theory of semantics, that is, a theory of how the semantic values (the truth and reference) of linguistic expressions are determined. Semantics and symbolic logic have then gone on to become two of the greatest success stories in the history of analytic philosophy, and no doubt this is the reason why Frege is regarded as one of the founders of the tradition, despite the fact that he was a German thinker, deeply rooted in a philosophical tradition that was quite different from the English-speaking empiricism that forms a more congenial historical background to analytic philosophy. I mentioned above the occasionally reoccurring anxiety in philosophy about the apparent lack of progress in the several thousand years' history of the subject. Semantics and logic have been seen by many as finally offering the prospect for real progress in philosophy, not just in semantic theory itself, but also as a tool to get a better grip on a wide range of philosophical issues. We can find a vigorous expression of this sentiment, for example, in Timothy Williamson's 2004 paper "Must Do Better". Williamson's idea of progress in philosophy is well expressed in these complimentary words about Michael Dummett's contribution to the realism/anti-realism debate:

> Instead of shouting slogans at each other, Dummett's realist and anti-realist would busy themselves in developing systematic compositional semantic theories of the appropriate type, which could then be judged and compared by something like scientific standards.
>
> (Williamson 2006, 179)

In what we may call "the semantic tradition", semantic theories and notions, like possible worlds, quantifiers, operators, domains of quantifications, connectives, and so on, have shaped and still shape the understanding of an astonishing range of philosophical topics, including as diverse issues as ontological realism (Chalmers et al. 2009), the analysis of knowledge and its relation to evidence (Williamson 2000), the metaphysics of modality (Kripke 1972), the nature of belief and desire (Richard 1990), the issue of cognitivism versus non-cognitivism in metaethics (Schroeder 2010), and many more.

One of the basic instruments in a semantic theory is to attribute a certain feature to each linguistic expression which Frege called "sense". *Sense determines reference* (or semantic value in general) at least in that sameness of sense entails sameness of reference; this commitment is crucial, for the whole point of the theory is to identify a feature of expressions that accounts for their semantic values. Though this gives, in itself, very little idea of what "senses" are, it is prima facie plausible to identify sense with the meaning of a linguistic expression. Frege held that shared meaning is possible only if senses are neither mental nor physical, but rather belong to a third realm of beings to which thinking subjects have the same access. The default assumption in the subsequent history of semantics tended to follow this way of thinking in assuming that "propositions" (the senses of declarative sentences) and "concepts" (the senses of sub-sentential expressions, the constituent of propositions) are abstract entities.

Proper names pose a particular problem for the idea that expressions have a sense or a meaning which determines their reference. Saul Kripke's *Naming and Necessity*, published first in 1972, was to become one of the most influential philosophical works of the 20th century, offering one of the best examples of how a focus on the semantic features of language can contribute to a whole range of philosophical problems, including metaphysics and the philosophy of mind. Kripke argued that names contribute their referent to complex expressions directly, without the mediation of senses. Hence what is expressed by names (the object it denotes) is often to be found outside thinking subjects. Kripke argued that similar considerations apply to natural kind terms denoting biological species or chemical kinds, like "gold" or "water" or "tiger".

The sense/reference framework has another important consequence for names, indexicals and natural kind terms. Parallel to Kripke, Hilary Putnam developed in his papers in the seventies a theory of natural kind terms similar to the one presented in *Naming and Necessity*. In his 1975 paper "The Meaning of 'Meaning'" (Putnam 1975a), Putnam invites us to consider the consequences of this theory with the help of a thought experiment. Imagine a planet called Twin Earth which is an exact replica of Earth, with qualitatively identical counterparts of all Earthly inhabitants, including our protagonist, Oscar. The one difference between Earth and Twin Earth is that the liquid they call "water" is in fact a different chemical compound, and hence when Oscar and Twin Oscar talk about "water", they refer to two different kinds.

A similar phenomenon arises in the case of names and indexical expressions. When Oscar and Twin Oscar use the name "Aristotle", they refer to different individuals: Oscar refers to Aristotle, and Twin Oscar to Twin Aristotle (as we would put it). Other influential cases – based also on expressions other than names and natural kind terms – are discussed in the work of Tyler Burge (Burge 1979). For example, Burge presents two linguistic communities which use the word "arthritis" in slightly different ways, but focuses on two subjects, who have the same views on arthritis. These two subjects, just like Oscar and Twin Oscar, are internally identical, but refer to different things. As we saw, one option in the case of names is to say that they are directly referring expressions, without a sense. But suppose it's implausible to say that some linguistic expressions which contribute to intelligent discourse are devoid of sense or meaning. Sense determines reference: sameness of sense entails sameness of reference, and hence difference of reference entails difference of sense. Therefore, the sense or meaning of "Aristotle" and "water" are different for Oscar and Twin Oscar (and similarly for Burge's protagonists).

Many of our linguistic expressions refer to things outside us. Hence it is obvious that at least some semantic features, namely, the references of many expressions constitutively depend on things outside thinking subjects. This is uncontroversial. If meaning is to determine reference, and two internally identical subjects – like Oscar and Twin Oscar – can refer to different things, then it seems that meanings also have to depend on external factors. It is important to see that this conclusion need not depend essentially on the Kripke/Putnam theory of natural kinds, or on alleged intuitions about the reference of the term "water". As long as we accept that two internally identical subjects can refer to different things by the use of names or indexicals (which is quite difficult to deny; indeed, we can stipulate such use of names), the requirement that sense determines reference entails that these subjects do not share their meanings either, despite their internal sameness. "Meanings ain't in the head", as Putnam famously declared.

2.2 The semantic conception of intentionality

The claim that *meanings* are not in the head is perhaps not that surprising after all. For example, it should be fairly uncontroversial that linguistic meaning depends on things outside an individual, namely on linguistic conventions being accepted by others in her linguistic community. Or it could depend on abstract senses that exist in the third realm beyond mental and physical beings. What about the idea that certain semantic features – other than reference – in my idiolect depend on things outside me? Even that is less than shocking. Semantic theories usually offer models which often include inevitable simplifications – this is especially true of formal semantic theories. All sorts of things can model all sorts of things. We can start with a model where the sense of a sentence is an ordered n-tuple of the senses of its constituents. Then we could be persuaded that names refer directly, without the mediation of a sense, and propose instead that the sense of sentences containing names should be modeled by an n-tuple that includes the reference, rather than the sense of the name. The point I want to stress is that in a way, this move is easy:

n-tuples, whether consisting "senses" or "references" can serve as good models; their usefulness will depend on the explanatory power of the model.

Putnam formulated the original claim about meanings, but the thesis assumed its real significance and became relevant to our current topic when it was broadened to include mental contents. One of the first to make this move was Tyler Burge (Burge 1979).[4] The general argument could proceed as follows. We start with noting that mental states like beliefs, or entertained thoughts, can be true or false. Moreover, not only beliefs, but also desires, perceptual experiences, certain emotions, and other mental states are *about* things in the world: they exhibit intentionality, or the mind's direction upon objects (see Chapter 8 on Intentionality). The next, crucial move is to understand intentional directedness on the analogy of semantic reference. This is not implausible: a belief is about things, which also serve as referents of expressions we use to express the belief. We might think that fundamentally the same idea is involved when a word refers to a thing, or an idea is about the same thing. This move offers the possibility of importing the conceptual tools of semantic theory into understanding the nature of mental states: we attribute a semantic content to a belief which is the same as the semantic content of the sentence we use to express the belief.

The semantic content of sentences, hence of beliefs, is nothing other than the sense or meaning of a sentence. We already know that meaning is outside the head: so the content of beliefs is also outside the head. Similar considerations will apply to other instances of intentional directedness. Hence some mental features are constitutively determined by things outside a thinking subject. This is the view known as *externalism* or *anti-individualism* about mental content, and it entails the rejection of the *internalist* Cartesian conception of the mind sketched in section 1. A solitary brain-in-a-vat or a subject deceived by an evil demon cannot have all the same mental states as we have, if the objects to which we refer don't exist in their world. Eliminating the world outside does not leave the inner world of thought intact, as Descartes believed. If we want thought to be about the world, then even what it is *possible* to think will depend on how things are external to us.

Lines of resistance to the externalist conclusion open accordingly. The requirement that sense determines reference leads to the externalist conclusion only if we assume that sense alone determines reference; for if sense plus something else determines reference, then from different references we cannot infer different senses (Farkas 2008, ch.7). Starting from the 2000s, there has been an intense debate in semantics about the role of context in determining truth-value (see Preyer and Peter 2007 for a representative cross-section of the debate), and a number of theories were developed which give up the principle that sense alone determines reference (MacFarlane 2005). Thus one could retain the semantic conception of intentionality and still resist the externalist conclusion. Alternatively, one could begin to question the idea that intentional directedness should be understood on the model of semantic reference (Crane 2014).

2.3 Two-dimensional views

A semantic theory is a theory of how the semantic value (truth, reference) of expressions is determined. The feature of expressions that determines their reference is variously called "meaning" or "sense" or "content". Some philosophers have suggested that meanings or contents have two different aspects that cannot be explained by a single notion. Just as in the case of semantic externalism, these "two-dimensional semantic theories" or "dual content theories" can be put forward about meanings (and, in this case, also about types of necessity), rather than about the mind. Chalmers (2006) gives a thorough overview of the various versions of this "two-dimensional" approach to contents.

David Kaplan, who is often regarded as the first to present a systematic two-dimensional framework (Kaplan 1977), distinguished between the character and the content of indexical expressions. On this view, the character remains constant for each use of the first person pronoun "I", and it expresses something like "the speaker of this utterance". However, the contents expressed by first-person sentences are different for different speakers: they are singular propositions which constitutively contain the subject of the utterance. Kaplan considers a Putnam-like scenario of Castor and Pollux, identical twins who are stipulated to have qualitatively identical internal states. Kaplan holds that the cognitive or psychological states (he uses the terms interchangeably) of the twins are exactly the same, even though they express different singular propositions when each says "My brother was born before me" (Kaplan 1977, 535). Kaplan follows Putnam's original formulation of the lesson of the Twin Earth story: semantic contents do, but psychological states don't determine reference. As mentioned before, this is a type of externalism, but not externalism about the mind.

Just like in the case of the Twin Earth story, the two-dimensional framework was subsequently modified, so that both dimensions were brought into the mental realm. The idea is that internally identical subjects in different environments (like Castor and Pollux, or Oscar and Twin Oscar, or me and my brain-in-a-vat counterpart) are similar in some mental respect, but different in another. For each pair, their mental states share their "narrow" contents, but differ in some of their "broad" contents (Fodor 1987).

The two-dimensional view has been seen by many as a judicious compromise between externalist and internalist views (Chalmers 2002). The broad content of mental states accounts for some of our practices in attributing mental states. For example, if we say that Castor and Pollux believe different things when they each think that "My brother was born before me", it is tempting to say that the difference in beliefs is a mental difference. At the same time, we can see why Kaplan was inclined to say that the twins are psychologically alike. If Castor and Pollux are both convinced that they are second-born, this may prompt similar actions. When we think about how the world appears from the subjective point of view, or how to explain actions in terms of the subject's mental states, it is tempting to discover mental *similarities* among internally identical agents.

Two-dimensional views, therefore, do not see broad and narrow features in competition: both contents can be attributed to the same mental state, for different purposes. However, someone could raise the following worry. When I consciously think to myself that "Water is wet" or "My brother was born before me", it does not seem at all that I am entertaining two thoughts on each occasion, with two different contents. With each conscious act of thinking, there seems to be only one thing that I grasp. So it is not very clear how the two different contents are present in my mind. One natural answer on behalf of the two-dimensional theory is to return to the observation, made earlier, that the semantic approach to mental content provides *models*, where operations on a structure of abstract entities model some or other function that contents are supposed to do – determine reference, or explain action, as the case may be. Mental contents can be modeled by sets of possible worlds, centered world, diagonal propositions, and so on, and the theory need not make a claim on the experienced reality of our mental life.

2.4 The extent of inner space

So far we have seen externalist theories which handle the issue of mental content through what we could broadly describe as the "modeling approach". In this section, we shall look at a rather different externalist view, defended in the works of Gareth Evans (Evans 1982) and John McDowell, which addresses the phenomenological-psychological reality of content. I shall use McDowell's 1986 paper "Singular Thought and the Extent of Inner Space" as a representative of this approach, since it explicitly tackles the issue of the boundaries of the mind.

McDowell's target in this paper is what he calls the "fully Cartesian" picture of the mind. On this picture, the mental realm is what is left after entertaining the possibility of radical deception, and consists of transparently accessible and infallibly known facts. Privileged access to the inner realm makes access to the rest of the world correspondingly problematic, opening a gap between the inner and outer world that is very difficult to bridge. The Cartesian conception puts "subjectivity's very possession of an objective environment in question" (McDowell 1986, 237). On McDowell's view, this is not simply the epistemological anxiety about the possible non-existence or radical different nature of the world; rather, the threat is that we cannot explain how thinking about a mind-independent world is so much as possible.

McDowell's answer is based on transforming Bertrand Russell's notion of acquaintance (Russell 1917). Acquaintance is an epistemic-psychological relation in which we stand to objects when we are directly aware of them, without an intermediary process of inference or knowledge of truths. When a particular is an object of acquaintance, it is a constituent of the singular proposition that forms the content of a judgment. McDowell makes it clear that, for Russell, unlike, for example, for Kaplan, singular propositions are not merely part of semantics, but they are intended as a "distinctive kind of configuration in psychological reality" (McDowell 1986, 228). However, for Russell, the psychological reality of singular propositions comes with a serious restriction on the range of objects that can enter into such propositions. Suppose – as McDowell himself would subsequently propose – that we allow external objects to be objects of acquaintance, and constituents of singular propositions. Since we can be mistaken about the presence of an external object, this move would open the possibility of an *illusion* of entertaining a singular proposition. This was unacceptable for Russell.

We can regain possession of the world if we allow that some of our mental states constitutively involve external objects, and thus "we are compelled to picture the inner and outer realms as interpenetrating, not separated from one another by the characteristically Cartesian divide" (McDowell 1986, 241). Some of the object-involving states are subjectively indistinguishable from states which do not involve objects, for example in a veridical perception and the matching perfect hallucination. On the fully Cartesian conception, the mental nature of subjectively indistinguishable states must be the same; otherwise we could mistake one mental state for another. McDowell wants to resist this move by giving up the claim that we are infallible about all aspects of mental states, and he accepts that mental states of very different nature can give rise to the same appearance:

> Short of the fully Cartesian picture, the infallibly knowable fact – its seeming to one that things are thus and so – can be taken disjunctively, as constituted either by the fact that things are manifestly thus and so or by the fact that that merely seems to be the case.
>
> (McDowell 1986, 242)

McDowell, like many others influenced by Oxford philosophy in the second half of the 20th century, can be seen as responding to a question raised prominently in P. F. Strawson's work: how can we explain the very idea of a subject possessing the experience of an objective environment (Strawson 1959, Chapter 2). One area where the question received an especially great amount of attention was perception. It seems a fundamental phenomenological fact about perception that it appears to present a mind-independent world. How is this possible? In the empiricist tradition, it was customary to view perceptual experiences as sensations, that is, as modifications of a subject's consciousness – but this leaves the fundamental phenomenological fact unexplained.

The "disjunctive" theory of perception was developed from the 1980s partly to answer this challenge (see also Chapter 4, Theories of Perception). The basic idea is hinted in the quote from McDowell (McDowell 1986, 242) : when something appears to be the case, it could *either* an object-involving fact manifesting itself in experience, *or* an indistinguishable mere appearance – hence the name "disjunctivism". The fact that some experiences constitutively involve an external object is meant to explain how we can make sense of the idea that perception presents a mind-independent world.[5] The important point for our purposes is that the mental nature of object-involving and non-object involving experiences are radically different, and this difference is due to facts external to the subject: the presence or absence of an object of perception. Disjunctivism and the relational views about experience are therefore forms of externalism about mental features.

Though Evans and McDowell have been as deeply influenced by the semantic theories of Frege and Russell as many of the externalist philosophers previously mentioned, their approach to the mind is somewhat different from those we placed in the "semantic tradition". It does not seem that they are attempting to offer models for various possible functions of mental features. Instead, they take as a starting point, and as psychologically real, the phenomenologically fundamental features of our thinking and experience: for example, the fact that we seem to be in possession of a conception of an objective world. Perhaps relatedly, McDowell has little interest in a scientistic conception of the mind. On the contrary, one of his main inspirations is Wilfrid Sellars's idea that a proper understanding of the mind is not possible in a merely causal-naturalistic explanatory framework (McDowell 1994). Hence the type of externalism that is motivated by the kind of considerations Evans and McDowell put forward does not fit into either of the broad trends we describe in this chapter: the modeling approaches presented in sections 2.1–2.3, or the naturalistic theories of section 3.

2.5 The boundaries of privileged access

According to externalists, Descartes was wrong in claiming that internally identical subjects always have the same mental features. It's been argued that this entails that Descartes was also wrong in claiming an epistemic privilege to the mental realm (see Brown 2004 for various aspects of the debate). More precisely, compared to internalism, externalism limits – according to this argument – the scope of privileged first-person knowledge of mental features. Indeed, it was claimed (Farkas 2008) that the restriction of privileged access is not a consequence, but rather a defining feature of externalist views. Arguably, this attitude was discernible, for example, in McDowell's considerations quoted in section 2.4: McDowell identifies the privileged epistemic status of mental facts as the central tenet of the fully Cartesian picture, and argues that by giving up this claim, we open the way towards making some of the external world constitutive of our mental states.[6]

It is interesting to mention here another influential view on the limitations of self-knowledge, represented in the work of Sigmund Freud. The two views are of course very different both in their theses and their motivations. But they can be both seen as undermining a central tenet of the Cartesian conception of the mind: in a manner of speaking, while externalists want to extend the boundary outwards, Freud suggested that the boundaries of the mind lie much deeper than the shallow heights reached by straightforward reflective awareness. This is the realm of the unconscious.

We have not addressed Freud in this chapter because Freud and psychoanalysis have had remarkably little effect on mainstream analytic philosophy, compared, for example, to continental philosophy, where Freud had much more of an influence, and compared to the rest of intellectual life and culture.[7] Unconscious mental states are the subject of much theorizing in analytic philosophy of mind, but the disciplines that analytic philosophers consult about these states are either cognitive psychology (for example, in studying the sub-personal states involved in learning or perceptual processes), or social psychology (for studying phenomena like implicit bias). Nonetheless, the broad influence of Freud's ideas probably contributed to undermining the Cartesian conception which is the main target of externalist views popular in the analytic philosophical tradition and which is also a target of many naturalist views of the mind discussed in the next section.

3. Naturalism about the mind

3.1 The functionalist-computationalist view

In Descartes' time, a philosopher interested in the study of the mind freely included anatomical, psychological, and biological considerations in his works. As with many other disciplines, the various sciences of the mind have subsequently become autonomous and separate from philosophy. Yet developments in the sciences continued to exercise a profound effect on philosophy, and this is especially apparent in analytic philosophy of mind in the 20th century. I have already alluded to the recurrent desire to place philosophy on a secure methodology that would offer a chance of progress comparable to progress in science. There have been two further, distinguishable, though often co-existent, manifestations of this impact.

The first is the doctrine of naturalism or physicalism. In the first half of the 20th century, especially after the development of the theories of relativity and quantum mechanics, it seemed that physics could offer an explanation of the world that was unparalleled in scope, depth, evidence, and explanatory power. The other natural sciences, even if not obviously reducible to physics, have links to physics that promised a unified theory of the world. This inspired a physicalist-naturalist program: aiming at an account of all mental phenomena that is compatible with the thesis that everything that exists figures in the theories of natural sciences. Though materialism was a notable philosophical position already in ancient philosophy, and from the 17th century onwards, it is characteristic of philosophy of mind in the second half of the 20th century that physicalism (both for defenders and opponents) dominated the agenda in a way it never had before (see Chapters 2, 3, 7 in this volume).

The second impact of the sciences is an increased interest in philosophy to approach the study of the mind from an interdisciplinary standpoint. This means actively trying to figure out how empirical results in psychology, evolutionary theory, or neuroscience may affect our philosophical theories of the mind. The two approaches are compatible, but independent: one could believe in a naturalist ontology but still rely mainly on the (broadly speaking) speculative methods of philosophy and not pay much attention to empirical work.[8] Or someone could reject a physicalist or naturalist ontology (together with a somewhat surprising number of natural scientists),[9] yet invest a lot of time in empirical studies of the mind in the hope that they illuminate our philosophical theories.

Starting in the late 1950s and early 1960s, the 20th century witnessed the development of a robust and sophisticated defense of a naturalist conception of the mind, and the emergence of cognitive science, an interdisciplinary approach to the workings of the mind (see Chapter 11, the Rise of Cognitive Science). One prominent idea both in naturalist theories and in cognitive science is that the mind could be understood on the analogy of computers (inspired by Turing's groundbreaking work for example in Turing 1950).[10] According to the classic functionalist-computational picture of the mind, our core cognitive processes can be understood as programs that manipulate certain representations stored in the brain. The central computing unit is connected to the periphery in two ways: our nervous system transduces stimuli that arrive from the world to our sensory organs, and also conveys certain tasks to be solved (for example by signaling that the body needs nutrition). The information arriving to the central system is used to build an inner representation of the world, which then helps the system to solve the tasks posed for it (for example, by computing the navigations needed to reach food). The solutions are then translated to action commands, which are communicated to another component of the periphery, the motor system (the result being that the organism moves towards the source of food).

One crucial point here is that in this so-called "sense-think-act cycle", the central thinking module, which is sandwiched between the periphery of perception and action, is conceived as running a highly abstract program; that is, a program that can be realized by very different physical mechanisms, and would be, in principle, compatible with a large variety of inputs and outputs, fashioned for all sorts of sensory organs and all sorts of bodies to be moved. This idea actually has very old roots: we saw a similar conception being present already in Aristotle and Descartes, in the view that pure cognition is independent both of the body, and the sensory-affective aspect of our mental life.

Descartes thought that everything material must work on mechanistic principles, and he simply could not imagine how a programmed mechanism could account for the creativity of human thought. Therefore, he held that the immaterial soul must be the home for rational cognition. Descartes' argument is based on some empirical-scientific assumptions that are clearly superseded today. As we shall see in section 3.4, the classic computationalist picture has come under increased criticism. But even if the picture needs correction, we should not underestimate the significance of having a conception of mental processes, the computational-functionalist conception, which makes sense – in a way that's consistent with a naturalist world-view – of something that completely baffled Descartes and others for centuries (see Rey 1997, Chapter 2).

There are at least three boundary issues raised by naturalism and the functionalist-computational theory of the mind. First, naturalist accounts of representations usually rely on an external individuation of mental content. Second, functionalism about the mind has the possible consequence that the physical basis of the mind extends beyond the boundaries of our organic body. Third, the classical computational conception was criticized for not taking into account the essential role of the "periphery" in cognitive processes. The resulting views – externalism about content, the extended mind hypothesis, and various versions of embodied cognition – assert the dependence of the mind on things outside the brain or the subject in rather different ways. I shall explain each of them in turn.

3.2 Naturalist reduction of content

Jerry Fodor has developed one of the most powerful and sophisticated defenses of the computational theory of the mind, through his landmark publications starting in the 1970s (Fodor 1975; 1987). Part of this project is to account for the fact that mental states seem to be about things in the world (see Chapter 8, Intentionality). As Fodor famously put it:

> I suppose sooner or later the physicists will complete the catalogue they've been compiling of the ultimate and irreducible properties of things. When they do, the likes of *spin*, *charm*, and *charge* will perhaps appear on their list. But *aboutness* surely won't: intentionality simply doesn't go that deep.
>
> (Fodor 1987, 97)

Aboutness in the computational theory of mind is approached through the notion of representation. The basis of the analogy with computer programs is that certain symbols, called "representations" are stored in the brain, and the machine – the mind, the brain – manipulates these symbols on the basis of their physical shapes (that is the only kind of feature detectable by a physical symbol-manipulator). The symbols represent various items in our environment, and this makes it possible for us to think and reason about them. If I believe that cats like cream, and I want give my cat a treat, I will decide to get some cream for him. But what makes it the case that a certain thought, realized by a symbol in the brain, represents cats, rather than, say, dogs? One plausible answer from a physicalist point of view is that there is some sort of causal or nomological connection between the presence of things in the world, and the presence of the representation. The crudest form of this would be the following: seeing a cat causes a certain brain-state which, in virtue of being caused by a cat, represents cats (or this particular cat). This very crude version is unsatisfactory, partly because it cannot account for misrepresentation: if all tokenings represent their causes, no tokening will ever be mistaken. Accounts that try to base representation on some sort of lawful connections or evolved functions face better prospects.

On a nomological account (Fodor 1987), symbols represent things whose presence has a lawful correlation with the symbol. This account can employ a certain version of the two-dimensional framework mentioned in section 2.3. Computations on symbols in the brain can explain one part of cognition and the narrow aspect of content; the lawful connections with the world can explain the broad aspect.

The Twin Earth scenario illustrates the consequences of the nomological view for the individuation of content. Oscar's "water" representations are nomologically correlated with the presence of H2O, Twin Oscar's "water" representations with the presence of XYZ. The content of their representations are different. The nomological view entails externalism about content as it was defined in section 2. An even more emphatic illustration of this comes from considering a certain version of the brain-in-a-vat scenario. In the virtual reality of brains-in-vats, presumably some complex part of the computer program is responsible for the tokening of representations in the brains, hence these are the prime candidates for standing in a lawful correlation with the presence of representations in the brain. The somewhat surprising conclusion is that brains-in-vats have actually mostly true beliefs about the world: since they represent bits of the computer program, and their world does consist of bits of the computer program, they are mostly right.

Starting in the 1980s, several authors (Dretske 1981; Millikan 1984; Papineau 1987) proposed alternative naturalist-reductive theories which analyze representation in terms of evolved functions. These views also entail externalism: if we imagined an artificial or accidentally created replica of a human being, her representational states would be different, since they would lack an evolutionary history (Davidson 1987). Naturalist theories are therefore usually committed to some form of externalism about mental content.

3.3 Extended mind

Most naturalist-physicalist theories of the mind rely on some version of functionalism, broadly understood. Central to this conception is the idea that what makes something a particular mental state depends on the role it plays in a cognitive system, but not on the physical constitution of the piece of machinery that realizes this role. This multiple realizability is often illustrated by stating that a certain belief or desire, or feeling pain, can be realized by neural states of quite different character in different species of animals, and possibly even by a creature who is made of inorganic material – as long as there is an isomorphism in the functional role the state plays in a larger system (Putnam 1960).

This raises the question of how much liberty we can take with the realization of functional roles. Andy Clark and David Chalmers proposed the following thought experiment (Clark and Chalmers 1998). Inga is an ordinary person who lives in New York and wants to visit the Museum of Modern Art. She recalls that the museum is on 53rd Street and sets off. Contrast her case with that of Otto, who suffers from long-term memory loss, and therefore enters all important information into a notebook that he carries with him and consults all the time. When Otto wants to visit the Museum of Modern Art, he looks up the address in his notebook, and sets off.

It is usually agreed that Inga has the belief that the museum is on 53rd Street even prior to recalling this information. On a functionalist theory, this state is defined in terms of having a certain functional role in Inga's cognitive system: taking into account her other mental states (for example a desire to visit a museum), it responds to certain inputs with certain outputs (for example setting off towards the museum). Clark and Chalmers argue that the information stored in Otto's notebook has exactly the same role in Otto's cognitive system, and therefore we should attribute the same belief to Otto, even before he consults his notebook. The fact that the notebook is to be found outside Otto's organic body is irrelevant here. Clark and Chalmers offer the following general consideration to support their claim:

> If, as we confront some task, a part of the world functions as a process which, *were it done in the head*, we would have no hesitation in recognizing as part of the cognitive process, then that part of the world is (so we claim) part of the cognitive process.
> (Clark and Chalmers 1998, 8)

The principle has subsequently become known as "the Parity Principle", and it is a consequence of a functionalist view of mental states. It is instructive to compare Otto and Inga with Ned Block's famous example in which he imagines the population of China realizing a system that is functionally equivalent to Block's brain: such a system would arguably lack mental states altogether, hence, Block argued, there has to be more to mentality than playing a functional role (Block 1980). But, unlike the Chinese network, both Inga and Otto are *bona fide* cognitive agents with mental states, so it makes perfectly good sense to ask whether they possess a particular mental state (ie. the belief that the museum is on 53rd Street) or not.

If functionalism is correct, this translates to the question of whether any state plays the appropriate role in their cognitive system. Functionalism asks us to disregard physical realization, for example the difference between brain tissue and pages of a notebook. Moreover, as Mark Sprevak has convincingly argued (Sprevak 2009), the spirit of functionalism also asks us to disregard the microfunctional differences that undoubtedly exist between Inga's and Otto's access to the relevant information. The macro-functional roles of the information stored in Inga's relevant brain-state and Otto's notebook are arguably the same. Therefore it seems we have to conclude that Otto also has the belief that the museum is on 53rd Street. The argument extends to any type of mental state which can be plausibly accounted for in terms of functional roles: for example, standing states like intentions or desires. It is less obvious whether, or how, the argument extends to episodes in the stream of consciousness whose identity arguably depends on their conscious or phenomenal character. Both Clark and Chalmers are inclined to think that consciousness does not extend in the way standing mental states do (Chalmers 2008; Clark 2010).[11]

The term "extended mind" suggests that the notebook is actually part of Otto's mind, or, put in more functionalist terms, the notebook is part of the physical reality that serves as a realizer for the functional states we attribute to Otto. This seems to be a dependence on things outside the subject that is different from the dependence in externalist theories discussed in section 2. We will return to this question in section 4.1.

3.4 Embodied cognition

The topic of "embodied" or "situated" cognition has received a lot of attention in cognitive science starting in the 1990s. The debates we have discussed so far have, by and large, been directly motivated by questions arising within philosophy: about the nature of intentionality, the proper account of representation, the philosophical theory of perception, the mind-body problem. In contrast, much of the historical and current background for discussing embodied cognition is found outside the usual disciplinary boundaries of philosophy. Part of the task of philosophers in this debate is, and has been, to distill the philosophical significance of certain ideas coming from the more empirical disciplines.

Robert Wilson and Lucia Foglia (2011) identify several key historical influences on the formation of embodied cognitive science, including three books that they regard as the first landmark publications in the area. In *Metaphors We Live By*, George Lakoff and Mark Johnson argued that many central cognitive processes are influenced by the use of metaphors, which, in turn, are deeply influenced by the kind of bodies human beings have and use in interacting with the world (Lakoff and Johnson 1980). Francisco Varela, in his book *The Embodied Mind*, co-authored with Evan Thompson and Eleanor Rosch, proposed an "enactive" program for cognitive science that questions "the assumption . . . that cognition consists of the representation of a world that is independent of our perceptual and cognitive capacities by a cognitive system that exists independent of the world" (Varela, Thompson and Rosch 1991, xx). Instead, cognitive structures emerge from the organism's interaction with the world: from the way sensory stimulation systematically changes as organisms and objects move (called "sensorimotor patterns" or "sensorimotor dependencies"). By using the term "embodied", the authors aim to highlight "first, that cognition depends upon the kinds of experience that come from having a body with various sensorimotor capacities, and second, that these individual sensorimotor capacities are themselves embedded in a more encompassing biological, psychological, and cultural context" (Varela et al. 1991, 173–174). As the quote also makes it clear, the scope of this thesis – unlike the extended mind thesis of the precious section – is meant to include conscious experiences, as well as standing states like beliefs.[12]

Continuing the list of key influences on embodied cognitive science, in robotics, Rodney Brooks (Brooks 1991a; 1991b) reported successful work in building robots based on a view of computational intelligence which did not rely on "independent information processing units which must interface with each other via representations. Instead, the intelligent system is decomposed into independent and parallel activity producers which all interface directly to the world through perception and action" (Brooks 1991a, 139). Brooks's insights feature prominently in Andy Clark's 1997 *Being There: Putting Brain, Body, and World Together Again*. Further historical influences mentioned by Wilson and Foglia include James Gibson's ecological view of perception (Gibson 1979), work on dynamical systems, and the dynamicist theory of cognitive development (Thelen and Smith 1994). Finally, a somewhat unexpected source of inspiration is to be found in the phenomenological philosophical tradition of the first part of the 20th century; in particular in the works of Husserl, Sartre, Heidegger, and Merleau-Ponty (see Chapter 1, The Phenomenological Tradition).

As these summaries of the origins of the embodied conception already indicate, the ideas coming together under the label of "embodied cognition" are rather diverse, and there isn't one single and specific thesis that represents the movement. We will now touch upon some of its central themes.

One dominant motif is a phenomenological reflection on mind and cognition, prominent in the works of philosophers like Merleau-Ponty and Heidegger. Phenomenologists point out that our view of the world is formed in close, and often unreflective, active interactions with things in the world, and those interactions, in turn, are essentially shaped by the nature of our body and sensory system. The resulting view is often styled as "anti-Cartesian", but it is instructive to see how it relates exactly to Descartes' actual views. Undoubtedly, this picture has a different flavor than the highly reflexive, contemplative, and abstract viewpoint that is often felt to be advocated by Descartes. There are many more, often metaphorical statements that aim to illustrate this contrast between "involvement" and "detachment", for example in the claim that once we get phenomenology right, we realize "that to perceive is to be in an interactive relationship with the world, not to be in an internal state that happens to be caused by the external world" (Cosmelli and Thompson 2011, 165). Arguably, many of these contrasts reveal an important difference in emphasis, but they hardly amount to serious doctrinal differences. After all, an interactive relationship is perfectly compatible with the idea that we have internal states caused by the world.

Second, though Descartes believed that the mind is an immaterial substance separable from the body, he fully acknowledged that as far as *actual* human psychology goes, sense-experience and the involvement of the body are crucial elements. "I am not merely present in my body as a sailor is present in a ship" (Descartes 1984, vol.2, 81), Descartes famously remarked.

As I mentioned in section 1, Descartes also had a partly empirical hypothesis about the role of the body in different mental processes. He thought that while brain states serve as proximal causes for sensory and affective mental states, the brain is not involved in pure thinking; instead, thinking takes place in the immaterial soul. Very few people today accept the existence of Cartesian immaterial substances, but it has been argued that the sharp Cartesian divide between pure thinking and the rest of mental phenomena survives in functionalist theories. As described in section 3.1, these theories hold that paradigmatic forms of cognition consist of centrally executed operations on highly abstract representations, sandwiched, but only contingently, between the input of a sensory system and the output to a motor system. A number of findings about the nature of cognition have been thought to undermine the classical computational picture.

Margaret Wilson (2002) provides a useful overview of some of these findings. First, cognition is situated: we often carry out cognitive tasks while perceptual information keeps coming in, and action is performed with a possible impact on the environment, both of which continuously modify the task at hand. Second, cognition is often under time-pressure that prevents building an abstract internal model of the world. Third, we off-load cognitive work on our body and on the environment: rotating the shapes in Tetris on the screen rather than in our head, we share the burden of holding and manipulating information with our environment. Fourth, much of cognition is directly for action, rather than for representation. All these ideas put considerable pressure on the claim that cognition is realized exclusively or even mainly by the kind of processes that figure in the classical computational view.

4. Varieties of "externalism"

4.1 Different conceptions of boundaries

The views presented so far all concern the boundaries of the mind in some sense. In this section, I will briefly compare these different senses. Susan Hurley distinguished between "what" and "how" externalism (Hurley 2010). "What" externalist theories (which include the theories we discussed in section 2) claim that some personal-level mental features – for example, content or phenomenal quality – are explained by external factors. Extended and embodied views belong to "how" externalism, on which external features "explain how the processes or mechanisms work that enable mental states" of specific types (Hurley 2010, 101). In earlier work (Hurley 1998), Hurley called how-externalism "vehicle" externalism, because it involves claims about the realizers or vehicles of mental states. In contrast, externalists of section 2 hold that we individuate certain mental states partly by their relations to their intentional objects – but this view need not say anything about vehicles. (I have refrained from calling embodied and embedded views "externalist", reserving this term only for what Hurley calls "what-externalism".)

Further differences between the different forms of "extensions" come to light if we consider the brain-in-a-vat scenario. In his review of Alva Noë's book *Action in Perception*, Ned Block illustrates his disagreement with Noë's enactive approach (which is a type of embodied view, on our classification) by speculating about a solitary brain-in-a-vat who, through an unlikely but not impossible chance fluctuation of particles, comes to existence in exactly the same physical state as the brain of an embodied human being (Block 2005). Block takes Noë to hold that the brain would not have the same experience as its embodied counterpart, and he argues that this is is implausible, because the body and the environment are merely causes of the experience, but not constitutive parts of the realizer of the experience.[13]

Block claims supervenience on the brain specifically for *experiences*, but not for all mental states. Though he is an internalist about experience, like the majority of philosophers of mind, he is an externalist about mental contents (the issue of extended mind is not addressed in the review). This way of presenting the matter suggests that all the different debates discussed in this chapter can be formulated in terms of which mental features do or do not supervene the brain or the body. However, Evan Thompson and Diego Cosmelli (2011) argued that setting up the opposition this way doesn't get to the heart of the enactive-embodied approach. Their interest is not the purely philosophical question about "the minimal metaphysical supervenience base" of experiences, but rather an explanatory framework for interdisciplinary research – for example, for research in neuroscience on the neural correlates of consciousness. On this latter approach, an interesting question is the bioengineering task of keeping a brain alive and functioning in a vat, and of providing stimuli that match our environment. Thompson and Cosmelli investigate this question in some detail, and find that the task is absolutely formidable, and the only way it could be done is to build something like a body for the brain and place it in an appropriate environment. They conclude:

> In the range of possible situations relevant to the explanatory framework of the neuroscience of consciousness, the brain in a vat thought experiment, strictly speaking, doesn't seem possible (because the envatted brain turns out to be an embodied brain after all).
>
> (Cosmelli and Thompson 2011, 173)

The extended mind hypothesis (Section 3.3) is usually classified together with, or even as one of the possible embodied views (Section 3.4), because of the apparent shared interest in the realization of cognitive processes (in other words, because of answering a how, rather than a what-question, to use Hurley's terminology). In fact, the motivations of the two views are rather different. The extended mind hypothesis, as explained above, is a consequence of the functionalist view that only functional roles matter and the nature of the physical realizer don't. Clearly, Otto's notebook could be replaced by a computer, by a tape recorder, by any kind of device that was capable of holding the abstract representations stored in Otto's notebook. This is quite alien to the spirit of embodied views, which emphasize the dependence of cognition on the particular shape of our bodies and the on the contingent variation of sensory stimulation with our interactions with the world. The two views are not incompatible, but, arguably, they limit each other's scope. States that are especially suitable for extension tend to employ multiply realizable, abstract representations – so these states are not strongly embodied. In contrast, embodied processes that depend on a contingent bodily setup are likely to resist extension (see also Clark 2008, part III).

4.2 Current state

Externalism, as defined in section 2, has become something like the orthodoxy in contemporary analytic philosophy of mind. Most philosophers who write on relevant topics are externalist at least about some mental features; that is, they hold that these features depend on factors external to a thinking subject.[14] Many are externalists about (at least some aspects of) content. Defenders of disjunctivist and relational views of perception are externalists about experiences. A further proposal which generated significant interest and debate was Timothy Williamson's claim that knowing is a state of mind (Williamson 2000). Since on this view, an ordinary knowing subject and her ignorant brain-in-a-vat counterpart have different mental states, this is also a form of externalism. In recent years, there has been some revival of an internalist defense (Farkas 2008; Mendola 2008), but this position remains in the minority.

The extended mind hypothesis, as discussed in section 3.3, remains a controversial thesis in philosophy, with committed defenders, committed opponents, and many agnostics. The findings described in section 3.4 give strong support to the claim cognitive processes significantly involve sensory input, motor output and interaction with the environment, so embodied cognitive science remains a robust research program. As we have seen in section 4.1 above, the focus of this program is often on empirical questions that go outside the usual disciplinary bounds of philosophy. But while the results strongly suggest that not all cognition is offline, abstract and representational, as Margaret Wilson (2002) notes, the same phenomena do not show that *no* cognition is performed in such a way. In his review of Varela, Thompson, and Rosch's *Embodied Mind* Daniel Dennett asked whether the enactive program was really revolutionary or rather a welcome shift in emphasis (Dennett 1993, 122). Dennett thought it was too soon to answer the question in 1993, and it is not obvious that the matter has been settled since then.

Notes

1 I would like to thank Tim Crane, Amy Kind, Philip Walsh, and Jeff Yoshimi for valuable comments on an earlier draft. Research for this chapter was supported by the Hungarian Scientific Research Fund, grant no. OTKA K-112542.
2 Descartes' *Meditations* are included in the second volume of his selected philosophical writings (Descartes 1984).
3 Frege's most important writings, including "On Sinn and Bedeutung" (1892) and "The Thought" (1918) are collected in Beaney 1997.
4 Putnam notes in a foreword to Pessin and Goldberg 1996 that at the time of writing "The Meaning of "Meaning"", he was not sure what the Twin Earth story entailed with respect to the mind (as opposed to meanings). But subsequently, he was persuaded by Burge and John McDowell that mental states also depend on factors outside us.
5 For defense of the disjunctive theory of perception, see McDowell 1982, Martin 2004. John Campbell is not a disjunctivist, but he also defends a form of externalism about perceptual experiences as a response to the question of how we can possess an objective environment; see his contribution in Campbell and Cassam 2014.

6 Brie Gertler (2012) assesses different detailed definitions of externalism, and concludes that there is no univocal thesis of externalism and internalism.
7 Here is an illustration: at the time of writing this chapter in October 2014, there are around 1,500 entries in the *Stanford Encyclopedia of Philosophy*, which is the most widely consulted internet reference work in analytic philosophy. Ninety-two of these entries (mostly on continental or feminist philosophy) refer to Freud, whereas, for example, Hilary Putnam is mentioned in 230 entries. The SEP entry on the "Philosophy of Psychiatry" does not contain a single reference to Freud's work. The term "psychoanalysis" is mentioned in 76 documents. In contrast, the number of documents that mention "cognitive science" is 175, "artificial intelligence" 119, "quantum mechanics" 138.
8 This would be true for example of U. T. Place, J.J.C. Smart, and David Armstrong, who published influential work defending physicalism in the 1950s and 60s; see Place 1956, Smart 1953 and Armstrong 1968.
9 I don't have statistics on the philosophical views of scientists, but it is interesting to note that most Nobel Prize winners in the 20th century who did research on the brain expressed some view in writing on the mind body-problem, and, with one exception, they were not physicalists. Charles Scott Sherrington (Nobel Prize 1932) held a "double aspect" theory; John Eccles (Nobel Prize 1963) was a dualist, Gerald Edelman (Nobel Prize 1972) defended non-reductive biologism, and Roger Wolcott Sperry (Nobel Prize 1981) defended a type of emergentism. The exception is Francis Crick (Nobel Prize 1962), who was an ardent physicalist.
10 Classic defenses of an early version of functionalism can be found in Putnam 1960 and 1967.
11 For various pros and cons in the debate, see the papers collected in Menary 2010.
12 For another development of the enactive conception, see Noë 2005.
13 For this type of criticism of the extended mind view, see also Adams and Aizawa (2010).
14 According to the 2009 survey conducted by PhilPapers, 51 percent of respondents accept or lean toward externalism, 20 percent accept or lean towards internalism, and 29 percent indicated "Other". However, we should note that many philosophers who accept dual content theories call themselves internalists, because they recognize some sort of narrow content in the contested cases. This hides the fact that they accept externalism about *some* mental features. For example, David Chalmers and Terry Horgan, philosophers who argued for a robust notion of narrow content, both claim they accept internalism, even though they both think that there is also an aspect of mental content which is broad. Horgan makes this clear in a comment: "I hold that the most fundamental kind of mental content is internalist (and phenomenally constituted), but that some thought-constituents also have a form of intentionality that constitutively depends in part on internal/external linkages" (PhilPapers Survey).

Bibliography

Adams, Fred and Ken Aizawa (2010). "Defending the Bounds of Cognition," in Menary (ed.): 67–80.
Armstrong, D. M. (1968). *A Materialist Theory of the Mind*. London: Routledge & Kegan Paul.
Beaney, Michael (ed.). (1997). *The Frege Reader*. Oxford: Blackwell Publishing.
Block, Ned (1980). "Troubles with Functionalism," in Block, Ned (ed.) *Readings in Philosophy of Psychology*. Cambridge, MA: Harvard University Press: 268–305.

Block, Ned (2005). "Review of *Action in Perception* by Alva Noë," *The Journal of Philosophy*, 102/5: 259–272.
Brown, Jessica (2004). *Anti-individualism and Knowledge*. Cambridge, MA: MIT Press.
Brooks, Rodney (1991a). "Intelligence without Representation," *Artificial Intelligence*, 47: 139–159.
Brooks, Rodney (1991b). "Intelligence without Reason," *Proceedings of 12th International Joint Conference on Artificial Intelligence*, Sydney, Australia: 569–595.
Burge, Tyler (1979). "Individualism and the Mental". Reprinted in Foundations of Mind: Philosophical Essays. Oxford: Clarendon Press, 2007: 100–150.
Campbell, John and Cassam, Quassim (2014). *Berkeley's Puzzle*. Oxford: Oxford University Press.
Chalmers, David (2002). "The Components of Content", in Chalmers, David (ed.), *Philosophy of Mind: Classical and Contemporary Readings*. Oxford: Oxford University Press: 608–633.
Chalmers, David (2006). "The Foundations of Two-dimensional Semantics", in Carpintero, M. Garcia, and Macia, J. (eds.), *Two-dimensional Semantics: Foundations and Applications*. Oxford: Oxford University Press: 55–140.
Chalmers, David (2008). "Foreword," in Clark (ed.): ix– xxix.
Chalmers, David, Manley, David and Wasserman, Ryan (eds.). (2009). *Metametaphysics*. Oxford: Clarendon Press.Clark, Andy (1997). *Being There: Putting Brain, Body, and World Together Again*. Cambridge, MA: MIT Press.
Clark, Andy (2008). *Supersizing the Mind: Embodiment, Action and Cognitive Extension*. Oxford: Oxford University Press.
Clark, Andy (2010). "Extended Mind Redux: A Response," http://opinionator.blogs.nytimes.com/2010/12/14/extended-mind-redux-a-response/.
Clark, Andy and Chalmers, David (1998). "The Extended Mind," *Analysis*, 58: 7–19.
Cosmelli, Diego and Thompson, Evan (2011). "Brain in a Vat or Body in a World: Brain-bound versus Enactive Views of Experience," *Philosophical Topics,* 39: 163–180.
Crane, Tim (2014). *Aspects of Psychologism*. Cambridge, MA: Harvard University Press.
Davidson, Donald (1987). "Knowing One's Own Mind", in *Proceedings and Addresses of the American Philosophical Association*, 60: 441–458.
Dennett, Daniel (1993). "Review of *The Embodied Mind: Cognitive Science and Human Experience* by Francisco J. Varela; Evan Thompson and Eleanor Rosch," *The American Journal of Psychology*, 106/1: 121–126.
Descartes, René (1984). *Philosophical Writings of René Descartes*. 3 volumes. Edited and translated by J. Cottingham, R. Stoothof, D. Murdoch and A. Kenny. Cambridge: Cambridge University Press.
Dretske, Fred (1981). *Knowledge and the Flow of Information*. Cambridge, MA: MIT Press.
Dreyfus, Hubert L. (1991). *Being in the World: Commentary on Heidegger's "Being and Time", Division 1*. Cambridge, MA: MIT Press.
Evans, Gareth (1982). *The Varieties of Reference*. Edited by John McDowell, Oxford: Clarendon Press.
Farkas, Katalin (2005). "The unity of Descartes's Thought," *History of Philosophy Quarterly*, 22/1: 17–30.
Farkas, Katalin (2008). *The Subject's Point of View*. Oxford: Oxford University Press.
Fodor, Jerry (1975). *The Language of Thought*. New York: Thomas Crowell.

Fodor, Jerry (1987). *Psychosemantics*. Cambridge, MA: Bradford Books.

Gertler, Brie (2012). "Understanding the Internalism-Externalism Debate: What is the Boundary of the Thinker?" *Philosophical Perspectives: Philosophy of Mind:* 51–75.

Gibson, J.J. (1979). *The Ecological Approach to Visual Perception*. Boston: Houghton Mifflin.

Hurley, Susan (1998). *Consciousness in Action*. London: Harvard University Press.

Hurley, Susan (2010). "The Varieties of Externalism," in Menary (ed.): 101–153.

Kaplan, David (1977). "Demonstratives," in Almog, J., Perry, J. and Wettstein, H. (eds.), *Themes from Kaplan*. Oxford: Oxford University Press, 1989: 481–563.

Kripke, Saul (1972). "Naming and Necessity," in Davidson, D. and Harman, G. (eds.), *Semantics of Natural Language*, 2nd edition. Dordrecht: Reidel Publishing Co.: 253–355.

Lakoff, George and Mark Johnson (1980). *Metaphors We Live By*. Chicago: University of Chicago Press.

Lau, Joe and Deutsch, Max (2014). "Externalism About Mental Content," *The Stanford Encyclopedia of Philosophy* (Summer 2014 Edition), Zalta, Edward N. (ed.). http://plato.stanford.edu/archives/sum2014/entries/content-externalism/.

McDowell, John (1982). "Criteria, Defeasibility and Knowledge," Reprinted in McDowell 1998: 369–394.

McDowell, John (1986). "Singular Thought and the Extent of Inner Space," Reprinted in McDowell 1998: 228–259.

McDowell, John (1994). *Mind and World*. Cambridge, MA: Harvard University Press.

McDowell, John (1998). *Meaning, Knowledge and Reality*. Cambridge, MA: Harvard University Press.

MacFarlane, John (2005). "Making Sense of Relative Truth," *Proceedings of the Aristotelian Society*, 105: 321–339.

Martin, M.G.F. (2004). "The Limits of Self-Awareness," *Philosophical Studies*, 120: 37–89.

Menary, Richard (ed.). (2010). *The Extended Mind*. Cambridge, MA: MIT Press.

Mendola, Joseph (2008). *Anti-Externalism*. Oxford: Oxford University Press.

Millikan, Ruth (1984). *Language, Thought and Other Biological Categories*. Cambridge, MA: MIT Press.

Noë, Alva (2005). *Action in Perception*. Cambridge, MA: MIT Press.

Papineau, David (1987). *Reality and Representation*, Oxford: Basil Blackwell.

Pessin, Andrew and Goldberg, Sanford (eds.). (1996). *The Twin Earth Chronicles*. Armonk, NY and London: M. E. Sharpe.

PhilPapers Survey (2009). http://philpapers.org/surveys/.

Place, U.T (1956). "Is Consciousness a Brain Process?" *British Journal of Psychology*, 47: 44–50.

Preyer, Gerhard and Peter, Georg (eds.). (2007). *Context-Sensitivity and Semantic Minimalism*. Oxford: Oxford University Press.

Putnam, Hilary (1960). "Minds and Machines," Reprinted in Putnam 1975b, 362–385.

Putnam, Hilary (1967). "The Nature of Mental States," Reprinted in Putnam 1975b, 429–440.

Putnam, Hilary (1975a). "The Meaning of 'Meaning,'" Reprinted in Putnam 1975b, 215–271.

Putnam, Hilary (1975b). *Mind, Language, and Reality*, Cambridge: Cambridge University Press.

Richard, Mark (1990). *Propositional Attitudes: An Essay on Thoughts and How We Ascribe Them*. Cambridge: Cambridge University Press.

Rey, G. (1997). *Contemporary Philosophy of Mind: A Contentiously Classical Approach*. Oxford: Basil Blackwell.

Russell, Bertrand (1917). "Knowledge by Acquaintance and Knowledge by Description," *Proceedings of the Aristotelian Society*, 1910–1911: 108–128.

Schroeder, Mark (2010). *Being For: Evaluating the Semantic Program of Expressivism*. Oxford: Oxford University Press.

Smart, J.J.C. (1953). "Sensations and Brain Processes," *Philosophical Review*, 68: 141–156.

Sprevak, Mark (2009). "Extended Cognition and Functionalism," *Journal of Philosophy*, 106(9): 503–527.

Strawson, P. F. (1959). *Individuals*. London: Methuen.

Thelen, E., and Smith, L. B. (1994). *A Dynamic Systems Approach to the Development of Cognition and Action*. Cambridge, MA: MIT Press.

Turing, Alan (1950). "Computing Machinery and Intelligence," *Mind*, 59: 433–460.

Varela, Francisco, Thompson, Evan and Rosch, Eleanor (1991). *The Embodied Mind: Cognitive Science and Human Experience*. Cambridge, MA: MIT Press.

Williamson, Timothy (2000). *Knowledge and Its Limits*. Oxford: Oxford University Press.

Williamson, Timothy (2006). "Must Do Better," in Greenough, P. and Lynch, M. (eds.), *Truth and Realism*. Oxford: Oxford University Press: 177–187.

Wilson, Margaret (2002). "Six Views of Embodied Cognition," *Psychonomic Bulletin and Review*, 9: 625–636.

Wilson, Robert A., and Foglia, Lucia (2011). "Embodied Cognition," *The Stanford Encyclopedia of Philosophy* (Fall 2011 Edition), Zalta, Edward N. (ed.). http://plato.stanford.edu/archives/fall2011/entries/embodied-cognition/

11

THE RISE OF COGNITIVE SCIENCE IN THE 20TH CENTURY

Carrie Figdor

1. Introduction

Cognitive science is the study of individual agency: its nature, scope, mechanisms, and patterns. It studies what agents are and how they function. This definition is modified from one provided by Bechtel, Abrahamsen, and Graham (1998), where cognitive science is defined as "the multidisciplinary scientific study of cognition and its role in intelligent agency." Several points motivate the modification. First (and least consequential), the multidisciplinarity of cognitive science is an accident of academic history, not a fact about its subject matter (a point also pressed in Gardner 1985). Second, the label "intelligent" is often used as a term of normative assessment, when cognitive science is concerned with behavior by entities (including possibly groups, as individual or collective agents) that are not considered intelligent, as well as unintelligent behavior of intelligent agents, for any intuitive definition of "intelligent".[1]

Third and most importantly, the term "cognition" is omitted from the definiens to help emphasize a position of neutrality on a number of contemporary debates. Cognition can often reasonably be equated with mental activity, but the mind has traditionally been associated or contrasted with the brain. The modified definition recognizes that whether or how much cognition is brain-based is a matter of considerable dispute (e.g., Clark 1997; Gallagher 2005; Adams and Aizawa 2008; Chemero 2011; Kiverstein and Miller 2015). That said, for reasons of brevity of exposition, I will often write in terms appropriate to the traditional brain-based framing of cognition.

In addition, the scope of cognition (and agency) is currently in flux. For example, if plants have cognition (Trewavas 2005; Calvo and Keijzer 2009), then brains and animal bodies are not required for cognition or agency. Other writers are more restrictive. For example, Von Eckardt 2003 sees the domain of cognitive science as the *human* cognitive capacities. My working assumption is that human-style cognition is a special case. Many people are most interested in human cognition. But what counts as cognitive will ultimately depend on the systems to which the basic conceptual framework of cognitive science can be fruitfully applied.

As conceptual history, the rise of cognitive science is the story of the articulation of the core concepts for explaining agency. This article explains five key innovations comprising the *basic explanatory package* of cognitive science. In traditional philosophical terms, they constitute the conceptual framework for explaining how the mind could be material. This package unifies the field despite the remaining conceptual and practical impediments of disciplinary boundaries, internal debates about how the package should be refined, and its incompleteness. It is assumed here that this package will be elaborated, not abandoned, in future work, just as the theory of evolution has continually unified biology despite tensions and controversies about its proper form.

The foundational ideas are associated with the main contributors and their main works; regrettably, discussion of the contributions of historical precursors and important contemporary figures is omitted for space reasons.[2] These ideas include the information-processing program (Alan Turing), neurons as information-processors (Warren McCulloch and Walter Pitts), feedback control of processing (Norbert Wiener), information as a measure of the structure of communication (Claude Shannon), and information-processing as a multiperspectival explanatory framework (David Marr). These ideas can be briefly described as follows, with details provided below.

Turing showed how recognizably rational behavior could be produced by an agent if very few distinct types of simple internal state transitions were sequenced in the right way. A human computer added columns of numbers, and so too could a simple Turing machine sequenced in the right way. McCulloch and Pitts showed how the basic internal machinery of the brain could be seen to realize these rational transitions. They mapped inferential steps involving propositions to transitions in states of neurons. Wiener described how the future behavior of such agents could depend on the impact of their prior responses on their environment. An agent can learn from experience when it can adaptively modify its behavior in response to experience that is itself a consequence of its prior behavior. Shannon showed how information could be understood and quantified in terms of the statistical or probabilistic structure inherent in communication. This structure is derived from conventional regularities that agents jointly create and can individually exploit to help achieve their goals. Marr showed that information-processing explanations shared an explanatory structure in which goals, processing steps, and physical operations would all be specified. This explanatory framework applied to non-rational as well as rational processes.

Of the five, Turing's and Shannon's contributions may be most fundamental: they articulated the core concepts of "processing" and "information" in "information-processing". In the case of Shannon, there are many other technical as well as colloquial concepts of information (Adriaans 2012). The admittedly controversial claim made here is that Shannon's concept is basic to cognitive science, and that its explanatory potential (unlike that of Turing's model) has barely begun to be elaborated (see, e.g., Isaac forthcoming, Figdor (MS)). I discuss its relation to the philosophical notion of representation or content in section 2.4.

A potential sixth core element of the package is a theory of the goals of and constraints on information-processing capacities at the agent level. Proposals for the social root of intelligence (e.g., Jolly 1966; Humphreys 1976; Dunbar 1998; Sterelny 2007) are attempts to make theoretical sense of agents' goals, assessments, expectations, and responses within their social contexts. Developing and integrating a basic framework of agentic goals vis-à-vis other agents is one of the main challenges facing 21st-century cognitive science.

The discussion below emphasizes the abstract nature of the core ideas. This feature has led, I believe, to some misunderstanding about the relation between cognitive science and the discipline-specific ways in which the ideas were initially appropriated, articulated, investigated, and deployed in explanation. For example, Turing's model did not come with fine print stating the limits of its explanatory power. As we are discovering, much can be done in artificial intelligence to satisfy military, industrial, and commercial aims without addressing the symbol grounding problem – the problem of fixing the reference of symbols or concepts. Solving this problem may be crucial for explaining some aspects of agency, but Turing's bare-bones model is not sufficient to solve it. That is why it is just a part of the basic explanatory package.

Similarly, the fact that post-behaviorist empirical psychology proceeded without looking at the brain is not the denial of an essential explanatory connection in cognitive science (nor, for that matter, in psychology). Significant advances in scientific investigation involving the brain had to wait until the 1990s. That was when the technology to measure ongoing neural activity with some degree of specificity during the performance of cognitive tasks became widely available. So when Searle (1980, 421) stated that "the whole idea of strong AI is that we don't need to know how the brain works to know how the mind works... [W]e can understand the mind without doing neurophysiology," this may be true of strong AI and parts of psychology yet false of cognitive science. The cognitive science-biology boundary is not yet fixed.

Finally, while the core ideas are abstract, they are fundamentally mathematical rather than philosophical, quantitative rather than qualitative. The genius of those contributing to the package was their ability to build conceptual bridges between intuitive conceptions of mind and non-intuition-based explanations of them. Philosophers have contributed significantly to cognitive science from the start – as critics (e.g., Searle 1980, Dreyfus 1992), integrators (e.g., Fodor 1983), collaborators (e.g., Churchland and Sejnowski 1992), champions (e.g., P. M. Churchland 1990; P. S. Churchland 1986), and theoreticians (e.g., Fodor 1975; Dennett 1987; Chalmers 1995). They will continue to do so not just in one or more of these roles (e.g. Block 2007), but also as disseminators (Hohwy 2014, Clark 2015), participants (Eliasmith 2013), and articulators of new social and moral concerns that arise as intuitions about human cognition and agency are challenged (Roskies 2010; Allen et al. 2000). We think about the mind differently now than we did 100 years ago, due to both theoretical and empirical advances. Future philosophical participation in cognitive science will have to take this change into account.

2. The basic explanatory package

We do resent the hiatus between our mental terminology and our physical terminology. It is being attacked in a very realistic fashion today.

McCulloch 1943 (from the Warren S. McCulloch Papers, cited in Piccinini 2004)

Cognitive science aims to explain agency in material terms – in particular, in mathematical terms that bridge logic (mind) and engineering (matter). Oddly, mathematics is frequently omitted from the list of disciplines contributing to cognitive science even though many pioneers of cognitive science, including Turing, Pitts, Wiener, and Shannon, were mathematicians. In contrast, neuroscience, philosophy, psychology, linguistics, and computer science are usually listed as constitutive disciplines (e.g., Bechtel et al. op.cit., 69–70; Miller 2003, 143; Heckathorn 1989), even though (like mathematics) most areas of these disciplines have nothing to do with cognitive science. Anthropology is also included even though it quickly parted ways from cognitive science (Bender et al. 2010). Sociology or "sociocultural studies" (Bechtel et al. op.cit., 93) is mainly noted for its absence (Bainbridge 1994, 408), underlining the lag in integrating social aspects of cognition.

The omission of mathematics may be due to the fact that, until Turing, we lacked an empirically plausible model of how the mind could be material. Without such a model, materialists could do little to counter the intuition, and philosophical position, that the mind is exempt from the mathematico-engineering, mechanical explanation of the rest of nature. Gottfried Leibniz (a mathematician) had the idea of a logical calculus in the 17th century, but he also denied that perception and consciousness could be implemented in a machine (Monadology 17).[3] With Turing's breakthrough, we could retrospectively identify percursors – more mathematicians. In the 18th century, Charles Babbage invented (but did not fully build) an analytical engine for general computing that operated on the same principles as the Jacquard loom, which used sequences of punchcards to organize sequences of the machine's weaving operations (Copeland 2008). George Boole (1854) found that mathematical operations performed on sets could also be logical operators that operated on propositions or sentential thought contents, suggesting that the resulting operations were laws of thought. Gottlob Frege (1879) added a logic that allowed for operations on parts of propositions, formalizing deductive inference.

The study of these ideas, blended in mathematical logic, unified the conceptual founders of cognitive science (Aspray 1985). The ideas themselves provided materialists with a clear engineering target: to build something that can do these logical operations. Doing this would at least get the ball rolling.

2.1 1936: Turing: software

Turing (1936) provided the first explanatory link between these logical operations and a machine that could perform them. He showed that any well-defined logical or mathematical problem that had an effective solution – that could be solved in a finite number of steps – could be solved by following simple state transitions in a sequence. Although a Turing machine was not a physical device, each step could be imagined physically as a series of squares on a tape plus a read-write device. The device would scan a square (start the transition), erase or print a 1 or 0 on the square (perform a simple operation), and move to the next square (end the transition). These state transitions could be realized by a physical device with appropriate on/off switches as 1s and 0s and a way to distinguish and respond to them. 1s and 0s are numerically, not psychologically, interpreted states, but the way was open to interpret thoughts as complex symbols that could be similarly manipulated. Turing also showed that given enough space and time a single sequence of simple steps – a universal Turing machine – could encompass any other sequence by embedding them (or inserting them as needed) in the larger sequence. Like a mind, a universal Turing machine was versatile ("general-purpose"): it could solve "any problem that can be reduced to a programme of elementary instructions" (Williams and Kilburn 1948).

But *can* all mental operations be reduced to a series of elementary instructions? Descartes argued that animals lacked minds because they lacked language, the means by which humans can express an infinite variety of thoughts. (He did not consider prelinguistic infants, inter alia.) But whether universal Turing machines were as versatile as minds did not have to turn on intuitive measures of versatility. As Alan Newell, Cliff Shaw, and Herbert Simon – pioneers in developing computer programs with psychologically interpretable states and transitions[4] – put it:

> [A] program incorporating such [elementary information] processes, with appropriate organization, can in fact solve problems. This aspect of problem solving has been thought to be "mysterious" and unexplained because it was not understood how sequences of simple processes could account for the successful solution of complex problems. The theory dissolves the mystery by showing that nothing more need be added to the constitution of a successful problem solver.
>
> (1958, 152)

"Dissolves" may be overstating matters, but the demystifying of mind had begun.

Turing's theory left open how an embodied universal Turing machine might be designed. The first programmable computers, which were built in the 1940s (Williams and Kilburn op.cit.; von Neumann 1945; Godfrey and Hendry 1993), were designed to meet engineering goals. For example, optimizing operational efficiency by means of central program-storage unit (a Central Control) entailed minimizing the flexibility of the operations (von Neumann 1966: secs. 2.2, 2.3). But so what, if any needed flexibility could be left up to a human programmer? Similarly, ease of repair could be optimized by building a "fragile" machine that would stop operating at an error (von Neumann 1966: 73), even if this meant they did not operate like brains, which isolated problems for working on them on the side.

Such engineering decisions should not be confused with limits on the explanatory potential of Turing's model. Dreyfus (1992) argued that computing can't explain human intelligence because the latter is context-sensitive and thus not rule-governed. Similarly, the fragility of von Neumann-style computers was treated as a bug by early champions of connectionism (e.g., Churchland 1990), an alternative computing design based on neurophysiology (described below). Fragility, flexibility, and context-dependence are concepts in the same family as the intuitive idea of versatility. Turing's model left open how any of these features might be realized in a universal Turing machine, and is consistent with a continuum of cognitive systems or agents of different degrees of versatility.

Nevertheless, the immediate assimilation of minds to computers by some psychologists and early AI researchers revealed exuberant hopes for how much mind could be explained with these first incarnations of Turing's model. Due to arguments showing that no formal logical system could be used to prove all formulas that we recognize as being true, Turing was aware that a simple Turing machine could not do everything a human mind could do (Copeland and Shagrir 2013). But Turing (1950) also linked his processing story to human linguistic behavior by proposing the Turing Test, in which an interrogator tries to determine if her hidden interlocutor is a human or a computer. He predicted a computer would pass the Turing Test within fifty years; it remains unpassed. Simon reportedly predicted in 1957 that a computer would beat a human chess champion within ten years; Big Blue beat Gary Kasparov in 1997.[5] Searle's (1980) Chinese-room thought experiment, which concludes that there is no understanding in a system that realizes an unelaborated Turing machine, provided a sharp rhetorical counter to these claims.

The early exuberance may also have reflected the fact that to experimental psychologists Turing's model provided a viable non-introspectivist alternative research programme to behaviorism. In the early days of scientific psychology, introspectivist or structuralist psychologists (such as Wilhelm Wundt and Edward Titchener) used the reports of trained introspectors as evidence for the workings of the mind. When introspectors disagreed, there was no objective criterion for determining who might be right. Such unresolvable conflicts discredited structuralism as scientific psychology. Radical behaviorism went to the opposite extreme: the only allowable evidence was observable behavior or environmental contingencies, and only behavior needed to be explained. Behaviorism in this radical form never took hold in developmental, comparative, social, perceptual, or clinical psychology, and was not dominant outside the US (Greenwood 1999; Miller 2003); even B. F. Skinner, its most well-known defender, was conflicted about it (Baars 2003). But where it was influential, its influence was profound: Neisser's 1967 *Cognitive Psychology*, hailed as the ur-text of post-behavioristic experimental psychology, had six chapters on vision, four on audition, and just one slim final chapter on higher cognition.[6]

As stored-program computing took off, experimental psychologists were facing a growing pile of anomalies that motivated looking inside the behaviorist's black box. Miller (1956) showed that short-term memory capacity stayed constant at around seven 'chunks' of information because items could be recoded into new 'chunks': for example, a 10-digit number is more easily remembered by being recoded into three chunks (e.g., 123–456–7890). This showed that internal cognitive machinery was needed to explain memory. Chomsky (1959) argued that children's linguistic output was governed by grammatical rules (or violated those rules in regular ways) that were underdetermined by the speech they heard as stimulus. This evidence of the 'poverty of the stimulus' (its inadequacy to explain the output) showed that internal operations were needed to explain language.

These and other results made the emerging cognitive science of information-processing highly attractive: it seemed "complicated enough to do everything that cognitive theorists have been talking about" (Miller et al. 1960, 43). What they had been talking about, inter alia, were ways to explain phenomena that made behaviorism implausible. Thus, psychologists took away from Turing the lesson that "if they could describe exactly and unambiguously anything that a living organism did, then a computing machine could be built that could exhibit the same behavior with sufficient exactitude to confuse the observer" (Baddeley 1994, 46).

No wonder, then, that Turing's model was immediately elaborated at a level appropriate to human-centered psychology: the symbols were interpreted as natural-language-like concepts or mental representations, and the rules were the rules of deductive logic or heuristics (Fodor 1975; Newell and Simon 1976; Miller, Galanter, and Pribram op.cit., 3). This 'rules-and-representations' research program came to be known as classical computationalism. The stored-program computer of von Neumann's design was the machine for which these first psychologically interpreted internal state transitions were developed. They were specified in the form of software programs written in high-level programming languages.

The autonomy of psychology from biology (or neuroscience in particular) should also be understood in this context. Off-loading problems that are not of direct interest, particularly if the technology for investigating them is not yet available, is a rational scientific strategy. As Newell, Shaw, and Simon (op.cit.: 163) put it: "Discovering what neural mechanisms realize these information-processing functions in the human brain is a task for another level of theory construction." The Turing-inspired research left open how much progress could be made without engaging with other levels of theory construction.

2.2 1943: McCulloch and Pitts: brainware

A materialist explanation of agency requires a theory of how physical agents could be cognitive systems. Assuming humans as the prototype of such an agent, McCulloch (a neurophysiologist) and Pitts (a mathematician) provided this theory. They proposed that neurons were biological logic gates.

A logic gate is a unit whose operations can be interpreted in terms of the truth table for the logical operations of 'and' and 'or', the operations in Boolean logic. An 'and' gate fires a pulse if and only if its two input channels both fire, mirroring the way a conjunction – A and B – is true if and only if both A and B are true. An 'or' gate fires if at least one of its two input channels fires, mirroring the way a disjunction – A or B – is true if and only if at least one of the constituent sentences is true. A McCulloch-Pitts neuron is an abstract biological analogue of an electrical switch or relay, a basic component of a von Neumann computer (von Neumann 1945: 4.2, 4.3; Wiener 1948: Ch. 5; Arbib 2000, 212). McCulloch-Pitts neurons were binary in operation, so their states could be associated with propositions: activation could be associated with truth values (on/1/true, off/0/false) and patterns of activation with inference. While such sparse coding (i.e., 1 activated neuron = 1 true proposition) is empirically wildly implausible, this interpretation is the simplest that directly links Turing's model, with its simple state transitions, to the activity of the basic operating units of actual brains.[7] This link presupposed the discovery by neuroscientist Santiago Ramon y Cajal that neurons do not form a continuous net but are discrete units that stand in electrochemical relations.

The McCulloch-Pitts theory inspired connectionist or neural network computing. Connectionist networks are virtual collections of McCulloch-Pitts neurons running on standard computers. They have simple units (nodes) with connections to other nodes. Input nodes are analogous to sensory neurons, output nodes to motor neurons, and "hidden" layers of nodes to neurons that mediate between input and output. Numerical weights on the connections regulate the amount of input (activation) passed or propagated from one node to another. When a node obtains sufficient net input from its incoming connections to reach or pass a firing threshold, it sends its output (fires) to the nodes to which it is connected by its outgoing connections. The weights on the connections at one stage of processing determine the activation pattern at the next stage.[8]

Connection weights implicitly contain the record of past activation and so collectively embody what the network has learned from experience. The weights are adjusted automatically or by a human modeler using a learning rule. For example, a simple Hebbian learning rule (after psychologist Donald O. Hebb) increases the numerical value assigned to the connection between two nodes that co-activate. This makes them more likely to be co-activated in the future, mimicking the neurophysiological feature that synaptic connections are strengthened when two neurons are co-activated (called long-term potentiation, or, as the slogan goes, "neurons that fire together wire together").

Connectionist-style modeling of cognitive capacities began in the 1940s and 1950s but was overshadowed by programming research until the 1986 publication of *Parallel Distributed Processing* (Rumelhart, McClelland, and the PDP Research Group 1986), which gathered papers on neural net research in perception, verb parsing, and other capacities. However, while early champions of connectionism approvingly contrasted their brain-like architecture with that of stored-program computing, McCulloch-Pitts neurons are no less abstract than the squares on a Turing machine tape. For example, there is no distinction between kinds of neurons and no means to represent the role of neuromodulators in realizing the context-dependence and variability of neural signaling (Dayan 2012; Izhikevich 2007). In fact connectionist networks are now used to model all kinds of networks (Baronchelli et al. 2013). Nodes and weighted connections (now also called edges) can represent, respectively, agents and the relative importance of interagent relations (Froese 2014); words and their frequency of association (Borge-Holthoefer and Arenas 2009; and ideas and the spread of innovation (Mason et al. 2008).

That said, there are important differences. In classical computing, there is one series of computations,, represented by symbolic-program-governed operations on squares of tape. (More than one series can be run in parallel, but they are equivalent to a single series.) In a connectionist network, multiple computations – each represented by the equation-governed activation of each neural logic gate – go on simultaneously. In classical computationalism the problem is to write a program that will generate the desired output given the input; in connectionism the problem is to get the connection weights set so that the desired output is generated from the input. These differences yield interesting differences in terms of their explanatory power. Serial, stored-program computing is terrific for modeling logical operations, while parallel, weighted-connection computing is terrific for partitioning data into classes by frequency of association.

The relations between these types of computing and between each type and psychological processes are still debated. One way this debate has been framed is whether connectionist networks describe a cognitive level directly or whether they implement classical computation (Fodor and Pylyshyn 1988; Smolensky 1991; Aizawa 1992). Currently, the activation patterns of the hidden layers in neural networks that are used to model brain activity have no clear psychological interpretation. Whether these patterns need to be so interpreted is also a matter of debate (Bechtel 2009).

2.3 1948: Wiener: feedback control

Turing's model did not say how symbols or rules for manipulating them could be modified. Since many agents learn from experience, their agency cannot be explained by Turing machines that lack an internal learning mechanism. Wiener provided a model of feedback control, building on ideas from 19th-century physicist James Clerk Maxwell.

Wiener (with his collaborator physiologist Arturo Rosenblueth) coined the term "cybernetics" (from the Greek for "steersman", 1961, 11) for the study of "control and communication in the animal and the machine" – physical systems, living or not. A feedback loop is an agent-environment causal loop (or an epicycle in it) that allows for adjustment of the agent's behavior (or a stage of it) in the light of what occurs in the environment as a result of its prior behavior. To use Wiener's example (1961, 7), the muscle motions involved in picking up a pencil require some sort of information that will guide the appropriate motor commands at each moment in a way that depends on how much farther away the pencil is at any moment. The motion of your arm, hand, and fingers at any time depends on the way the environment now affects your eyes (the source of the visual input of your arm position relative to the pencil) which depends on the motion you made a moment ago.

Cybernetics complicated the core explanatory package structurally and conceptually. In a simple Turing machine, the dependency between two states is set by a rule. Providing the initial input is like tapping the first domino in a series. In a simple feedforward neural network – in which connections propagate activation in one direction, from input to output – activation in nodes closer to output nodes cannot affect activation in nodes closer to input nodes. The updating of the network's connection weights by the network modeler is analogous to thought-insertion. In both cases, internal feedback loops are needed to enable outputs at a later stage to be used as input in an earlier stage. Of course, a system may be able to get feedback but not be able to use it to alter its behavior. Where there is feedback control, there is also the capacity to change behavior by using feedback. Where in addition the change in behavior is adaptive, or responsive to environmental contingencies, there is also learning.

In this way, cybernetics also introduced the concepts of goals, expectations, and assessments into the basic explanatory package: a system that has the capacity to generate and use feedback to control its behavior adaptively is a system with goals (or final states), expectations (intermediate states), and ways to assess its input in the light of these expectations and goals. The feedback control concept applies to "a learning system that *wants* something, that adapts its behavior in order to maximize a special signal from the environment" (Sutton and Barto 1998: Preface). Understanding such a system requires understanding the many ways in which it is coupled with its environment.

Like the other elements of the core explanatory package, the cybernetic model is abstract enough to apply to a wide range of systems. Like them, too, cybernetics was elaborated early on in psychological terms. Miller, Galanter, and Pribram (1960) adopted the model to describe "how actions are controlled by an organism's internal representation of its universe." Their motivation was clear:

> The men who have pioneered in this area [of computing and programming] have been remarkably innocent about psychology – the creatures whose behavior they want to simulate often seem more like a mathematician's dream than like living animals.
>
> (op.cit.: 3)

They theorized that stimulus and response were stages of the same complex feedback loop, which they called a TOTE unit ("Test-Operate-Test-Exit"). What an organism did was guided by the outcomes of TOTE units, which could be organized hierarchically (that is, feedback loops within feedback loops). Such complications were critical for the information-processing paradigm to even begin to explain human agency.

More recently, the cybernetic idea is reflected in the predictive error minimization or Bayesian brain model of whole-brain function (Friston 2010; Clark 2015; Hohwy 2014), presaged by Rosenblueth, Wiener, and Bigelow (1943). A Bayesian model is one in which a system's states (often interpreted as its beliefs or hypotheses) are updated using Bayes's theorem. The theorem calculates the adjustments in the level of belief or credence one should have in a hypothesis in the light of new evidence and one's prior credence in that hypothesis. On the predictive brain model, the brain (or a structure within it) compares a new input value to an expected value, calculates the difference or error, if any, between the expected value and the actual input value, and makes an adjustment so that at the next stage its subsequent input is closer to its expectation. The system can adjust the hypothesis that generated the initial expected value to get a new expectation and then act much as it did, or it can adjust its subsequent behavior to get new input that will more closely match its expected value, or a bit of both.

When a feedback control loop is spatiotemporally tight, it is tempting to argue that a system does not require internal models or representations to explain its behavior. To borrow van Gelder's (1995) illustrative example, the Watt governor for a steam engine continuously and mutually adjusts linear motion and centrifugal force because these forces are realized by mechanically coupled parts (a throttle valve, a spinning spindle with weighted arms). But not all feedback control loops are so tight or so closely linked to sensorimotor capacities (as with Weiner's own example of reaching for a pencil). For example, reinforcement learning, when rewarded behavior becomes more frequent, falls squarely within the cybernetic model and yet requires non-behavioristic explanation. As the predictive brain hypothesis is critically examined, the debate over the need for representational notions in neural networks (and, by implication, brains) is likely to expand to include the concepts of goals, expectations, and assessments that are integral to cybernetics.

2.4 1948: Shannon: information

So far, the explanatory package has focused on the "processing" in "information-processing". But what is information? Shannon's (1948) answer, building on Nyquist (1924) and Hartley (1928), is derived from his theory of communication. Communication is information transfer between agents. A core concept of information can be extracted from agents' coordinated communicative actions, which can be quantified.

Warren Weaver, Shannon's collaborator and communicator, distinguishes three basic problems in communication: the technical problem of accurate transfer of information from sender to receiver (was the message transmitted accurately?); the semantic problem of interpretation of meaning by the receiver as compared to the intended meaning of the sender (was the message understood in the intended way?); and the effectiveness problem of the success with which the meaning conveyed to the receiver leads to the receiver's desired conduct (did the message lead the receiver to respond as the sender intended?). Answers to the latter two questions are constrained by answers to the first. As Shannon (1948, 1) notes, the semantic aspect of communication, and specifically the problem of reference, is irrelevant to "the engineering problem" of information transfer. It does not follow that his solution to the engineering problem is irrelevant to explaining reference or intentionality – that is, the ability of minds to represent aspects of the external world in such a way that it is also possible for them to *mis*represent those aspects). To the contrary, the theory describes the characteristics of a communication system that make reference possible. The link from reference to intentional contents – paradigmatically, thoughts about objects and their properties – will depend on how language and thought are related. For brevity, I assume here that at least some contentful mental states are partly, if not determinately, encoded in brain states (Dennett 1975), and that language expresses these contents, however imperfectly.

Shannon's theory "is specifically adapted to handle one of the most significant but difficult aspects of meaning, namely the influence of context" (Weaver 1949):

> The concept of information applies not to the individual message, as the concept of meaning would, but rather to the situation as a whole, the unit information indicating that in this situation one has an amount of freedom of choice, in selecting a message, which it is convenient to regard as a standard or unit amount.

In philosophy, a linguistic context is typically an extra-linguistic setting in which an utterance occurs, described in qualitative terms – who is talking to whom, when, where, about what. Here, a linguistic context is the structure of the language to which the message belongs and which constrains the meanings that can be communicated. This linguistic context is quantified in the theory, and a quantitative concept of information can be extracted from it. As Weaver (op.cit.: 11) puts it, "information relates not so much to what you do say, but to what you could say." Shannon's theory, like the other elements of the core explanatory package, is apt for many kinds of agents and communication systems, such as neural signalling (Dayan and Abbott 2001). But, for brevity, I focus on the primary case of human linguistic communication.

In human language, the basic constraints on the set of possible messages is given by the statistical structure of the language in which source and receiver participate. The statistical structure of a language is reflected in its written form, which encodes the spoken form that directly expresses thought. The first letter of a sentence is maximally uncertain; it is most informative (has the most information) in that it constrains all subsequent letter choices while the only constraint on it is that the language contains that letter.[9] The frequencies of and relationships between letters can be quantified. The more the first choice constrains the second, the less information the second letter will contain: if the first letter is "Q" then given the features of English it is overwhelmingly likely that the next letter will be "U". English is about 50 percent redundant (for strings of up to eight letters): about half the letters or words we use are chosen by us, and about half are determined by the statistical structure of English. This is why we can figure out badly garbled or incomplete messages.[10]

In short, in communication the U is redundant; it contains no more information than was given by the choice of Q; its presence is far from random; it is highly probable given the selection of Q; its entropy is low; we experience no surprise upon seeing a U; once you see a Q you already know what comes next. These are all ways of expressing the same probabilistic relationship that is the basis of the unit of information. A unit of information is a measure of how much freedom a source has in selecting a message. Information transfer can be quantified in terms of the probabilities assigned to each message in a set of possible messages that a sender could select to send to the receiver. The larger the set of possible messages, the more source freedom; the more source freedom, the more receiver uncertainty regarding which message will be selected. Greater freedom of choice, greater uncertainty, and greater quantity of information go hand in hand (Weaver 1949).

What is not stated explicitly in Shannon's theory is the fact that the statistical structure captured in letter frequencies encodes some (but not all) of the conventions that create a language, distinguishing utterances or inscriptions from noise. Meaningfulness involves further conventions, a prominent account of which has been developed by Skyrms 2010, following Lewis 1969 and, before him, Grice 1957 (see also Isaac (forthcoming) and Figdor (MS), among others in this vibrant area of new research). Other places to look for insight into conventions these might well be anthropology (Bender et al. 2010) and other cultural and social sciences. The concept of information in standard informational or teleoinformational theories of content (e.g. Dretske 1988; Millikan 1984; Neander 2017) is in effect pure reference, divorced from and independent of communication. Shannon's theory prompts thinking of reference as the upshot of additional constraints on communication, while leaving open how constrained a communication system must be, and which constraints it must have, in order for agents using that system to count as having representations (or intentionality) in the philosophical sense.[11]

In this vein, Weaver (op.cit.:14) speculatively adds into the communication process a step of statistical semantic decoding after the engineering receiver decodes the signal back into a message (e.g., the pulses of Morse code into English letters). This "semantic receiver" – currently just a black box – would match the statistical semantic characteristics of the message to the statistical semantic characteristics of the totality of receivers or the subset of them that the source wishes to affect. Within this black box, the causal relations of informational semantics would appear as statistical or probabilistic patterns of agent-world interaction. From this perspective, the man in Searle's (op.cit.) Chinese room does not understand the symbols he manipulates because his rulebook only embodies, metaphorically, the engineering receiver.

2.5 1982: Marr: explanation

While many of the elements in the core explanatory package were discovered or derived from work that occurred during World War II, the post-war period involved the institutionalization of cognitive science and the development of these ideas within recognized institutional and disciplinary strictures. (Sept. 11, 1956 – the second day of a three-day Symposium on Information Theory at MIT – has been cited (Miller 2003, 142; Bechtel et al. op.cit.: 37) as an unofficial birthdate of cognitive science.) Marr, a vision scientist, drew some general explanatory lessons from the emerging information-processing framework. Reacting to his contemporaries' focus on the physiology of single neurons in visual processing, Marr held that a full explanation of vision would require understanding not just physical mechanisms but also their organization and contexts of operation.

Marr (1982, 24) proposed that explaining any information-processing system required answering three different sorts of questions about it. These could be described and conceptualized in terms of three explanatory levels or analyses (Bechtel and Shagrir 2015; Shagrir 2010). The computational level involved explaining the why or goal of a particular kind of processing: What is the problem that the system need to solve? The algorithmic level involved explaining how this goal could be achieved in terms of the steps or state transitions leading to it: What sorts of representations and rules are used to solve the problem? The implementation level involved explaining how physical structures might realize these state transitions: What physical mechanisms instantiate these representations and their processing? Marr's approach yielded a common explanatory currency for integrating cognitive science research across disciplines, from neurobiology to cognitive psychology, and expanded later by Marr's collaborator Thomas Poggio to include social phenomena.

Marr, with Poggio and Ellen Hildreth, illustrated this approach by reframing visual processing into the same classical computational terms that were being used to explain higher cognitive capacities. Information-processing was not just about playing chess, but also perceiving objects. Systems within human agents could also be understood in the same basic information-processing terms. For example, activity in a particular area of V1 was for edge detection (computational level). It achieved this goal using rules for calculating zero-crossings (algorithmic level); and neural and other biological and biochemical machinery in this area of V1 implemented these algorithms. V1 is the most common label for the tip of the occipital lobe, at the back of the brain, where visual information is initially processed after passing through the retinas and subcortical brain structures. Additional processing in other visual areas would eventually yield a 3D image of an object.

The three levels of analysis could apply to many complex systems. Answers to any one of questions would provide constraints on answers to the others. So explaining any one system would require referring to systems at other levels:

> It is a feature of such [complex information-processing] tasks, arising from the fact that the information processed in the machine is only

loosely constrained by the physical properties of the machine, that they must be understood at different, though inter-related, levels.

(1981, 258)

In the case of vision, without answers at all three levels, describing the activity of neurons in response to specific stimuli, and even how these neurons are connected, would not yield an explanation of the phenomenon of vision. The need for multiple explanatory levels is hardly limited to cognition (O'Malley et al. 2013).

Other than in machine vision, Marr's emphasis on finding algorithms by which visual-feature outputs are computed (as in edge detection) has been superceded by a greater focus on real-world perception and embodied cognition (e.g., O'Regan and Noe 2001) and neural network computing methods (e.g., Olshausen and Field 1996). Debate over the necessity for symbolic representations in cognitive science has also sparked debate regarding the necessity for the algorithmic level in particular, given the classical computational terms in which Marr stated his theory. The relative independence of the levels, or the answers to the questions, has also been a matter of debate (although Marr and Poggio emphasized their interdependence). More recently, the contemporary search for canonical neural computations (Carandini 2012) pushes the explanatory framework downwards, while Poggio (2012, 1021) pushes it outward by adding learning and development to the three original levels.

Conclusion: what lies ahead?

As long as the mind remains a black box, there will always be a donkey on which to pin dualist . . . intuitions.

Greene and Cohen 2004, 1781

The first century of cognitive science was largely a matter of formulating the basic explanatory package for materialism and exploring how much could be explained by these ideas. Different disciplines interpreted that framework in the ways most suited to their available technologies, training, and immediate explanatory goals. We do not yet have a comprehensive materialism, but there are advances going on in every direction.

One important example may be theories of consciousness (Dehaene et al. 1998; Oizumi et al. 2014; Tononi and Koch 2014), which had largely been left to philosophers (e.g., Chalmers op.cit., Block 1995) during "a century of taboo" in science (Baars 2003, fn. 1). This acceptance of consciousness as a scientific explanandum has been accompanied by efforts to accept reports of introspectively accessible conscious states as valid evidence (Jack and Roepstorff 2002; 2003). Clinical cases (e.g., detection of neural activity in vegetative-state patients), research in animal cognition, and advances in robotics are contributing to this final rejection of radical behaviorism and dualism.

New discoveries in neuroscience are also altering traditional ways of thinking about the mind. For example, the perception/cognition distinction is under siege given the discovery of the huge cortical allocation in higher primates to visual processing and new theories of vision in which the goal of vision is recognizing meaningful social stimuli (Nakayama 2010, 15). In memory research, our intuitive concept of memory as something stored in the brain, rather than constructed and elaborated in context, seems to get human memory wrong and computer memory right. Neuroimaging studies show overlap in brain areas involved in remembering past experiences and imagining or simulating possible future experiences. This suggests that remembering and imagining may be forms of a single process for preparing for the future, rather than distinct processes of recalling a stored representation and engaging in stimulus-independent thought (Schacter et al. 2012).

While the 21st century has already been dubbed the century of the brain (Flavell 2000), it is also likely to be the century of the social (see also Bechtel et al. op.cit.: 90). The fact that early conceptual innovations regarding social cognition arose from field work with animals (e.g. Jolly op.cit.) may explain why they were not integrated earlier: the very idea of animal cognition was and to some degree remains a matter of debate (Shettleworth 2010). But enactivist and embodied cognitive research points in the opposite direction from that recommended in Fodor's (1980) brief for methodological solipsism, a pragmatic recommendation for research modeled on Descartes' solipsistic method for discovering the essence of mind. This push away from solipsism has been a thread within cognitive science for some time (e.g. Thelen and Smith 1994; Gibson 1979; Brooks 1990; 1991). Social context is now being theorized in terms of multi-agent systems engaged in cooperation, communication, and learning.

It seems likely that the basic conceptual package for explaining agency will soon be fully elaborated in outline if not in its empirical details. Near the start of the last century, psychologist Karl Lashley summed up the materialist viewpoint as follows:

> The vitalist cites particular phenomena . . . and denies the possibility of a mechanistic account of them. But he thereby commits what we might call the egotistic fallacy. On analysis, his argument reduces every time to the form, "*I* am not able to devise a machine that will do these things; therefore no one will ever conceive of such a machine.
>
> (1923, 269)

If one substitutes "dualism" for "vitalism", a similar remark might be made regarding cognitive science at the start of the 21st century. Dualism will always remain conceivable, but an empirically testable theoretical framework for materialism is just a matter of time.

Notes

1 For example, Newell and Simon's (1976) physical symbol system hypothesis – that a physical symbol system has the necessary and sufficient means for intelligent action – covered humans and computers alike. They agreed that only systems of sufficient complexity and power could exhibit general intelligence, but intelligent action was not necessarily human action.

2 Besides Bechtel et al. op.cit., Boden 2006 is an authoritative and comprehensive discussion. Aspray 1985: 120 provides a detailed chronology of key relevant works.

3 The influence of Leibniz's logic on 19th-century logicians is disputed (Peckhaus 2009), although Wiener (1961: 12) calls Leibniz the "patron saint" of cybernetics and Shannon (1948: 52) in turn credits Wiener as an important influence. What is indisputable is that the isolated idea of a logical calculus had no impact on the development of a materialist alternative to dualism prior to Turing, who relied directly on Boole, as did Shannon; meanwhile, Pitts was a student of Carnap, and Newell, Shaw, and Simon demonstrated the information-processing paradigm's possibilities when their Logic Theorist program provided a more elegant proof of a theorem from Russell and Whitehead's Principia Mathematica than the one in Principia (which led them to try, without success, to publish this result in a paper that listed Logic Theorist as a co-author).

4 Newell, Shaw, and Simon (1958) developed the first list-processing language (IPL) for an information-processing system of psychologically interpretable transitions, rather than transitions in terms of 1s and 0s (Boden 1991, 10).

5 I am unable to find a precise citation for the widely reported quotation attributed to Simon in which the prediction is made. Even if apocryphal, the prediction does capture the enthusiasm of these early AI pioneers.

6 Radical behaviorism did leave two important legacies. First, the demand for observable behavioral evidence of psychological claims ("methodological" behaviorism) is now entrenched. Second, by focusing on behavior rather than consciousness, behaviorism "helped to break down the distinction between the mental behavior of humans and the information processing of lower animals and machines" (Aspray (1985, 128).

7 Von Neumann suggested a further analogy: the Central Control and Memory of a standard stored-program computer were intended to "correspond to the associative neurons in the human nervous system" (von Neumann: 3, sec. 2.6; sec. 4.0, 4.2) – that is, the hidden layers of a connectionist network.

8 This description of neural networks best fits feedforward networks, such as those in the PDP Research Group papers cited below. In these networks, activation passes from input to hidden to output layers, and the output is what the nodes in the output layer compute. Another important strand of connectionism stems from Hopfield (1982), who designed a recurrent network. In a recurrent network, every node provides input to every other node, and the network's output is a stable activation pattern of the whole network.

9 In languages with non-alphabetic scripts (e.g. Chinese), the set of conventions behind the statistical structure of communication (discussed below) are presumably divided up differently from the way they are in alphabetic languages.

10 At http://karpathy.github.io/2015/05/21/rnn-effectiveness/ the text that the network modeler's system generates illustrates the way that the statistical structure of English constrains letters to the extent that meaningful text emerges.

11 Note that Dretske's (1981; 1983) appropriation of Shannon amounted to a causal theory of content of individual thoughts; as Dretske himself admits (1983, 82), he took very little from Shannon's actual theory.

Bibliography

Adams, F. and Aizawa, K. (2008). *The Bounds of Cognition*. Oxford, UK: Wiley-Blackwell.

Adriaans, P. (2012). "Information," *The Stanford Encyclopedia of Philosophy* (Fall 2013 edition), Zalta, E. (ed.), http://plato.stanford.edu/archives/fall2013/entries/information/.

Aizawa, K. (1992). "Connectionism and Artificial Intelligence: History and Philosophical Interpretation," *Journal of Experimental and Theoretical Artificial Intelligence*, 4: 295–313.

Allen, C., Varner, G. and Zinser, J. (2000). "Prolegomena to Any Future Artificial Moral Agent," *Journal of Experimental and Theoretical Artificial Intelligence*, 12(3): 251–261.

Arbib, M. (2000). "McCulloch's Search for the Logic of the Nervous System," *Perspectives in Biology and Medicine*, 43(2): 193–216.

Aspray, W. (1985). "The Scientific Conceptualization of Information," *Annals of the History of Computing*, 7(2): 117–140.

Baars, B. (2003). "The Double Life of B. F. Skinner," *Journal of Consciousness Studies*, 10(1): 5–25.

Baddeley, A. (1994). "The Magical Number Seven: Still Magic After all these Years?" *Psychological Review*, 101(2): 353–356.

Bainbridge, W., Brent, E., Carley, K., Heise, D., Macy, M., Markovsky, B. and Skvoretz, J. (1994). "Artificial Social Intelligence," *Annual Review of Sociology*, 20: 407–436.

Baronchelli, A., Ferrer-i-Cancho, R., Pastor-Satorras, R., Chater, N. and Christiansen, M. (2013). "Networks in Cognitive Science," *Trends in Cognitive Sciences*, 17 (7): 348–360.

Bechtel, W. (2009). "Constructing a Philosophy of Science of Cognitive Science," *Topics in Cognitive Science*, 1: 548–569.

Bechtel, W., Abrahamsen, A. & Graham, G. (1998). "The Life of Cognitive Science," in Bechtel, W. and Graham, G. (eds.), *A Companion to Cognitive Science*. Oxford: Basil Blackwell: 1–104.

Bechtel, W. and Shagrir, O. (2015). "The Non-Redundant Contributions of Marr's Three Levels of Analysis for Explaining Information-Processing Mechanisms," *Topics in Cognitive Science*, 7: 312–322.

Bender, A., Hutchins, E. and Medin, D. (2010). "Anthropology in Cognitive Science," *Topics in Cognitive Science*, 2: 374–385.

Block, N. (1995). "On a Confusion about a Function of Consciousness," *Behavioral and Brain Sciences*, 18: 227–287.

Block, N. (2007). "Consciousness, Accessibility, and the Mesh between Psychology and Neuroscience," *Behavioral and Brain Sciences*, 30(5–6): 481–499.

Boden, M. (1991). "Horses of a Different Color?" in Ramsey, W., Stich, S. and Rumelhart, D. (eds.), *Philosophy and Connectionist Theory*. Hillsdale, NJ: Lawrence Erlbaum Associates.

Boden, M. (2006). *Mind As Machine: A History of Cognitive Science*. Oxford: Oxford University Press.

Boole, G. (1854). *An Investigation of the Laws of Thought on Which Are Founded the Mathematical Theories of Logic and Probabilities*. Dover: Constable.

Borge-Holthoefer, J. and Arenas, A. (2009). Navigating word association norms to extract semantic information. In N. A. Taatgen and H. van Rijn (eds.), *Proceedings of the 31st Annual Conference of the Cognitive Science Society*, 621–2777.

Brooks, R. (1990). "Elephants Don't Play Chess," *Robotics and Autonomous Systems*, 6 (1-2): 3–15.
Brooks, R. (1991). "Intelligence Without Representation," *Artificial Intelligence*, 47: 139–159.
Calvo, P., and Keijzer, F. (2009). "Cognition in Plants," in Baluščka, F. (ed.), *Plant- Environment Interactions: Signaling and Communication in Plants*. Berlin and Heidelberg: Springer-Verlag.
Carandini, M. (2012). "From Circuits to Behavior: a Bridge too Far?" *Nature Neuroscience*, 15(4): 507–509.
Chalmers, D. (1995). *The Conscious Mind*. Oxford: Oxford University Press.
Chemero, A. (2011). *Radical Embodied Cognitive Science*. Cambridge, MA: MIT Press.
Chomsky, N. (1959). "A Review of B.F. Skinner's *Verbal Behavior*," *Language*, 35(1): 26–58.
Churchland, P.M. (1990). "On the Nature of Theories: A Neurocomputational Perspective," in Savage, W. (ed.), *Scientific Theories* (Minnesota Studies in the Philosophy of Science vol. 14): 59–101.
Churchland, P.S. (1986). *Neurophilosophy: Towards a Unified Science of the Mind-brain*. Cambridge, MA: MIT Press.
Churchland, P.S. and Sejnowski, T. (1992). *The Computational Brain*. Cambridge, MA: MIT Press.
Clark, A. (1997). *Being There: Putting Brain, Body and World Together Again*. Cambridge, MA: MIT Press.
Clark, A. (2015). *Surfing Uncertainty: Prediction, action and the embodied mind*. Oxford: Oxford University Press.
Copeland, B.J. (2008). "The Modern History of Computing," *The Stanford Encyclopedia of Philosophy* (Fall 2008 edition), Zalta, E. (ed.). http://plato.stanford.edu/archives/fall2008/entries/computing-history/.
Copeland, B. J. and Shagrir, O. (2013). "Turing Versus Godel on Computability and the Mind," in Copeland, B. J., Posy, C. and Shagrir, O. (eds.), *Computability: Turing, Godel, Church, and beyond*. Cambridge, MA: MIT Press.
Dayan, P. (2012). "Twenty-five Lessons From Computational Neuromodulation," *Neuron* 76: 240–256.
Dayan, P. and Abbott, L. (2001). *Theoretical Neuroscience: Computational and Mathematical Modeling of Neural Systems*. Cambridge, MA: MIT Press.
Dehaene, S., Kerszberg, M. and Changeux, J.-P. (1998). "A Neuronal Model of a Global Workspace in Effortful Cognitive Tasks," *Proceedings of the National Academy of Sciences USA*, 95(24): 14529–14534.
Dennett, D. (1975). "Brain Writing and Mind Reading," in Gunderson, K. (ed.), *Language, Mind, and Knowledge*. Minneapolis: University of Minnesota Press: 403–415.
Dennett, D. (1987). *The Intentional Stance*. Cambridge, MA: MIT Press.
Dretske, F. (1981). *Knowledge and the Flow of Information*. Cambridge, MA: MIT Press.
Dretske, F. (1983). "Precis of Knowledge and the Flow of Information," *Behavioral and Brain Sciences*, 6: 55–90.
Dretske, F. (1988). *Explaining Behavior*. Cambridge, MA: MIT Press.
Dreyfus, H. (1992). *What Computers Still Can't Do: A Critique of Artificial Reason*. Cambridge, MA: MIT Press.
Dunbar, R. (1998). The Social Brain Hypothesis. *Evolutionary Anthropology* 6: 178–190.

Eliasmith, C. (2013). *How to Build a Brain: A Neural Architecture for Biological Cognition.* New York and Oxford: Oxford University Press.

Figdor, C. (MS). Shannon + Friston = Content. Under review.

Flavell, J.H. (2000). "Development of Children's Knowledge about the Mental World," *International Journal of Behavioral Development* 2000, 24 (1): 15–23.

Fodor, J. (1975). *The Language of Thought.* Thomas Y. Crowell.

Fodor, J. (1980). "Methodological Solipsism Considered as a Research Strategy in Cognitive Psychology," *Behavioral and Brain Sciences,* 63: 63–73.

Fodor, J. (1983). *The Modularity of Mind.* Cambridge, MA: MIT Press.

Fodor, J. and Pylyshyn, Z. (1988). "Connectionism and Cognitive Architecture: A Critical Analysis," *Cognition,* 28: 3–71.

Frege, G. (1879). Begriffschrift, eine der Arithmetischen nachgebildete Formelsprache des reinen Denkens. *Revue Philosophique de la France Et de l'Etranger,* 8: 108–109.

Friston, K. (2010). The free-energy principle: a unified brain theory? *Nature Reviews Neuroscience,* 11(2): 127–138.

Froese, T., Gershenson, C. and Manzanilla, L. (2014). "Can Government be Self-Organized? A Mathematical Model of the Collective Social Organization of Ancient Teotihuacan, Central Mexico," *PLoS One,* 9(10): e109966.

Gallagher, S. (2005). *How the Body Shapes the Mind.* New York: Oxford University Press.

Gardner, H. (1985). *The Mind's New Science.* New York: Basic Books.

Gibson, J.J. (1979). *The Ecological Approach to Visual Perception.* Hillsdale, NJ: Lawrence Erlbaum Associates.

Godfrey, M. and Hendry, D. (1993). "The Computer as von Neumann Planned It," *IEEE Annals of the History of Computing,* 15(1): 11–21.

Greene, J., and Cohen, J. (2004). "For the Law, Neuroscience Changes Everything and Nothing," *Philosophical Transactions: Biological Sciences,* 359 (1451): 1775–1785.

Greenwood, J. (1999). "Understanding the 'Cognitive Revolution' in Psychology," *Journal of the History of the Behavioral Sciences,* 35(1): 1–22.

Grice, H.P. (1957). "Meaning," *Philosophical Review,* 66(3): 377–388.

Hartley, R. (1928). "Transmission of Information," *Bell System Technical Journal,* 7(3): 535–563.

Heckathorn, D. (1989). "Cognitive Science, Sociology, and the Theoretic Analysis of Complex Systems," *Journal of Mathematical Sociology,* 14(2–3): 97–110.

Hohwy, J. (2014). *The Predictive Mind.* New York: Oxford University Press.

Hopfield, J. (1982). "Neural Networks and Physical Systems with Emergent Collective Computational Abilities," *Proceedings of the National Academy of Sciences of the USA,* 79 (8): 2554–2558.

Humphrey, N. (1976). "The Social Function of Intellect," in Bateson, P. and Hinde, R. (eds.), *Growing Points in Ethology.* Cambridge: Cambridge University Press: 303–317.

Isaac, A. (forthcoming). The Semantics Latent in Shannon Information. *British Journal for Philosophy of Science.* https://doiorg.proxy.lib.uiowa.edu/10.1093/bjps/axx029.

Izhikevich, E. (2007). *Dynamical Systems in Neuroscience: The Geometry of Excitability and Bursting.* Cambridge, MA: MIT Press.

Jack, A. and Roepstorff, A. (2002). "Introspection and Cognitive Brain Mapping: from Stimulus-response to Script-report," *Trends in Cognitive Sciences,* 6(8): 333–339.

Jack, A. and Roepstorff, A. (2003). "Why Trust the Subject? Editorial Introduction to Trusting the Subject? The Use of Introspective Evidence in Cognitive Science," *Journal of Consciousness Studies,* 10 (9–10): v–xx.

Jolly, A. (1966). "Lemur Social Behavior and Primate Intelligence," *Science* (New Series), 153 (3735): 501–506.

Kiverstein, J. and Miller, M. (2015). "The embodied brain: towards a radical embodied cognitive neuroscience," *Frontiers in Human Neuroscience* (9), article 237, doi: 10.3389/fnhum.2015.00237.

Lashley, K. (1923). "The Behavioristic Interpretation of Consciousness I and II," *Psychological Review*, 30 (4): 237–272 and 30 (5): 329–353.

Lewis, D. (1969). *Convention*. Cambridge, MA: Harvard University Press.

McCulloch, W. and Pitts, W. (1943). "A Logical Calculus of the Ideas Immanent in Nervous Activity," *Bulletin of Mathematical Biophysics*, 5: 115–133.

Marr, D. (1982). *Vision: A Computational Investigation into the Human Representation and Processing of Visual Information*. San Francisco, CA: W. H. Freeman and Company.

Mason, W. A., Jones, A. and Goldstone, R. L. (2008). "Propagation of Innovations in Networked Groups." *Journal of Experimental Psychology*, 137(3): 422–433.

Miller, G. (2003). "The Cognitive Revolution: A Historical Perspective," *Trends in Cognitive Sciences*, 7 (3): 141–144.

Miller, G. (1956). "The Magical Number Seven, Plus or Minus Two," *Psychological Review*, 63: 81–97.

Miller, G., Galanter, E. and Pribram, K. (1960). *Plans and the Structure of Behavior*. New York: Holt, Rinehart & Winston.

Millikan, R. (1984). *Language, Thought, and other Biological Categories*. Cambridge, MA: MIT Press.

Nakayama, K. (2010). "Introduction: Vision Going Social," in Adams, Jr., R. N. Ambady, R., Nakayama, K. and Shimojo, S. (eds.), *The Science of Social Vision*. New York and Oxford: Oxford University Press: 3–17.

Neander, K. (2017). *A Mark of the Mental: in defense of informational teleosemantics*. Cambridge: MIT Press.

Neisser, U. (1967). *Cognitive Psychology*. New York: Meredith Publishing.

Newell, A. (1982). "The Knowledge Level," *Artificial Intelligence*, 18: 87–127.

Newell, A. (1993). "Reflections on the Knowledge Level," *Artificial Intelligence*, 59: 31–38.

Newell, A., Shaw, J. and Simon, H. (1958). "Elements of a Theory of Human Problem Solving," *Psychological Review*, 65(3): 151–166.

Newell, A. and Simon, H. (1976). "Computer Science as Empirical Inquiry: Symbols and Search," *Communications of the ACM (Association for Computing Machinery)*, 19(3): 113–126.

Nyquist, H. (1924). "Certain Factors Affecting Telegraph Speed," *Bell System Technical Journal*.

Oizumi, M., Albantakis, L. and Tononi, G. (2014). "From the Phenomenology to the Mechanisms of Consciousness: Integrated Information Theory 3.0," *PLoS Computational Biology*, 10 (5): e1003588.

Olshausen, B., and Field, D. (1996). "Emergence of Simple-Cell Receptive Field Properties by Learning a Sparse Code for Natural Images," *Nature*, 381: 607–609.

O'Malley, M., Brigandt, I., Love, A., Crawford, J., Gilbert, J., Knight, R., Mitchell, S., and Rohwer, F. "Multilevel Research Strategies and Biological Systems," *Philosophy of Science*, 81(5): 811–828.

O'Regan, J.K., and Noe, A. (2001). "A Sensorimotor Account of Vision and Visual Consciousness," *Behavioral and Brain Sciences*, 24: 939–1031.

Peckhaus, V. (2009). "Leibniz's Influence on 19th Century Logic," *The Stanford Encyclopedia of Philosophy* (Spring 2014 edition), Zalta, E. (ed.). http://plato.stanford.edu/archives/spr2014/entries/leibniz-logic-influence/.

Piccinini, G. (2004). "The First Computational Theory of the Brain: A Close Look at McCulloch and Pitts's 'Logical Calculus of Ideas Immanent in Nervous Activity'." *Synthese*, 141(2): 175–215.

Poggio, T. (1981). "Marr's Computational Approach to Vision," *Trends in Neurosciences*, 10: 258–262.

Poggio, T. (2012). "The Levels of Understanding Framework," revised. *Perception*, 41: 1017–1023.

Rosenblueth, A., Wiener, N. and Bigelow, J. (1943). "Behavior, Purpose, and Teleology," *Philosophy of Science*, 10(1): 18–24.

Roskies, A. (2010). "How Does Neuroscience Affect Our Conception of Volition?" *Annual Reviews Neuroscience*, 33: 109–130.

Rumelhart, D., McClelland, J., and the PDP Research Group (1986). *Parallel Distributed Processing: Explorations in the Microstructure of Cognition*. Vol. 1: Foundations, and Vol.2: Psychological and biological models. Cambridge, MA: MIT Press.

Schacter, D., Addis, D., Hassabis, D., Martin, V., Spreng, R.N., and Szpunar, K. (2012). "The Future of Memory: Remembering, Imagining, and the Brain," *Neuron*, 76(4): 677–694.

Searle, J. (1980). "Minds, Brains, and Programs," *Behavioral and Brain Sciences*, 3: 417–424.

Shagrir, O. (2010). "Marr on Computational-Level Theories," *Philosophy of Science*, 77 (4): 477–500.

Shannon, C. (1948). "A Mathematical Theory of Communication," *Bell System Technical Journal*, 379–423, 623–656.

Shettleworth, S. J. (2010). *Cognition, Evolution, and Behavior*. Oxford: Oxford University Press.

Skryms, B. (2010). *Signals: Evolution, Learning, and Information*. Oxford: Oxford University Press.

Smolensky, P. (1991). "Connectionism, Constituency and the Language of Thought," in Loewer, B. and Rey, G. (eds.), *Meaning in Mind: Fodor and His Critics*. Oxford: Blackwell.

Sterelny, K. (2007). "Social Intelligence, Human Intelligence, and Niche Construction," *Philosophical Transactions of the Royal Society B* 362: 719–730.

Sutton, R., and Barto, A. (1998). *Reinforcement Learning: An Introduction*. Cambridge, MA and London: MIT Press. http://webdocs.cs.ualberta.ca/~sutton/book/ebook/the-book.html.

Thelen, E., and Smith, L. (1994). *A Dynamical Systems Approach to Development of Cognition and Action*. Cambridge, MA: MIT Press.

Tononi, G., and Koch, C. (2014). "Consciousness: Here, There, but Not Everywhere". arXiv preprint arXiv:1405.7089.

Trewavas, A. (2005). "Green Plants as Intelligent Organisms," *Trends in Plant Sciences*, 10: 413–419.

Turing, A. (1936). "On Computable Numbers, with an Application to the Entscheidungsproblem," *Proceedings of the London Mathematical Society* Series 2, 47: 230–265.

Turing, A. (1950). "Computing Machinery and Intelligence," *Mind*, 59(236): 433–460.

van Gelder, T. (1995). "What Might Cognition Be, if Not Computation?" *Journal of Philosophy*, 92 (7): 345–481.

von Eckardt, B. (2003). The Explanatory Need for Mental Representations in Cognitive Science. *Mind & Language* 18 (4): 427–439.

von Neumann, J. (1945). "First Draft of a Report on the EDVAC. Moore School of Electrical Engineering, University of Pennsylvania," Reset typescript online at: www.virtualtravelog.net/wp/wp-content/media/2003-08-TheFirstDraft.pdf.

von Neumann, J. (1966). *Theory of Self-Reproducing Automata*. Edited and completed by Arthur W. Burks. Urbana and London: University of Indiana Press.

Weaver, W. (1949). "The Mathematics of Communication," *Scientific American*, 181(1): 11–15.

Wiener, N. (1948). *Cybernetics, or Control and Communication in the Animal and the Machine*. New York: John Wiley & Sons.

Wiener, N. (1961). *Cybernetics*. New York: M.I.T. Press.

Williams, F. and Kilburn, T. (1948). "Electronic Digital Computers," *Nature*, 162 (4117): 487.

12

HOW PHILOSOPHY OF MIND CAN SHAPE THE FUTURE

Susan Schneider and Pete Mandik

A bright metallic thread of future-oriented thinking runs through the tapestry of the philosophy of mind, especially in those parts of the field that have grappled with the possibility of minds as machines. Can a robot feel pain? Can a suitably programmed computer think actual thoughts? Could humans survive the total replacement of their nervous system by neural prosthetics? As the pace of technological change quickens, what was once purely speculative is becoming more and more real. As society moves further into the 21st century, what are the ways that philosophy of mind can shape the future? What challenges will the future bring to the discipline? In this chapter, we examine a few suggestive possibilities. We begin with what we suspect will be a game changer – the development of AI and artificial general intelligence (AGI). We then turn to radical brain enhancements, urging that the future will likely introduce exciting new issues involving (inter alia) the extended mind hypothesis, the epistemology of evaluating the thoughts of vastly smarter beings, mind uploading, and more.

1. The rise of the machines: some philosophical challenges

These last few years have been marked by the widespread cultural recognition that sophisticated AI is under development, and may change the face of society. For instance, according to a recent survey, the most cited AI researchers expect AI to "carry out most human professions at least as well as a typical human" within a 10-percent probability by the year 2024. Further, they assign a 50-percent probability by 2050, and a 90-percent probability by 2070 (Muller and Bostrom 2014).[1] AI critics, such as John Searle, Jerry Fodor and Hubert Dreyfus, must now answer to the impressive work coming out of venues like Google's *DeepMind* and exhibited by IBM's *Watson* program,[2] rather than referring back to the notorious litany of failures of AI in the 1970s and 1980s.

Indeed, silicon seems to be a better medium for information processing than the brain. Neurons reach a peak speed of about 200 Hz, which is about seven orders of magnitude slower than current microprocessors (Bostrom 2014, 59). Although the brain compensates for some of this with massive parallelism, features such as "hubs," and so on, crucial mental capacities such as attention rely upon serial processing, which is incredibly slow, and has a maximum capacity of about seven manageable chunks (Miller 1956; Schneider 2014). Additionally, the number of neurons in a human brain is limited by cranial volume and metabolism, but computers can occupy entire buildings or cities, and can even be remotely connected across the globe (Bostrom 2014; Schneider 2014).

Of course, the human brain is more intelligent than any modern day computer. Intelligent machines can in principle be constructed by reverse engineering the brain, however, and improving upon its algorithms, or through some combination of reverse engineering and judicious algorithms that aren't based on the workings of the human brain. In addition, an AI program can be downloaded to different locations at once, is easily modifiable, and can survive under a variety of conditions that carbon-based life cannot. The increases in redundancy and backups that programs allow mean that AI minds will be hardier and more reliable than their biological counterparts.

We've noted AI experts' projections that sophisticated AI may be reached within the next several decades. By "sophisticated AI" what is meant is **artificial general intelligence** (AGI). An AGI is a flexible, domain-general intelligence – an intelligence that can integrate material from various domains, rather than merely excelling at a single task, like winning *Jeopardy* or playing chess. Philosophers have debated the possibility of AGI for decades, and we hope they will help shape the global understanding of AGI in the future. For instance, perhaps some philosophers will discover a distinctively philosophical reason for believing that, despite the successes of Watson and *DeepMind*, experts will (and must) hit a wall when it comes to creating AGI – perhaps computers can excel at domain specific reasoning but general purpose reasoning is not amenable to computational explanation. Or perhaps the resources of the philosophy of mind will not unearth a deep obstacle to AGI, but instead provide insights that will aid in its development.

In any case, within society at large, the earlier skepticism about AGI has given way. Indeed, there is now a general suspicion that once AGI is reached, it may upgrade itself to even greater levels of intelligence. As David Chalmers explains:

> The key idea is that a machine that is more intelligent than humans will be better than humans at designing machines. So it will be capable of designing a machine more intelligent than the most intelligent machine that humans can design. So if it is itself designed by humans, it will be capable of designing a machine more intelligent than itself. By similar reasoning, this next machine will also be capable of designing a machine more intelligent than itself. If every machine in turn does what it is capable of, we should expect a sequence of ever more intelligent machines.
>
> (Chalmers 2010)

In a similar vein, Nick Bostrom's *New York Times* bestselling book *Superintelligence: Paths, Dangers and Strategies* (2014) argues that a superintelligence could supplant humans as the dominant intelligence on the planet, and that the sequence of changes could be rapid-fire (see also Kurzweil 2005). Indeed, due in large part to Bostrom's book, and the successes at *DeepMind*, this last year marked the widespread cultural and scientific recognition of the possibility of "superintelligent AI."[3]

> **Superintelligent AI**: a kind of artificial general intelligence that is able to exceed the best human level intelligence in every field – social skills, general wisdom, scientific creativity, and so on
> (Bostrom 2014; Kurzweil 2005; Schneider 2009a; 2015).

Superintelligent AI (SAI) could be developed during a *technological singularity*, a point at which ever more rapid technological advances, especially, an intelligence explosion, reach a point at which unenhanced humans can no longer predict or even understand the changes that are unfolding. If an intelligence explosion occurs, Bostrom warns that there is no way to predict or control the final goals of a SAI. Moral programming is difficult to specify in a foolproof fashion, and it could be rewritten by a superintelligence in any case. Nor is there any agreement in the field of ethics about what the correct moral principles are. Further, a clever machine could bypass safeguards like kill switches and attempts to box it in, and could potentially be an existential threat to humanity (Bostrom 2014). A superintelligence is, after all, defined as an entity that is more intelligent than humans, in every domain. Bostrom calls this problem "The Control Problem." (Bostrom 2014).

The control problem is a serious problem – perhaps it is even insurmountable. Indeed, upon reading Bostrom's book, scientists and business leaders such as Stephen Hawking, Bill Gates, Max Tegmark, among others, commented that superintelligent AI could threaten the human race, having goals that humans can neither predict nor control. Yet most current work on the control problem is being done by computer scientists. Philosophers of mind and moral philosophers can add to these debates, contributing work on how to create friendly AI (for an excellent overview of the issues, see Wallach and Allen 2010).

The possibility of human or beyond-human AI raises further philosophical questions as well. If AGI and SAI are developed, would they be conscious? Would they be selves or persons, although they are arguably not even living beings? Of course, perhaps we are putting the cart before the horse in assuming that superintelligence can even be developed: perhaps the move from human-level AGI to superintelligence is itself questionable (Chalmers 2010)? After all, how can humans create beyond-human intelligence given that our own intellectual resources are only at a human level? Quicker processing speed and a greater number of cognitive operations do not necessarily result in a qualitative shift to a greater form of intelligence. Indeed, what are markers for "beyond human intelligence", and how can we determine when it has been reached?

In his groundbreaking paper on the singularity, Chalmers suggests even more issues that philosophers could explore:

> Philosophically: The singularity raises many important philosophical questions. . . . The potential consequences of an intelligence explosion force us to think hard about values and morality and about consciousness and personal identity. In effect, the singularity brings up some of the hardest traditional questions in philosophy and raises some new philosophical questions as well.
> . . . To determine whether an intelligence explosion will be a good or a bad thing, we need to think about the relationship between intelligence and value. To determine whether we can play a significant role in a post-singularity world, we need to know whether human identity can survive the enhancing of our cognitive systems, perhaps through uploading onto new technology. These are life-or-death questions that may confront us in coming decades or centuries. To have any hope of answering them, we need to think clearly about the philosophical issues.
>
> (Chalmers 2010)

What sorts of things can philosophers do to help tackle the issues raised by AI, the singularity, and other technologies on the horizon? We recommend an approach that draws on thought experiments of the sort traditionally considered by philosophers of mind, but tempered by knowledge of contemporary advances in science and technology.

Philosophers often view thought experiments as windows into the fundamental nature of things – hypothetical situations in the "laboratory of the mind" that depict something that exceeds the bounds of current technology or even is incompatible with the laws of nature, but that is supposed to reveal something philosophically enlightening about the topic in question (Schneider 2009b). Thought experiments can entertain, illustrate a puzzle, lay bare a contradiction in thought, and move us toward further clarification. Yet experimental philosophers have countered that thought experiments are not trustworthy guides to philosophical issues because they covertly rely upon intuitive judgments about possibility that are hostage to features like our cultural and economic backgrounds.

Emerging technologies introduce a host of real world cases – cases that seem nomologically and technologically possible – rather than relying upon dubious intuitions about what is possible in remote possible worlds like zombie worlds (worlds in which no entity is conscious, even the entities that act like they are) or Cartesian worlds stocked with disembodied minds. And, in the domain of emerging technologies – this arena in which science fiction meets science fact – philosophy quite possibly becomes a matter of life and death, as we will further discuss shortly (Chalmers 2010; Schneider 2009b; Mandik 2015).

In what follows, we identify more ways that philosophers of mind can help shape the 21st century. We begin with a fictional scenario that introduces issues about the extended mind hypothesis. We then turn to several interrelated philosophical problems, based upon this scenario and others that we introduce.

2. The ethics of brain enhancement, the extended mind, and human integration into a post-singularity world

Consider the following thought experiment, modified from Schneider (2009a):

> Suppose it is 2025 and being a technophile, you purchase brain enhancements as they become readily available. First, you add a mobile internet connection to your retina, then, you enhance your working memory by adding neural circuitry. You are now officially a cyborg. Now skip ahead to 2040. Through nanotechnological therapies and enhancements you are able to extend your lifespan, and as the years progress, you continue to accumulate more far-reaching enhancements. By 2060, after several small but cumulatively profound alterations, you are a "posthuman." To quote philosopher Nick Bostrom, posthumans are possible future beings, "whose basic capacities so radically exceed those of present humans as to be no longer unambiguously human by our current standards."
>
> (Bostrom 2017)
>
> At this point, your intelligence is enhanced not just in terms of speed of mental processing; you are now able to make rich connections that you were not able to make before. Unenhanced humans, or "naturals," seem to you to be intellectually disabled – you have little in common with them – but as a transhumanist (a proponent of the sorts of cybernetic and genetic modifications that, in the extreme case, leads to posthumans), you are supportive of their right to not enhance.
>
> (Bostrom 2017; Garreau 2004; Kurzweil 2005)
>
> It is now 2250 AD. Over time, the slow addition of better and better neural circuitry has left no real intellectual difference in kind between you and AI. Your mental operations have been gradually transferring to the cloud, and by this point, you are silicon-based. The only real difference between you and an AI creature of standard design is one of origin – you were once a natural. But you are now almost entirely engineered by technology – you are perhaps more aptly characterized as a member of a rather heterogeneous class of AI life forms.

Of course, this is just a thought experiment, but it is hard to imagine people in mainstream society resisting opportunities for superior health, intelligence, extreme longevity and efficiency. Indeed, the advanced technologies wing of the defense department (DARPA) is now working on brain chips, electronic prosthetics implanted in the brain, providing intriguing examples of "cyborgs."

There are many philosophical issues that this thought experiment raises. Let us consider a few.

2.1 The extended mind, 2.0

Despite being implanted *in* brains, brain chips strike us as providing better support for the extended mind hypothesis than Clark and Chalmers's original examples of laptops and notepads. (The extended mind hypothesis is the proposal that the physical substrate for the human mind is not restricted to the human central nervous system, but can sometimes or perhaps always include external physical items, as when one's memories are stored in external media such as notebooks and hard drives. See Chapter 10). For it can be objected that laptops and notepads do not seem to exhibit a sufficiently rich cognitive integration with the brain to justify the claim that the mind is extended beyond the brain. Instead, information from notebooks and laptops enters into cognitive and perceptual systems through sensory transducers. When one forgets their laptop or notebook, they only have recourse to the processing of their brain. The brain itself seems to be the true unit of mentality. In contrast, brain implants could become well-integrated with the biological brain, for the inputs from the implants do not enter the cognitive system through sensory transducers, but could in principle function like actual minicolumns or brain regions.

You might object that it is unclear what's "extended" about neural prostheses. If they aren't outside of the body, how do they make the mind "extended"? But if one believes the mind is just the brain, then this makes the mind extended. Further, these implants need not be in the skull, they could be located elsewhere in the body, or even on the cloud, for instance. What is crucial is that they are as well integrated as components of the brain normally are. Would brain or cloud-based implants provide better support for the view that the mind is extended? Further, can consciousness (as opposed to mere information processing) really extend beyond the biological brain? That is, can silicon minicolumns or microchips be part of the neural basis of conscious experience? These are issues well-worth considering, we believe, as we move to a future with neural enhancements and therapies that extend beyond the biological brain.

2.2 Human integration into a post-singularity world

Let us continue our thought experiments further into the future. Suppose that it is now AD 2250 and some humans have upgraded to become superintelligent beings, through gradual cognitive enhancements, including cloud-based computations. But suppose you resist any upgrades – you opt to stay a "Natural" – a member of a group resisting enhancements (Garreau 2004). Having conceptual resources beyond your wildest imagination, the superintelligent beings generate an entirely new budget of solutions to longstanding, central philosophical problems, such as the mind-body problem, the hard problem of consciousness, and the problem of free will. They univocally and passionately tell you that the solutions are obvious. But you and the other Naturals throw your hands up; these "solutions" strike you and the other unenhanced as gibberish (Schneider 2009b).

You think: Who knows, maybe these "superintelligent" beings were engineered poorly; or maybe it is me. Perhaps the unenhanced are "cognitively closed," as Colin McGinn has argued, being constitutionally unable to solve major philosophical problems (McGinn 1993). The enhanced call themselves "Humans 2.0"; they claim the unenhanced are but an inferior version. They beg you to enhance. What shall you do? What shall you make of your epistemic predicament? You cannot grasp the contents of the superintelligent beings' thoughts without significant upgrades. But what if their way of thinking is flawed to begin with? In that case, upgrading will surely not help. Is there some sort of neutral vantage point or at least a set of plausible principles with which to guide you in framing a response to such a challenge?

This scenario is merely one example of the kind of issues that will come to the fore as machines outsmart humans, and as some humans themselves enhance their intelligence in ways that allow them to outthink ordinary humans, at least in certain domains. Understanding how to approach such situations requires fruitful collaboration between philosophers of mind, epistemologists, AI specialists, and others.

2.2.1 The ethics of brain enhancement decisions

Should we embrace postbiological intelligence? Enhancement decisions will require deep deliberation about metaphysical and ethical questions that are both controversial and difficult to solve: questions that require reflection about personal identity and the nature of mind, among other issues, and which draw from empirical work in cognitive science. As we explain below, enhancing by moving from carbon to silicon may not be something that preserves your conscious experience or personal identity. Given this, a precautionary stance suggests that we should not enhance unless it is confirmed that consciousness is preserved. For the enhancement is supposed to increase the quality of your life, enabling your survival and giving you more time on the planet as a subject of experience. However, in contrast to a precautionary stance is an attitude of "metaphysical daring" (Mandik 2015). Being metaphysically daring involves making a kind of bet about metaphysical issues such as whether a naturally originating mind could have its consciousness or identity preserved across a transformation from tissue to silicon chips. Metaphysically daring future humans and posthumans may reap the benefits of an enhanced substrate. Indeed, as Mandik argues, systems that exhibit high degrees of metaphysical daring may, in making many more copies of themselves in the form of digital backups, be more fit in a Darwinian sense than their more cautious evolutionary competitors. Of course, part of what makes the attitude *daring* is the lack of certainty about whether it is correct that such benefits are forthcoming (Mandik 2015).

Given both the lack of certainty on such matters and their life-or-death nature, a pluralistic society should recognize the diversity of different philosophical views on these matters, including a wide range from the metaphysically daring to the metaphysically cautious, and not assume that science itself can answer questions about whether radical forms of brain enhancement are justifiable, or are even compatible with survival, given different views on personal identity and the nature of mind. A good place to further illustrate these observations is with a very extreme "enhancement" case that has been in the news a good deal recently: mind uploading.

3. Mind uploading ("Whole Brain Emulation")

Science fiction has long depicted scenarios in which a person in distress, such as Johnny Depp's character in *Transcendence*, uploads his or her brain in last ditch effort to avoid death. The idea behind uploading is that the person's brain is scanned, and a software model of it is constructed that is so precise that, when run on ultra-efficient hardware, it thinks and behaves in exactly the same way as the original brain. The process of scanning will likely destroy the original brain, as in *Transcendence*, although non-destructive uploading has also been discussed as a more distant possibility (Blackford and Broderick 2014). Uploading is akin to migration to the cloud, but it can be more rapid fire, bypassing your cyborgization. Uploaded beings can be computationally identical to the original human, but they could also become vastly smarter, and less like an ordinary human, as with *Transcendence*.

You might think that if uploading could be developed, day-to-day life would be drastically improved. For instance, on Monday at 6:00 PM, you could have sushi in Tokyo; by 7:30 PM, you could be sipping wine nestled in the hills of the Napa Valley; you need only rent a suitable android body in each locale. Airports could become a thing of the past. Bodily harm matters little to you, for you just pay a fee to the rental company when your android surrogate is injured or destroyed. Formerly averse to risk, you find yourself skydiving and climbing Everest. You think: if I continue to backup, I will live forever. What a surprising route to immortality.

Oxford University's *Future of Humanity Institute* has a brain emulation project that is taking the first steps toward developing uploading. The *OpenWorm* project has successfully uploaded a worm (*C elegans*) and downloaded it to a Lego robot, which behaved like a worm. Uploading could be perfected during a technological singularity. So suppose, like Will Caster, Johnny Depp's character in *Transcendence*, you have just learned you have only a few weeks to live. You recall Steven Hawking's remark: "I think the brain is like a programme . . . so it's theoretically possible to copy the brain onto a computer and so provide a form of life after death" (Collins 2013). So you wonder: could I truly transfer my consciousness to a computer?

Metaphysics has now become a matter of life and death for you. Would you survive? Philosophers, such as Nick Bostrom and David Chalmers, tend to respond with guarded optimism. But let's consider a literary example to see if even guarded optimism is well-founded. In Robert Sawyer's novel *Mindscan* the protagonist, Jake Sullivan, tries to upload to avoid dying of a brain tumor. He undergoes a non-destructive uploading procedure, and although the contents of his brain are copied precisely, he wakes up after the procedure, still on the operating table, and is astonished to find that he is still stuck in his original body. His consciousness did not "transfer"! Sullivan should have read the personal identity literature in metaphysics, which asks: in virtue of what do you survive over the time? Having a soul? Being a material being? Having the same memories and thought patterns as your earlier self? In deciding whether you could survive uploading, it is important to consider the metaphysical credentials behind each of these views (Schneider 2009a). (See also Chapter 5 on personal identity.)

One reason Jake should have been suspicious is that objects generally follow a continuous trajectory through space over time – but here, for Jake to "transfer" to his upload, his brain would not even move, and his consciousness would somehow travel inside a computer and then, at a later point, be downloaded into an android. And the stuff that makes up the new Jake would be entirely different. Further, an upload can be downloaded to multiple places at once. But, plausibly, at most only one of these creatures would really be Jake. Which one? Finally, notice that Jake survived the scan. So why believe that any of the uploads is him, rather than the original Jake? In the macroscopic world around us, single objects do not reside in multiple locations at once.

At best, so-called mind uploaders merely create computational copies of themselves that are forms of artificial intelligence (AI). But a copy is not the same as the original. It's a *copy* (Schneider 2014). But if uploads are copies, why be confident, to go back to our original case of your migration to the cloud, that moving to the cloud really preserves your identity? Of course, maybe Derek Parfit is correct. Perhaps there is no identity to begin with (Parfit 1984). In this case, survival is not an issue for you. You may opt to upload for other reasons though – perhaps you believe that creating a psychological duplicate is somehow beneficial.

Or maybe there really is survival, but we are like programs, which can be uploaded and downloaded? In this latter case, maybe uploading can preserve identity because the mind is a program. A program is abstract, like a musical score or equation, and is not a concrete object like a coffee cup, a brain, or a chair. On this sort of view, minds, as programs, are abstract in the sense that the plot of a novel or a song's melody is abstract. If an author emails their latest novel to their publisher, and the publisher prints thousands of copies of the novel, there's only one story here, not thousands. If human minds are abstract in this sense, then the scenario of nond-estructive uploading involves only a single mind, just as there can be a thousand bound copies of a single novel (Mandik 2015, 146–147).

What case can be made for regarding minds as abstract? As Mandik points out:

> Much of what we think, want, and experience is abstract. I can think that there's a dog chasing a cat without there being some particular dog or particular cat that I am thereby thinking about. As Quine (1956) points out, the desire I express in saying "I want a sloop" can just be me wanting relief from slooplessness without there being some certain sloop that I want. Regarding experiences and "what it is like" to have them: I can experience a patch of red on separate occasions, and what it is like to have the experience on the one occasion may be exactly like what it is like on the other occasion. Tye (1995) characterizes all phenomenal character as "abstract" in this sense. If what matters for having my mind is something that can be characterized as abstract in these ways, the possibility opens of a deep analogy between a human life and the story of a novel.
> (Mandik 2015, 147)

The view that the mind is abstract in a way that would allow for continuity through uploading is not without its opponents. For instance, Schneider has argued the mind is not a program. For a program or algorithm is like an equation and is abstract. In the fields of philosophy of mathematics and metaphysics, abstract entities are by definition non-spatial, non-causal, atemporal, unchanging, and non-physical. We can tell introspectively that time passes, so minds are temporal, and minds (or more specifically, mental property tokenings, or mental events) are causal, and, relatedly, they experience chance. An equation or algorithm is not located anywhere – although inscriptions and program instantiations are. Our minds and thoughts have concrete locations in space. At best, the mind is a *program instantiation*, which is a concrete entity – a physical object (Schneider, forthcoming).

Regardless of whether we regard the survival conditions of minds as more like the survival conditions for ordinary physical objects or instead like abstract entities such as songs or stories, the important thing is that these are all very controversial positions, relying on certain convictions about the nature of the self, and they militate for different decisions about radical brain enhancement.

As the 21st century unfolds, enhancement decisions will not merely require scientific information about whether uploading can be developed, or whether various minicolumns in your brain can be replaced with silicon implants. They will require philosophical deliberation about the nature of self and mind.

We will revisit radical brain enhancement shortly, for we have yet to explore the important question of whether a silicon being, whether it be you or merely an uploaded copy of you, could be conscious.

4. The hard problem of AI consciousness

When we deliberate, hear music, see the rich hues of a sunset, and so on, there is information processing going on in the brain. But above and beyond the manipulation of data, there is a subjective side – there is a felt quality to our experience. Chalmers's hard problem of consciousness asks: why does all this information processing in the human brain, under certain conditions, have a felt quality to it? Why aren't we "zombies" in the philosopher's sense, being creatures that lack inner experience (Chalmers 2008)?

As Chalmers emphasizes, this problem doesn't seem to have a scientific answer. For instance, we could develop a complete theory of vision, understanding all of the details of visual processing in the brain, but still not understand why there are subjective experiences attached to these informational states. Chalmers contrasts the hard problem with what he calls "easy problems", problems involving consciousness that have eventual scientific answers, such as the mechanisms behind attention and how we categorize and react to stimuli (Chalmers 2008). Of course these scientific problem are difficult problems; Chalmers merely calls them "easy problems" to contrast them with the "hard problem" of consciousness, which he thinks will not have a purely scientific solution.

We now face yet another perplexing issue involving consciousness – a kind of "hard problem" concerning machine consciousness, if you will:

The Hard Problem of AI Consciousness: Would the processing of a silicon-based superintelligent system feel a certain way, from the inside?

A sophisticated AI could solve problems that even the brightest humans are unable to solve, but still, being made of a different substrate, would its information processing feel a certain way from the inside (Chalmers 2008; Searle 1980; Schneider 2015)?

This is not just Chalmers's hard problem applied to the case of AI. For the hard problem of consciousness assumes that we are conscious – after all, each of us can tell from introspecting that we are conscious at this moment. It asks *why* we are conscious. Why does all your information processing feel a certain way from the inside? In contrast, the Hard Problem of AI Consciousness asks *whether* AI, being silicon-based, is even capable of consciousness. It does not presuppose that AI is conscious. These are different problems, but they are both hard problems in their own right – problems that science alone cannot answer.

Ned Block has raised a similar problem, which he calls "The Harder Problem of Consciousness" (Block 2002; McLaughlin 2003). In essence, Block focuses on the case of a "superficial functional isomorph" (SFI) of a human – a being "that is functionally isomorphic to us with respect to those causal relations among mental states, inputs, and outputs that are specified by 'folk psychology'" (Block 2002, 399). According to Block, a SFI need not be conscious, because for all we know, the capacity for consciousness may depend upon a system's underlying substrate, and a silicon-based functional isomorph may lack the right substrate (Block 2002). Block aptly calls attention to the epistemic difficulty of determining whether a different realization would be conscious.

Is our problem just Block's "Harder Problem of Consciousness" then? Block develops his line of thought by focusing on a case of a SFI. In contrast, our hard problem of AI consciousness applies to systems that are not reasonably considered functional duplicates of us, by either armchair folk psychological attributions or scientific functionalist assessments (i.e., psychofunctionalism). It applies to systems that are incredibly different from us with respect to their cognitive and perceptual capacities, such as superintelligences or AGIs not designed to be humanlike. Further, Block's problem arises only for proponents of what he calls "Phenomenal Realism," a view that counts among its commitments that no "a priori or at least armchair analyses of consciousness (or at least armchair sufficient conditions) are given in non-phenomenal terms, most prominently in terms of representation, thought or function." In contrast, our problem can be raised while being neutral about the ultimate status of such analyses. For all we know, there is some as yet unforeseen but correct armchair analysis of consciousness in terms of information processing functions. We are nonetheless currently in the position to be deeply perplexed about *whether* an AI performing such functions would thereby be conscious.

The problem is more general than Block's problem then: simply put, silicon may not be the right medium for consciousness.

Our problem is also related to biological naturalism, a position that is commonly associated with John Searle that has historically denied that AI can be conscious (see Searle 1980). But unlike Searle, we do not find the Chinese Room thought experiment compelling (see Schneider 2015 and Mandik 2017 for discussion).[4] We do not wish to *deny* that machines can be conscious. Instead, we consider it an *open question* whether silicon-based beings can be conscious.

We gain a better understanding of the hard problem of AI consciousness by asking: what considerations may be fueling this problem? Perhaps the problem is fueled, at least in part, by a kind of other minds problem, applied to the case of machines. The case of machines is certainly more challenging, because in the human case, we feel others are minded because of their behavior as well as the fact that they have a physiology that is similar to ours. The case with machines is more challenging, because of a lack of physiological similarity, and it gets quite difficult if a machine's cognitive and perceptual systems are not even loosely similar to our own, as we may not even have similar behaviors to go on.

An other-minds problem, on its own, may fuel the problem, but it does not strike us as being a compelling reason to deny consciousness to AGIs or SAIs. Ethical considerations suggest that it is best to be charitable in these cases, for any mistake could wrongly influence the debate over whether such creatures might be worthy of special ethical consideration as sentient beings. As Asimov's robot stories illustrated, any failure to be charitable to AI could come back to haunt us, as they may treat us as we treated them. Indeed, AIs could pose a "hard problem of carbon-based consciousness" about us, asking if biological, carbon-based entities have the right substrate for experience. After all, how could AI ever be certain that we are conscious?

The Problem of Other Minds is not the only concern that fuels the Hard Problem of AI Consciousness, however.[5] A further, related concern is the following. Carbon molecules form stronger, more stable chemical bonds than silicon, which allows carbon to form an extraordinary number of compounds, and, unlike silicon, carbon has the capacity to more easily form double-bonds. This difference has important implications in the field of astrobiology, because it is for this reason that carbon, and not silicon, is said to be well-suited for the development of life throughout the universe (Bennett and Shostak 2012). If these chemical differences impact life itself, we should not rule out the possibility that these chemical differences also impact whether silicon gives rise to consciousness, even if they do not hinder silicon's ability to process information in a superior manner. This is not an endorsement of biological naturalism, but is a consideration indicating that it is not yet clear whether AI can be conscious.

If the answer to the AI hard problem is that silicon cannot be the basis for consciousness, then superintelligent machines – machines that may even one day supplant us – will exhibit a vastly superior form of intelligence, but they will lack inner experience. Just as the breathtaking android in the movie *Ex Machina* (2015) convinced Caleb that she was in love with him, so too, a clever AI may convincingly behave as if it is conscious.

Further, if subsequent reflection on the AI hard problem reveals that even beings with artificial brains that are computationally like those of humans cannot be conscious, then, in an extreme, horrifying case, humans upload, and only nonhuman animals are left to feel the spark of insight, the pangs of grief, or the warm hues of a sunrise. This would be an unfathomable loss, one that is not offset by a mere net gain in intelligence. Even the slightest chance that this could happen should give us reason to proceed in the development of uploading and brain implant technologies with caution. These issues urgently need to be addressed.

4.1 A solution?

Is there a means to answer the AI Hard Problem? Two scenarios are suggestive.

First, although it is unlikely, we could find silicon-based *natural* intelligence on a planet – silicon-based life that arose through chemical processes, rather than being constructed by a biological species. If these creatures have a phenomenological vocabulary – a vocabulary of what it is like to experience the world – it would not be due to their being programmed by a biological species to act as if they had experience. Further, their phenomenological vocabulary cannot be a mere mimicry of the behavior or vocabulary of a biological species that evolved separately and had contact with them. What we need is pure, untainted silicon phenomenology, if you will.

If untainted naturally occurring silicon-based phenomenology was discovered, this would make more plausible the claim that artificial silicon-based systems could support phenomenology. Of course, even in this case some may still doubt whether artificial systems could be conscious (based, for instance, on considerations about teleofunction or John Searle's alleged derived/non-derived intentionality distinction) (Searle 1983).

Let's turn now to a second suggestion for making progress on the Hard Problem of AI Consciousness. Let us return to the case of one's migration to the cloud. In the process of migrating, neurons that form the neural basis of one's consciousness are gradually replaced by silicon chips. If, during this process, a prosthetic part of the brain ceases to function normally – specifically, if it ceases to give rise to the aspect of consciousness that that brain area is responsible for – then there should be behavioral indications, including verbal reports. An otherwise normal person should be able to detect, or at least indicate to others through odd behaviors, that something is amiss, as with traumatic brain injuries involving the loss of consciousness in some domain, such as blindsight or blindness denial. This would indicate a "substitution failure" of the artificial part for the original component.

But should we really draw the conclusion, from a substitution failure, that the underlying cause is that silicon cannot be a neural correlate of conscious experience? Why not instead conclude that scientists failed to program in a key feature of the original component – a problem which science can eventually solve? But after years and years of trying, we may reasonably question whether silicon is a suitable substitute for carbon when it comes to consciousness. This would be a sign that the answer to the hard problem of AI consciousness is negative: AI cannot be conscious. But even a longstanding substitution failure would not be *definitive*, for there is always the chance that our science has fallen short. But this scenario would provide some evidence for a negative answer.

Readers familiar with Chalmers's "absent qualia, dancing qualia" thought experiment may object that we've missed something, for Chalmers's thought experiment supports the view that consciousness supervenes on functional configuration: if you fix the psychofunctional facts, you fix the qualia. But we are disputing that functional isomorphism occurs in the first place. We consider it an open question.

If silicon systems cannot be conscious, then the functional facts cannot be fixed. When it comes to consciousness, carbon and silicon are not functionally interchangeable. For why would a silicon system, S2, be a psychofunctional isomorph of the original system, S1, after the transfer? S2s replaced brain region, or minicolumn, being made of silicon, will always differ causally from the replaced component. For wouldn't the new silicon component somehow signal to other brain areas that there is a defect in consciousness, as with neurophysiological deficits?

Could the silicon chip be doctored, so as to signal consciousness when consciousness was absent though? This is a tricky question. It could be the case that there are some observational false positives, in which case, we may fail to rule out certain cases of non-conscious systems. But would it then be a genuine functional isomorph of a carbon system? It is not clear that it would be, for the brain chip would need to prevent signaling to other brain areas that consciousness is lacking.

The conscious system would not. Our example does not require rejecting the view that qualia supervenes on functional organization, then.

Conclusion

The practical and intellectual challenges we foresee philosophers of mind helping to meet have here fallen into four groups. The first group of challenges centered on the possibility of superintelligent artificial intelligence, a technology that may potentially populate our world with nonhuman selves bestowed with capacities that meet or exceed our own. The second group of challenges concern brain enhancement, extreme cases of which might result in beings more posthuman than human. Even more extreme transformations formed the core of the third group of challenges, those that centered on the hypothetical technology of mind uploading, which might constitute a way for human minds to survive indefinitely through digital backup, or might instead be merely a very expensive form of suicide. Fourth and finally, we raised the hard problem of AI consciousness, a special form of the problem of determining whether a given entity is such that there's something it feels like to itself "from the inside." There's an ethical element to this problem, for we recognize an ethical imperative not to inflict avoidable suffering upon any being, whether they be natural or artificial.

We surely have just scratched the surface in exploring ways that philosophy of mind can help shape the future. Despite the numerous ways that will surely escape our foresight, we are confident that the technological changes that await us, in particular those involving information processing technology, will pose problems that science alone cannot equip society to solve.

Notes

1 Further, there is growing concern among policymakers and the public that AI will eventually outmode humans, leading to technological unemployment (Frey and Osborne, 2013).
2 *DeepMind* is a British artificial intelligence company acquired by Google in 2014. The IBM's *Watson* program is a natural-language processing computer system that famously competed on *Jeopardy!* in 2011.
3 Worries about technological unemployment do not assume that AGIs will be superintelligent; indeed, people can become unemployed due to the development of domain-specific AI systems that are not even at the level of being AGIs.
4 In Searle's famous Chinese Room argument, Searle appeals to the thought experiment of the "Chinese Room" to argue against the possibility of artificial systems being genuinely intelligent. In the thought experiment, Searle runs a program for understanding Chinese despite himself understanding only English. Observers outside of the Chinese room send and receive messages to and from the room that lead them to believe the room's inhabitant is perfectly conversant in Chinese. But Searle is orchestrating the message exchange solely in virtue of following instructions written in English.
5 For discussion of the Chinese Room Thought experiment, see (Schneider 2015 and Mandik 2017).

Bibliography

Bennett, J., and Shostak, S. (2012). *Life in the Universe*, 3rd ed., Boston: Addison-Wesley.

Blackford, R., and Broderick, D., (2014). *Intelligence Unbound: The Future of Uploaded and Machine Minds*. Boston: Wiley Blackwell.

Block, N. (2002). "The Harder Problem of Consciousness," *The Journal of Philosophy*, XCIX: 1–35.

Bostrom, D. (2017). The Transhumanist FAQ: v 2.1. World Transhumanist Association.

Bostrom, N. (2014). *Superintelligence: Paths, Dangers, Strategies*. Oxford: Oxford University Press.

Chalmers, D. J. (2010). "The Singularity: A Philosophical Analysis," *Journal of Consciousness Studies*, 17, 7–65.

Chalmers, D. J. (2008). "The Hard Problem of Consciousness." in Velmans, Max and Schneider, Susan (eds.), *The Blackwell Companion to Consciousness*. Oxford: Wiley-Blackwell.

Collins, N. (2013). "Hawking: 'in the Future Brains Could Be Separated From the Body,'" *The Telegraph*, 20 September.

Corabi, J., and Schneider, S. (2012). "The Metaphysics of Uploading," *Journal of Consciousness Studies*, 19.

Frey, C. and and Osborne, M. (2013). https://www.oxfordmartin.ox.ac.uk/downloads/academic/future-of-employment.pdf

Garreau, J. (2004). *Radical Evolution: The Promise and Peril of Enhancing our Minds, our Bodies – and What it Means to be Human*. New York: Doubleday.

Kurzweil, R. (2005). *The Singularity is Near: When Humans Transcend Biology*. New York: Viking.

McGinn, C. (1993). *Problems in Philosophy*. Oxford: Oxford University Press.

McLaughlin Brian (2003). P. A Naturalist-Phenomenal Realist Response to Block's Harder Problem, *Philosophical Issues* 13, 163–204.

Mandik, P. (2015). Metaphysical Daring as a Posthuman Survival Strategy, *Midwest Studies in Philosophy*, 39(1), 144–157.

Mandik, P. (2017). "Robot Pain," in Corns, J. (ed.), *The Routledge Handbook of Philosophy of Pain*. New York: Routledge: 200–209.

Miller, G. A. (1956). The magical number seven, plus or minus two: Some limits on our capacity for processing information. *Psychological Review* 63 (2), 81–97. doi: 10.1037/h0043158. PMID 13310704.

Müller, V. C., and Bostrom, N. (2014). "Future Progress in Artifi-cial Intelligence: A Survey of Expert Opinion," in Müller, Vincent C. (ed.), *Fundamental Issues of Artificial Intelligence*. Synthese Library. Berlin: Springer.

Parfit, D. (1984). *Reasons and Persons*. Oxford: Oxford University Press.

Quine, W. V. O. (1956). Quantifiers and Propositional Attitudes, *Journal of Philosophy*, 53, 177–187.

Schneider, S. (2009a). "Mindscan: Transcending and Enhancing the Human Brain," in Schneider, Susan (ed.), *Science Fiction and Philosophy*. Oxford: Blackwell Publishing 241–255.

Schneider, S. (2009b). "Science Fiction Thought Experiments as a Window into Philosophical Puzzles," in *Science Fiction and Philosophy*. Chichester: Wiley-Blackwell.

Schneider, S. (2011). *The Language of Thought: A New Philosophical Direction*. Boston: MIT Press.

Schneider, S. (2014). "The Philosophy of 'Her'," *The New York Times*, 2 March.

Schneider, S. (2015). "Alien Minds," *Discovery* (an astrophysics trade anthology, based on a NASA/Library of Congress Symposium), Steven Dick, Cambridge: Cambridge University Press.

Schneider, S. (forthcoming). "The Mind is not the Software of the Brain (Even if it is Computational)", ms.

Searle, J. (1980). Minds, Brains and Programs, *The Behavioral and Brain Sciences*, 3, 417–457.

Searle, John R. (1983). *Intentionality: An Essay in the Philosophy of Mind*. Cambridge: Cambridge University Press.

Tye, Michael (1995). *Ten Problems of Consciousness: A Representational Theory of the Phenomenal Mind*. Cambridge, MA: MIT Press.

Wallach, W. and Allen, C. (2010). *Moral Machines*. Oxford: Oxford University Press.

INDEX

Note: page numbers in *italic* indicate a figure on the corresponding page.

aboutness 67, 207, 268
access, privileged 263, 265–266
acquaintance 71, 120n11, 154, 170n6, 263–264
action: broad causation and 189–190; in computationalism 267; embodied cognition and 273; exclusion problem and 181–182; in functionalism 267; in identity theory 61; intentionality and 263; in Külpe 161; mental causation and 180–181; in physical symbol system hypothesis 296n1; reasons and 180–181; in Wittgenstein 248–251
Adorno, Theodor 28
adverbialism 108, 110–111
agency: and anomalism problem 181; in cognitive science 280–283; and feedback control 288; in materialism 286–287, 295; scope of 280; and TOTE units 289–290; in Wittgenstein 250–251
Alexander, Samuel 88, 177–178
animalism 137–143, 144nn9,14–15
anomalism 180–184; anomalous monism 31, 181–183
Anscombe, G.E.M. (Elizabeth) 12, 108–109, 179, 184, 186
anti-individualism 258–266
Aristotle 64, 206, 209, 219, 257, 267
Armstrong, David 62, 95–96
artificial general intelligence (AGI) 304–305

artificial intelligence (AI) 31, 42n13, 285, 303–307, 311–317
associationism 82
Austin, J. L. 106
Ayer, A. J. 105, 167

Babbage, Charles 283
Bain, Alexander 82–83, 226n15
Baldwin, J. M. 81
Baldwin, Thomas 80
bat argument 69–70
Bayesian model of perception 116
Beauvoir, Simone de 10, 22, 27
behaviorism 2–4; analytical 83, 85; cognitive science and 285; consciousness and 82–87; criticisms of 56–57; functionalism vs. 64–65; introspectionism and 148–149; logical 54; methodological 83, 85; mind-body problem in 53–57; philosophical 54–55; psychological 53–54; radical 53–54
Berkeley, George 105
Black, Max 88
Block, Ned 68, 74n19, 89, 93, 95–97, 273–274, 313–314
Boole, George 283, 296n3
Boring, Edwin G. 58, 88
Bosanquet, Bernard 104
Bostrom, Nick 304–305, 307, 311
boundaries 273–274
Bradley, F. H. 104

320

INDEX

brain enhancement 308–310
brain mapping *see* neural localization
brainware 286–288
Brentano, Franz 29, 108, 157, 159, 200–210, 219–223, 226nn7,9,15, 228nn50,54
British Empiricists 16, 112, 161–163, 248–249
British idealism 104–105
Broad, C. D. 83, 105, 151–152, 177
Broca, Paul 4, 194n3
Brodmann, Korbinian 5
Brooks, Rodney 271–272
Burge, Tyler 17, 189, 260–261
Butler, Bishop 127, 144n13

Caird, Edward 104
Campbell, John 275n5
Carnap, Rudolf 28–30, 54, 85, 87–88, 296n3
Cartesian conception of mind 256–258
c-fibers 58–59, 63–64, 66, 194n8
Chalmers, David 71–72, 91–92, 262, 269–270, 276n14, 304, 306, 308, 311, 313, 316
Chinese Room 67, 292, 314, 317n4
Chisholm, Roderick 57, 108, 201–202, 213–217, 227n39
Chomsky, Noam 3, 30, 42n11, 56–57, 90, 286
Churchland, Patricia 19n3, 282
Churchland, Paul 73, 73n4, 116, 117, 119, 282, 285
Church-Turing thesis 7
Clark, Andy 269–270, 272
cognition: in cognitive science 280; consciousness and 87, 94–98; in Descartes 257, 267; embodied 7, 24, 118, 267, 271–273, 294; pure 257; social 24, 26–27, 31, 295
cognitive science: agency in 283; behaviorism and 285, 296n6; brainware and 286–288; computationalism and 286; cybernetics and 288–289; defined 280; domain of 280; explanation in 293–294; explanatory package of 281, 283–294; feedback control and 288–290; future of 294–295; information in 290–292; Marr and 293–294; McCulloch and 286–288; Pitts and 286–288; Shannon and 290–292; software and 284–286; Turing and 284–286; Wiener and 288–290
computationalism 266–268, 286, 288
computer revolution 7–9
Comte, Auguste 156–157, 159
conceivability argument 72
conceptual analysis 25, 29, 91, 251–253
connectionist networks 12, 18, 287–288, 296n7
consciousness 22; in artificial intelligence 312–317; behaviorism and 82–87; in Brentano 219–223; cognition and 87, 94–98; disappearance of 82–87; and explanatory gap 87–94; intentionality and 94–98, 216–225; perception and 79–83, 219–220; physicalism and 87–94; thought and 79–83
constructivism 12, 113–119, 163
content theory 79–80
Cosmelli, Diego 274
Crowther, Paul 120n9
cybernetics 288–289, 296n3
cyborgs 308
cytoarchitectonic method 5

Davidson, Donald 74n13, 181–182, 195n12
Democritus 58
Dennett, Daniel 71, 85, 96–97, 275
Derrida, Jacques 28
Descartes, René 52, 72, 175, 191, 248, 256–258, 265–267, 272, 284
directedness 67, 200–201, 207, 216, 261
direct realism 31, 106, 108, 111–112, 115–116
disassociation paradigm 227n43
disjunctivism 106, 111–112, 264–265, 275, 275n5
downward causation 39–40, *40*, 177–178, 194n5
Drake, Durant 192–193
Dreyfus, Hubert 26, 258, 303

321

INDEX

dualism 52, 175, 179; cognitive science and 295; intentionality and 201; mental causation and 191–194; Wittgenstein and 235
Dummett, Michael 258

ecological perception 117–119
eliminativism 54, 56, 73n4
embodied cognition 7, 24, 118, 267, 271–273, 294
emergence 40, *40*, 43n27
emergentism 176–177, 190, 194n5, 276n9
empiricism, British 16, 112, 161–163, 248–249
emulation, whole brain 310–312
epiphenomenalism 39, 61, 70, 176, 178, 183, 185, 190–191, 193–194, 194n5, 195n12
essences, in Husserl 24–25
Evans, Gareth 109, 263
exclusion problem 180–181, 184–188
experimental psychology 148, 158
explanatory gap 87–94
extended mind 269–271, 307–308
externalism 258–266, 273–275, 276n14
externalism problem 181, 188–190

Farber, Marvin 30
Farrell, B. A. 90
feedback control 288–290
feedforward networks 296n8
Feigl, Herbert 58, 61, 90
Ferrier, David 194n3
Field, Hartry 227n34
first-person access 167–168
Firth, Roderick 153, 155–156, 167
fission problem 131–132
Flourens, Pierre 4
Fodor, Jerry 62, 86–87, 89, 183, 188–189, 268, 303
Foglia, Lucia 271
formal ontology 30
Frege, Gottlob 59, 227n39, 233, 258–259, 283
Freud, Sigmund 8, 87, 265–266, 276n7
functionalism 21–22, 31; analytic 66; behaviorism vs. 64–65; cognitive system and 269–271; conceptual 66; criticisms of 67–69; intentionality and 218–219; mental states in 64–66; mind-body problem in 63–69; naturalism and 266–268; qualia in 68–69; Wittgenstein and 251–253

Gage, Phineas 4–5
Gall, Franz Joseph 4
Gates, Bill 305
Gertler, Brie 276n6
Gestalt psychology 26; first-person access and 167; hyletic data and 42n16; introspection and 163–166; perception and 113–117; psychophysical isomorphism and 120n12; structuralism and 113–114
Gibson, J. J. 12, 117–118, 272
"given" 79–83
grammar, pure 30
Green, T. H. 104
Grice, H. P. 127, 129
Gurwitsch, Aron 26, 28, 42nn16,18
Guthrie, Edwin R. 3

Hamilton, William 156
harmony, pre-established 193
Hawking, Stephen 305, 310–311
Hebb, Donald O. 287
Hebbian learning rule 287
Heidegger, Martin 22, 25–27, 29, 42n13, 258, 272
Helmholtz, Hermann von 112–113, 115–117
Hempel, Carl 54, 91, 180, 195n14
Hempel's dilemma 195n14
higher-order representation 95
higher-order thought 95
Hildreth, Ellen 293
Hobbes, Thomas 58, 64, 73n1, 87
horizon structure 23–24, 34–35, 42n13
HOT theory 95–97
Hull, Clark 3, 83
human animal 137–141
Hume, David 34, 129, 179–181, 184, 196n22, 233, 249
Hurley, Susan 273–274

322

INDEX

Husserl, Edmund 23–26, 28–30, 32–39, 41n3, 43nn20–21, 81–82, 107–108, 164–165
Huxley, T. H. 176, 193
hyletic data 36, 42n16

idealism, British 104–105
identity *see* personal identity
identity theory 21, 73n8; case for 58–62; mind-body problem in 57–63
illusions 105–106
imaging 6, 295
immediate retrospection 157, 162–163
improper category objection 179
indexical expressions 259–260
individualism 17, 258–266
information: in cognitive science 281–282, 284, 286, 290–292; in computationalism 13; in constructivism 115–116; and extended mind 269–270; intentionality and 215–216; perception and 118; in physicalism 71, 90
inner-object model 16, 233–238, 240, 248–250
inner space 263–265
intentionalism 95–97, 108–110
intentionality 22, 31; in Brentano 202–210, 219–223; in Chisholm 213–216; consciousness and 94–98, 216–225; dualism and 201; functionalism and 218–219; judgments and 210–211; logic and 202; in Meinong 210–213; mental phenomena and 204–208; perception and 206; phenomena and 203–206; phenomenology and 217–218; physicalism and 215; psychology and 202–203; representationalism and 202, 216–225; semantic 260–261; in Twardowski 210–213
interactionism 176, 191–192
introspection: behaviorism and 148–149; careful 155; conscious experience and 152–153; first-person access and 167–168; Gestalt psychology and 163–166; perception and 149–156; phenomenological method and 163–166; restricted 159–160; scientific role of 156–168; in sense-datum theory debate 149–156, 168; systematic 160–163; transparency and 168–170
inverted qualia argument 68–69, 82, 89, 94

Jackson, Frank 22, 70–71, 74n22, 90–93, 218
James, William 78, 80, 82–83, 157–158, 171nn11,14, 177, 194n3, 249
Jaynes, Julian 85
Joachim, Harold 104

Kant, Immanuel 116, 256
Kaplan, David 17, 262–263
Kim, Jaegwon 64, 184–186, 188, 195n12
knowledge argument 70–71
Koffka, Kurt 12, 14, 114, 164–166
Köhler, Wolfgang 114, 118, 164
Kripke, Saul 73n8, 196n19, 259
Külpe, Oswald 159–163

Ladd, George Trumbull 80
Lashley, Karl 5, 295
Leibniz, Gottfried 193, 283, 296n3
Levinas, Emmanuel 26–27
Levine, Joseph 90–91
Lewis, C. I. 78, 81–82, 86, 91–92, 109, 151
Lewis, David 62
Libet, B. 40
Locke, John 127, 129, 143n3
logical positivism 28, 54, 85, 87, 105
logic gate 18, 287
Lovejoy, Arthur 177

Mach, Ernst 163
Malcolm, Norman 184, 195n13
Malebranche, Nicolas 193
Marr, David 118, 281, 293–294
Martin, M.G.F (Michael) 82, 112, 169–170
materialism 52, 87, 90–93, 266; agency and 286, 295; behaviorism and 53; identity theory and 88; reductive 176; *see also* physicalism

323

Maxwell, James Clerk 288
McCulloch, Warren 281, 283, 286–288
McCulloch-Pitts neurons 287–288
McDowell, John 112, 263–265
McGinn, Colin 90, 309
McTaggart, J.M.E. 104
meaning: consciousness and 80; in Husserl 29; information and 290–291; in inner-object model 234; intentionality and 260–261; in logical behaviorism 54; reference and 260; in semantic theory 259; in verificationism 55; in Wittgenstein 241–245
Meinong, Alexius 210–213
Melden, A. I. 179–180, 184
mental causation: anomalism and 180–184; downward 178; in dualism 191–194; epiphenomenalism and 178, 193–194, 194n5; exclusion problem and 180–181, 184–190; externalism problem and 181; illustration of 175; interactionism and 191–192; many problems for 180–190; naturalist approaches to 176–178; occasionalism and 193; in parallelism 192–193; physicalism and 195n14; pre-established harmony and 193; property dependence approaches and 187–188; realization and 187–188; reasons as causes in 178–180; supervenience and 187–188
Merleau-Ponty, Maurice 27–28, 36, 42n15, 107–108, 118
Millikan, Ruth 74n, 120n15, 216, 227n37, 269, 292
Mill, James 82
Mill, John Stuart 156–157, 162
mind-body problem: in 20th-century philosophy 52–73; in behaviorism 53–57; in functionalism 63–69; in identity theory 57–63; and multiple realizability 62–63; phenomenology of 37–41, *38*, *40*; and qualia 69–72
mind uploading 310–312, 317
modularity 117
monism 31, 52, 73, 106, 181–183
Moore, G. E. 78–80, 82, 105, 149–152
moral programming 305

Morgan, Lloyd 177
multiple realizability 62–63, 187, 195n15, 269

Nagel, Thomas 7, 68–70, 89–90, 92–93
names 259–260
naturalism 87–88, 176–178, 256, 266–273, 314–315
neo-Hegelians 104
neural localization 4–7, 11, 13
neural networks 287, 296n8
Newell, Alan 284, 296n1
no-criterion argument 239, 253n3
Noe, Alva 273

object-directedness 67, 200–201, 207, 216, 261
occasionalism 193
Olson, Eric 133, 136, 138, 140
ontological dependence 30
operant conditioning 2–3

pain 58–59, 63–64, 66, 194n8, 236–237, 240
parallelism 192–193
Parfit, Derek 131–133, 135–137
Parity Principle 270
Pavlov, Ivan 3, 83
Penfield, Wilder 5
perception: adverbialism and 110–111; Bayesian model of 116; consciousness and 79–83, 219–220; constructivism and 114–117; disjunctive theory of 264–265; disjunctivism and 111–112; ecological 117–119; Gestalt psychology and 113–114; in Heidegger 25–26; in Husserl 25, 37–38; illusions in 105–106; inner 159–160; intentionalism and 108–110; intentionality and 206; introspection and 149–156; in Merleau-Ponty 27–28; objects of 104–112; qualia and 107; representationalism and 108–110, 120n11; sense-data theory and 105–108, 149–156; structuralism and 113–114
percepts 115
perceptual content 31–36

INDEX

perceptual process 112–119
perceptual relation 104–112
personal identity: animalist challenge in 137–141, 144n14; fission problem in 131–132; memory and 127–128; non-branching approach to 132–133; ontological problem in 141–143; and "plurality of worms" 133–134; and psychological continuity 126–131, 144n15; questions about 126; in reductionism 135–137, 144nn11,13; stage view of 134–135
phenomenalism 106, 163
phenomenological reduction 23
phenomenology: defined 22; functionalism and 22; genetic 23–24; in Heidegger 25–26; in Husserl 23–24; intentionality and 217–218; introspection and 163–166; in Levinas 26–27; of mind-body problem 37–41, *38*, *40*; overview of 22–28; and perceptual content 31–36; proprietary cognitive 98; in relation to philosophy of mind 28–31
physical, as term 119n2
physicalism 52, 60, 63, 66, 69–73, 87–94; intentionality and 215; mental causation and 195n14; *see also* materialism
physical symbol system hypothesis 296n1
Pitts, Walter 281, 286–288
Place, U. T. 58, 73n1, 88, 186, 194n6
Poggio, Tomaso 293
positivism, logical 28, 54, 85, 87, 105
predicative structures 35–36
pre-established harmony 193
Price, H. H. 81, 105, 151–152; 154–155, 168, 170n6
privileged access 263, 265–266
psychological continuity 126–131, 144n15
"Psychology as the Behaviorist Sees It" (Watson) 2
psychophysical isomorphism 120n12
"pure grammar" 30
Putnam, Hilary 57, 62–63, 66, 259, 261–262, 276n7

qualia: bat argument and 69–70; consciousness and 81–82, 89, 93; in functionalism 68–69; knowledge argument and 70–71; and mind-body problem 69–72; perception and 107; zombie argument and 71–72
quasi-memory 127–128
Quine, W. V. 85, 87–88
Quinton, Anthony 129–130

"raw feels" 82–87
realism, direct 67, 106, 200–201, 207, 216, 261
realizability, multiple 62–63, 187, 195n15, 269
reductionism 98, 135–137, 144nn11,13, 186, 196n18
reductive materialism 176
referentialism 234, 248
Reid, Thomas 106
representationalism 31, 36, 95–96, 108–112, 115, 120n11, 168–170, 202, 216–225
retrospection, immediate 157–158, 162
Ricoeur, Paul 28
Rosenblueth, Arturo 288, 290
Rosenthal, David 95
Russell, Bertrand 78–79, 105–106, 177, 233, 249, 263–264, 296n3
Ryle, Gilbert 29, 54, 56, 84, 179, 184, 186

Santayana, George 176, 193
Sartre, Jean-Paul 27
Schlick, Moritz 58
Schutz, Alfred 26
science: introspection and 156–168; *see also* cognitive science
Searle, John 31, 42n12, 67–68, 91, 303, 314, 317n4
Sellars, Roy Wood 176–177
Sellars, Wilfrid 30, 265
semantic intentionality 260–261
semantic tradition 258–260
sensationalism 162–163
sense-data theory 105–108, 149–156, 168
sensorily manifest 33
Shannon, Claude 281, 290–292, 296n3
Shaw, Cliff 284, 296n3
Sherrington, Charles 194n3

INDEX

Shoemaker, Sydney 93, 130, 140, 187
Simon, Herbert 284, 296n1
singularity, technological 305–310
Skinner, B. F. 2–3, 53–54, 83, 285
Smart, J.J.C. 58, 60, 88–89, 109, 186, 194n6
software 284–286
spatiality 191
split-brain subjects 5, 7, 13
Sprigge, T.L.S. 90
Stein, Edith 26
Stout, G. F. 80–81, 96
Strawson, P. F. 167, 225, 228n56, 264
structuralism 12, 112–115, 160, 162, 285
superficial functional isomorph (SFI) 313
superintelligent artificial intelligence (SAI) 305, 314

technological singularity 305–310
Tegmark, Max 305
Thomasson, Amie 29
Thompson, Evan 274
Thorndike, Edward 83
thought: consciousness and 79–83; in Wittgenstein 245–248; *see also* cognition; consciousness
thought experiments 306; *see also* Chinese Room; Twin Earth
Titchener, Edward B. 82–83, 88, 112, 148, 159–163, 285
Tolman, E. C. 83, 86, 89
TOTE unit 289–290
transparency 32, 168–170, 202, 224–225, 228n56
Turing, Alan 7–9, 267, 281, 283–286, 296n3
Turing test 7–9, 285
Twardowski, Kazimierz 210–213, 227n24
Twin Earth 259, 262, 269
two-dimensional views 262–263
Tye, Michael 93, 168
type physicalism 63, 66; *see also* identity theory

understanding: in Wittgenstein 241–245; *see also* cognition

verificationism 54–55, 239
Vienna Circle 85
Vienna school 28
volition 249; *see also* will
voluntary action: in Wittgenstein 248–251; *see also* action

Ward, James 83
Watson, John 2, 53–54, 83–84, 194n3
Weaver, Warren 290–292
Wernicke, Carl 4
Wertheimer, Max 12, 113–114, 163
what-externalism 273
Whitby, Blay 9, 19n8
whole brain emulation 310–312
Wiener, Norbert 18, 281, 288–290, 296n3
Wiggins, David 131
will: emergence and 41; in Libet 40; reasons and 181; in Wittgenstein 248–251
Williams, Bernard 131
Williamson, Timothy 258, 275
Wilson, Margaret 273, 275
Wilson, Robert 271
Wittgenstein, Ludwig: agency in 250–251; anomalism and 184; behaviorism and 29, 54–56, 84–85, 88; Cartesian framework and 178; conception of philosophy by 233–234; and conceptual analysis 251–252; and dual explanation solutions 186; dualism and 235; functionalism and 251–253; influence of 251–253; and inner-object model 234–235, 249–250; instantaneous experience of complex contents in 241–245; meaning in 241–245; and no-criterion argument 239, 253n3; and other minds 235–240; pain in 61, 236–237, 240; referentialism and 234; sensations and 235–240; thinking in 245–248; Turing and 9; understanding in 241–245; voluntary action in 248–251; will in 248–251
Wundt, Wilhelm 80, 112, 148, 159–160, 164, 171nn11,14, 194n3, 285

zombie argument 71–72, 92, 306